William Caxton and early printing in England

William Caxton and early printing in England

LOTTE HELLINGA

THE BRITISH LIBRARY

First published in 2010 by
The British Library
96 Euston Road
London NW1 2DB

British Library Cataloguing in Publication Data
A catalogue record for this publication is available from The British Library

ISBN 978-0-7123-5088-4

Designed by Tony Kitzinger
Colour reproduction by Dot Gradations Ltd, Essex
Printed and bound in England by Henry Ling Limited, at the Dorset Press, Dorchester DT1 1HD

Contents

The crafte of Printynge ...
hathe ben the cause of many thynges
and great chaunges, & is lyke to be
the cause of many straunge thynges
here after to come

John Rastell, c. 1530

Foreword

Early in 2007 the eleventh volume of the *Catalogue of books printed in the XVth century now in the British Library* was published, containing very full descriptions of books printed in England before the year 1501, in so far as represented in the national collection. The publication of this volume, the final part of the catalogue (vols xii and xiii had preceded it) brought to conclusion the commitment undertaken about a century earlier by what was then the library of the British Museum, to publish extensive bibliographical descriptions of the world's most representative collection of incunabula. Since the publication of the first volume in 1908, 'BMC' – as it became known – was recognized as a work of authority that documented the spread of printing in Europe in the fifteenth century. It is a work for specialists, either in the history of printing and printed books or, to a lesser extent, of the transmission of texts in the early modern period.

The question arose now whether some results of all the detailed work published in the most recent volume of the catalogue (BMC xi) might be made accessible to readers to enjoy the history of England's early printers for its own sake, without the ballast of scholarly apparatus and argument. Another limitation that might be discarded for a work written with the general reader in mind, was the traditional time-limit set for the BMC-volumes, the end of the fifteenth century. Instead, the lifespan of the second generation of printers in England, Richard Pynson and Wynkyn de Worde, which ended in 1535 and practically coincided with fundamental changes in the freedom with which printers could operate, suggested a terminal date that might make better sense.

A 'story' derived from academic writing is a distinct genre. Despite the advantages of fewer constraints, writing it – as I was invited to do – does not come easily to someone more used to addressing a supposed audience of specialists, each statement underpinned by a structure of footnotes proferring evidence of one kind or other. Remaining truthful to the results of earlier detailed investigations, and presenting such results within a much wider spectrum of facts, requires restraint. In attempting to tell a coherent story I had to omit a great deal of factual detail. But by producing a picture in a larger setting than was possible within the constraints of the catalogue of a collection, however wide its range, new interpretations of relations between printers and their environment presented themselves and are discussed. Therefore this book is also submitted as a new offering to those already familiar with the subject. I wish to alert bibliographically-minded readers that in matters of dating I have followed the chronologies established for BMC xi and also presented in the reprint of E. Gordon Duff's bibliography of printing in England and for the English market published in 2009. Dates in the present book sometimes deviate from datings in earlier bibliographies, notably from STC.

Readers of the present book wishing to pursue the absent detail – among which the devil is known to lurk – are referred to the section 'Further reading', where I acknowledge the bibliographical works and secondary literature on which my story is mainly based. The bibliographical works provide the full picture of the production of printed books in England; secondary literature sets the context, and recent specialist studies led me to new interpretations, such as, for example, of the roles David Aubert and Colard Mansion may have played in Caxton's early publications in Flanders (an episode not covered in BMC xi).

The present book is a story of printers, but not a story of what happened to the thousands of books they produced after they had left their presses, the readers they reached, and how later they were valued by bibliophile collectors and by textual scholars. That is the story of an evolution that took place over centuries, and may perhaps be told on another occasion. But the time-span covered by this book, a period of some sixty years, is long enough to show how the work of printers in England reflects the developments that took place when printed books were becoming familiar objects to an ever widening circle of readers. Printers responded to the demands and expectations of a new generation that began to treat books in less solemn ways; the changes brought about by their developing taste are still visible to us. It was therefore a great pleasure to be encouraged to select a large number of illustrations. That sequence has its own tale to tell, for example by the development of typographical form, and the transition of the function of colour in the book, painted and printed, that gave way to the profusion of woodcuts and printed decoration in sixteenth-century printing. In the early years, black blocks of printed text were articulated with the use of red, usually added by hand. In the sixteenth century, English printers seem to have revelled in the shapes that could be formed out of movable type, their use of space on the page occasionally bizarre, but charged with meaning. Typography was given a modulated and sometimes resonant voice.

Friends and former colleagues have lent me much support in completing this book. Tony Curwen and David Paisey very generously agreed to assume the role of my imagined 'non-specialist' reader. Both read an early draft, and produced numerous corrections and suggestions for greater fluency and clarification, all gratefully received. At a later stage the text was read – this time explicitly with expert eyes – by Nicolas Barker, Professor A. S. G. Edwards, and John Goldfinch, the two latter engaging once again with the text in proof. I feel most indebted for their comments and corrections. Professor Mary Erler offered valuable advice to the sections on devotional publishing and the contemporaries of Wynkyn de Worde and saved me from error. Finally, Alix Christie read the text in proof and contributed suggestions from her quite different professional experience. I am grateful to my former colleague Philippa Marks for advice on bindings and providing rubbings for figs 39, 58, and 96.

Most of the illustrations are taken from manuscripts and printed books in the collections of the British Library. For additional material I am grateful for permission to reproduce items from:

All Souls College, Oxford (fig. 37);
Bodleian Library, Oxford (figs 15a, 24, 67);
Cambridge University Library (fig. 45);
H. E. Huntington Libray, San Marino, California (fig. 16);
John Rylands University Library, Manchester (figs 69, 112);
Koninklijke Bibliotheek, The Hague (fig. 9);
Lambeth Palace Library, London (fig. 40);
State Library of Victoria, Melbourne (fig. 97).

I feel particularly indebted to Dr Heribert Tenschert for his generosity in making images available for the reproduction of two illuminated pages from the beautiful manuscript in his possession of the *Dialogue des créatures* written for Colard Mansion (figs 7 and 19).

I am grateful to David Way, British Library Publishing, for his invitation to write this book, for encouragement, and for unstinting support by him and his team for its production. Tony Kitzinger undertook its design, and, as on previous occasions, it was a delight to see the book taking shape in his hands.

Lotte Hellinga
Spring 2010

Introduction

Printing was slow to come to England. By the time the first book printed in England came off a small press in an outbuilding of Westminster Abbey in mid-1476, the art of printing with movable type had been developing on the continent of Europe for about twenty years, and the new technique, perceived as almost magical, was beginning to change the world for ever. The 'invention of printing' may from a distance of some 550 years appear as a single revolutionary event, but it took over half a century for the technique to be fully accepted, developed and exploited, and for products of printing presses, books and other printed matter, to become common goods throughout much of the Continent. The main subject of this book is how England responded in its own way to this lengthy process.

The story I tell ends in 1535 with the death of Wynkyn de Worde, the last survivor of the second generation of printers in England. His death coincided with the introduction of new legislation which formally ended the activities of aliens (of whom he was one), who had played an important, although by then diminishing part in every aspect of the book trade in England. The new statute was introduced not only to protect the commercial interests of indigenous printers, publishers and booksellers; it was precisely at this time that authorities recognized that the printing press was an instrument for the dissemination of the new doctrine of Lutheranism. They intended to prevent the introduction of heretical texts, either by local printing or import from overseas by foreign booksellers who had settled in London.

Between 1476 and 1535 printing and publishing in the British Isles took place almost entirely in England – a brief episode in Edinburgh in 1508–10 being the sole exception. Within the kingdom, the few printing enterprises in the provinces, even those involving the universities of Oxford and Cambridge, were all short lived. The early printers and publishers settled mainly in a relatively small area, in Westminster and London: two distinct centres at the time, each with its own metropolitan character.

England's first printer, William Caxton, issued the first book of his Westminster business – a modest pamphlet in Latin – after gaining on the Continent considerable experience of the trade in printed books. He had spent most of his life as a successful London Mercer, though living overseas. Based for some thirty years in the Flemish city of Bruges, he reached in due course a position of eminence among his English colleagues in the Low Countries, and was appointed their official representative, or 'Governor'. During a brief interval in Cologne he had ample opportunity to observe not only the new technique and the new trade mechanisms required for the distribution of mass-produced printed books, but also the impact this new phenomenon was beginning to have. As he absorbed this, his commercial sense mingled with the notion that texts he enjoyed and loved, or might even write himself, could now be multiplied and made available to friends and strangers alike. He decided to risk joining the adventurous new enterprise, and became a printer.

Caxton was of an independent mind. Even at this remove we can perceive his versatility, his ability to respond to varying influences and circumstances. The last twenty years of his life in which he pursued his printing career, from 1472 to his death in 1492, saw a succession of tumultuous political changes which dramatically changed the lives of many of his patrons and clients, and could not have left him unaffected. By adapting, time and again, to the rapidly changing world around him, he created for printing in England a distinct character that was to persist in those who followed him.

The main production of Caxton's press in Westminster was a sequence of books in the English language. Only a few years after he had started, other printers began to operate in Oxford, in the City of London, and in the Benedictine abbey of St Albans. Like Caxton, almost all of them (with the possible exception of the printers at St Albans) had first worked elsewhere in centres of printing as far-flung as Rome and Cologne, but unlike Caxton, none of them were Englishmen. Few of their books were in English; they printed mainly texts in Latin and in the legal language used at the Chancery and the Inns of Court which is known as Law-French. The presentation of their books and the styles of their printing types show unmistakably where they first learned the trade and from where they brought their materials. Seen together with Caxton's style of printing, which was initially much influenced by that of Flemish manuscripts of his time, the overall image of the first ten years of printing in England is surprisingly cosmopolitan.

In 1486 a distinct period ended with the cessation of printing in Oxford and St Albans, and (temporarily) in Westminster and London. After a short interval Caxton resumed his publishing business, and after his death in 1492 the new generation, consisting before 1504 of only three printing houses (those of Richard Pynson, Wynkyn de Worde, and Julian Notary), continued to develop the genres which had proved to be reliable while also seeking new and independent directions. The sudden end of the smaller enterprises in 1486 may be ascribed to the deaths of one or perhaps two of their owners, but it is noticeable that thereafter the production of theological and other academic books in Latin did not recover. Such works had been the focus of the presses at Oxford and St Albans. Demand for printed books in Latin was rising in England, and consequently in the book trade the balance shifted from production at home to importation from the main producers in Europe. Printers in England (and the two in Scotland) could not, or more probably would not, compete with the trade in imported books, which many of them also imported and sold. The dominance of the import trade, known as the Latin trade, dictated the nature of book production in the British Isles for centuries. Most of what printers chose to print was material that could not conveniently be obtained from the great centres of book production on the Continent. It was to be even longer before publishing in England and Scotland became a major force on the world market. During all that time, books printed in the British Isles tended to be 'national' in character, published for the home market, whether the subjects were the common law of the land, education, history, literature or entertainment, and (before the Reformation) Catholic liturgy, mainly of Salisbury use. Apart from schoolbooks for teaching Latin and liturgies, they were mostly in English or Law-French. The great printing houses of the Continent produced a steady stream of Latin works, from the classics of law, theology and literature (in ever improved versions), to modern works, all aimed at the whole world of learning, of the '*literati*', including those in Britain.

By sheer mechanical force the invention of printing accelerated a cycle of communication that had existed for thousands of years, driven by the human gifts of language and intellectual curiosity. The written word had existed since the beginnings of script to reach across space and time. With the mechanical means to multiply texts by a factor of many hundreds and even thousands, the existing circuit of demand, production, and distribution not only functioned faster, it expanded exponentially and required an increasingly complex cycle of interplay between perceived demand, production, and channels of dissemination. Within each printing house the production process perpetually linked compositors and pressmen as they prepared and completed the printing of books, sheet by sheet, in step with each other, creating small cycles within the larger cycle of book production.

The present book does not examine early printing techniques in detail. For the first half-century of printing there are hardly any direct sources from which to draw, since images of printers at work or verbal descriptions in printers' manuals appeared only later. What we understand of the early techniques is all derived from what we can observe in the books themselves. The men whose hands actually created them, the compositors and pressmen, remain utterly unknown to us as individuals. A printing house was a community of workers living together, at its head the master printer whose name it bore; such households were the principal form of organization. From early in the sixteenth century the main English master printers, Richard Pynson and Wynkyn de Worde, probably belonged to the guild of producers of (manuscript) books, the London text-writers and illuminators, who early in the fifteenth century had formed a minor city-guild, the Mistery of Stationers. Until Pynson and De Worde became Stationers, men working in printing houses were not bound by the formal rules of a guild. Occasionally their names were recorded as members of a household of aliens, as for example the household of Johannes Lettou in the City of London, whose servants were in 1483 all recorded as 'Theutonici'. In 1534 Wynkyn de Worde named in his will many of his former and present journeymen and servants without specifying what their tasks in the printing house were or had been. He also counted several bookbinders among his friends and beneficiaries, but binding belonged to the retail business, and binders were not part of the production cycle in a printing house. Many printers, however, dealt also in imported books, and worked regularly with individual binders. Richard Pynson began his commercial life in the leather business as a glover and bookbinder before becoming a printer.

Even more remote than men working in the printing houses were the producers of the materials from which books were made. Paper used in England was made in mills on fast-flowing rivers in the Piedmont in Italy, and in Normandy and the north-east of France. Their product was bought up by wholesalers who traded it along the established commercial routes; when it passed through customs in English ports its arrival was recorded, and some of these records still survive. Until the 1550s the only paper mill in the British Isles was that of John Tate in Hertfordshire, which in the 1490s briefly provided De Worde with fine paper. Vellum or parchment, made from animal skins – rarely used in England for books – could be procured locally. No record is known to exist of the trade in typographical materials, which were almost all imported.

Printing is often called an art, publishing less so. In the early days the two terms were often interchangeable, as the early printers usually had to master the art of publishing themselves: gauging whether there would be demand for texts they considered for publication, printing them in a form they hoped would be acceptable or even attractive to the imagined reader, and marketing them. The early printers in England showed varying degrees of interest and skill in undertaking this complex set of tasks, in the quality of texts, their aesthetic presentation, and even in their market potential. Their priorities shifted over time in response to the rapid changes that were taking place in the world around them. We shall see that in the early decades of the sixteenth century the book trade consisted mainly of men who limited themselves to dealing in the ready-made product, or who undertook work on commission. What the few early printers had in common was that, even when they had to combine the two distinct functions of the trade, they were producers first and sellers second.

Who were these people who brought printing to England? What creative impulses drove them to choose this complicated and often financially risky process?

The chances of finding satisfactory answers to these questions without indulging in fiction are slim. With the exception of William Caxton we know little about them: at best a few biographical details, some formal records, some appearances in the courts of law, and records of death. The books they left us are scattered over many libraries. But database compilation and imaging technology have made those books more accessible today than they have ever been. Moreover, a century of secondary literature, especially rich in recent years, has accumulated about the first printers and their books. So now is a good time to survey their work again, to examine how printing in England began to unfold over a period of sixty years, spanning three generations of printers. In this brief survey it is the books, and the circumstances of their production, that will be our principal guides when seeking to answer that difficult question: Who were these people?

morderitis et comeditis: videte ne ab
invicē cōsumamini. Dico aūt i xristo.
5 Spiritu ambulate: ⁊ desideria carnis
non pficietis. Caro enim concupiscit
adversus spiritū: spirit⁹ aūt advsus
carnē. Hec enim sibi invicem advers͡ā-
tur: ut non quecūq; vultis illa facia-
tis. Qđ si spiritu ducemini: nōn estis
sub lege. Manifesta sunt autē opera
carnis: que sunt fornicatio·immūdi-
cia·impudicicia·luxuria·ydolorū servi-
tus·veneficia·inimicicie·cōtēciones·e-
mulationes·ire·rixe·dissensiones·se-
cte·invidie·homicidia·ebrietates·
comessationes·⁊ hijs similia: q̄ pdico
vobis sicut pdixi: quoniā qui talia
agunt regnū dei nō consequent̄. Fru-
ctus aūt spiritus est caritas·gaudiū·
pax·paciencia·benignitas·bonitas·
longanimitas·mā̄suetudo·fides·mo-
destia·continēcia·castitas. Adversus
huiusmodi non est lex. Qui autem
sunt xristi: carnem suā crucifixerunt
cum viciis et concupiscentijs. vi
Si vivimus spiritu: spiritu ⁊ ambu-
lem⁹. Non efficiamur inanis glo-
rie cupidi: invicem pvocātes: invicem
invidentes. Fratres: ⁊ si pocupat⁹ fu-
erit homo i aliquo delicto·vos q̄ spiri-
tuales estis huiusmodi instruite i spi-
ritu lenitatis: considerās teipm ne ⁊ tu
tempteris. Alter alteri⁹ onera portate:
⁊ sic adimplebitis legē xristi. Nā si qs
existimat se aliquid esse cū nichil sit:
ipse se seducit. Opus autem suū pbet
unusquisq;: ⁊ sic in semetipso tātū glo-
riā habebit: ⁊ nō i altero. Unusquisq;
6 enim onus suū portabit. Cōmunicet
aūt hijs qui cathezizat̄ verbo: ei qui
se cathezizat in omnibꝫ bonis. Noli-
te errare. De⁹ nō irridetur. Que enim
seminaverit homo: hec et metet. Qui

qui seminat in carne sua: de carne et
metet ⁊ corruptionē: qui aūt seminat
in spiritu: de spiritu metet vitā eternā.
Bonū autē facientes nō deficiamus:
tempore enim suo metem⁹ nō deficien-
tes. Ergo dum tempus habem⁹ ope-
remur bonū ad oīnes: maxime autē
ad domesticos fidei. Videte qualibꝫ 6
litteris scripsi vobis mea manu. Qui-
cunq; enim volūt placere in carne hij
cogunt vos circūcidi: tantū ut crucis
xristi psecutionē nō paciant̄. Neq; eni
qui circūcidūtur legem custodiūt: sed
volūt vos circūcidi ut in carne vestra
gloriētur. Michi aūt absit gloriari
nisi in cruce dūi nostri ihesu xristi: per
quē michi mūdus crucifixus est: ⁊ ego
mūdo. In xristo enim ihesu neq; circū-
cisio aliquid valet neq; pputiū: sed no-
va creatura. Et quicunq; hāc regulā
secuti fuerint: pax sup illos ⁊ misericor-
dia ⁊ sup israhel dei. De cetero nemo
michi molestus sit. Ego eni stigmata
dūi ihesu i corpore meo porto. Gracia
dūi nři ihesu xristi cum spiritu vřo fres
amen. Explicit epla ad galathas. Incipit
prolog⁹ in eplam ad ephesios.
Ephesij sunt asyani. Hij
accepto verbo veritatis p-
stiterūt i fide. Hos collau-
dat aplus scribēs eis a ro-
ma de carcere p tychicū dyaconē.
Incipit epla ad ephesios. i.
Paulus aplus xristi P.a.
ihesu p volūtatē dei
omnibꝫ sanctis qui
sūt ephesi: et fidelibꝫ
in xristo ihesu. Gra-
cia vobis et pax a
deo patre nostro: et dn̄o ihesu xristo.
Benedict⁹ de⁹ et pater dūi nostri ihesu
xristi q̄ benedixit nos i omī benedictione

1

Before Caxton

William Caxton first encountered printing when in 1471–2 fate took him to Cologne for eighteen months. The first printer there had arrived only six years earlier, in 1465, a mere ten years after the first printed book was completed. How and why printing had spread in so brief a time determined the course of Caxton's career.

European printing as we know it began in the city of Mainz, on the middle reaches of the Rhine, and it was along this main European artery for commerce that the technique spread in its first years. Its inventor, Johann Gutenberg, had experimented with forms of printing for many years, and fragments of those early experiments survive; there are also some documents, equally fragmentary witnesses to a life full of strife and toil. When his invention came to fruition in 1455 with the completion of a great Latin Bible, the new technique was greeted with joyful amazement. Gutenberg's Bible, printed in an edition of some 180 copies (of which about forty-five were printed on vellum) found buyers over a wide geographical area. We know that at least two copies reached England soon after printing was completed, for the style of the rich decoration of their margins and initials shows that it was painted in London, in approximately the same decade. Other copies can similarly be shown to have reached Trier, Cologne, Augsburg, Leipzig, and Erfurt at an early date, and also places as far-flung as Lübeck, Flanders, Utrecht, Vienna, and northern Italy. Yet, in spite of the successful sale of the Bible, mainly to abbeys and large monasteries, Gutenberg was not able to build a viable publishing business himself. This was achieved by his former partners in the venture, the financier Johann Fust and a younger man, Peter Schoeffer. They, the inventors of publishing, founded a firm that produced a sequence of very large books: psalters, bibles, civil and canon law, works by the Church Fathers and other theological literature, and the most beloved author of the Classics, Cicero. Johann Fust died in 1466, but Schoeffer, by then his son-in-law, continued the business which remained established in Mainz for several generations.

From the autumn of 1462 the city of Mainz was torn apart by a conflict among the Church and the secular authorities that lasted for several years. Gutenberg, exiled from Mainz, became one of its many victims, whereas Fust and Schoeffer printed with impeccable impartiality the broadside decrees issued by the chief combatants – the Emperor, the Pope and the two archbishops – whereas the

Fig. 1. A single vellum leaf, including part of the letters of St Paul, is all that remains of a copy of Gutenberg's great Bible. It was illuminated in London not long after its printing was completed in Mainz. Later, the copy was demolished, and this leaf ended up in the binding of a smaller book. Early in the eighteenth century it was rescued, rather the worse for wear, by John Bagford who sold it to Hans Sloane as a specimen of early printing. *Biblia latina*. [Mainz, Johann Gutenberg, 1455]. London, BL, IC. 56a, fol. [DD]7 recto.

previous production of large volumes was suspended until peace was restored. The violence in Mainz may have induced printers who had worked with Gutenberg and his successors to leave the area, for it was during this period that printers, many of them identifying themselves as natives of the Rhine region, swiftly spread out in several directions. Printing businesses had already begun to operate in Strasbourg (1460) and Bamberg (1461), and were followed by Cologne (1465), Basel (by 1468), Augsburg (1468), and Nuremberg (1469). Two printers from the Rhine area set up a press in 1465 in the Benedictine Abbey of Subiaco in the mountains not far from Rome, and moved to that city two years later. Other printers from the German lands moved to Italy and began businesses in Venice (1469), Milan (1470), and Naples (by 1470, possibly earlier), soon followed by other towns. In France, the Sorbonne press in Paris was established in 1470. In all these big cities the printing press arrived to stay. Gutenberg's experiments preceding the invention were probably shrouded in secrecy, but once the first printed books had come out, we can trace a story of expansion over a large area.

By 1471, when Caxton arrived in Cologne, printers had thus settled in twelve cities, seven in the German-speaking lands, four in Italy, and one in France. As presses were established, an ever growing number of punchcutters and typefounders, printers and compositors, the possessors of rare new skills, travelled as 'aliens' to foreign parts, and with them they carried the tools and specialized materials, the punches (original hand-cut characters used to make matrices), matrices (moulds in which type was cast) or cast type, that were indispensable to the trade. Presses were built on the spot. There is therefore nothing unusual in finding that most of the early printers in England were foreigners. All this migration of people and materials was possible because, in the early years, printing was mainly in Latin, the language of the Church and the lingua franca of the world of learning, a world without language barriers. The travelling printers, however, would find that in most of the great trading centres merchants who were compatriots were organized in 'nations', which enjoyed privileges and formal protection from the host city. In these communities they could share their native tongue and culture, and printers were welcome to join them. But trade connections within such cities ranged much wider, and the mercantile world was multilingual, in many vernacular languages.

The introduction of printing intensified what was already emerging as a cultural division, or what may be viewed as the coexistence of two parallel worlds. There was the world of the *literati*, the clerics, the academically educated, lawyers and doctors, who communicated in a single language, Latin. And then there was the multilingual vernacular

N princip
Obmissis d
dici tota er
uetus & nc
deo tanq̃ c
tanq̃ crea
tore & glo
diuidit̃ in q̃ttuor partes uideli
tales. Et quia uetus testament
Ezech. i. ca. Ideo no. testa. di
correspondet Euangelium. L
Apostoloꝝ. Libris historialibu
correspondet liber Apoca. C
legales uidelicet quinq̃ libros M
communitati populi adunati.
unius dei quod fit in libro Ger
hoc in Exo. & duobus libris se
explicatio & hoc fit in Deuter
nature humane productionem
ad electionem fidelis populi &
generationum ut patebit infra
facta est propter hominem na
plante propter animalia. anim
& iuuamentum. Corpora etia
scd̃m ꝙ dicitur Deutero. iiii. ca
& omnia astra celi & errore de
in ministerium cunctis gentibu
generaliter. Secundo hominis
Circa primum tria facit scripti
distinctionis seu formationis ib
dispositionis ibi. Dixit autem d
omnem diem. opus distinctioni
sequentibus. & septimo die requ
sententiam Hieron. in epistola
libris principium Genes. est ta
apud Hebreos non legatur. &
cibus expositiõibus tam doctor
confusio est tam intelligentie
expositionum illarũ maxime c
insistere scd̃m gratiam a domi
opiniones seu expositiones solle
qui istos sex dies exponit non
cognitionem angelicam relata
angelica duplex est. Vna est
omnis creatura ad deum cõpa
in uerbo & hec dicitur matutin

Fig. 2. Books printed by the first printers in Rome were often decorated in a style that became characteristic for most of Italy. The Bible commentary by Nicolaus de Lyra was their largest publication by far.

Nicolaus de Lyra, *Postilla super totam Bibliam*. Rome, Conradus Sweynheym and Arnoldus Pannartz, 1471–2. London, BL, IC. 17180, fol. [a]4 verso (detail).

world in which courts and their entourages had a very visible role, but in which the extensive mercantile classes and their organizations proved to be a growing power. The mercantile world was literate in its own way, in vernacular languages, and so was the smaller world of privileged, often highly literate women. Although printing belonged in the first instance to the Latin world, a slow and eventually successful process of conquest by the vernacular languages was set in motion not long after its invention. Caxton and his successors in England had an important, even decisive, part to play in it.

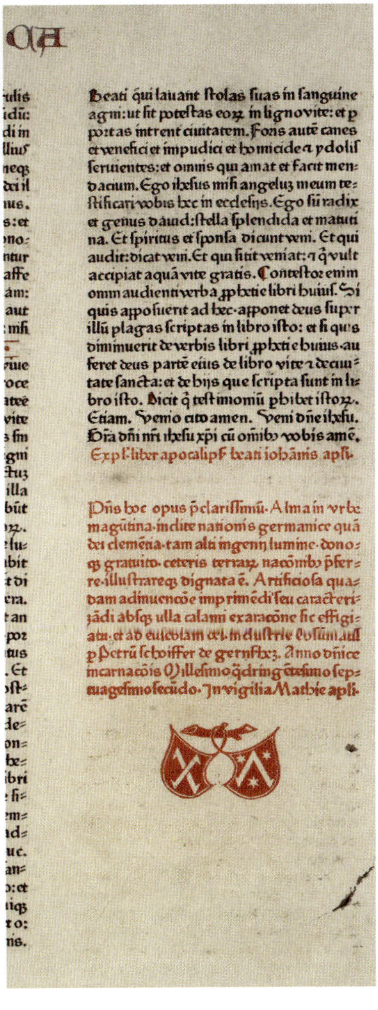

Fig. 3. This is an example of one of the many voluminous works published in Mainz. Schoeffer's device is printed below the lengthy colophon.

Biblia latina. Mainz, Peter Schoeffer, 1472. London, BL, IC. 168, fol. [kk]7 recto (detail).

Gutenberg's Latin Bible and the earliest books printed by Fust and Schoeffer in Mainz were probably printed with the strong backing of the Benedictine order, and in all likelihood the order gave practical support to their rapid distribution over a wide area. Although the Church remained an important client and backer of printers by commissioning the printing of liturgies and other major works, most printers had also to work on a speculative basis, relying on the book trade. What printers were to discover once their workshops were well established was that expansion, the multiplication of texts, could get ahead of itself. The need to sell what were in effect 'mass-produced' artefacts in order to recoup costs and continue production was a novel development with which the printers came to terms only gradually, and for which they had to find new business models. Fust and Schoeffer in Mainz seem to have avoided problems by a combination of institutional backing and well-perceived demand. But some years later, Konrad Sweynheym and Arnold Pannartz, the two printers who in 1465 had together been the first to settle in Italy in the abbey of Subiaco, and then in 1467 in the city of Rome itself (both were clerics, respectively from the archdioceses of Mainz and Cologne), complained bitterly that they were left with thousands of unsold copies of their fine editions, printed at great cost. Early in 1472 they published a letter addressed to Pope Sixtus IV, begging for his support, in which they added up the number of books they had printed in a period of just over six years, editions of the Church Fathers, an extensive Bible commentary, and many Classical authors. Thanks to their complaint we know that their edition sizes were usually 275 or 300 copies. The total of 'volumina' (or copies) they list of some forty separate editions adds up to the astounding figure of 12,475.

The first printers in Venice, who from the time they first set up their presses in 1469 enthusiastically produced books of monumental proportions, apparently fell into the same trap, and had to reduce their output for a while. But they recovered soon, for in Venice they had the advantage of operating in one of the Western world's greatest commercial centres. It was a pattern that was widely followed. In continental printing, existing trade routes for all kinds of goods, by land or by sea, proved to be the key to successful publishing enterprises. All through the first century of printing, the book trade was consolidated in great commercial cities, the nodes in these routes, which were also financial centres where venture capital could be found. Nowhere were more books printed than in Venice, but Milan, Nuremberg, Basel, Strasbourg, Cologne, and Paris, and in later years Lyon, Antwerp, and Leipzig, were the most influential centres of book production, exporting masses of books along the routes they commanded. Conversely, in small towns, universities, and monasteries, presses often disappeared after a few years, even if they had started out with strong local support.

Early printers depended for the distribution of their books on well-established networks, systems of agents and middle men; printing history is therefore inseparable from mercantile history. Many of the great commercial cities were connected by trade alliances. The Hanseatic League connected towns in northern Germany and Scandinavia with ports on the Baltic and with an entrepôt as far east as Novgorod, deep in Russia. It was in the interest of other cities to foster good relations with the League, often formalized in treaties. Bruges and London, although themselves not Hanseatic cities, offered special protection to merchants belonging to the League, and in the City of London the German merchants had a fortified establishment at the Steelyard, on the north bank of the Thames. Not less important for England was the fleet of Venetian galleys that twice a year put in at Bruges and Southampton with cargoes of luxury goods, including books.

The commercial centres offered another advantage: the presence of wealthy merchants who might either become partners with printers (as Johann Fust did in Mainz), or became patrons and backers without a formal association. In either form of participation they provided financial security and stability. Only occasionally do we know them by name. In Venice, the Frankfurt merchant Peter Ugelheimer was the financial backer, patron and friend to some of the early printers in the city, as is known from documents, and also from copies of their books he owned, all with *de luxe* painted decoration. The fortunate survival of account books shows in detail how in the 1470s Girolamo Strozzi, a member of the international trading *compagnia* of this Florentine family, multinationals of their time, financed the Italian translation of three important books – Pliny's Natural History and two histories of Florence – and subsequently had them printed in Venice. The accounts document that Girolamo Strozzi took an active part in their distribution in Italian cities through agents for the *compagnia*, and that they also sent copies to Bruges and London. Export of Italian books, destined for the mercantile communities in Flanders and England, is an exception. Generally, books

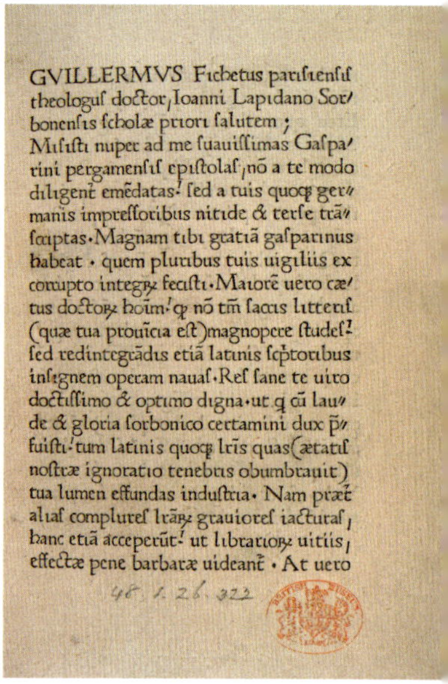
GVILLERMVS Fichetus pariſienſiſ theologuſ doctor, Ioanni Lapidano Sor-
bonenſis ſcholæ priori ſalutem ;
Miſiſti nuper ad me ſuauiſſimas Gaſpa-
rini pergamenſiſ epiſtolaſ, nõ a te modo
diligent̃ emẽdatas: ſed a tuis quoq; ger-
manis impreſſoribus nitide & terſe trã-
ſcriptas. Magnam tibi gratiã gaſparinus
habeat · quem pluribus tuis uigiliis ex
corrupto integrꝝ fecisti. Maiorẽ uero cæ-
tus doctorꝝ hoĩm: q nõ tm̃ ſacris litteriſ
(quæ tua prouĩcia eſt) magnopere ſtudeſ:
ſed redintegrãdis etiã latinis ſcptoribus
inſignem operam nauaſ. Reſ ſane te uiro
doctiſſimo & optimo digna · ut q cũ lau-
de & gloria ſorbonico certamini dux p̃-
fuiſti: tum latinis quoq; lrĩs quas (ætatiſ
noſtræ ignoratio tenebris obumbrauit)
tua lumen effundas induſtria. Nam præt
aliaſ compluteſ lrãꝝ grauioreſ iacturaſ,
hanc etiã acceperũt: ut librariorꝝ uitiis,
effectæ pene barbaræ uideant̃ · At uero

Fig. 4. The press at the Sorbonne, the first in France, was established in 1470 on the initiative and with the protection of two professors, Guillaume Fichet and Jean Heynlin. They appointed three printers from southern Germany who imported materials from the same region, including a roman type that appears to be specified by Fichet. The professors chose this text to set their pupils an example of writing good Latin.

Gasparinus Barzizius, *Epistolae*. Paris, Michael Friburger, Ulrich Gering, Martin Crantz, [c. 1470]. London, BL, IA. 39002, fol. [a]1 recto.

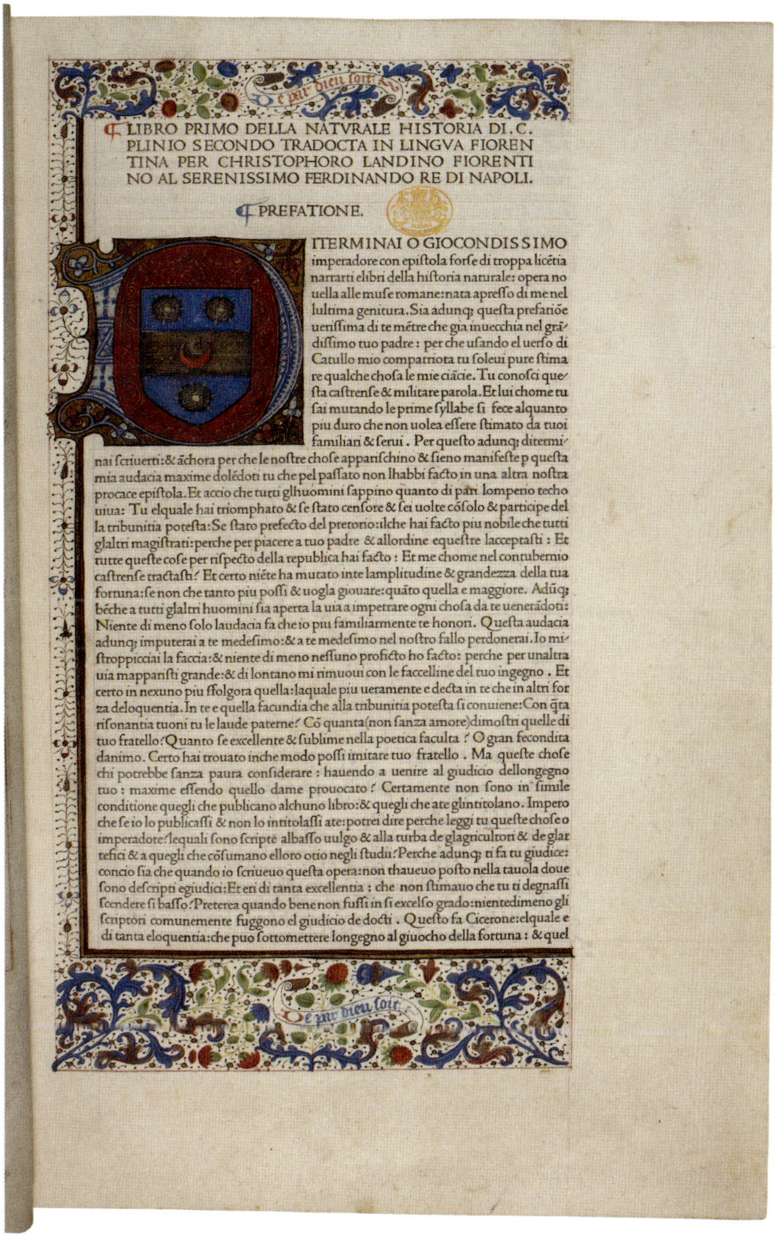

Fig. 5. Pliny's classic was translated on the initiative of the Florentine merchant Girolamo Strozzi. His account books document that he also financed its printing in Venice, and that he marketed it himself. The first owner (a Frenchman) had the book lavishly decorated.

Gaius Plinius Secundus, *Historia naturalis*. Translated into Italian by Cristoforo Landino. Venice, Nicolas Jenson, 1476. London, BL, C. 3.d.2, fol. [a]5 recto.

printed in vernacular languages were not intended for the world market but for smaller areas, strictly defined by language. In this case it was a prominent merchant who took the initiative to have important works translated from Latin into a vernacular language, and supported their publication in print as well as their wide distribution. The initiatives Caxton took were remarkably similar.

2

Caxton in Bruges: merchant and diplomat

Caxton was one of the most communicative publishers of all time. From his first publication in the English language, the *Recuyell of the histories of Troy*, published in 1473 when he was residing in Flanders, he preceded with extensive prologues many of the works he translated and printed, sometimes for good measure adding epilogues at the end. In these garrulous pieces he takes the reader into his confidence and reveals what led him to publish the text that followed, often translated by himself, his motives for its selection, reflecting on the value it might have for others, his recommendations and reservations. His engaging prose can speak to us directly, even today. The learned works printed in Mainz, Rome, and Venice often ended with enigmatic, punning colophons in sophisticated Latin, difficult to unravel. He would have come across some of them, but such mannerism was not for him. It seems that he wished to distance himself from this kind of publishing, underlining the cultural distinction by declaring that he did not belong to that world. He saw himself, he repeatedly wrote, as a 'simple person' – at least compared with such intricate manifestations of learning.

In contrast to the revelations he made during his later years, from which a self-portrait emerges such as we have of few other publishers, we know almost nothing of Caxton's youth, except some records of his formal steps on the career ladder and the usual activities of a merchant. From the time when he had reached the apex of that career, in 1462, with his appointment as Governor of the English Nation in Bruges, a good deal of archival documentation survives that allows us to follow his activities, but his own voice is not heard until he began printing in English. Yet, even with this paucity of personal detail, much more is known of the formal antecedents of Caxton's life before he became a printer than of the lives of any of the other early printers in England.

Caxton himself informs us in the first of his prologues to the *Recuyell of the histories of Troy* that he was born in the Weald of Kent, and that he had lived for thirty years overseas, 'for the most part in the countries of Brabant, Flanders, Holland, and Zeeland'. He leaves it to us to guess the date of his birth and his parentage. In all likelihood he belonged to a family of Caxtons who for several generations had been Mercers and a branch of which lived in the weavers' town of Tenterden in Kent,

Fig. 6. In the earliest of his prologues Caxton relates the conversation with Margaret of York in which she commanded him to complete the translation of the *Recuyell* (after correcting his English). He dared not disobey her.

Raoul Lefevre, *Recueil des histoires de Troies*, in the translation by William Caxton entitled *Recuyell of the histories of Troy*. [Ghent?], William Caxton, [c. 1473]. London, BL, C.11.c.1, fol. [a]3 recto.

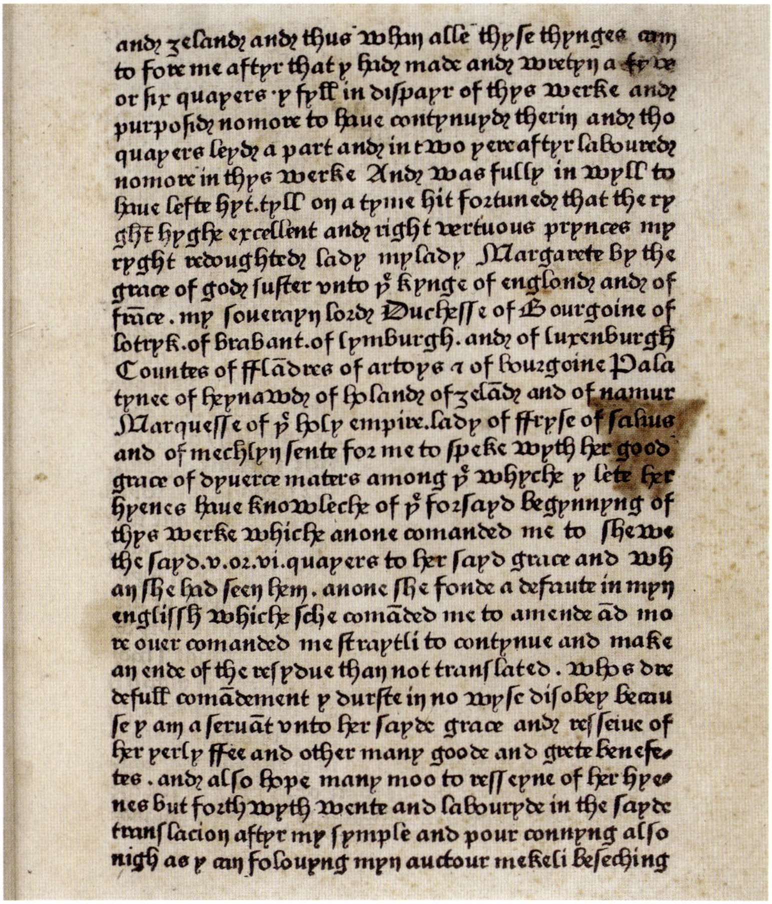

and zelande and thus whan alle thyse thynges cam
to fore me aftyr that y had made and wretyn a fyve
or six quayers . y fyll in dispayr of thys werke and
purposid nomore to haue contynuyd therin and tho
quayers leyd a part and in two yere aftyr laboured
nomore in thys werke And was fully in wyll to
haue lefte hyt . tyll on a tyme hit fortuned that the ry
ght hyghe excellent and right vertuous prynces my
ryght redoughted lady my lady Margarete by the
grace of god suster unto yͤ kynge of englond and of
frāce . my souerayn lord Duchesse of Bourgoine of
lotryk . of brabant . of lymburgh . and of luxenburgh
Countes of fflādres of artoys & of bourgoine Pala
tynee of heynawd of holand of zelād and of namur
Marquesse of yͤ holy empire . lady of ffryse of salins
and of mechlyn sente for me to speke wyth her good
grace of dyuerce maters among yͤ whyche y lete her
hyenes haue knowleche of yͤ forsayd begynnyng of
thys werke whiche anone comanded me to shewe
the sayd . v . or . vi . quayers to her sayd grace and wh
an she had seen hem . anone she fonde a defaute in myn
englissh whiche sche comāded me to amende ād mo
re ouer comanded me straytli to contynue and make
an ende of the resydue than not translated . whos dre
defull comādement y durste in no wyse disobey becau
se y am a seruāt unto her sayde grace and resseiue of
her yerly ffee and other many goode and grete benefe
tes . and also hope many moo to resseyue of her hye
nes but forthwyth wente and labourde in the sayde
translacion aftyr my symple and pour connyng also
nigh as y can folowyng myn auctour mekeli beseching

which may well be his birthplace. We may deduce that he was born sometime between 1420 and 1424 from the earliest document in which he appears in person, the record of his enrolment fee to the Mercers' Company, paid in 1438. In his teens he was apprenticed to a prominent Mercer in London, Robert Large, and the custom was that such apprenticeships lasted from seven to ten years. We do not know when he moved to Flanders, but given his statement written in the early 1470s that he had lived there for thirty years, this was probably some time in the 1440s, during his apprenticeship. The first time his name appears in a document as present in Bruges is in 1450. By then in his late twenties, he was a freeman of the Mercers' Company. Two years later he took the Company's livery, as noted in its accounts.

Sporadic records show that during the decades he lived 'overseas' Caxton occasionally visited London to complete transactions, but that he lived in Bruges among the English merchants organized as the English Nation, enjoying privileges granted centuries earlier by the Counts of Flanders. Their official residence in Bruges was the 'Domus Anglorum', 'The House of the Englishmen', but there is no record that he actually lived there.

Within the system of privileges and protection granted by diverse authorities, mercantile interests had to be negotiated and defended; they were a major lever in the continual shifting of power between the three neighbouring countries, flexing their muscles as newly emerging modern nation-states: the kingdoms of France and England, and the duchy of Burgundy that over the generations had expanded from its original French territory as far northwards as what is now the Netherlands. In Caxton's time, the War of the Roses erupted once again in England. Meanwhile the kingdom of France and the duchy of Burgundy coexisted as major powers in a precarious balance. Both varied their alliance to England's reigning monarchs according to the political weather. The dukes of Burgundy had never-fulfilled aspirations to turn their extensive territories into a third kingdom, reconstituting the middle kingdom of Charlemagne's son Lothair. Flanders and Brabant were their richest lands, and their flourishing cities, Lille, Brussels, Mechelen, Ghent, and Bruges, were the dukes' preferred residences for their opulent courts. Until the final decades of the fifteenth century, Bruges was pre-eminent among them as a centre of international trade and finance, with its settlements of organized 'nations' of merchants, and with particularly close connections with Florence, Genoa, and Venice. The Italians imported luxury goods for which there was a rising demand in the prosperous Flemish cities, but Bruges was also a gateway to the German lands in the east, and Holland and Zeeland in the north. Bruges, therefore, was a colourful, cosmopolitan centre for culture and trade, until, in the late 1470s, its political tide began to turn, and, coincidentally, the creek from the North Sea that led to its harbour silted up. From then on Antwerp took over its metropolitan and cultural role.

From Bruges the English Mercers could cover a large area with their trade, which would include a variety of goods but consisted principally of woollen cloth, brought from England and sold in the cities of Flanders, Brabant, and Holland in competition with the local weaving industry. Much business was done at the seasonal fairs that took place at fixed times in Antwerp, Bergen op Zoom, Middelburg, and in Bruges itself. Cloth had supplanted raw wool as the main import from England, for wool had to be traded through the Staple at Calais, with the drawback that it attracted heavy taxes. For these reasons the Mercers were predominant among the English merchants in the Low Countries, their headquarters in Bruges being controlled from London by the Court of Merchant Adventurers. That Court was the authority that appointed the Governor of the English Nation, and in 1462 it chose Caxton for the position.

In a region where so much importance was attached to trade, and where for its sake the value of peace was much appreciated (especially by Duke Philip the Good of Burgundy during his lengthy reign), much was achieved by diplomacy. Conferences and diplomatic missions occurred frequently, in which, along with noblemen and prelates, prominent merchants participated. In those circumstances, particular to the era, the Governor of the English Nation had an influential role as diplomat. It is in this function that we can catch occasional glimpses of Caxton associating with high-ranking envoys sent by the English king, contacts that would be as crucial for his later career as printer-publisher as were his wide experience in the world of commerce and his friendships with fellow Mercers.

Although the sparse official record shows exceptionally favourable circumstances, there are factors that do not form part of it, which were at least as decisive for the later part of Caxton's life. The most obvious, if hidden, fact is that he not only rose to eminence among his peers, but that he must also have prospered in the trade, providing sufficient capital to finance his printing business, and to all appearances comfortably so.

At least as significant for his future as man of letters was that he was fortunate to witness at first hand in Flanders a period of exceptional creativity in literature and in the production of beautiful books. In the course of the fifteenth century the manuscript book had flourished in the cities of Flanders and Brabant as an exuberant expression of courtly culture. In the years Caxton resided in Bruges and travelled across the region, its cities, Bruges in particular, saw a 'golden age' in the arts, as sometimes springs up when prosperity attracts and inspires a variety of talents. In Flanders and Brabant this age has left lasting traces, most famously in painting and also in sculpture, architecture, music, tapestry, literature and historiography, but most prolifically of all in manuscripts illuminated with painted miniatures. Several traditions in manuscript production combined to reach artistic heights rivalled in its time only in a few cities in Italy and France. The mighty abbeys and other religious houses in Flanders had included scriptoria since the thirteenth century. Some of the manuscripts of this period, soberly decorated, still exist. In the same period, libraries containing works of learning began to be formed. They contrast with a new, secular, tradition that originated at the French courts, where in the fourteenth century we see manuscripts of French texts, not only decorated, but enriched by miniatures painted with immense refinement. The most famous collection of such manuscripts was that of the French King Charles V, which contained some thousand volumes, dispersed by the end of the fourteenth century. By then the dukes of Burgundy had started to continue the tradition.

Duke Philip the Good, who died in 1467, was a great patron of arts and letters, and his library the most famous of its time. Many of its 900 or so manuscripts are still extant in the Royal Library in Brussels.

With its mainly literary, historical, and religious texts in French, it has often been taken as the model that determined Caxton's choice of texts to translate and publish, but its influence was less direct, for in its time it was not the only such library, and around it flourished a culture of literary patronage and bibliophily. Other collections, belonging to Philip's sons, to lesser nobility, and to civil servants in the Burgundian administration, had much in common with the ducal library, albeit on a smaller scale. The manuscripts in Burgundian collections were often of texts commissioned from authors by their patrons and produced by scribes and illuminators who were great artists in their own right. One major library in Bruges belonged to the Adorno family, merchants of Genoese extraction, who included humanist manuscripts in their collection, and even drew up plans to make it publicly accessible. A library of even greater fame was that of Seigneur Loys (or Louis) de Gruuthuse, Seigneur de Bruges, a Bruges nobleman and patron of the arts, whose outstanding collection of manuscripts was mainly produced by the same artists as worked for the ducal library. We shall see that for Caxton's first patron, Margaret of York, Duchess of Burgundy, some sixteen lavishly illuminated manuscripts, several containing texts written especially for her, were produced over a period of not more than nine years.

Although numerous manuscripts were commissioned by various patrons, less spectacular books could be found at the bookshops in Bruges that clustered round the church of St Donatian. In the course of the century the city had become a centre for all aspects of the trade in manuscript books, and even became specialized in producing a particular genre: the books of hours that include daily prayers in the order prescribed by the liturgy. Books of hours served the private devotion of thousands of Christians, and had become very popular in the fourteenth century. In Bruges, their production, decorated in a characteristic style, became a local industry, with exports on a large scale, the business regulated by the local government which in 1426 issued rules for limners (illuminators) and miniaturists, protecting the local trade. In 1454 the Guild of St John the Evangelist (later 'St John and St Luke') was established, and as the trade had expanded, the original regulations were reinforced, and strict terms were imposed in 1457 by the council of the city's aldermen, at a time when Caxton resided in Bruges: only citizens of Bruges were allowed to produce books and to sell them, and anyone in a trade connected with books (as scribe, illuminator, binder or bookseller), had to join the guild and pay its dues.

It requires scant imagination to see Caxton as familiar with the reading habits of several layers of society, and aware of manuscript production and the book trade in the Flemish cities – as well as its restrictions. French was the language of the many prose texts multi-

Fig. 7. This manuscript was probably commissioned from Colard Mansion by Loys de Gruuthuse, portrayed in the dedication miniature, although his coat of arms and motto are not included in its border. The painter is designated as 'The Bruges Master of 1482'. The *Dialogus creaturarum* is a moralising bestiary written in the 14th century, consisting of 121 dialogues between many of God's creations, and some mythological beasts. Mansion translated a Latin version, published with many woodcut illustrations from 1480 onwards. See also fig. 19.

Maino de Maineri, *Dialogus creaturarum moralizatus*, in a translation from Latin into French by Colard Mansion entitled *Dialogue des créatures*. Manuscript, Bruges, Colard Mansion, 1482, fol. 1 recto. Collection Heribert Tenschert, Bibermühle, Switzerland.

plied in manuscripts, especially history, but also devotional literature and philosophy, lightened with chivalry and romance. Flanders was a bilingual country, Flemish being the language commonly used in its cities, not only in the streets and on the quayside but also among educated people; the deans of the Guild of St John kept their accounts in Flemish, for example. French was the language of high society and of high culture. Caxton was familiar with both; his translation of *Reynard the fox*, which he printed in 1481–2 and 1489, shows subtle understanding of a Dutch prose version. All his other translations are from French originals. From the comments that accompany his later translations into English, we can infer that he read many of these texts during the years when he was overseas. For his reading he would not have depended on the magnificent manuscripts written and painted in the Flemish ateliers for the great of the land, but he was steeped in the high culture that they represented, even when transmitted in manuscripts of more modest style.

seulement de theseus et de
philottes au grant regret de
ceulx de thebes qui conuin
neirent roy sur eulx. Lapus
le filz du roy agenor dassirie
pource quil auoit espousee
la fille du roy creon nommee
Jocasta

Comment hercules mist a
mort le roy laomedon et des
truisit troyes la seconde fois

Hercules donc et
theseus et philo
tes sen allerent
de thebes et cheuaucherent
en plusieurs lieux querans
leurs auentures et passans
par licie dont hercules fut
fait roy. Ilz se trouuerent
vng iour en mirmidone
ou pallais du roy eson ou
estoit Jason qui auoit em
prins de nagier en lisle de
colcos et faisoit lors ses ap
prestes. Quant hercu
les eut este festoye de Jason
et du duc peleus et il sceut
lentreprinse de Jason qui
vouloit conquerir le veaur
re dor. Il iura quil laccompai
gneroit et se fortune lui es
toit contraire quil sauen
tureroit en son emprinse
mener a fin. Quen feroye
le long compte Jason et her
cules preparerent vne tres
bonne nef et monterent
en mer et ne renouuelle
rent point leurs viures jus
ques a ce quilz vindrent au
port de troyes. mais encore
ne les renouuellerent ilz
point a ce port. Car le roy la
omedon estoit lors en troyes
quil auoit moult fortiffiee
et sachant estre descendu
en son port vng nauire de
grecz Il leur manda quilz
se partissent et quil estoit
ennemy des grecz. Jason

3
Caxton and Margaret of York, Duchess of Burgundy: his first translation

Against this background, a sequence of events acted as a catalyst in setting Caxton on his path as translator. It also brought him into closer contact with the entourage of the English court. The early years of Caxton's governorship in Bruges had seen a sharp decline in the relations between the Burgundians and England. Duke Philip the Good, cranky and bellicose in old age, decided to form an alliance with the French king against England, and to forbid the importation of English cloth, which led the English Mercers to leave Bruges and settle, temporarily, in Utrecht, just outside the Burgundian territories. Philip's son and heir Charles, although not less bellicose, chose to take a contrary course, and signed a secret treaty of friendship with King Edward IV while his father was still alive. After Philip had died in June 1467, Charles, now 'le Téméraire' or 'the Bold', sought openly to form an alliance with England against France. Friendship blossomed into a plan for a dynastic marriage between Charles and Margaret of York, the younger sister of Edward IV. Such a marriage necessitated protracted negotiations, re-establishing the relationship between the two powers and their mutual rights. Caxton probably had a role in these meetings, or was at least present, and thus it was that he met some of the prominent men who were to be patrons of his printed works, among them John Russell, then an envoy in the English delegation led by the Bishop of Salisbury, and Anthony Woodville, Lord Scales. The marriage was celebrated in Bruges in July 1468 in a week of festivities, with processions, jousts, pageants, and extravagant banquets, described with wonder by the chroniclers of the time. It was a sumptuous and above all colourful celebration of the House of Burgundy and its ancestry. Caxton was in a position to observe this display of Burgundian pomp from a ringside seat, and it led directly to his first work of translation.

Fig. 8. Hercules was the Greek hero who allegedly founded the dynasty of the Dukes of Burgundy. Here he is depicted killing Laomedon, in a manuscript written and painted in Flanders for Edward IV. See also fig. 23.

Raoul Lefevre, *Recueil des histoires de Troies*, here entitled *Le livre nomme Hercules*. Manuscript, probably Bruges, c. 1480. London, BL, Ms Royal 17 E. ii, fol. 171 verso.

Caxton's translation into English of what became known as the *Recuyell of the histories of Troy* is famous as the first book printed in English. The text was written in celebration of the tradition that the mythological heroes of ancient Greece were the forefathers of the dukes of Burgundy. The myths and the symbolism around this tradition throw light on why Caxton chose to translate this particular text, and hence on his transition from diplomat to translator and

Fig. 9. The opening miniature in this manuscript represents a meeting of the knights of the Order of the Golden Fleece held in 1468, the first chaired by Charles the Bold; Edward IV was made a knight of the order on this occasion. Not all the knights pictured were in fact present. All are dressed in ceremonial cloaks and wear chains with the golden fleece which is also illustrated in the border. In front are the four serving officers.

Statutes of the Order of the Golden Fleece. Manuscript, Flanders, c. 1470–73. The Hague, Royal Library, Ms 76 E 10, fol. 5 verso.

eventually publisher. The images of the Burgundian tradition may seem remote from the history of English printing, but they were very much a part of the world in which Caxton lived and thought; understanding what they meant to successive Burgundian rulers offers clues to the value Caxton and his contemporaries attached to them, and thus to the origin of the first book printed in English.

The famous Flemish portraits of the dukes, their male offspring and entourage, and their portrayal in miniatures, all feature the emblem of the Order of the Golden Fleece, its device, still recognizably in the shape of a sheep's fleece, hanging from a heavy golden chain. The order was founded in 1430 by Duke Philip the Good, and was to remain one of the most enduring and famous of the medieval orders of chivalry. It was similar in its ideals of nobility and support of Christianity to the English Order of the Garter on which it was modelled. Although Christianity was the leading principle of the Order, its patron saint being St Andrew, its imagery was pagan, entirely based on Greek mythology, in particular on the voyage of the Argonauts to Colchis at the end of which Jason won the Golden Fleece. Several generations before the Order was founded the court of Burgundy fostered the legend that the dukes were descended from the ancient hero Hercules, who early in his eventful life had been one of the Argonauts, and who had on his return from Colchis destroyed the city of Troy – its first destruction. Retaliation and further destruction followed, eventually leading to the Trojan War and the third destruction of the city by the Greeks.

On a later journey, on his way to Spain – as the the Burgundian legend was told in the time of Philip the Good's grandfather – Hercules had passed through Burgundy and married Alise; she gave birth to a son, who became the founder of the dynasty. There were tapestries in Burgundian castles depicting Hercules and the Argonauts. Philip the Good, brought up in the tradition, was more attracted to Jason and the Argonauts than to Hercules, and when he founded the Order of the Golden Fleece he conceived it as a band of thirty-one knights, tested in hardship to achieve a common purpose, a clear parallel to the Argonauts led by Jason. Connotations of a crusade, the soul of Christianity substituted for the fleece of the myth, were deliberate, as was the symbolism of the Lamb of God, one of the most powerful and universal symbols of Christianity in the late Middle Ages. Jan van Eyck's glorious Ghent altarpiece depicting the veneration of the Lamb was completed in 1432, only two years after the Order was established. The Order's emblem and symbolism is conspicuous in all its outward manifestations, its chapter meetings and the pomp surrounding them, the tapestries that were displayed on great occasions, and the fine manuscripts with the Order's statutes and other texts it inspired. But in an order committed to the protection of the Christian faith (and which indeed contemplated a Burgundian crusade) there was persistent tension between the pagan emblems and biblical symbols. Notably, objections were made to taking Jason, a hero of very dubious virtue, as an emblem of moral leadership, and it was suggested that the Old Testament hero Gideon would be more appropriate, and could even be adopted without the need to change the Order's name or its main symbol: in Gideon's story as related in the Book of Judges, his faith in God was tested by means of a sheep's fleece.

As the duke, a literary patron on the grand scale, encouraged the retelling of the story of Jason, Medea and the Argonauts, the mythical Jason's immorality and infidelity were gradually disguised and reshaped. In this vein the first chancellor of the Order, Jean Germain, wrote a version of the story, partly inspired by the Christian interpretation of Ovid's *Metamorphoses* known as the *Ovide moralisé*. Several years later, Raoul Lefevre (allegedly Philip's chaplain, about whom hardly anything is known) rewrote the story of Jason and the golden fleece once again and dedicated it to Philip the Good, apparently having undertaken the writing of this version on his own initiative. For his *L'Histoire de Jason*, completed in 1460, Lefevre turned such early sources as were available to him into a chivalric romance, inserting other stories taken from the *Ovide moralisé*, with the result that Jason emerged as a conquering knight with a perhaps not impeccable reputation, but no longer a byword for infidelity. The duke must have approved, for he then commissioned from Lefevre the sequel, the history of the Trojan War describing the four successive destructions of the city of Troy: the first two by Hercules on his return from Colchis, the third by the Greeks as the outcome of the Trojan War, and the fourth not mythical at all but during the first Mithridatic War (90–85 BC). However, when Lefevre had completed his *Recueil des histoires de Troies* in 1464, he had covered only the two destructions by Hercules, who was treated as the main protagonist. He thus reverted to the earlier focus of the ducal ancestry.

Three years later Charles the Bold succeeded his father, and in 1468, shortly before his marriage to Margaret of York, he chaired for the first time a chapter meeting of the Order (see fig. 9). There it emerged that this highly erudite warrior felt a closer bond to the heroic figure of Hercules than to Jason. Weeks later, as part of the wedding celebrations, twelve short plays were staged in which episodes in the life of Hercules were mimed. Clearly, whoever wished to flatter the new duke would do better giving his attention to Hercules than to Jason. This cannot have escaped Caxton, who proceeded to translate Lefevre's *Recueil*, despite the logic of the narrative, which begins with Jason and the Argonauts.

When Caxton's English *Recuyell of the histories of Troy* appeared in print, it included five separate statements about the circumstances of and reasons for the translation, written by himself. It is the first time he offers us his beguiling prose. Not only does its tone set him apart from the intricate language of Latin culture usually found in printed books at the time, he also distances himself from the high-flown expressions customary at the French-speaking court. When reading his words it is crucial to appreciate his sincerity – which has been doubted by some scholars – while at the same time bearing in mind that his simplicity may sometimes disguise a rather more complex background situation. As in all texts written in earlier times, there is room for interpretation.

The opening of the work contains two statements of particular interest, since they relate the circumstances in which Caxton made his translation. The book begins with a plain and apparently precise statement (distinctive only by being printed in bright red), which must have been written when the translation was completed, and we

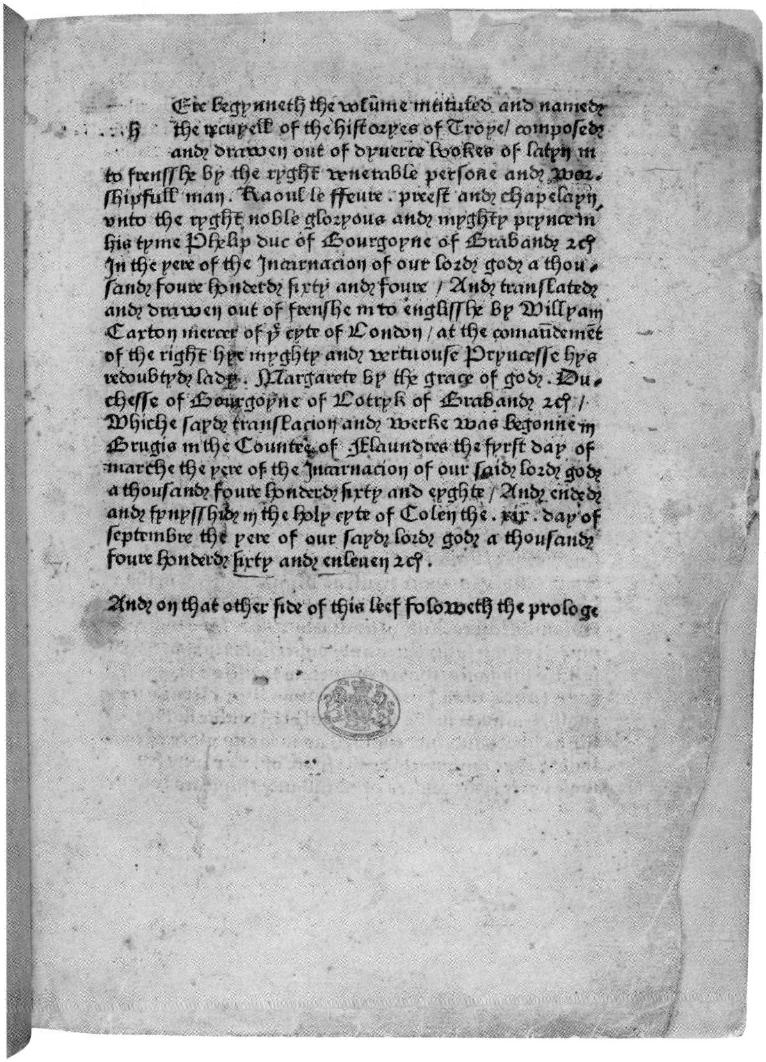
h ere begynneth the volume intituled and named the recuyell of the historyes of Troye / composed and drawen out of dyuerce bookes of latyn in to frensshe by the ryght venerable persone and worshipfull man . Raoul le ffeure . preest and chapelayn vnto the ryght noble gloryous and myghty prynce in his tyme Phelip duc of Bourgoyne of Braband etc In the yere of the Incarnacion of our lord god a thousand foure honderd sixty and foure / And translated and drawen out of frenshe in to englisshe by Willyam Caxton mercer of ye cyte of London / at the comaundement of the right hye myghty and vertuouse Pryncesse hys redoubtyd lady . Margarete by the grace of god . Duchesse of Bourgoyne of Lotryk of Braband etc / Whiche sayd translacion and werke was begonne in Brugis in the Countee of Flaundres the fyrst day of marche the yere of the Incarnacion of our said lord god a thousand foure honderd sixty and eyghte / And ended and fynysshid in the holy cyte of Colen the . xix . day of septembre the yere of our sayd lord god a thousand foure honderd sixty and enleuen etc .

And on that other side of this leef foloweth the prologe

Fig. 10. The opening page of the *Recuyell of the histories of Troy*, the first book printed in English. The date of the translation ('between 1468 and 1471') can be interpreted in different ways.

The text was printed in red. Space was left open for painting or drawing an initial H, but this copy was left without such decoration.

Raoul Lefevre, *Recueil des histoires de Troies*, in the translation by William Caxton entitled *Recuyell of the histories of Troy*. [Ghent?], William Caxton, [c. 1473]. London, BL, C.11.c.1, fol. [a]2 recto

might have expected to find it at the end, in the form of a colophon as was customary. As it is, it announces the work as if it were a title page, a feature of printed books which was as yet undeveloped. The work, says the red text, was begun in Bruges on 1 March 1468 and finished in Cologne on 19 September 1471, and was commissioned by Margaret, Duchess of Burgundy. Stated with authority, this sounds clear enough, but it is not as simple as it sounds.

In the first place the date '1 March 1468' raises a question: is it given in the style of the modern calendar, the year beginning on 1 January, or in the style of Flanders, where the year was usually taken to begin on Easter Day, or perhaps in the English style, the year beginning on Lady Day, 25 March? All three styles were commonly used, and none would have been inappropriate for Caxton, but if it was either the Easter style (which in 1469 fell on 2 April) or Lady Day, the year would not have been 1468 but in modern usage 1469. The other statement in this short preface, that the translation was commissioned by Margaret, Duchess of Burgundy, would appear to settle this question: Margaret of York was not a Duchess of Burgundy before her marriage in July 1468. But now the much more extensive prologue that immediately follows the initial statement informs us about the circumstances of the beginning of the translation, and this raises further doubts. Caxton writes that he had begun the translation to make the text available in England as well as in other countries, that after making some headway, proceeding recklessly 'like a blind Bayard', he had found the task unexpectedly difficult, and doubting his abilities had set it aside for a year or two, until he happened to show it to the young English duchess, in whose service he was by then. A dynastic marriage leads to the need to educate a young princess in the unfamiliar language and ways of her husband's court, delightfully reported by Caxton in a dialogue that anticipates Shakespeare's Princess Catherine learning English. As in *Henry V*, an older confidant instructs the young spouse; except that this young spouse is respectfully depicted as a woman of remarkable determination: '...anon she fonde a defaute in myn englissh whiche she comanded me to amende and moreover comanded me straytli to contynue...' and complete the translation.

Although there is ample documentary evidence to show that the years immediately after the ducal marriage were a busy time for Caxton the Governor, he duly worked on the translation, visiting Margaret's court when she resided in Bruges or in Ghent. Meanwhile, however, Caxton revealed in his prologue that he had begun his work of translation speculatively, without the commission by a patron – acting in the mould of the Burgundian authors who over more than a generation had established a pattern of dedicating literary and historical works to the highest in the land, in the expectation of commissions for further writing. Raoul Lefevre was only one among many examples that might be followed. Caxton the diplomat with a penchant for vernacular literature may even have conceived the idea for this translation during Charles's approaches to Edward IV in the year before Duke Philip died, or perhaps during the negotiations for the marriage treaty, when many eminent Englishmen were in close contact with the court of Burgundy. The translation would have been an inspired piece of diplomacy, explaining the cultural background of one of the parties to the other, an occasion for not too subtle flattery. Or, the first inspiration may have been the preparations for the wedding celebrations with their pageantry on the themes of Burgundian ancestry and symbolism, the works of Hercules in the forefront in honour of Duke Charles. Such situations would support March 1468 as the time when the translation was begun, but there is no way to be certain. Caxton's choice of text, the *Recueil* with the tales of Hercules favoured above those of Jason (which he translated later) is clearly connected to

Charles the Bold, but if he ever had an English patron in mind other than Margaret of York, this was not the occasion to tell us.

If Caxton adopted the pattern of seeking literary patronage that he had observed during his many years in Flanders, Margaret chose also to make a highly Burgundian gesture when early in her marriage she commissioned the translation of a work in the literary or historical tradition. The choice of text could hardly be bettered as a work entirely to her husband's taste. Although Charles has gone down in history as the fighter-duke who was killed in battle while pursuing a vain military ideal, he was, like his father, a very considerable patron of the arts and literature. He is pictured by his contemporaries when solemnly receiving manuscripts from authors, scribes, or artists, but also more playfully, lurking behind a pillar to spy on his scribe. Margaret followed the Burgundian model energetically, but as we shall see, without sharing Caxton's taste either for texts or for their presentation in print.

In the years it took Caxton to complete the translation of the *Recueil* (whether he had started it in 1468 or 1469) and later again its printing, a sequence of events took place that affected him deeply. As far as Caxton was concerned, the years 1469–70 seem to have brought business as usual for the Governor, testified by records of messages and gifts of wine from various cities in the Low Countries. But meanwhile the situation in England became extremely unstable in a renewed eruption of the War of the Roses. In rebellions throughout the kingdom, Edward IV was successively imprisoned, released, embattled, and finally overthrown. He fled early in October 1470 by ship from King's Lynn. Penniless, he landed on the Dutch coast where he was rescued by the governor of the county of Holland, the Bruges nobleman Loys de Gruuthuse, who offered him hospitality, first in The Hague, and later in his palatial mansion in Bruges. During this humiliating exile, with the Lancastrian king Henry VI back on the throne, Edward's presence was at first barely tolerated by his brother-in-law Duke Charles. However, by early 1471 the duke began to see strategic advantage in supporting Edward, and helped him return to England in March that year. Edward's forces won in a series of battles, and on 11 April 1471 he was restored to the throne and began his second reign, consolidated by further victories in May.

In none of the records of these events is Caxton's name so much as mentioned, yet it is unthinkable that the king's presence in Bruges would not have required some form of response from him, either as the Governor of the English Nation, or as the servant of the king's sister Duchess Margaret. Would Caxton have been placed in an awkward position of divided loyalties: which king was he formally representing? Or was he perhaps obliged to keep his distance, in line with the Burgundian court? There is an indication that at some point during this episode he must have put a foot wrong: in June 1471, shortly after Edward's restoration to the throne, we find Caxton in Cologne, granted a residence permit for one month, twice extended, to the end of 1472. Obviously, he was no longer Governor; at an unknown date a fellow Mercer, John Pickering, was appointed as his successor. Also, on 8 March 1472, halfway through the period of his residence in Cologne, Caxton was granted by Edward IV a pardon 'for all manner of crimes before 4 March last'. Whatever crimes Caxton had committed at a time which in the prologue to the *Recuyell* he described as 'troublous ... and of grete devysions', the period of clearly enforced lack of official duties gave him the opportunity to take further steps on the evolutionary path that was to characterize the last twenty years of his life.

4
Caxton in Cologne

The official documents in the city of Cologne's record of 'strangers', with their custom of giving precise dates, give substance to the testimony written more than twenty years later by Wynkyn de Worde, Caxton's successor in Westminster. One of De Worde's most ambitious publications, an illustrated English translation of a lengthy medieval natural history, Bartholomaeus Anglicus, *De proprietatibus rerum*, concludes with a long, sonorous poem. In it De Worde states that the work was previously published by 'William Caxton first prynter of this book / In laten tonge at Coleyn'.

Initially, however, before his first encounter with the printing business, Caxton enjoyed 'good leyzer beyng in Coleyn and have none other thynge to doo at this tyme in eschewyng of ydlenes, moder of all vices' – none other than completing the translation of the *Recueil des histoires de Troies*, that is. The threat of idleness must have mainly occurred in his first months in the city, for these words in one of his prologues to the translation of the *Recueil* can only refer to a time before 19 September 1471, the date of its completion. After that date he very successfully eschewed it with his first publishing venture.

If the cities of Flanders and Brabant were places full of colour, it may not be unfair to think of Cologne in black and white. Instead of secular courts and their culture, its dominating presence was its university with a high reputation for the scholasticism of Thomas Aquinas and his followers. The city was an archiepiscopal see – the building of its enormous medieval cathedral was not finished until the nineteenth century – and it was famous for its many monasteries and convents. But apart from this concentration of austere learning, its position on the Rhine at the crossroads of trade routes made it an important commercial hub, and it was one of the great centres of the Hanseatic League. It is therefore not surprising that modernity did not take long to find its way there, in the form of printing houses.

When Caxton arrived in Cologne in the summer of 1471, one printing house had been active there for just over five years, and from 1470 the city's printing industry had been expanding rapidly. The first printer in Cologne was a cleric, Ulrich Zell, who in 1464 had moved down the Rhine from Mainz, where he had worked in the printing house of Johann Fust and Peter Schoeffer. Perhaps driven away by the political troubles in Mainz, he settled in his new environment by matriculating in the university, which gave him certain civic rights. Early in 1466 he completed the first of what was to be a steady stream of small quarto editions of theological and a few Classical texts. They were well suited to the requirements of Cologne's university with its important theological faculty, but his market was larger. Even its first printer knew how to exploit Cologne's foremost position as a centre of trade in north-west Europe, and its trading routes in all directions of the compass. Zell maintained in particular his close relations with the printers in Mainz. Peter Schoeffer included books printed by Zell in an advertisement he issued *circa* 1469, and he may even have commissioned from Zell the printing or reprinting of certain titles. The connection is also apparent in the appearance of Zell's books, for they were printed in the typographical style first used in Mainz by Fust and Schoeffer with printing types possibly obtained from them. Zell's consistent production of quarto editions complemented the equally steady output of large folio editions in Mainz, and undoubtedly he also traded in books printed there. Part of Zell's business may have functioned as a branch office for the more affluent Mainz printers, until at the end of the 1470s Schoeffer's trade in books changed direction, and he became a wholesaler of works printed by others. By then Zell's printing house had gained sufficient momentum to continue on its own. This business model – a flourishing printing house opening a 'branch office' elsewhere – will be met again in England, especially in Oxford, where the two earliest printing houses were in all likelihood established on the initiative of printers in Cologne.

If Zell managed to work as an independent printer, finding various means to finance his business, the success of his endeavours did not escape the attention of several of Cologne's enterprising merchants, who were used to dealing in many kinds of commodities. In the year before Caxton's arrival a business pattern began to emerge in which a merchant would act as publisher, occasionally being named as such in colophons. The merchant would engage a printer to produce a few books for him, and he would then market the books along with other goods in which he traded. None of these merchants published on a large scale, and this phase in the book trade in Cologne lasted only a few years – for then other printers set up successful larger printing houses – but these years, from around 1470 to 1474, include the time when Caxton was in the city. One merchant, a prominent citizen, may be singled out as a likely acquaintance of Caxton. Johann Helman had represented Cologne merchants in the Low Countries, and he was of similar age to Caxton. He is known to have backed printers and to have imported paper on a large scale. Like Johann Fust in Mainz, he was the father-in-law of an active printer, in his case Heinrich Quentell, founder of a business that continued for several generations. Although Helman's interest in printing cannot be documented earlier than *circa* 1478, it is thought probable that he was involved before that year. Merchants who took an interest in the printing business were likely to have been congenial to Caxton, and it may have been from them that he took his cue.

From this distinct phase in Cologne publishing in the years 1470 to 1474, just about fifty editions of quarto books survive produced by several different printers. Like almost all of Zell's books they were small quartos in Latin, but they were printed in quite different printing types that form a complicated but coherent group. Whereas Zell's types were in the style termed 'fere humanistica', adopted by the printers in Mainz for their great folio editions, and designed to please the eye of any scholar in the Latin-reading world, the type of the other contemporary Cologne quartos was based on the script forms traditional in several monasteries of Cologne. It was a script that was strongly influenced by the distinct style of the Brethren of the Common Life, also known as 'Frater script', and therefore associated with the monastic orders that were influenced by the religious movement of the Devotio Moderna (Modern Devotion) towards a simpler and more austere religious life.

The maker of this type must have intended to design a distinctive 'Cologne' style for the books, conforming to the hands found in manuscripts written in Cologne, rather than emphasizing a particular spiritual character. He can be identified as Johan Veldener, named after the small town of Velden in the bishopric of Würzburg; he was a gifted punchcutter who was to have a profound influence on the early years of printing in English and in England.

Identifying the publishers and printers of these fifty or so small books is difficult, because the evidence is unusually fragmented. Names of printers and dates are rarely given; moreover the typographical differences are only slight, because there was in fact just one fount of type cast for different clients, constantly in development. It has taken generations of scholarship to unravel the printing history

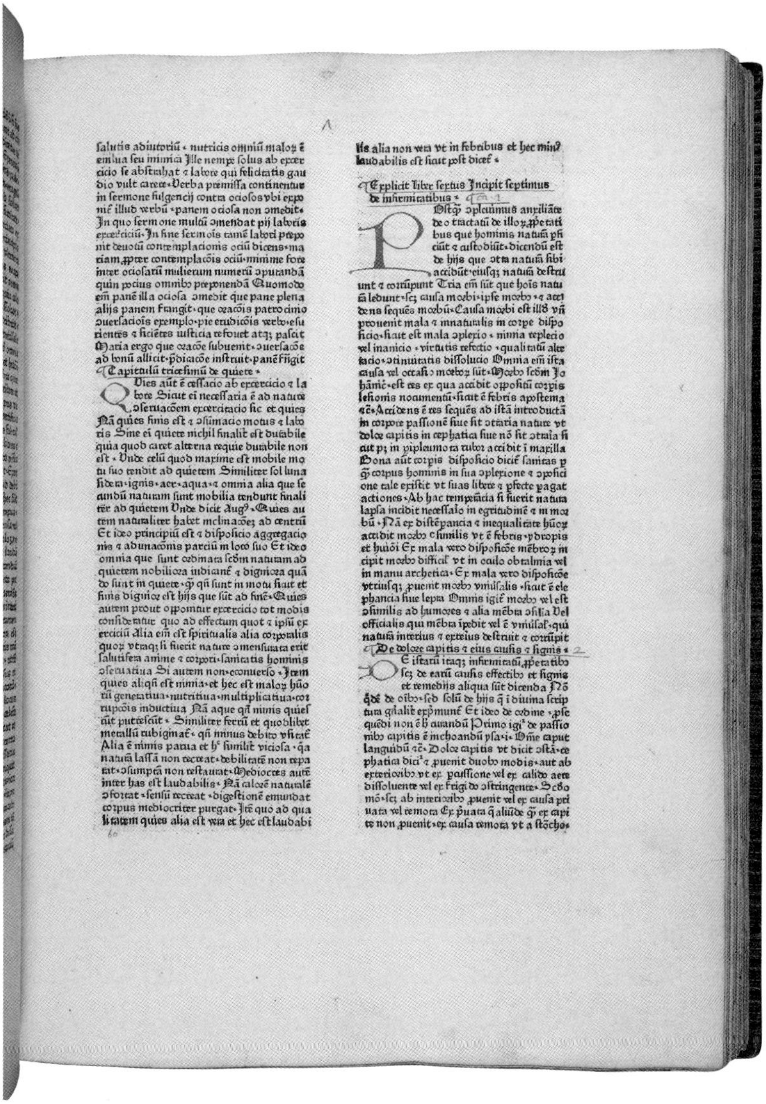

Fig. 11. The first book printed for Caxton in Cologne. The printing type is characteristic for Cologne and particularly close to that of the Printer of Dares (see fig. 13), but the size of the book resembles those printed in Mainz, as seen, for example, in fig. 3.

Bartholomaeus Anglicus, *De proprietatibus rerum*. [Cologne, William Caxton, 1472]. London, BL, IC. 3772, fol. [f] 5 recto.

of Cologne in those few years, and to grasp the intricate pattern created by some unnamed printers who were commissioned by certain Cologne merchants to print books of the kind that could be marketed along with other merchandise. The type for all of them was provided by Johan Veldener, who may or may not have printed a few of those books himself.

But for Wynkyn de Worde's testimony in his English edition of Bartholomaeus Anglicus, *De proprietatibus rerum* (translated in the fourteenth century by John Trevisa), published *circa* 1496, more than twenty years later, we would not have known that Caxton was responsible for the publication of three books in Latin closely related to the work of the anonymous Cologne printers. They are linked to them by the state of the Veldener type in which they were printed, but unlike the characteristically small Cologne books, they are three substantial folio editions.

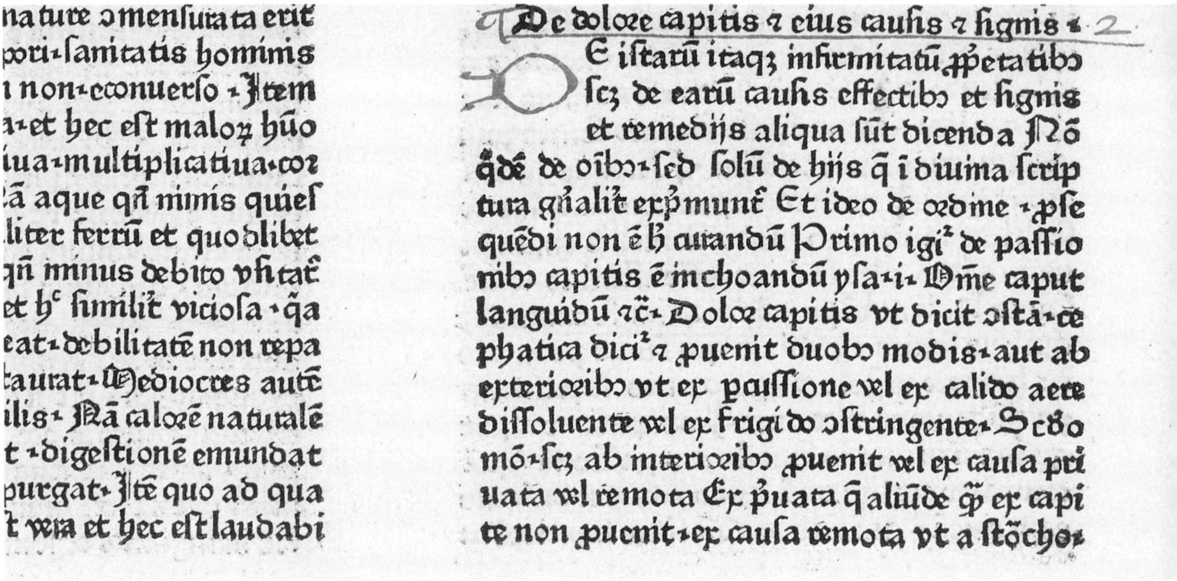

Fig. 12. Caxton's Cologne type, actual scale. Detail of the page shown in fig. 11.

By far the largest of the three books, almost 500 pages printed on paper of the extra-large size known as 'royal', is the original Latin text of Bartholomaeus Anglicus (figs 11, 12). The state of its type connects it with that in two more modest books, printed in a folio format on standard-sized 'chancery' paper. They are *De vita et moribus philosophorum* by Walter Burley and the *Gesta Romanorum*, both collections of stories with a moral attached. All three are Latin works of English origin, and perhaps Caxton selected them for their Englishness, although by this time all three texts were well known in continental Europe. From the early ownership of many surviving copies it is clear that they were not destined to be traded to England, but that they found buyers in the German lands and in adjoining areas like Liège (in modern Belgium).

The printing of an outsize folio format requires a large press, even when the work is printed one page at a time, as the Bartholomaeus Anglicus was. Only once before, probably in 1470, had a book been printed in Cologne with those dimensions (and with almost the same number of pages). Its printing type reveals that the printer was Ulrich Zell, but this publication had not been at the behest of one of the local merchant publishers. It was probably commissioned from him by Peter Schoeffer in Mainz, for it is an edition of the first part of the *Summa* of the great Thomas Aquinas, of which a second part had been published in Mainz in 1467 in a book of similar dimensions, as well as a related Aquinas text in 1469. Apparently, Schoeffer (working alone after the death in 1466 of his father-in-law and partner Johann Fust) did not have in 1470 the capacity to produce the first part while his presses were busily engaged on other large projects. The book Zell produced for him (without an imprint to reveal its origin) is

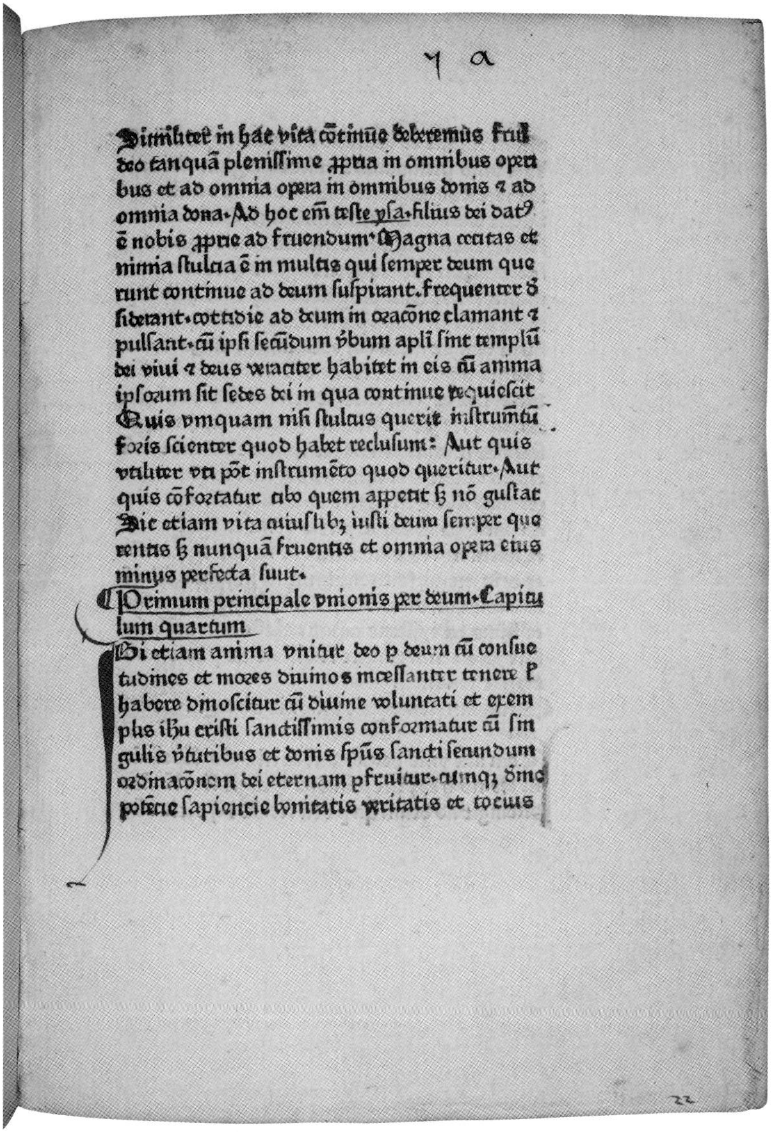

Similiter in hac vita cõtinue deberemus frui
deo tanquã plenissime ꝓpria in omnibus operi
bus et ad omnia opera in omnibus donis ⁊ ad
omnia dona. Ad hoc enim teste ysa. filius dei dat⁹
ē nobis ꝓprie ad fruendum. Magna cecitas et
nimia stulticia ē in multis qui semper deum que
runt continue ad deum suspirant. frequenter de
siderant. cottidie ad deum in oracõne clamant ⁊
pulsant. cũ ipsi secũdum v̄bum apli sint templũ
dei viui ⁊ deus veraciter habitet in eis cũ anima
ipsorum sit sedes dei in qua continue requiescit
Quis vmquam nisi stultus querit instrumentũ
foris scienter quod habet reclusum: Aut quis
vtiliter vti põt instrumẽto quod queritur. Aut
quis cõfortatur cibo quem appetit ꝫ nõ gustat
Sic etiam vita ciuiū lib; iusti deum semper que
rentis ꝫ nunquã fruentis et omnia opera eius
minus perfecta sunt.
¶ Primum principale vnionis per deum. Capitu
lum quartum
Si etiam anima vnitur deo p deum cũ consue
tudines et mores diuinos incessanter tenere ꝑ
habere dinoscitur cũ diuine voluntati et exem
plis ihu cristi sanctissimis conformatur cũ sin
gulis v̄tutibus et donis spũs sancti secundum
ordinacõnem dei eternam perfruitur. cumq; dine
potencie sapiencie bonitatis veritatis et tocius

Fig. 13. One of the small quarto books printed by anonymous printers in Cologne, the type representing handwriting common in several Cologne monasteries.

Thomas Aquinas, *Tractatus de beatitudine eternitatis*. [Cologne, Printer of Dares, before December 1472]. London, BL, C. 9.a.25/1, fol. [d]1 recto.

practically indistinguishable from the large folio editions Schoeffer published at this time (see for example fig. 3). Zell must have found it worth his while to get a large press built for him that would accommodate the royal folio format for this book, conforming in size with the Mainz editions of Aquinas. Thus it was that about a year later Caxton could find in Cologne a large press, not in use, on which to print the Bartholomaeus Anglicus in a presentation worthy of a large and important text; it was a presentation that despite its characteristic Cologne type could easily have passed as a product of the prestigious printing houses of its time in Mainz, Basel, or Strasbourg, and would be aimed at the same market. Fortunately, it is preserved in many copies, none of which were in England at an early date.

In Cologne Caxton encountered printed books in much larger quantity than he had ever seen in Bruges; moreover, he was for the first time in a place where books were printed, and he observed the interest his merchant colleagues took in commissioning the printing of books, and their active participation in all aspects of the trade. He decided that his financial position allowed him to follow this model, but to do so on a larger scale, and he may well have been inspired by an enterprising merchant like Johann Helman, and even more by the ambitious and successful printing business in Mainz, where Johann Fust's capital input had allowed the development of a flourishing firm.

Caxton took the necessary practical steps. There is no indication as to how he chose and procured the manuscripts for the texts he decided to publish, nor is there any clue to identify an adviser and/or editor who must have been on hand to supervise the processes of publishing Latin texts. Although all three works have English associations, manuscripts to serve as printer's copy could equally well have been found outside England. At the same time Caxton had to equip his printing shop. For his outsize book he procured a considerable quantity of the large-format royal paper – a product for which supply could not always be assured – and another supply of standard-size chancery paper for the two other books; he ordered a large quantity of type from Johan Veldener (for the setting of large pages requires more type than that of small pages); and he engaged a printer, who can probably be identified as Johann Schilling, who worked for a few years in Cologne before departing for Basel and Vienne-en-Dauphiné. Johann Schilling must have headed a small team of two or three more skilled men to assist with typesetting and to work the press while Caxton obtained the use of the large press from Ulrich Zell.

In the course of this process, Caxton must have learned a great deal about the mechanics of printing, about organizing a printing house and the marketing of its products. But the term 'printer', traditionally applied to everyone whose name appears in the imprints of early books, should not mislead us into thinking that Caxton himself set type or pulled at the press. Instead, he wielded his pen to translate or write texts, and did so until the end of his life. He was a publisher, the organizer and financier of a printing business, and was exceptional in contributing so many of the texts that were thus multiplied and sent into the world as a new form of books.

By the time the three books were printed, and many copies of them sold and dispatched, it was Christmas 1472. Caxton's time in Cologne was up, and he departed for Bruges, the translation of the *Recueil* in his baggage, and – presumably – in his head a vision and even a plan for what he could do with it.

5
Caxton's plans for a printing house

The decisions Caxton took in 1473, the first year after his return to Flanders from Cologne, were a sequence of perhaps still tentative steps, but they determined the nature of his publishing business throughout its existence. We must therefore consider in some detail the situation he faced and the options open to him.

We may first listen to what he declares himself, in his prologues to the two English translations he published in 1473–4, the *Recuyell of the histories of Troy* and *The game of chess*. Having accomplished the translation of the *Recuyell*, he writes, 'be cause I haue promysid to dyverce gentilmen and to my frendes to addresse to hem as hastely as I myght this sayd book / Therfore I have practysed and lerned at my grete charge and dispense to ordeyne this said book in prynte'. In the second edition of *The game of chess* he wrote retrospectively in 1483: 'by cause thys sayd book is ful of holsom wysedom and requysyte unto every astate and degree / I have purposed to enprynte it'.

The prologues are public statements, couched in careful wording, and we can be certain that much remained unsaid. We have to supply our own words when we try to present a fuller picture of the considerations that led Caxton to his life-changing decisions.

Immediately on his return he put into action a decision to publish in print his translation into English of the *Recueil*. In the course of 1475 this was followed by the decision to continue publishing in English, and to base his publishing enterprise in Westminster. Two discoveries made in the previous years led to these decisions: first, he had found confidence in his own literary skills in his mother tongue. There is every sign that he enjoyed having accomplished the translation of a substantial book, and he did not wish to leave it at that. His second discovery, following immediately on this feat, was of the multiplication of texts in print, and the trade in printed books.

We have already seen that by the early 1470s a considerable trade in printed books had developed. This was almost entirely of books in Latin, printed for the world of learning, books that could be marketed over a very wide area. When Caxton himself briefly had a taste of the trade in the early 1470s, he must have decided that this particular kind was not for him. Publishing Latin works required the backing of scholars for selecting works and editorial control of the text during the printing process. This could not satisfy Caxton's own interest in presenting texts; it was not his world, nor the world of the predominantly French-language literary culture in Flanders. His decision to publish in the vernacular was at that time still very unusual, driven in the first place by his wish to publish his own works in English.

In 1473, only a few printers had undertaken to print in vernacular languages; these were unconnected initiatives, widely dispersed. Looking at a map of Europe, and Caxton's position on it, we would see that he was quite remote from any towns where books in vernacular languages were produced. None are likely to have come to his knowledge before he started his own enterprise.

In vernacular printing we should distinguish between ephemera of strictly local use, such as almanacs and proclamations, and more substantial works with a potentially larger market, although of course limited to a particular language area. On the map, the town nearest to Caxton where vernacular printing had taken place was Mainz. Some pamphlets in German are even among Johann Gutenberg's early experiments. His successors in Mainz printed in the 1460s a few almanacs and – interestingly – at least five broadsheet public proclamations. Five German literary works of some substance and strikingly illustrated were printed in the years between 1461 and 1464 in Bamberg by Albrecht Pfister. Southern Germany was also the area where a much more constant production of German works was to begin, in Augsburg from around 1471 and in Ulm from 1473. But by far the most substantial work in the German language was a translation of the Bible, printed in Strasbourg by Johann Mentelin (before June 1466) and by Heinrich Eggestein (not after 1470). These two editions were obviously undertaken in the expectation of finding a ready market.

There is nothing to suggest that Caxton was aware of any of these enterprises, and it is even less probable that he knew that in Italy printing in the vernacular had suddenly started to bloom. From 1470 or 1471 on, along with many minor texts, the greatest Italian works by Dante and Boccaccio were published repeatedly, and there was in those early years also an Italian translation of the Bible. Although the many printers in Italy who undertook vernacular printing can hardly have served Caxton as models on which to base his business, there are similarities with a later phase in his publishing career, when he produced editions of earlier masterpieces of English literature by Chaucer, Gower, and Lydgate.

Apart from one or possibly two works in Spanish (the *Statutes* of Segovia and perhaps Jacobus de Voragine's *Golden legend* printed in Seville), by the beginning of the year 1473 this is the complete tally of printing in vernacular languages. There was as yet none in French.

These scattered examples of vernacular printing could not therefore offer a single business pattern for marketing printed vernacular books, as had so rapidly developed for books in Latin. The market for substantial works, certainly outside Italy, could not as readily be defined as that for Latin works, and it would vary in every area. Creating a market, creating a demand for vernacular texts in print, and especially literary texts, was therefore a considerable challenge. Without a precedent to follow – as had been available to him in Cologne – Caxton had to find his own solutions. Initially, he found his model in the earlier form of book production on a large scale, that of French-language manuscripts, which for decades had flourished in Flanders and neighbouring areas.

Even here, the relationship of the talented authors and artists, creators of hundreds of manuscripts that still survive as major works of art, with the patrons at the Burgundian court and with other noble bibliophiles on whom they were dependent, did not conform to a single, uniform pattern. There were distinct roles in the process of creation, and they could be balanced in different ways. In the first place, notions of authorship might include translation, editing, and compilation as well as writing original works. The scribe of a manuscript, often a courtier in the service of a patron, might also be its 'author' in this wider sense. Only the limners and painters of miniatures had a distinct function, and occasionally appear individually in accounts, apparently working under a separate arrangement. The author might work exclusively for one particular patron, as for example Charles Soillot for Duke Philip the Good and after his death for Charles the Bold, whereas others worked successively, or even simultaneously, for more than one patron.

Patronage was a key factor, but concealed behind the always florid introductory statements setting out the reasons for producing a particular work and praising the patron, and the many miniatures depicting the respectful dedication by a kneeling author to a grandee surrounded by his courtiers, a more subtle interaction was going on. Authors and scribes were professionals, and although undoubtedly they sought to influence their patrons, they would also try to find new clients, and to this end might produce work on a speculative basis. We have seen that already with Lefevre's first work, *L'Histoire de Jason*, and indeed with Caxton himself, casually showing his 'first quires' of the *Recuyell* to Duchess Margaret. Others were primarily book dealers. Jean Wauquelin, for example, was established as a scribe and dealer in Mons from where he sold books to the ducal library. In Bruges, Colard Mansion was probably a book-dealer rather than a professional scribe, and his most prominent patron and client was Seigneur Loys de Gruuthuse. Caxton had the opportunity to observe the variations in the relationships between patrons and book producers during his many years in Flanders, and especially when as Governor of the English Nation in Bruges he came into closer contact with the great and the good. Apart from the printing houses in Cologne, he took his cue from the scribal ateliers in Flanders, and he may well have approached more than one of them for assistance and possibly seeking cooperation. There is some evidence that Colard Mansion took part in Caxton's printing business in late 1474 or 1475, but there may well have been another associate before him.

Recent publications about the production of manuscripts in the Burgundian era make it seem possible that Caxton worked initially with one of the most prolific and experienced authors and scribes of his time. David Aubert was from 1453 in the service of Duke Philip the Good, after working for a bibliophile nobleman, Jean de Créquy, who had a fine taste for literature, but modest aspirations for the appearance of manuscripts. Some works, written for him on paper, were later copied for the ducal library as manuscripts of great splendour written on vellum. Aubert first served the duke in administrative functions, in the tradition of his family, but is later named as 'escripvain' (or 'scribe'), and also as compiler and translator. Between 1458 and 1467 he produced a sequence of some twenty-five major manuscripts, often dated and signed off at the successive cities in the ducal lands where the court resided, in Hesdin, Brussels, Ghent, and Bruges, his atelier moving with the court. The manuscripts were probably written by a small team of scribes under his supervision, but some are signed as written in his own hand, 'manu propria'. Many of his works are provided with extensive and flattering prologues, praising the duke's patronage. After a period of working exclusively for the duke, he found other clients among the great Burgundian bibliophiles, Guillaume Bourgeois, Philippe de Croy, and Antoine de Bourgogne, Duke Philip's natural son known as the Grand Bâtard. After Philip's death in 1467 it seems that Aubert reverted to mainly administrative duties, including the care of the ducal library, until Margaret of York commissioned him to produce a number of spectacular manuscripts, the earliest of which was completed early in 1475 in Ghent (where she then mainly resided) – after Caxton's *Recuyell* and *The game of chess* were printed.

It would seem that Aubert fulfilled many of the creative and organizing roles that we recognize as those of a publisher, but he did not take the same commercial risks. As far as we know, his manuscripts were always commissioned by a patron, undoubtedly after he had recommended a text, and this was often a text he had either translated or edited. The painting of the miniatures seems to have been independently commissioned, for there are records of separate payments for these in the ducal accounts, at least for the manuscripts produced before 1468, but cooperation had to exist between scribe and illuminator.

Margaret of York became Aubert's main patron when he resumed his role as scribe and author after a gap of some five or six years. Her patronage alone offers a link with Caxton, but there are a few more indications that Caxton was – at the very least – well aware of Aubert's

Fig. 14. The representation of an author dedicating his work to a patron, traditional in miniatures, was given the novel form of a copper engraving, its design ascribed to 'the Master of Mary of Burgundy'. The portraits of Caxton, the author/printer, and Margaret, his dedicatee, are probably realistic. The engraving survives in only one copy of the *Recuyell*.

Raoul Lefevre, *Recueil des histoires de Troies*, in the translation into English by William Caxton entitled *Recuyell of the histories of Troy*. [Ghent?], William Caxton, [*c*. 1473], engraving affixed to fol. [a]1 recto (detail). San Marino (California), H. E. Huntington Library.

manuscripts, his talents and skills, and the nature of his business. The most obvious is the style of Caxton's first printing type ('Type 1'), found in only five books, two in English and three in French, all traditionally ascribed to Caxton as printer. It is a close approximation to the wide, sloping hand adopted by Aubert for the manuscripts produced in his atelier – not necessarily all written by himself. The style contrasts with that of Caxton's second type ('Type 2'), that he took with him to Westminster, but that was used before his departure in a French book, the *Cordiale*, and in a very fine Book of Hours. Type 2, more upright and rounded, is closer to the style of script in one of the manuscripts (known as 'La penitance d'Adam') ascribed to the atelier of Colard Mansion, and conforms more to the style of other scribes working in Flanders in the period (see figs 15, 16, 22, 26–8).

Another possible association with David Aubert is the copper engraving that survives in only one copy of the *Recuyell*, representing the dedication of the book to the Duchess. It is the only illustration – much reproduced – known in Caxton's work before 1481, its technique an innovation in itself and found elsewhere in only a few early printed books, the *Recuyell* probably the earliest. The mise en scène of the traditional image of the dedication is particularly lively: the author – Caxton – kneels at the feet of his patroness and hands her the book – a novelty, a printed book! – as the demure ladies of her court divide their attention between the event and the pets attending the ceremony; a lot of whispering goes on in the back row. The design has been recognized as the work of an anonymous artist, known as 'the

Master of Mary of Burgundy', who from 1476 painted the miniatures in several manuscripts written and signed by David Aubert.

There are less material elements in Aubert's way of work that Caxton may consciously have followed: Aubert, the almost-publisher, his identity as author and translator emphasized in his prologues, made clever use of patronage, and produced work for several clients even though he was a functionary of the ducal court. Some of these features also apply to Colard Mansion, albeit on a smaller scale, but there is no indication that he ever counted the dukes of Burgundy or Margaret of York among his patrons. The latter's patronage is the strongest factor Aubert and Caxton have in common.

If we now return to trying to read Caxton's mind in the early months of 1473, we see uppermost the plan to present his works in print. The books would be much more modest in appearance than the richly produced bibliophiles' manuscripts, and more akin to the paper manuscripts of literary texts such as David Aubert had written in his early days for Jean de Créquy. Printed works, as Caxton had learned in Cologne, carried a considerable commercial risk, for after incurring the cost of production they required a plan for selling them. That risk might be mitigated by patronage, on the model of the scribal book production of the Burgundian lands.

Now, with the presence of Margaret of York and her patronage of his translation of the *Recueil des histoires de Troies*, he was in a position to follow the Burgundian model for a work in English, and to turn it into the novel medium of print. Within a year of publishing the *Recuyell* it was followed in print by another translation, Jacobus de Cessolis's *The game of chess*, dedicated to George, Duke of Clarence, brother of Margaret and of Edward IV (see fig. 16). What Caxton seems to have hoped to achieve was to persuade the English royal court to follow the Burgundian example of patronage, granting him a semi-official but well-recognized role as author and translator; English courtiers might even rise to the same level of enthusiasm as the collectors in the duchy of Burgundy were showing for French works. Even at this early stage, his ultimate ambition would have been aimed at the king. During his brief exile in Bruges in 1470–71, when he was the guest of Loys de Gruuthuse, Edward IV had surely become aware that it was fashionable to amass luxurious manuscripts, but it was not until 1478–80 that he commissioned the writing and painting in Flanders of a substantial number of them. Caxton, nevertheless, may have speculated on this incipient interest. Whether illustrious patronage would help to sell printed books, experience would show. It was a bold experiment.

Practical steps had to follow the plans that we may assume had formed in Caxton's mind. Setting up a printing house from scratch is a complicated business.

Equipment had to be built, a punchcutter and a typefounder had to

Fig. 15. This manuscript was produced by David Aubert for Margaret of York. The miniature, ascribed to the Master of Mary of Burgundy, represents Margaret kneeling in prayer with her ladies; the robed figure standing in the background has features of her spouse Charles the Bold, including the chain with the golden fleece.

Traités moraux et religieux. Manuscript, Ghent, David Aubert, 1476. Oxford, Bodleian Library, Ms Douce 365, fol. 115 recto.

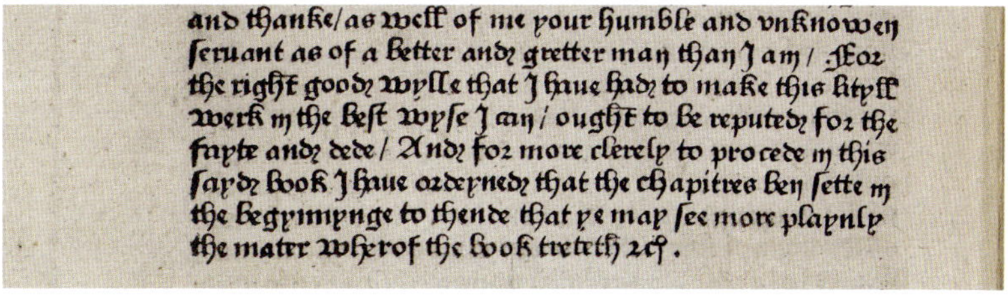

and thanke/as well of me your humble and unknowen
servant as of a better and gretter man than I am / For
the right good wylle that I have had to make this lytyl
werk in the best wyse I can / ought to be reputed for the
fayte and dede / And for more clerely to procede in this
sayd book I have ordeyned that the chapitres ben sette in
the begynnynge to thende that ye may see more playnly
the mater wherof the book treteth &c.

Fig. 16. Caxton's first Flemish printing type (Type 1) may be modelled on the style of script preferred by David Aubert (see above fig. 15 and below fig. 18). The type is here seen at the end of the prologue to Caxton's translation of *The Game of chess* which he dedicated to George, Duke of Clarence, brother of Edward IV and Margaret of York.

Jacobus de Cessolis, *De ludo scaccorum*, in the translation from a French version by William Caxton entitled *The game of chess*. [Ghent?] William Caxton, 1474. London, BL, G. 10543, fol. [a]2 verso (detail).

be engaged so that a regular supply of type would be available, large supplies of paper bought and printing ink, a new commodity, expertly prepared. And finally compositors and press crews had to be engaged and probably trained, since not all would have had previous experience in a printing house. As to compositors, here we meet a question to which there is no answer: did he engage Englishmen, who knew the language, or could compositors be expected to reproduce any language that was put in front of them – as they did for centuries to come? There is no sign in the setting of the two English books that the compositors misunderstood the language, and it is therefore probable – in the absence of proof – that Caxton found Englishmen and had them trained in the new skill.

Above all, as long as he was still based in Flanders, Caxton had to overcome an important obstacle: in Bruges, his residence for so many years, the strict regulations of the city and the guild would not allow anyone who was not a citizen of Bruges (a '*poorter*'), to carry out a business that had anything to do with book production. Whether a book was written by hand or 'mechanically' written, as the expression at the time was, the trade was forbidden to aliens. As representative of English interests, as Caxton still was, he could not obtain a citizen's rights. He could finance a business, but he would have to find a local associate to carry out the actual work. And so he had to decide whether strictly regulated Bruges was the best place for this innovation, or whether it would be wiser to start somewhere else.

6

The first books printed in English: a tale of the known and the unknown

In bibliographical scholarship, the first two books printed in English, the *Recuyell* and *The game of chess*, along with five others – four in French and a Latin Book of Hours for the use of Salisbury – are all considered as having been printed by or for Caxton. It has hitherto been generally agreed that this took place between 1473 and the end of 1475, though opinion has vacillated by one or two years. Today, bibliographers unanimously designate all seven books as printed in Bruges. But were they?

Bibliography has its origin in systems of classification, and therefore tends to use simplified labels for the known and eschew the unknown, always with the risk of attaching such labels to what under close scrutiny might better remain unclassified. In the case of the earliest books ascribed to Caxton in Bruges the unknowns are manifold, for none of the seven books now accepted as belonging to this first phase of English publishing includes a statement of where it was printed, nor is there any external documentation to supply such information.

Bibliographical classification is based on material evidence presented by the books themselves. It relies in the first place on the identification of printers according to the founts of type they used. For the group of seven books ascribed to Caxton 'in Bruges', two founts are distinguished, Type 1 and Type 2. Recently, investigations of the paper supplies used in these books has ranged the successive supplies in a sequence which established an unambiguous chronological order for the seven books. First came the *Recuyell* printed in Type 1 (the fount in the style of David Aubert's handwriting), followed by the shorter *The game of chess*, which bears the date 31 March 1474. Then, without date, came two works in French, the original French version of the *Recueil des histoires de Troies*, like the English edition a quite substantial work, and a much shorter religious text, a meditation on the Penitential Psalms by Pierre d'Ailly, at the time a popular text, both printed in the same type. Next, but still at an unknown date, Type 2 was introduced in the exquisite small Sarum Hours. On the basis of material evidence it is now agreed that the Hours were indeed printed in Bruges, and not in Westminster as previously thought. Sixth, also in Type 2, was a French version of the *Cordiale*, or *Traité des quatre dernières choses*, a text on preparation for death that Caxton later, in Westminster, was to print in English as *Cordyal* or *The four last thinges*. Lastly, and surprisingly, paper research has shown that a French book in Type 1, *L'Histoire de Jason*, did not immediately follow the sequence of other books in Type 1, nor does it have any paper in common with the *Cordiale*, but it appears to have been printed at a later date on isolated supplies not connected with any other printed books, probably after Caxton's departure to Westminster.

The discipline of bibliography has no difficulty in linking all seven books firmly with Caxton, for in the two books in English he names himself as having 'ordained' them in print. It follows that the three books in French that were printed in the same fount of type should also be ascribed to him. Type 2 is equally firmly associated with Caxton, for he used it for about six years as his main type in Westminster, and it was undoubtedly owned by him. In this neat arrangement the name of Colard Mansion is also supplied as Caxton's associate, although the only material link between them is the primitive and unsatisfactory technique for printing initials with red, surrounded by text in black, which appears in the *Cordiale*, and is also found in Colard Mansion's work. That Mansion was resident in Bruges and started publishing printed books under his own name in 1476, the same year as Caxton started to print in Westminster, added further substance to this notion.

Against the certainties of the bibliographers, who attach the label 'Bruges' to all seven books, the result of almost 150 years of observation and recording, historians who wish to reconstruct the events – how and where these books came to be produced – struggle with uncertainties that increase as more players who may possibly have been involved in this process are introduced into the scene. Research into the period has expanded, a few new documents have come to light, and the spotlight shines on new figures who emerge from the shadows of history.

There are now at least four, possibly five, historical figures known to have played a role in these events: Caxton himself, Margaret of York, Johan Veldener, Colard Mansion, and – we may now speculate – David Aubert. (A subsidiary figure is Margaret's brother, the Duke of Clarence, to whom *The game of chess* was dedicated.) As knowledge and understanding of these five major players has grown, so the interpretation of their interaction has changed – the figures sliding as if in a kaleidoscope into different but always neatly fitting configurations. Their backdrop, however, remains constant. It is the area from Bruges in the west to Cologne in the east, and between them the cities of Louvain, Ghent, Audenarde, and the other great towns of Flanders and Brabant. Over the years, Caxton had visited most of them, as is apparent from loose remarks strewn among his translations. But, Bruges and Cologne apart, he knew Ghent best, for he wrote in his prologue to the *Recuyell* that he had stayed there, working on the translation, before leaving for Cologne.

When we review briefly how Caxton's episode of printing in the Low Countries has been presented in the past, we may start by looking back to the first extensive biography of Caxton, written by the printer William Blades and published in 1861–3. There, we find Caxton alone holding centre stage, firmly situated with his printing house in Bruges, because it had long been his customary place of residence; Colard Mansion, known as a scribe and later a printer in Bruges, was associated with him as an assistant or pupil. It was Blades who noted the similarity in technique of red printing between the *Cordiale* and Colard Mansion's later work, and made much of it. Conversely, the idea was later mooted, and then again contradicted, that it was Colard Mansion who taught Caxton to print. Whichever way these roles were divided, Caxton was initially perceived as a craftsman who had mastered the art of printing, and headed a team consisting of a few assistants. Forty years later Johan Veldener entered the picture when E. Gordon Duff noted that Veldener was the first to use some of Caxton's Type 2 in one of his own books printed in Louvain. Then the documents recording Caxton's stay in Cologne were brought to light, while in Cologne itself the role of Veldener as punchcutter began to be understood, and new interpretations of the complicated history of the first years of printing in Cologne emerged in studies by Severin Corsten and Paul Needham. As a result, Veldener was brought forward as the main expert in all matters typographical who supported Caxton with founts of type and advice for at least ten years,

Fig. 17. Nicolas Finet, canon of Cambrai and confessor of Margaret of York, wrote for her this devout treatise. The manuscript presentation copy has the dimensions of a small prayer book, to be held in the hand. Its opening miniature, showing Margaret in prayer before the risen Christ, is ascribed to a follower of the Brussels painter Dreux Jean. The border includes her coat of arms and a flowerpot with marguerites on which part of her motto 'bien en aviegne' is just visible.

Le dyalogue de la duchesse de bourgogne a Ihesu Crist. Manuscript, Brussels, *c.* 1468–70. London, BL, Ms Add. 7970, fol. 1 verso, 2 recto.

and helped him set up his printing house, somewhat at the expense of Colard Mansion's reputation. By the time of the celebrations for the Caxton quincentenary in 1976, the word 'entrepreneur' was frequently applied to Caxton, and he was no longer perceived as an active craftsman-printer, but rather as a publisher. The addition of the name of David Aubert is new, for not until recent years has he been studied, his manuscript production surveyed, and the importance of his role in book-production in Flanders fully grasped; his oeuvre far exceeds that known to have been produced in the atelier of Colard Mansion.

When we try to create a new picture of what happened in 1473 and the early months of 1474, the period during which the workshop that printed the *Recuyell* and *The game of chess* was set up from scratch, we can be sure of the whereabouts of only two of the five main actors: Margaret of York's main residence was in Ghent and Colard Mansion was dean of the Guild of St John in Bruges until the end of 1473.

Margaret of York was from 1470 undoubtedly deeply interested in books, but her mind was not on printing nor on the history or pseudo-history she had encouraged Caxton to pursue. Instead, she commissioned devotional texts, all in French, and had them executed in spectacular manuscripts produced by the foremost scribes and illuminators in Brussels and Ghent, David Aubert among them. Until the death of Charles the Bold in January 1477, no fewer than sixteen such manuscripts were produced for her. In many of them she appears in the miniatures in person, a slim, wimpled figure in colourful cityscapes or interiors, her spouse sometimes pictured by her side or hovering in the background (see figs 15, 17). Her pictorial presence in the manuscripts may be likened to altarpieces in which the donor is explicitly represented in an act of devotion. Caxton's art could never satisfy the need for such religious expression.

Caxton's own life records are patchy between the time he left Cologne, at the end of 1472, and 1475, when he became an exceedingly busy man. He seems gradually to have regained his position as a prominent merchant and English diplomat. In the late summer of 1473 he was appointed as one of the ambassadors in lengthy negotiations with the Hansa merchants which were held in Utrecht. From August 1474 his role is much clearer; at that time he was present at the convent of the Carmelites in Bruges as a witness to the solemn conclusion of the negotiations with the Hansa, finally confirmed in Bruges on 20 April 1475. A month later he had embarked in the company of a Burgundian administrator on a tour of small ports in Holland and Zeeland as representative of Edward IV, charged with chartering ships in preparation for an invasion of France that Edward and the Duke plotted to carry out together. His progress in May and June can be traced by a trail of accounts in Dutch archives for the cost of receptions and dinner, and there is even a copy of a letter by him preserved in the city archive of the northern town of Hoorn, written in more than adequate Dutch, regarding this mission. On 4 September he was back in Bruges, once again witnessing the treaty with the Hansa. This is the last time we see him in a public function 'overseas'. Not long afterwards, or at least before the summer of 1476, he left for Westminster. Whatever Caxton did immediately upon his return from Cologne, the printing business was not his sole occupation, and from the summer of 1474 he would not have had time to lead a printer's business actively, and must have relied on an associate.

Of the three who might have assisted Caxton in his printing venture, Veldener's role seems least in doubt. His entire career as punchcutter and printer is a peripatetic sequence. He left Cologne at about the same time as Caxton, and matriculated at the University of Louvain at the end of July 1473, which would have given him the right to open a printing business in the city. In the following years he printed two books that probably preceded his first dated work, published in 1475 (this is the book with a few lines in Caxton's Type 2 mentioned above). During the same period he helped the Brethren of the Common Life in Brussels with the installation of their printing house and provided their founts of type, which are related to his own founts and those used in Cologne. There is no reason to assume that he was always present in Louvain once he was matriculated at the university.

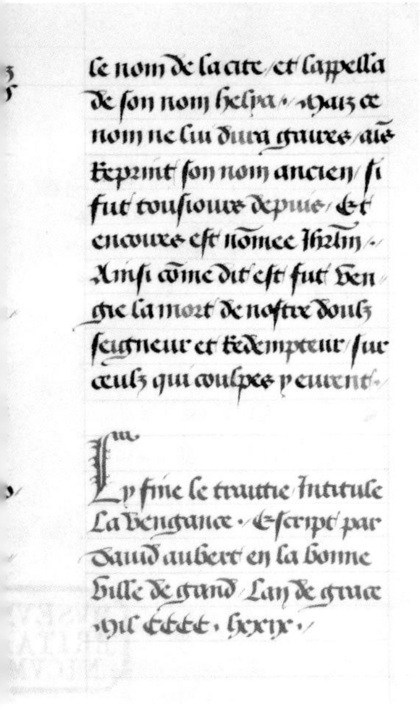

Fig. 18. The script of David Aubert. According to its colophon this, his last known manuscript, was written in his own hand.

La vie passion et mort pour le sauvement du monde and *La vengeance de la mort de Jhesu Crist.* Manuscript, Ghent, David Aubert, 1479. London, BL, Ms Royal 16 G.iii, fol. 193 recto (detail).

One outcome of an analysis of the printing of the *Recuyell*, presented in 1976 at the time of the Caxton celebrations, was that it seemed likely that an experienced compositor had set the early pages of the beginning of two sections of the book, including the opening page printed in red (see fig. 10). It was, and still is, tempting to hazard a guess that this was Veldener, after he had cut the many punches for Type 1 (a complicated fount that followed its scribal model), cast it, and also helped to install a workshop. We know for certain that in 1475 he produced Caxton's Type 2, because of its fleeting appearance in one of his own books.

David Aubert's career had been equally nomadic, working on translation and producing beautiful manuscripts wherever the ducal court would take him. This period of his activity ended in 1469, two years after the death of Philip the Good. He seems not to have worked at all for Charles the Bold, but instead fulfilled a few commissions for other Burgundian grandees, including Antoine 'le Grand Bâtard', the illegitimate half-brother of Charles. There seems to be no documentation of where and how he spent the five or six years after 1469 until he settled in Ghent by the beginning of 1475, the date he wrote in the colophon of the first of the manuscripts written there by him for Margaret of York: 'A este escript en sa ville de Gand par David son escripvain, l'an de grace mil CCCC soixante et quatorse, le premier du mois de fevrier.' (The year 1474 combined with a date before Easter must be interpreted as 1475 in the modern calendar. We have already encountered the same style of dating with the dates Caxton mentions in his prologue to the *Recuyell*.) In Ghent Aubert produced in an intensive burst of work six or seven magnificent manuscripts for Margaret of York, the last in 1476. Another followed later, in 1479. Opinions remain divided over the interpretation of the year-dates and whether one or two manuscripts should be ascribed to his hand, to his atelier or simply, on the basis of style, to 'Ghent'.

The role of Colard Mansion, whose presence in Bruges is seemingly so well documented, turns out to be the most problematic of the five. Before 1476 all we know with certainty about him is that he was a translator, and that he was associated with the book trade. His literary activity seems to be the main characteristic he has in common with David Aubert, and indeed with Caxton. There is even doubt about Mansion's work as a scribe. He may have been a book dealer who could organize the writing and illumination of manuscripts, and he may have had a small atelier. His first appearance on the scene is in the accounts of the Guild of St John the Evangelist in Bruges, where his first annual contribution is recorded in 1457/8, the year when the city council confirmed in strong wording its earlier restriction of any form of book trade to members of the guild. In the accounts Mansion's profession is not specified.

The earliest record of a transaction is not until 1467, when he sold a manuscript of *Romuléon* – not necessarily written by him – to the ducal library. Two translations are known to be his: *La pénitance d'Adam* (undated, but thought to be of the mid-1470s), commissioned by Loys de Gruuthuse who was undoubtedly his most prominent patron, and in 1482 the delightful *Dialogue des créatures*. Both texts were copied in very fine illuminated manuscripts (two are known of each), written in different hands, all of which may be ascribed to his atelier, but probably none to himself. [figs 7 and 19]

However, Mansion's fame rests not on the manuscripts, or even his translations, but on the twenty-four books he published between 1476 and 1484. Their main printing type exceeds in elegance the script of the manuscripts with which he is associated, and they include four books that stand out as rivalling in presentation and scale the most extravagant manuscripts of the period: his Boccaccio, *De la ruine des nobles hommes et femmes*, of 1476, some copies of which include copper engravings, probably designed by the same hand as the engraving in Caxton's *Recuyell* (see fig. 14); a French version of Boethius, *De consolatione philosophiae*, in 1477, in which he left spaces open for miniatures; Jean Boutillier, *La somme rural*, in 1479, printed in a new, somewhat more modest fount of type; and his own adaptation of the *Ovide moralisé* in 1484, illustrated with striking woodcuts. The other works are smaller but very well chosen, and include such literary gems as Alain Chartier's *Quadrilogue invectif*, *La danse des aveugles* by Pierre Michault, and *Le purgatoire des mauvais maris*.

We have to remind ourselves, however, that all this well-deserved fame was earned in the years from 1476. Before then there is little evidence of the extent to which Mansion was active in any area of the book trade. The accounts of the Guild of St John provide the outsiders' view of his career. Between 1457/8 and 1474 he appears most years in the accounts, but not in 1469 and 1470; he fulfilled the function of dean in 1471–3. Some extensive and unusual notes in the accounts reveal a fickle side of his nature which posterity has preferred to overlook. When he was dean he took the initiative for building a new altar for the guild (which was based in the Bruges abbey of Eekhout), and put up the sum of three pounds in loan, to be paid back by voluntary subscriptions of fellow members. The financial aftermath of this devout and public-spirited project was, however, chaotic, if not downright irregular. His successor as dean, Jos Scheede, was left with a mess to clear up, a process which he carefully recorded in the accounts, his irritation shining through. He notes, circumstantially, that Mansion, when dean, had ordered him to lend him a sum of money for the altar; at least thirteen members of the guild voluntarily contributed various sums. But in addition Mansion had withheld the guild's revenue from other sources, and was now, we

Fig. 19. Colard Mansion, pictured as an author, translator, and publisher, supervises two scribes who are copying manuscripts for him. Through the window parts of a church and other buildings are seen, suggesting a view of Bruges. The oversized sun and moon, already traditional in printed editions as illustrations of the first dialogue of the *Dialogus creaturarum*, are also a Flemish-language pun on Mansion's name: 'maan' and 'son'. See also fig. 7.

Maino de Maineri, *Dialogus creaturarum moralizatus*, in a translation from Latin into French by Colard Mansion entitled *Dialogue des créatures*. Manuscript, Bruges, Colard Mansion, 1482, fol. 7 recto. Collection Heribert Tenschert, Bibermühle, Switzerland.

may infer, claiming more than was his due. Scheede calculated it all in a written statement, called in May 1474 a meeting in the hostelry Het Vlieghende Hert, where he presented Mansion with the statement and the (small) amount still due to him, in the presence of four named witnesses and many other members of the guild ('veel meer andere ghildebroeders').

This confrontation may have soured Mansion's relations with the guild. Between 1474 and 1480 he paid only once an annual contribution (in 1479), despite intense activity as a printer during most of those years, but he reappears in the accounts in 1481 to 1483. In 1484 Mansion fled Bruges ('profugit' is the term used in a note), abandoning his shop and leaving behind him debts which he may have incurred in producing the sumptuous *Ovide moralisé*.

Mansion excelled in creating projects on a grandiose scale, manuscripts, printed books, and even an altar. But business sense is also a must for a successful publisher, and there he was clearly falling short. Money was his undoing.

Once again we can try to position these five figures in a new and coherent picture, filling with hypotheses the gaps where facts are absent and querying the hypotheses that have crept into acceptance as fact. The difference this time is that the (still incomplete) data can now be set against the larger backdrop of manuscript production in Flanders and the subsequent production of printed books in Bruges, Audenarde, and Ghent which strove to equal the finest manuscripts in scale, quality and style.

We may find a cue for a new interpretation in the style of Caxton's two printing types and their connection with distinct scribal hands. 'Early printed books imitated manuscripts' is a pronouncement incunabulists usually feel compelled to contradict, pointing out that typography progressed as a process of rapid simplification of script forms, a logical consequence of the complexity of the manufacture of type. In the beginning printing was called 'mechanical writing', and 'mechanical' implies the loss of all the variation that is produced by the writing hand, even at its most professional. Subtle differentiations in script forms according to the position of a letter in a word were phased out, separate letter forms replaced 'tied letters' or 'ligatures' (combined letters) that reproduced the connected aspect of script. Medieval scribes were in the habit of saving space and time by using many abbreviations and contractions, a convention that in typography was gradually abandoned for the sake of clarity and convenience for the reader. This process can be observed within the first twenty to thirty years of printing, although it progressed at different rates according to circumstances and requirement. We can see it very clearly in the successive founts created by Johan Veldener. In Cologne, Brussels and Flanders he successfully represented traditional forms of script of quite distinct styles, in very complicated founts with many abbreviations and ligatures. In his later work he appears to have accepted the simplifications that would make a fount much more efficient to work with.

The first founts of type used by Caxton during his time in Flanders are very clearly typographical representations (or imitations) of hands found in Flemish manuscripts. Books printed in these types exhibit an undeniable kinship to such manuscripts, although they are more modest and lack the colourful extravagance of the work of the Flemish ateliers. To achieve for Type 1 the effect of David Aubert's own hand and that of manuscripts written for him, a very extensive, complicated fount was cut, with many ligatures and variant character

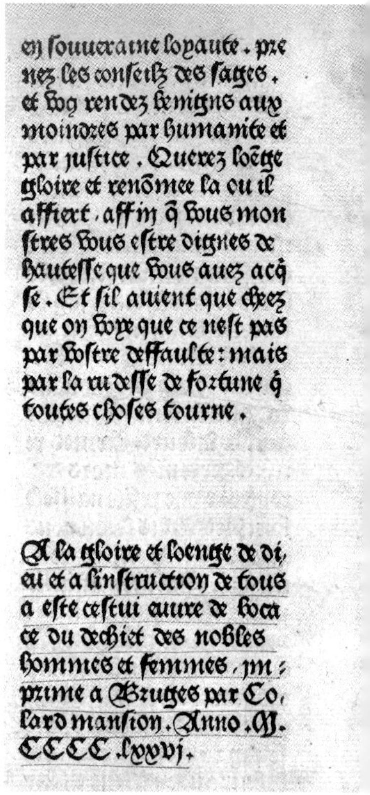
en souueraine loyaute . pre
nez les conseilz des sages .
et vous rendez benignes aux
moindres par humanite et
par justice . Querez louenge
gloire et renomee la ou il
affiert . affin q̄ vous mon
strez vous estre dignes de
haultesse que vous auez acq̄
se . Et sil auient que chez
que on voye que ce nest pas
par vostre deffaulte : mais
par la rudesse de fortune q̄
toutes choses tourne .

A la gloire et louenge de di
eu et a linstruction de tous
a este cestui euure de boca
ce du dechiet des nobles
hommes et femmes . im
prime a Bruges par Co
lard mansion . Anno . M .
CCCC . lxxvj .

Fig. 20. Colard Mansion's main text type was designed on an exceptionally generous scale, shown here on the final page of the Boccaccio. This very large book is one of the first he published.

Giovanni Boccaccio, *De casibus virorum illustrium*, in the translation into French by Laurent de Premierfait entitled *De la ruyne des nobles hommes et femmes*. Bruges, Colard Mansion, 1476. London, BL, IC. 49402, fol. [G]9 verso (detail).

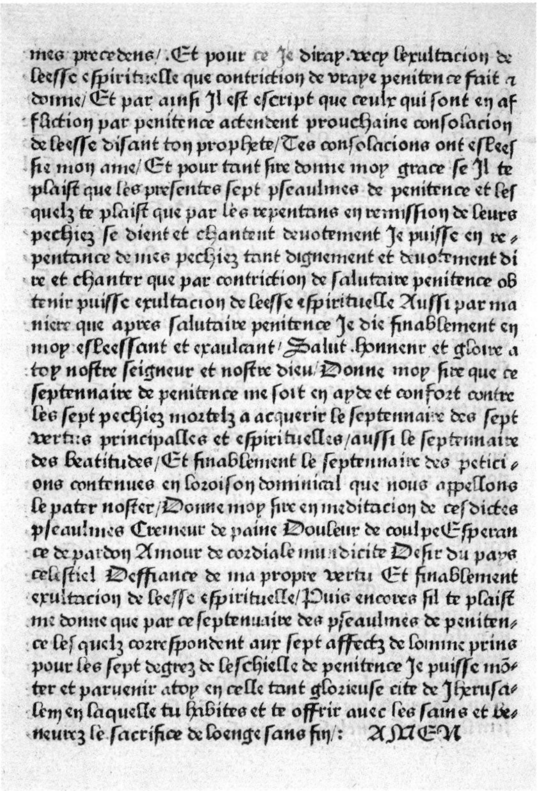

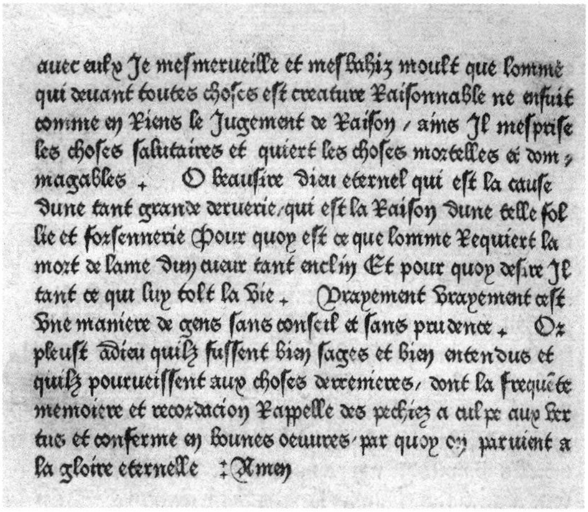

Fig. 22. Caxton's text type in the Flemish 'bastarda' style (Type 2), designed by Johan Veldener, was introduced in the last two books printed for him 'overseas', before he took it to Westminster. This French version of the *Cordiale* was probably printed for him in 1475 by Colard Mansion in Bruges.

Cordiale: Les quattres choses derrenieres, French translation by Jean Mielot of the *Cordiale quattuor novissimorum*. [Bruges, Colard Mansion for William Caxton, c. 1475]. London, BL, IB. 49437, fol. [i]7 verso (detail).

Fig. 21. Pierre d'Ailly, diplomat and bishop of Cambrai (d. 1420) was the author of many philosophical and theological works in Latin and French. The present work, a meditiation on the penitential psalms, is similar to the works of devotion written for Margaret of York. Since it is printed in the same type as Caxton's *Recuyell* and *Game of chess*, but very different in content, it may be a publication by David Aubert produced after Caxton had left Ghent.

Petrus de Alliaco, *Les sept degrés de l'échelle*. [Ghent? David Aubert? c. 1474]. London, BL, IB. 49408, fol. [d]9 verso.

forms. It takes up a lot of horizontal space, and economy did not dictate its design (see figs 6, 10, 16). In Burgundian manuscripts, economy never appears to have been an important consideration to their scribes. Type 2 is upright, rounded and bold, but despite being more compact it is not more economical, for being cast on a larger body it took up more vertical space (see fig. 22). It is almost as extensive and complicated as Type 1, and appears to be a stylistic precursor of the even larger, very beautiful type with which Colard Mansion began to print in 1476 (see fig. 20).

If we now assume that these stylistic resemblances signify that Caxton had first formed an association with David Aubert, and that this was followed by an association of shorter duration with Colard Mansion before he left for Westminster, we may propose a new configuration of the five main figures in the story, and tell it once again.

When Caxton left Cologne at the end of 1472 he did not head immediately to Bruges, but returned to Ghent, where he had attended the court of Margaret of York until the summer of 1471 and where she was still in residence. There he put into action his plan to print his translation of the *Recuyell*. According to its prologue he was still in her service, and, although he does not inform us of the nature of that service, it brought him again closer to the English court and

Margaret's royal relations. He may have hoped to create for himself at the English court a position similar to that of the book producers – translators and scribes – he had observed working so productively and prestigiously at the court of Burgundy. Printing his two English translations may have appealed to him as a form of distribution and communication, but, despite his commercial enterprise in Cologne, he may not have entertained strong commercial expectations for his initial plans for printing in English.

In Ghent he came to know David Aubert, who after many years of producing spectacular manuscript books had reverted to such functions of court officialdom as were traditional in his family. There are no manuscripts known to be written by him between 1469 and 1475. We may now hypothesize that Caxton formed an association with Aubert in which both had a stake, their aim being to produce by mechanical writing some books on paper in English and in French. These would be less ambitious than Aubert's great manuscripts, perhaps something along the lines of the well-chosen texts he had written in the service of Seigneur Jean de Créquy, before he worked for Philip the Good. Caxton procured the services of Johan Veldener to design a fount to represent David Aubert's script mechanically, and he engaged him also to install the printer's workshop and instruct (at least two) compositors. We can only speculate whether Caxton and Aubert shared both expenses and risks. Veldener fulfilled his commitment, and when he had set a few pages and had convinced himself that all was in working order, he would have returned to his other business in Louvain and Brussels – we may note that Louvain is a good deal nearer to Ghent than to Bruges. Caxton had his two English books printed, and their marketing, in so far as they were to be offered for sale, was his responsibility. But then the workshop in Ghent produced the two books in French, Lefevre's *Recueil* and Pierre d'Ailly's *Méditations*, and they were much more in Aubert's line of business. This must bring us towards the end of 1474. By this time Caxton had left Ghent (for we see him active in Bruges), and had left Type 1 there with Aubert, who did not immediately continue publishing in print after completing the two French books. Margaret of York commissioned him to write for her a number of luxurious manuscripts, the first completed on 1 February 1475, and he was fully occupied with this commission, free of any financial risk, for the next eighteen months to two years. But at the end of all that activity Aubert produced one more book in French printed in Type 1, to complement the *Recueil* and complete the oeuvre of Raoul Lefevre: *L'Histoire de Jason*. As we have already noted, records of the paper stocks show that the supplies used for this book were not related to those found in the books previously printed in Type 1, nor to any other printed books, and the work may have been published by Aubert as late as 1477. It is impossible to determine whether Caxton – by then in Westminster – had any share in its publication.

Early in 1475 Caxton, back in Bruges and back in favour with the king, had already conceived the plan to move to Westminster to begin printing there, this time with a stronger commercial basis. He commissioned from Veldener another fount of type (Type 2) that he wished to take with him, and this time he chose a more common Flemish style as his model, one that was also favoured by Colard Mansion; a matching fount for typographical contrast (Type 3, first seen in 1476 in Westminster) was to be delivered later. He himself was kept very busy in the middle of that year with his diplomatic mission on behalf of the king, but he entered into an agreement with Colard Mansion, who himself may have been beginning to plan the setting up of his own printing house in Bruges (as he was allowed to do as a citizen, if in those years a not altogether regular member of the guild). Mansion – commissioned by Caxton – tried out Type 2 in the Sarum Hours, a small volume for private devotion, to be held in the hand. It was printed in octavo format, a common size for manuscript books of hours, but at that time still an exceptional format to appear in print. Small-size manuscript books of hours had long been a specialism of the Bruges scribes and illuminators, who exported them on a large scale for use in many different dioceses. Into the Sarum liturgy of the printed version (for the diocese of Salisbury, and the common use in England) two additions were introduced, the Commemorations of the Three Kings and of St Barbara, who were particularly venerated in the Low Countries and in Cologne. The only substantial fragment of the Hours that still exists, printed on vellum, was beautifully illuminated in the traditional Bruges style. Mansion followed this with the larger French *Cordiale*, using a new supply of paper, the remnants of which Caxton shipped to Westminster, along with his Type 2 in the form of a very competently cast fount, and probably further equipment for a new printer's workshop.

For the sake of bibliographical clarity this rearrangement may be summarized as in Table 1.

TABLE 1. Caxton's seven Ghent/Bruges editions

Recuyell (English):	Type 1 [1473, Ghent? Caxton with David Aubert]
Game of chess (English):	Type 1 [1474, Ghent? Caxton with David Aubert]
Recueil (French):	Type 1 [1474, Ghent? David Aubert]
Méditations (French):	Type 1 [1474, Ghent? David Aubert]
Sarum Hours (Latin):	Type 2 [1475, Bruges, Colard Mansion for Caxton]
Cordiale (French):	Type 2 [1475, Bruges, Colard Mansion for Caxton]
Histoire de Jason (French):	Type 1 [1477? Ghent? David Aubert?]

7
Caxton and his patrons in Westminster

The two dedicatees of the English books printed in Flanders failed to give Caxton encouragement either as a printer or as a translator. The preference of the first, Margaret of York, for religious texts came from deeply felt devotion and found expression in the richly illuminated manuscripts she commissioned. The second, her brother the Duke of Clarence, never appears to have appreciated Caxton's gift, although the translation dedicated to him, the allegory on the game of chess, fitted the complexities of his political intrigues to perfection. If it had been Caxton's aim to engage Edward IV's attention for his books rather than for his services as a diplomat and representative, there was no sign of success. It was not until the late 1470s that the king began to assemble a royal library, at a time when Caxton was busily publishing in Westminster, but he did so strictly following the luxurious example of Burgundian collections, and his model was specifically the library of his former host, Loys de Gruuthuse. He commissioned at least twenty very fine manuscripts from the great Flemish workshops, many of historical works, and several had a close connection with manuscripts in the Gruuthuse library. They included – surely to Caxton's chagrin – an elaborately illustrated *Recueil des histoires de Troies*. The king and the printer were briefly on parallel courses that never converged.

Lack of encouragement from that quarter does not seem to have diminished Caxton's determination to spend his remaining years on translating and other literary delights. Publishing, however, notably publishing in print, required very careful consideration. After his first tentative steps he had enough experience to face the question whether either of the models with which he had experimented until then, large-scale commercial publishing in Latin as in Cologne, or book production under noble patronage as in Flanders, could be adapted for the commercial publishing of works in English. The brief episode in Flanders with the two English books may have been enough to alert him to the limitations of noble patronage where printed books were concerned. The essence of publishing printed books, producing texts in multiple copies, is that the larger part of those copies has to reach buyers not known to the publisher. Caxton's future work was to rely only partly on the influence of patrons, and he managed to strike a balance between works published with some measure of protection from a patron, and works published independently, without any such support.

Fig. 23. Among the manuscripts Edward IV commissioned in Flanders for his royal library was the original French version of Lefevre's work. The miniature shows the rebuilding of Troy after the first destruction. The border decoration includes the king's coat of arms. See also fig. 8.

Raoul Lefevre, *Recueil des histoires de Troies*, here entitled *Le livre nomme Hercules*. Manuscript, probably Bruges, c. 1480. London, BL, Ms Royal 17 E.ii, fol. 250 recto.

One thing was obvious, that a secure market for books printed in English could be found only in England, and it was there he would have to move. The main centre of the manuscript book trade in England was already well established in the City of London around St Paul's Churchyard, but Caxton decided on a different vantage point. There is no document to show how his arrangement with Westminster Abbey came about. The earliest record from the incomplete Abbey accounts is the rental of a 'shopa' from Michaelmas (29 September) 1476 – which should not be taken to mean that he could not have been there at some earlier date.

We may note that the arrangement was of advantage to both parties. For Caxton its situation could hardly be bettered. The abbey and its precincts gave him the opportunity to make his presence as well as his books known to clients and potential patrons, to the many

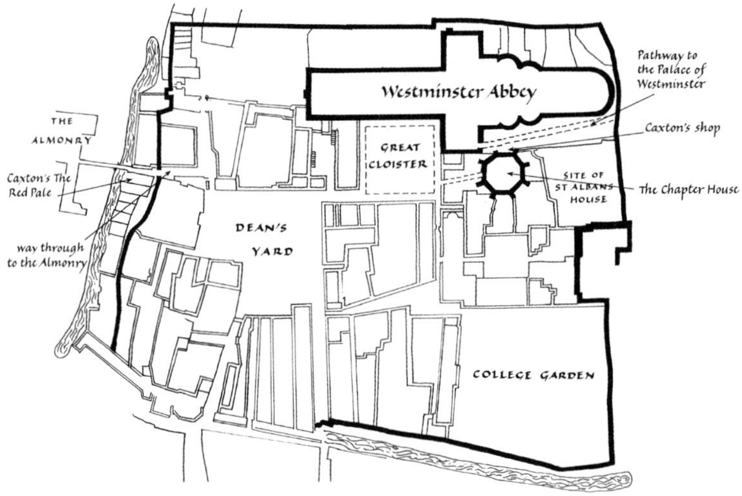

persons passing in and out of the abbey and in and out of the Palace of Westminster – courtiers, members of parliament, prelates and others serving the abbey, and those attending its services. Its proximity to the palace would favour a relationship with the royal court, however unpromising this may have appeared at first. King and Chancery were as yet blind to the advantages a nearby printing press might offer.

Caxton's location in Westminster also opened the way to finding a wider circle of clients among merchants mainly based in the City of London, Mercers and others. St Paul's Churchyard in the City of London would not be too distant from the abbey to advertise books for sale in Westminster: 'Late hym come to westmonester in to the almonerye at the reed pale', is the invitation to a potential client in Caxton's famous advertisement *circa* 1477, the wording suggesting that it was displayed not in Westminster itself, but at a manageable distance. It has also been suggested that Caxton preferred Westminster over London as the abbey precincts would give him independence from regulations and restrictions imposed by the Mercers' Company, the City, or the guild or company in which the book trade had begun to organize itself.

The abbey may have been equally aware of possible advantages in having a printer at hand. The Benedictine Order had stood at the cradle of printing in Mainz, where it was probably influential in the printing of the first Latin Bible, and where a few years later a psalter according to the Benedictine liturgy was produced in print. In 1470 Adrianus de Brielis, formerly an abbot of the abbey of St Jakob near Mainz, oversaw for Peter Schoeffer the printing of a magnificent edition of the letters of St Jerome. In the mid-1460s the first printing in Italy took place at the Benedictine abbey of St Scolastica at Subiaco, and in 1471 a monk at Subiaco tried to persuade the abbot of Göttweig near Melk in Austria to make use of the press for printing a breviary

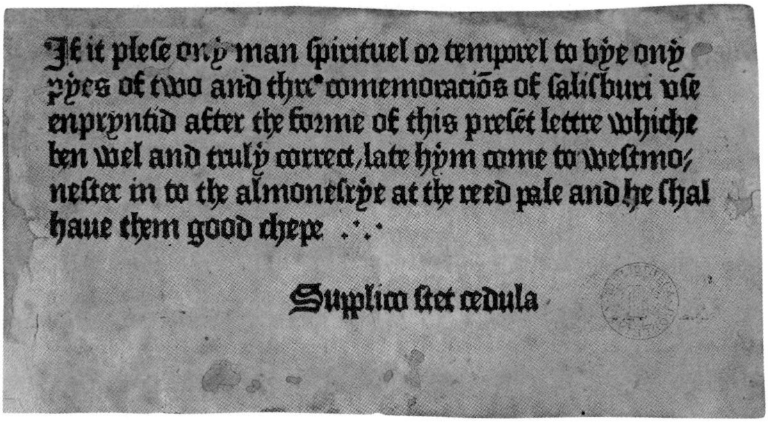

If it plese ony man spirituel or temporel to bye ony
pyes of two and thre comemoracios of salisburi vse
enpryntid after the forme of this preset lettre whiche
ben wel and truly correct, late hym come to westmo-
nester in to the almonesrye at the reed pale and he shal
haue them good chepe . . .

Supplico stet cedula

Fig. 24. Caxton's advertisement. Offered for sale is the *Ordinale Sarum* (or Sarum Pye), a directory for the liturgical year for the use of Salisbury (and most of England). In the space of six lines Caxton draws attention to the type, the accuracy of the text, and the low price of the work; he gives his address as 'The Red Pale' in the almonry of Westminster Abbey. The final line 'stet' (leave) indicates that this 'cedula' (leaflet) was indeed publicly displayed. The advertisement functions also as a specimen of the formal type that was designed by Johan Veldener (Caxton's Type 3) to match the bastarda text type (Type 2).

Advertisement. [Westminster, William Caxton, *c.* 1477]. Oxford, Bodleian Library, Douce frag.e.1.

for a number of Benedictine houses, since multiplication in print might lead to uniformity and harmony in the liturgy of the congregations. In Augsburg the abbot of St Ulrich and Afra set up a printing press at great expense, which produced a sequence of substantial books *circa* 1473–6. Within the Benedictine Order there was therefore by 1476 considerable precedent for using the printing press, and other orders were soon to follow suit. In England, the first religious house to introduce printing after Westminster Abbey was the Benedictine Abbey of St Albans.

Westminster Abbey was not, however, going to venture on such headlong risks and invest in a printing office, as had happened at Subiaco and Augsburg, where the enterprises were short-lived (and as later they turned out to be at St Albans). Perhaps the abbey encouraged Caxton to settle in its precincts, but he was a rent-paying tenant for three convenient spaces, the house named 'The Red Pale' in the almonry, a shop or booth adjoining the chapter house, and a storage space above a gate. Nevertheless, this was a privileged location, and in return Caxton might have been expected to multiply in print such Latin works as the abbey judged necessary or convenient. However, Latin works printed by Caxton at Westminster are few. Since several survive only as fragments, we may guess that a number have been lost without even leaving a snippet of evidence that they ever existed. Or we have to assume that he never quite fulfilled the abbey's expectations. Yet, in so far as they exist, the Latin works are with three exceptions all religious, the exceptions related to the influence of the court and diplomacy. There are handbooks for the priesthood, books of hours, and a Latin psalter, signs that Caxton not only sought to extend his client base, but also what in modern terms would be called the product range, works for which customers could be assured, certainly in the environment of the abbey. For textual accuracy of liturgical and related works he could expect the support of experts on the spot.

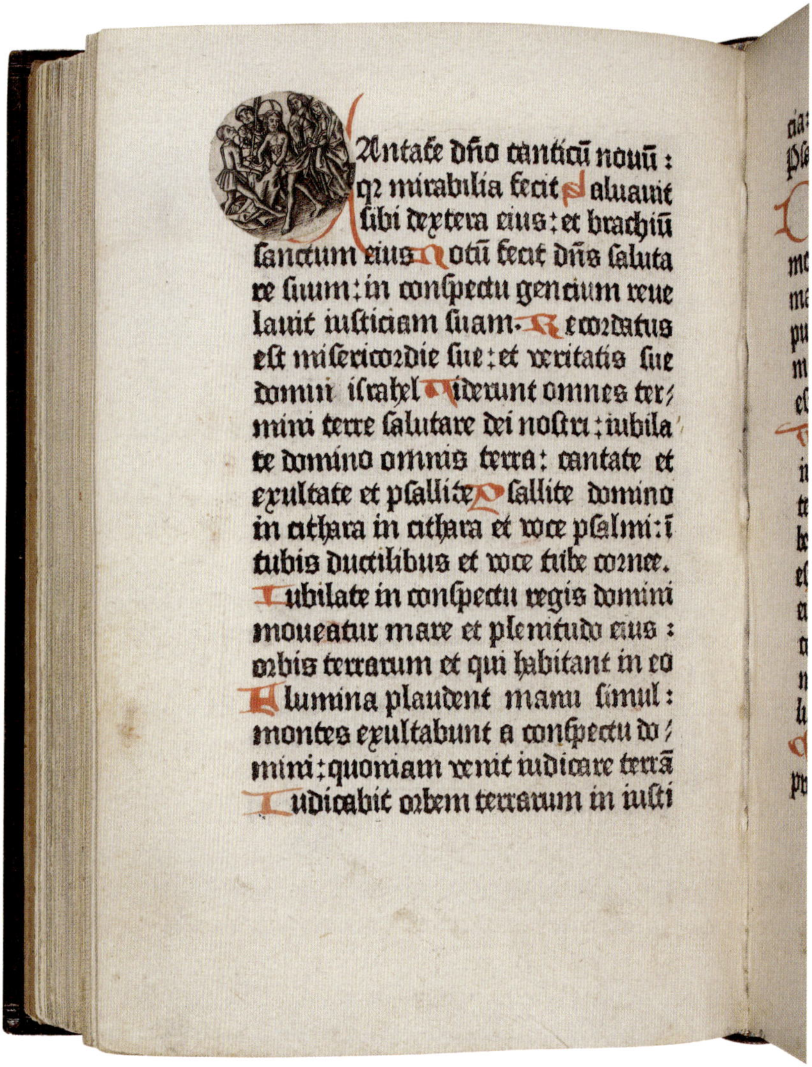

Fig. 25. Caxton used for his psalter the formal Type 3. The space for an initial and all capitals are crudely filled in with red ink. A later user embellished the book by inserting small engravings with scenes of Christ's passion in the margins or covering the red initials. The engraver is identified as the fifteenth-century 'Master E. S.'.

Psalterium. [Westminster, William Caxton, *c.* 1481]. London, BL, IA. 55038, fol. n3 verso.

Of a different nature were the editions of single-leaf indulgences, probably printed in many hundreds of copies of which only a few are left. In so far as they survive they indicate some further connections, for they were certainly printed to order of a papal delegate if it was a papal indulgence or of the head of a religious house if the indulgence was for its benefit. One of the papal commissaries was John Kendale, who was based at St Margaret's Church, adjoining the abbey, but Caxton also printed indulgences for the confraternities of the Hospital of St Mary Rounceval at Charing Cross and of the Dominican convent in Arundel (see fig. 27).

The only item printed in Westminster with a firm date attached in the year 1476 is a (Latin) papal indulgence, issued by John Sant, abbot of Abingdon. The unique surviving copy was sold on 13 December 1476, the date filled in by the pardoner whose task it was to sell indulgences. Its printing was preceded by that of five small books, all

Fig. 26. The first edition of *The Canterbury tales* is the first major book Caxton printed in England, completed late in 1476 or early in 1477. The Flemish bastarda text type (Type 2) appeared not in disharmony with this most English of texts. The beginning of the Miller's Tale is emphasized with a red initial and a paragraph mark painted by hand, both probably added in the printing house.

Geoffrey Chaucer, *The Canterbury tales*. [Westminster, William Caxton, 1476–7]. London, BL, G. 11585, fol. [g]8 recto.

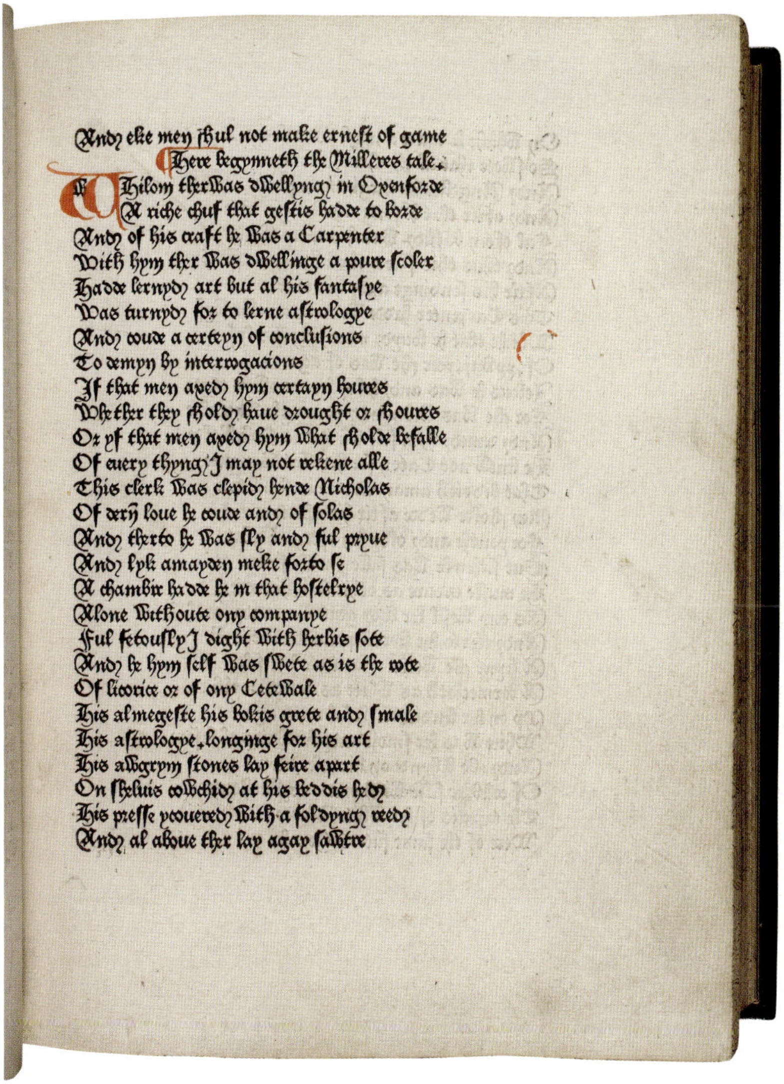
And eke men shul not make ernest of game
Here begynneth the Milleres tale.
Whilom ther was dwellyng in Oxenforde
A riche chuf that gestis hadde to borde
And of his craft he was a Carpenter
With hym ther was dwellinge a poure scoler
Hadde lernyd art but al his fantasye
Was turnyd for to lerne astrologye
And coude a certeyn of conclusions
To demyn by interrogacions
If that men axed hym certayn houres
Whether they sholde haue drought or shoures
Or yf that men axed hym what sholde befalle
Of euery thyng I may not rekene alle
This clerk was clepid hende Nicholas
Of derñ loue he coude and of solas
And therto he was sly and ful pryue
And lyk a mayden meke forto se
A chambir hadde he in that hostelrye
Alone withoute ony companye
Ful fetously dight with herbis sote
And he hym self was swete as is the rote
Of licorice or of ony Cetewale
His almegeste his bokis grete and smale
His astrologye. longinge for his art
His augrym stones lay feire apart
On shelvis cowchid at his beddis hede
His presse ycouered with a foldyng rede
And al aboue ther lay a gay sawtre

undated, but a date may be surmised for the earliest of them. It was a pamphlet of seven small pages, a short oration in Latin held years before, in February 1470, by John Russell, acting as an ambassador for Edward IV at the investiture of Charles the Bold as Knight of the Garter. It was probably printed in the early summer of 1476, shortly before Russell was appointed Bishop of Rochester in July. Publication of the text in print by its author would have been a not too subtle act of self-promotion to assure his appointment to the see – which was in the gift of the king. This chain of circumstances suggests the possibility that Russell, who knew Caxton from his successive embassies at the Burgundian court, had a hand in the deal with Westminster Abbey.

Soon after he was settled in Westminster, bringing to an end the lengthy preamble with many distractions on his path towards a new phase in his life, Caxton took his boldest step, manifesting what he intended to do as a publisher, and at the same time making his most enduring gift to English literature: the printing of Chaucer's *Canterbury tales*. The number of surviving manuscripts of the work, then about three-quarters of a century old, is relatively high. Caxton's masterstroke was that in order to publicize printing in English he chose a work that was already popular among people who could afford manuscripts. When printed it would become available to readers 'of every astate and degre', as he put it some seven years later in the prologue to his second edition, a readership that might be as varied as the pilgrims in the tales. Deliberately or not, the text itself seems to define the widening of the public he hoped to reach with what he could produce in his new printing house. There is no record of a wife of Bath, a shipman or a miller owning or even reading Caxton's first edition, but there were merchants who did. One surviving copy, at Merton College in Oxford, testifies to such readers in the bright colours that decorate its margins with emblems of the Haberdashers' Company in the City of London.

Caxton himself wrote in the prologue to the second edition that he had sold the book to 'many and diverse gentylmen', and it turned out that the dissemination of the work to more readers than had been possible in manuscripts initiated a critical process that was to continue over the centuries. One of the gentlemen, writes Caxton, compared the printed book with another manuscript source, and pointed out that the order of the tales should be changed, that lines were missing, and that other lines did not belong to the authentic text. In 1483 Caxton reprinted the work using the gentleman's (or rather, the gentleman's father's) manuscript as the basis for corrections which to the modern eye look rather haphazard. He would not be the last to find that the popularity of the text, and the multitude of earlier sources, would force the conscientious editor who aims to produce a coherent text into baffling dilemmas.

His concern for the text, however, reveals a real sense of responsibility for an adequate representation of the author's work, without defects, without false lines, respecting its integrity as it had come down from the past. In a pristine state, untouched by blemishes, the work would be fully relevant to readers of Caxton's own time, as if it were 'new'.

The printing of the first edition, completed late in 1476 or early in 1477, was innocent of any awareness of deficiencies. None of the surviving copies (only one of them wholly perfect) contains a prologue or epilogue in which Caxton explains his reasons for publishing the work, as he did in so many books. We must assume that there never was any; without the protection of a patron he seems to have launched it as his own independent enterprise. Despite its shortcomings it was – still is – a strikingly handsome book, a sizeable

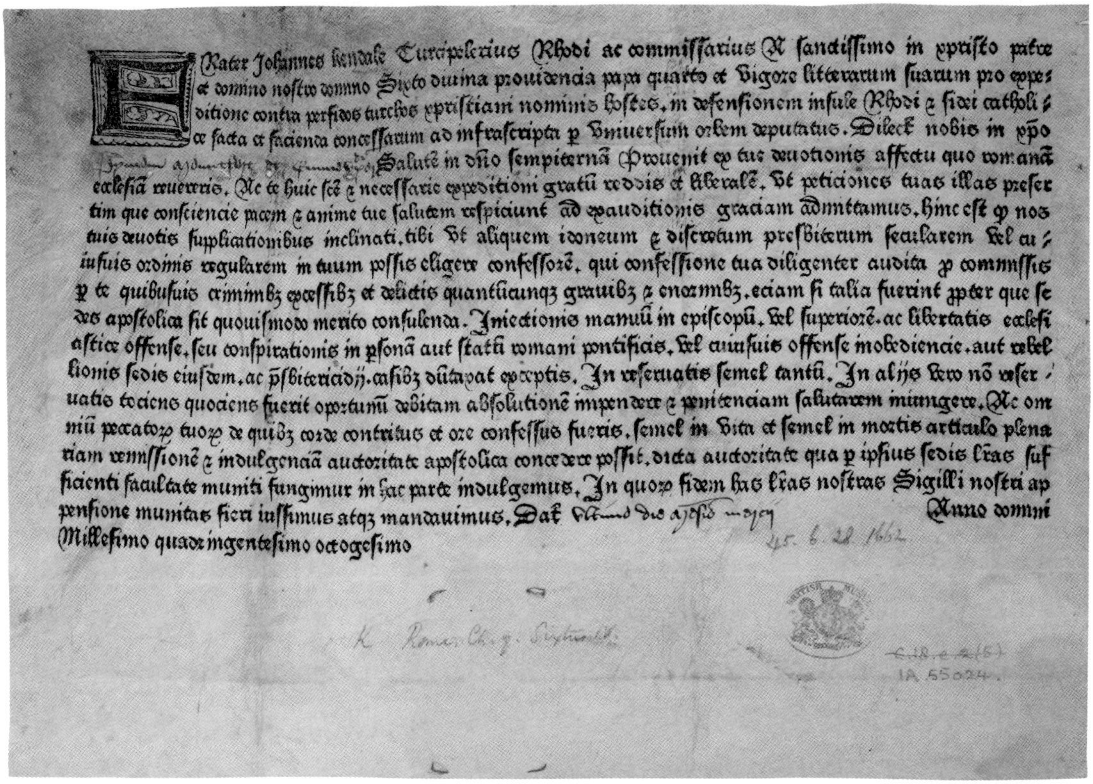
FRater Johannes kendale Turcipelerius Rhodi ac commissarius A sanctissimo in xpristo patre
et domino nostro domino Sixto diuina prouidencia papa quarto et vigore litterarum suarum pro expe-
ditione contra perfidos turcos xpristiani nominis hostes. in defensionem insule Rhodi et fidei catholi-
ce facta et facienda concessarum ad infrascripta p vniuersum orbem deputatus. Dilect nobis in xpo
Salute in dño sempiternā Prouenit ex tue deuotionis affectu quo romanā
ecclesiā reueretis. Ac te huic sce et necessarie expeditioni gratū reddis et liberale. Vt peticiones tuas illas preser
tim que consciencie pacem et anime tue salutem respiciunt ad exauditionis graciam admittamus. hinc est q nos
tuis deuotis supplicationibus inclinati. tibi Vt aliquem idoneum et discretum presbiterum secularem vel cu-
iusuis ordinis regularem in tuum possis eligere confessore. qui confessione tua diligenter audita p commissis
p te quibusuis criminibz excessibz et delictis quantūcunqz grauibz et enormibz. eciam si talia fuerint ppter que se
des apostolica sit quouismodo merito consulenda. Iniectionis manuū in episcopū. vel superiorē. ac libertatis ecclesi
astice offense. seu conspirationis in psonā aut statū romani pontificis. vel cuiusuis offense inobediencie. aut rebel
lionis sedis eiusdem. ac p̄sbitericidij. casibz dūtaxat exceptis. In reseruatis semel tantū. In alijs vero nō reser-
uatis totiens quociens fuerit oportunū debitam absolutionē impendere et penitenciam salutarem iniungere. Ac om
niū peccatorū tuorū de quibz corde contritus et ore confessus fueris. semel in vita et semel in mortis articulo plena
riam remissionē et indulgenciā auctoritate apostolica concedere possit. dicta auctoritate qua p ipsius sedis lras suf
ficienti facultate muniti fungimur in hac parte indulgemus. In quorū fidem has lras nostras Sigilli nostri ap
pensione munitas fieri iussimus atqz mandauimus. Dat Anno domini
Millesimo quadringentesimo octogesimo

Fig. 27. This indulgence in favour of the Knights of St John in their defence of Rhodes against the Turks was granted by pope Sixtus IV. It was issued by John Kendale, the papal commissary in England. The names of the purchasers of this copy are filled in: Simon Mountfort and his wife Emma, and the document is dated '1480, the last day of March'. This indulgence was printed by Caxton on vellum, and it was the first time he used a woodcut initial.

Indulgence. [Westminster, William Caxton], 1480. London, BL, IC. 55024.

volume of 374 leaves, Caxton's new type that he had brought from Flanders generously displayed in the well-spaced lines of verse. Comparison with the two English books printed in Flanders shows that in just two or three years he had come a long way.

The publication of *The Canterbury tales* marked the beginning of a period of continuous activity that was sustained until the end of 1485 or early 1486, and – after an interval of very low production – resumed in 1489 until Caxton's death in the early months of 1492. In all those years he was by far the most prolific printer in England, and dominated the printing of works in English. The works that were reprinted, also after his death, show that several were highly successful in finding readers and creating a demand. Caxton's selection of the English works he printed was remarkably balanced, in that roughly half were written by authors other than himself, mainly consisting of the already well-established authors of English literature: Chaucer, Lydgate, and Gower. A few publications were earlier translations, including Chaucer's translation of Boethius's *Consolation of philosophy*, and Nicolas Love's translation of the Latin *Meditationes Vitae Christi*, relating episodes of the life of Christ, a work that had been popular throughout the fifteenth century and was reprinted many times. History, or pseudo-history, was Caxton's most favoured topic, as he progressed from Lefevre's pseudo-history of the Argonauts and Troy

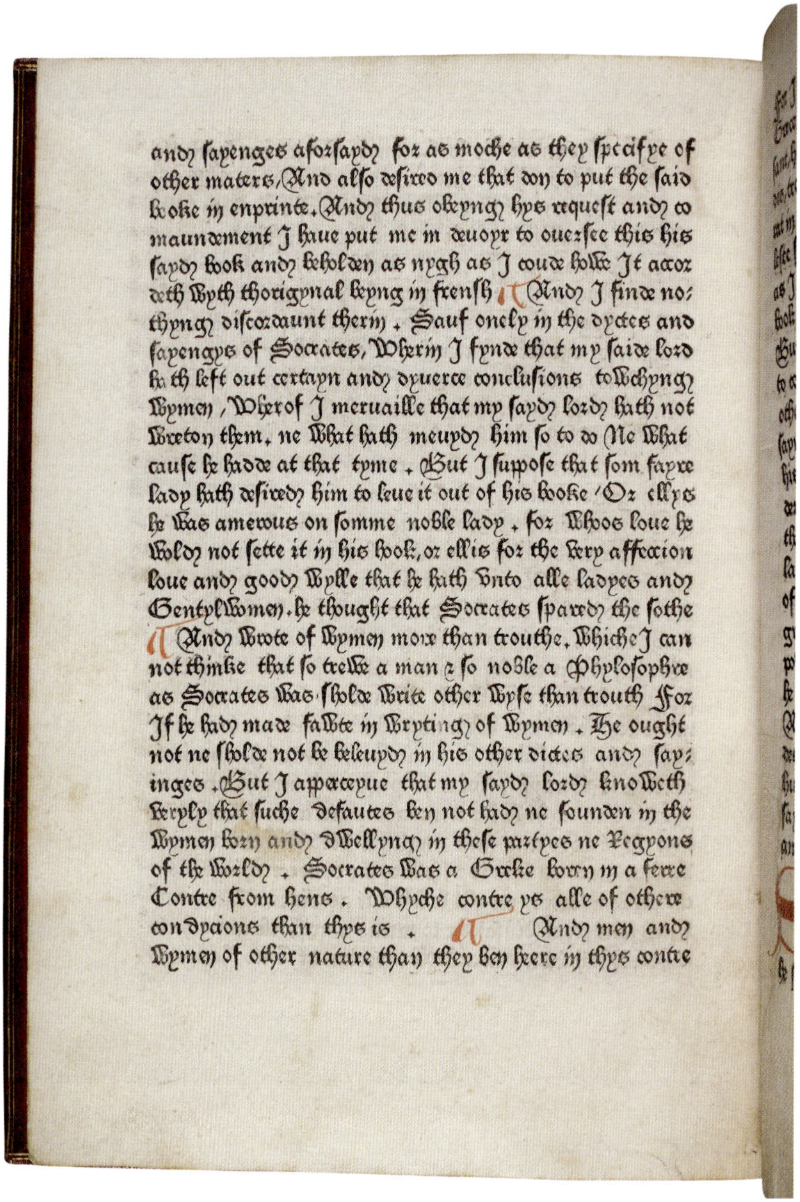

and sayenges aforsayd for as moche as they specifye of
other maters, And also desired me that don to put the said
booke in enprinte. And thus obeyng hys request and co
maundement I haue put me in deuoyr to ouersee this his
sayd book and beholden as nygh as I coude howe It accor
deth wyth thorigynal beyng in frensh ¶ And I finde no:
thyng discordaunt therin. Sauf onely in the dyctes and
sayengys of Socrates, Wherin I fynde that my saide lord
hath left out certayn and dyuerce conclusions towchyng
wymen, Wherof I meruaille that my sayd lord hath not
wreton them, ne what hath meuyd him so to do Ne what
cause he hadde at that tyme. But I suppose that som fayre
lady hath desired him to leue it out of his booke, Or ellys
he was amerous on somme noble lady, for whos loue he
wold not sette it in his book, or ellis for the very affeccion
loue and good wylle that he hath vnto alle ladyes and
Gentylwomen. he thought that Socrates spared the sothe
¶ And wrote of wymen more than trouthe. Whiche I can
not thinke that so trewe a man & so noble a Phylosophre
as Socrates was sholde write other wyse than trouth For
If he had made fawte in wryting of wymen. He ought
not ne sholde not be beleuyd in his other dictes and say:
inges. But I apparceyue that my sayd lord knoweth
verily that suche defautes ben not had ne founden in the
wymen born and dwellyng in these partyes ne regyons
of the world. Socrates was a Greke born in a ferre
Contre from hens. Whyche contre ys alle of othere
condicions than thys is. ¶ And men and
wymen of other nature than they ben here in thys contre

Fig. 28. In his extensive epilogue Caxton teased Anthony Woodville, his noble patron, suggesting that this eligible widower had found it strategic to omit some text potentially offensive to a lady's ears.

The dicts and sayings of the philosophers, translated from the French by Anthony Woodville, Earl Rivers. Westminster, William Caxton, 1477. London, BL, C. 10.b.2, fol. [k]2 verso.

to the real English history of the *Chronicles of England* and John Trevisa's translation of Higden's *Polychronicon*, and derived from it the *Description of Britain*. The stories of two Christian worthies, Godfrey of Boloyne and Charlemagne (which he translated), and the newcomer Thomas Malory's *Morte Darthur* all straddle the area of romance and history.

The other half of his publications in English consisted of prose written by himself, the extensions to the *Chronicles of England* and the *Polychronicon*, and above all his translations of twenty works, ranging in size from the colossal *Golden legend* to Alain Chartier's *Curial*, a pamphlet of six leaves, and, most famously, the prologues and epilogues that accompanied many of his publications. To the astounding quantity of printed translation should be added that of the very large

Ovide moralisé, not printed and known only in a fine manuscript, and the also very substantial *Vitas patrum*, or *Lives of the Fathers*, completed on the last day of his life and posthumously published by Wynkyn de Worde. In all, his own prose amounts to some three million words, according to an estimate by George D. Painter. He also undertook considerable editorial work, for example in Malory's *Morte Darthur*, improving its structure and using as a source for expansion and emendation the *Chronicles of England* that he had published five years earlier. While his compositors set type, and his pressmen printed, Caxton wielded his pen, apparently without pause.

Three of the translations Caxton printed in 1477–9 are by his most important patron, Anthony Woodville, Earl Rivers. In 1477 Caxton printed for the first time the English translation of the *Dicts and sayings of the philosophers*, a then popular compilation of originally Arabic versions of pronouncements of sages of antiquity – Colard Mansion brought out an edition in French – that he was to reprint twice. In an elaborate epilogue he explains that the translation was undertaken by Earl Rivers, 'the noble and puissant lord' who had requested him to read it critically. Caxton detected omissions: Earl Rivers had skipped the misogynistic remarks by Socrates, and Caxton took it upon himself to supply that section of text; as always, his first concern was for the customer who must not be short-changed by a defective text. Musing on what the delicate reasons might have been for the translator to be so wary of offending women – 'or ellis peraventure that the wynde had blowe over the leef at the tyme of translacion of his booke' – he wrote a playful, teasing passage, suggesting a certain intimacy between author and publisher, despite his professions of respect for Earl Rivers's high rank. Earl Rivers was a brother of Elizabeth Woodville, the queen consort of Edward IV. On behalf of his brother-in-law Rivers had been an important presence at successive negotiations with the dukes of Burgundy, and he may have made Caxton's acquaintance on some of these occasions, or at the celebrations of the marriage of Margaret of York. He was chivalrous, a famous jouster, and also a man of letters, but not a collector in the mould of the Burgundian nobles, although a few precious manuscripts may have come his way by inheritance. As his reputation at the court rose, he was appointed to several important functions, and in 1473 Edward trusted him sufficiently to put him in charge of the education and household of Edward, Prince of Wales, then three years old. The king himself had drawn up an elaborate and detailed scheme for the upbringing of his heir, who had a separate court at Ludlow on the Welsh border. Rivers's advice may be surmised behind several other of Caxton's publications of the period that were either dedicated to the young prince or might have contributed to his education. This productive interaction came to a sudden end in the spring of 1483,

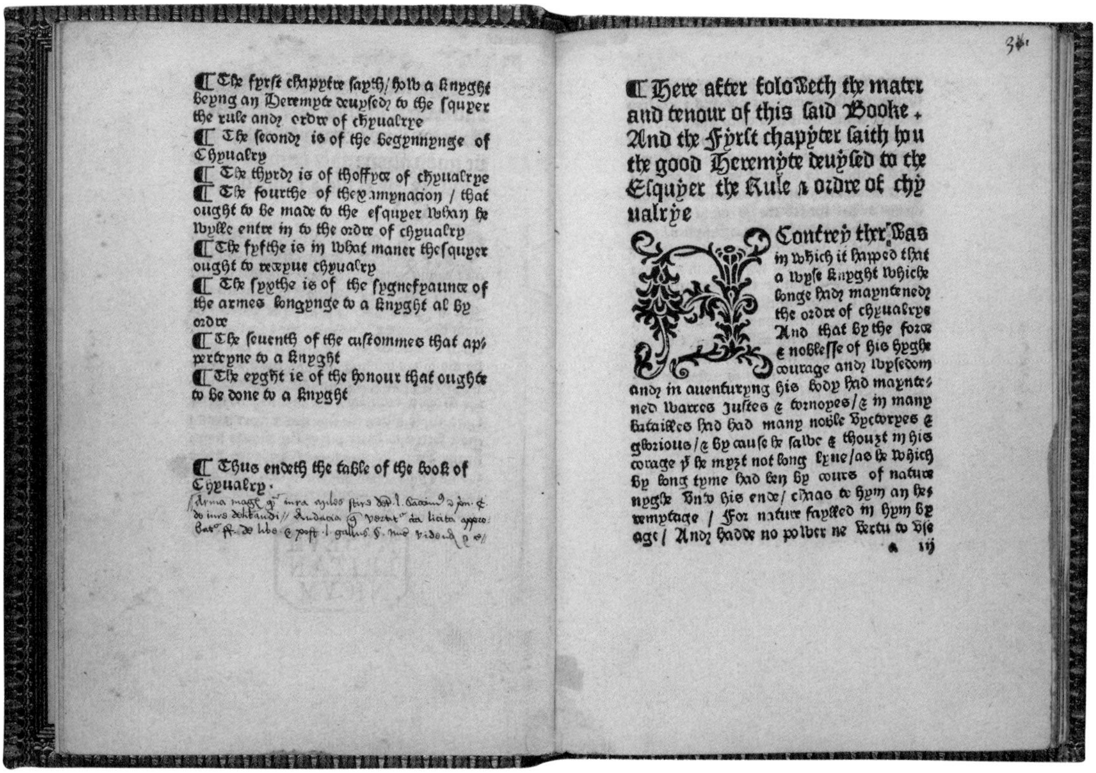
Here after foloweth the matere and tenour of this said Booke. And the Fyrst chappyter saith how the good Heremyte deuysed to the Esquyer the Rule & ordre of chyualrye

Thus endeth the table of the book of Chyualry.

when, only weeks after the death of Edward IV, Rivers was first imprisoned, then executed, one of the first victims of the usurpation of Richard III.

The execution of Earl Rivers was the first of many dramatic episodes that took place between 1483 and 1485. Yet Caxton, who witnessed much of this from nearby, gives no direct indication of how he was affected by what happened around him. He had been acquainted with several players in this high drama, and he had lost the patron who had engaged more with his work than any other. Personal in tone as many of his prologues and epilogues were, much remained unexpressed.

Until the end of 1485 or even early in 1486, and therefore well after the Battle of Bosworth that ended Richard III's reign in August 1485, the production of Caxton's printer's shop continued steadily with the momentum he had created, ending with the completion of several major works. Then it dwindled to only a few small books in 1487, not fully to resume until 1489. As we shall see, in the intervening years he probably busied himself importing books rather than printing them.

The gap between two periods of productivity may at least partly be understood as a slightly delayed effect of the changes in the monarchy. Shocking though Earl Rivers's execution must have been for Caxton, it did not necessarily threaten his status. Had Richard III's reign been longer, the new king might well have been inclined to

Fig. 29. Caxton dedicated this small book to Richard III. The text by the Catalan author Ramon Lull (d. 1315) was intended for the education of young nobles and had a long and influential manuscript tradition in Catalan and French. Caxton attached an extensive epilogue in praise of English heroes beginning with king Arthur.

The book is set in the small text type (Type 4) modelled on the larger Flemish bastarda, and Type 3 is used for the title and first line of text. It begins with a table of contents (of which the end is shown). The floral initial was used in the same year in his *Aesop*.

Ramon Lull, *The book of the order of Chivalry or Knighthood*, translated from a French version by William Caxton. Westminster, William Caxton, [1484]. London, BL, IA. 55071, fol. a2 verso, a3 recto.

make good use of the press. Richard was decidedly more bookish than his brother Edward, and had a small library of interesting manuscripts. One sign of appreciation of the press by himself or his chancery is the publication in print of the statutes of the first parliament of his reign, commissioned from the printers in the City of London. Particularly significant is the statute issued in 1484 that exempted all foreigners engaged in every kind of trade in books, whether manuscript or printed, from protective restrictions pertaining to other trades. In 1484 Caxton dedicated a small but important book to Richard, his own English translation of Ramon Lull's *Order of chivalry*, requesting in its epilogue 'that he [the king] commaunde this book to be had and redde unto other yong lordes, knyghtes and gentylmen within this royame that the noble ordre of chyvalrye be herafter better used and honoured'. Patronage could hardly be more openly solicited.

After the Battle of Bosworth, the arrival of the new monarchy brought a period of uncertainty in government, which also affected many among the new reading classes. The balance Caxton sought to strike between sponsored and own-risk publishing was at that time disturbed. Once the dust had settled, a good three years into his reign, the new king, Henry VII, and even more so his mother, Lady Margaret Beaufort, began to take an active interest in the press and directed Caxton, who was again, briefly, the only printer in the realm, to translate and print several works for them, giving renewed impetus to printing in England.

Caxton never held the formal title 'King's Printer'; the position was not instituted until 1504, and once he had arrived in Westminster he made a determined and successful bid to find clients and readership beyond the circles of the court and nobility. Even so, the two distinct periods in Caxton's publishing in England were both influenced by the ruling monarchies – the first mainly through Earl Rivers, despite Caxton's several approaches to the king. Some of the successes of the earlier period were carried over by reprints in the later years; nevertheless, there are good reasons to consider the two periods separately, and take first a more detailed look at some of the works Caxton printed between 1476 and the end of 1485.

8
Books multiplied: Caxton's publications until 1486

Following the publication of John Russell's Latin oration and before *The Canterbury tales*, Caxton printed in 1476 four small books, some especially for children, followed after *The Canterbury tales* by at least eight more, together known collectively as 'the early quartos'. The first four are short texts in verse by John Lydgate, *The horse, the sheep and the goose*, *The churl and the bird*, a little English text teaching table manners with the Latin title *Stans puer ad mensam*, and a similarly improving text, the Latin *Disticha*, ascribed to Cato with the English translation of Benedict Burgh, who had become in June 1476 a canon of St Stephen's Chapel of the Palace of Westminster. The second lot, printed later than *The Canterbury tales*, included reprints of the two Lydgate poems and of Cato, and added two short poems by Chaucer, *Anelida and Arcite* and *The parliament of fowls*, Lydgate's *Temple of glass*, and another text by Lydgate teaching good manners, *The book of courtesy*, known as *Little John*; most delightful of all, even to a very young child, is the Latin *Infantia Salvatoris*, legends of the miracles performed by the 'infantulus Jesus' according to the Apocrypha. They were all standard reading texts for the very young, and, failing any information from Caxton himself on this point, there is no way of knowing at whose behest he printed them. They may have been primarily intended for the school at the abbey's almonry, Caxton's new neighbours, or Benedict Burgh may have been his adviser, but they would have found a ready market among all whose occupation it was to teach young children. 'Fayrer ne wyser ne bet-bespoken children in theyre yongthe ben nowher than ther ben in London,' wrote Caxton several years later in the last of his editions of Cato. Yet it is hard to escape the idea that Earl Rivers in his capacity as governor of the Prince of Wales and his younger brother may have been interested in using these little books for his charges in the household in Ludlow. Reading was high on the king's list of educational priorities for the princes. Rivers's publication of his own translations shows that he had embraced the notion of sharing his work with a large, to him unknown public, as Caxton put it: 'enprinted and so multiplied to goo abrood emonge the peple'.

The Caxton quartos are all extremely rare, known from only one or two copies each. They show very clearly a strategy many early printers followed, at which Caxton was adept: to give customers the oppor-

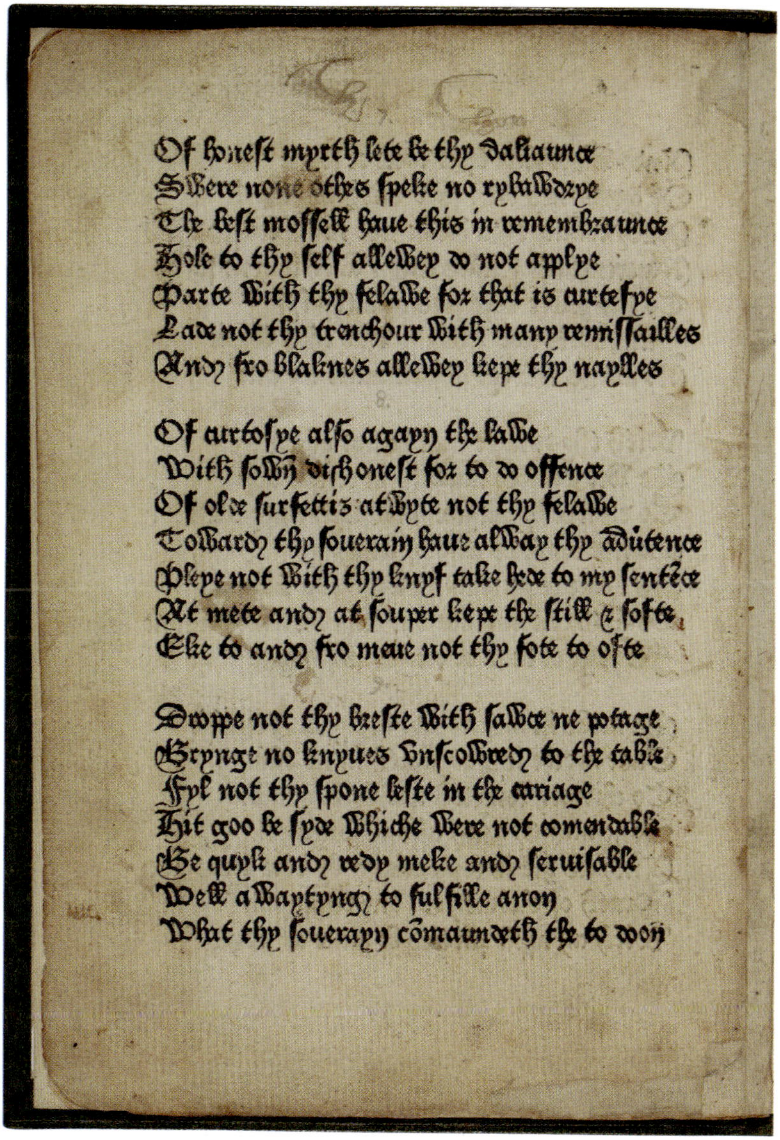
Of honest myrth late be thy daliaunce
Swere none othes speke no rybawdrye
The best morsell haue this in remembraunce
Hole to thy self alleway do not applye
Parte with thy felawe for that is curtesye
Lade not thy trenchour with many remyssailles
And fro blaknes alleway kepe thy nayles

Of curtosye also agayn the lawe
With sowh dishonest for to do offence
Of olde surfettis abrayde not thy felawe
Towarde thy souerayn haue alway thy aduertence
Pleye not with thy knyf take hede to my sentence
At mete and at souper kepe the still & softe
Eke to and fro meue not thy fote to ofte

Droppe not thy breste with sawce ne potage
Brynge no knyues vnscowred to the table
Fyl not thy spone leste in the cariage
Hit goo besyde which were not comendable
Be quyk and redy meke and seruisable
Well awaytyng to fulfille anon
What thy souerayn comaundeth the to doon

Fig. 30. Among the first books printed in Westminster in 1476 is a courtesy book, Lydgate's instructive verse teaching children table manners: 'No black nails, please. Don't play with your knife!'. Caxton may have published such small books as a gentle introduction to seeing English texts in the new medium of print.

John Lydgate, *Stans puer ad mensam*. [Westminster, William Caxton, 1476]. Cambridge University Library, Oates 4070, fol. [a]2 verso.

tunity to select a number of compatible small, or even not so small books to be combined and bound to order into one substantial volume. This was not an innovation, for a combination of texts written by different scribes is also often found in manuscript codices, with a list of contents at the beginning. It worked undeniably better with printed books, since the products of the new art of printing were often uniform in appearance, yet it was possible to make them into books which suited individual requirements and taste. Most of the surviving Caxton quartos come from one or the other of two substantial volumes, split up in the eighteenth or nineteenth centuries. It would therefore be wrong to imagine them as delicate little books in children's hands, unless we are thinking of the many copies that did not survive. For Caxton they all belonged to a single coherent publishing enterprise. But they could also be bought singly. Testing the market by floating small books with poetic texts in English – printed! – around the time of the publication of *The Canterbury tales* was an ingenious way of attracting buyers and readers to a medium that was new to them.

As far as printing for Earl Rivers and Edward, Prince of Wales is concerned, we are on somewhat surer, but not entirely solid, ground with a book that Caxton dedicated to the young prince early in 1477, his translation of Raoul Lefevre's *L'Histoire de Jason*. The final page of the text ends with a short dedication to the prince 'now in his tendre iongth [youth]' with the wish that he would be remembered perpetually – a wish that has come true, but, alas, as one of the princes murdered in the Tower. In the prologue Caxton refers to his earlier translation of the *Recueil* for Margaret of York, and writes that under the protection of Edward IV, himself a Knight of the Golden Fleece, he had undertaken the translation, 'not presumyng to presente it unto his Highnesse for as moch as I doubte not his good grace hath it in Frensh which he wele understandeth... But I entende ... to presente this sayde boke unto the most fayr ... yong lorde, my Lord Prynce of Wales ... to th'entent he may begynne to lerne rede Englissh...' This is all very elegant, respectful, and tender, and may well be seen as a response to the king's instruction of 1473 that he 'be reade before him such noble storyes as behoveth to a prynce to understande'. But Caxton may not have been quite as sincere as he sounds. Some five hundred years after these words were printed, typographical analysis and careful recording of the paper used for this book brought to light the fact that the present prologue replaces an earlier one. The investigation is too complicated and detailed to relate here, but we may briefly consider whether there had first been another dedicatee and, if so, who this might have been.

Caxton took out and replaced two sheets (eight pages) after the book was completed, the first half of them containing the prologue. Perhaps the original was simply replaced because the formulation was not according to a protocol prescribed for such a ritualistic occasion, and a circumstance of that nature cannot be ruled out, but there is another possibility. Although the book is undated, investigations have shown that the printing of the *History of Jason* followed that of *The Canterbury tales* and preceded the *Dicts of the philosophers*, and must therefore have taken place in 1477, probably early in the year. Written by the same author, Raoul Lefevre, the *History of Jason* is closely linked to the *Recuyell of the histories of Troy*, and in the French-language manuscript tradition the two works are usually paired. As we have discussed already, both texts relate parts of the mythical ancestry of the House of Burgundy, Jason and the Golden Fleece preceding the destruction of Troy. The *History of Jason*, celebrating the Order of the Golden

Fleece, was originally written first. We have already considered why Caxton chose the *Recuyell*, its protagonist Hercules, as an appropriate text to flatter Margaret of York and entice her patronage. It would be logical for Caxton to present his translation of *Jason* to his patron, complementing the translation of the *Recueil*. But there seems to have been a reluctance to print the *Jason*. The French version of *Jason* (not dedicated to anyone) was printed in Flanders later than the *Recueil*, perhaps even as long as three years later, in 1477; it is doubtful that Caxton (by then established in Westminster) had anything to do with its publication. The English translation of *Jason* was also published some four years later than Caxton's *Recuyell*. During Margaret's marriage to Charles the Bold there was an ever more pressing reason for such reluctance to present this text to her. Duke Charles did not have a male heir, and Margaret of York did not bear him any children. It was a painful subject, which caused undoubtedly much rumour and gossip. There is a poignant miniature illustrating her anxiety. A magnificent manuscript of Pierre de Vaux, *La vie de Sainte Colette* was ordered by the duchess to be presented to the abbey of the Poor Clares in Ghent. The manuscript opens with a miniature showing the ducal pair kneeling together in prayer in front of the altar of the saint, and in an inscription in her own handwriting the duchess begged the nuns to pray for her. The abbey (which still owns the manuscript) was a site for pilgrimages relating to child-bearing, and to this day houses a maternity clinic.

The *History of Jason* begins with a graphic description of a dynastic crisis: an aging king and a fair young queen, 'long to geder withoute havyng generacion, wherof their dayes were full of bewaylynges and of litill playsir in the goodes of fortune. But they were contynelly in the temples and oracles...' But then, by a near-miracle, Jason is born, and the queen dies in childbed. No text could be less suitable for a dedication to Margaret of York, even more so when in January 1477 news broke that Charles the Bold had been killed in battle before Nancy. It was a dynastic disaster that pitched the Burgundian Netherlands into an acute crisis, and was to determine the country's destiny for centuries to come.

We can only note the coincidence of dates, and wonder. Caxton's substitution of the text of his dedication is seamless to readers unconcerned with watermarks or compositors' practices: we were not meant to know. There can be no doubt, however, that the story of Jason fitted to perfection Edward IV's desire for stories to be read to his son. Someone must have made the connection, and it is quite probable that this was Earl Rivers, who was at that time in contact with Caxton regarding his own translation of the *Dicts of the philosophers*, first printed in the same year.

The *Dicts* was followed early in 1478 by Rivers's translation in verse of the French *Moral proverbs* of Christine de Pisan, a small book of only eight pages. Caxton ends it with an envoy in his own verse:

> Go thou litil quayer / and recommaund me
> Unto the good grace / of my special lorde
> Therle Ryveris. for I have enprinted the [thee]
> At his commandement. folowyng evry worde
> His copye / as his secretaire can recorde
> At westmestre of feverer the .xx. daye
> And of kyng Edward / the xvii. yere vraye
> Enprinted by caxton
> In feverer the colde season

We may note Caxton's protestation that he followed the translator's words very carefully, invoking the earl's secretary as witness. This may hark back to what happened the previous year with the *Dicts*. At Earl Rivers's request Caxton had 'overseen' it, that is corrected the text, but his amendments may not all have been to the Earl's liking, and in the second edition, printed in 1480, a number of textual corrections are found. Probably they were made by the translator himself, for they are first found in a manuscript of the translation that was prepared for presentation to Edward IV, with a traditional dedication miniature at the beginning, and at the end the date 24 December 1477. Earl Rivers must have used a copy of the first edition and annotated it, his corrections to be incorporated by the scribe who wrote the presentation version, and later by Caxton's compositors for the reprint. It is a telling example of a printed book, an expendable object, being used for the further development of a text. A year later, in February 1479, Earl Rivers had another translation from the French ready, and by this time author and printer seem to have found themselves in harmony, for there are no signs of revision. The text is the *Cordyal* or *The four last thinges*, a text on preparation for death that highlights yet another aspect of Rivers's persona: he was deeply pious. Rivers used again a printed book for his work, the French *Cordiale* printed for Caxton in Bruges.

Earl Rivers's influence in the early years in Westminster probably went beyond the publication of his own translations. In 1481 he may have encouraged the publication of the English translation of Cicero's *De amicitia* by John Tiptoft, Earl of Worcester, along with other Cicero translations, which Caxton dedicated to Edward IV. It is generally thought that it was Rivers who provided the French version of Alain Chartier's *Curial*, a savage satire of life at a royal court which Caxton printed in 1483. Finally, there are good arguments for assuming that it was through his mediation that Caxton could make use of the manuscript of Thomas Malory's *Morte Darthur* that was the basis for his edition of 1485 (completed well after Rivers's execution).

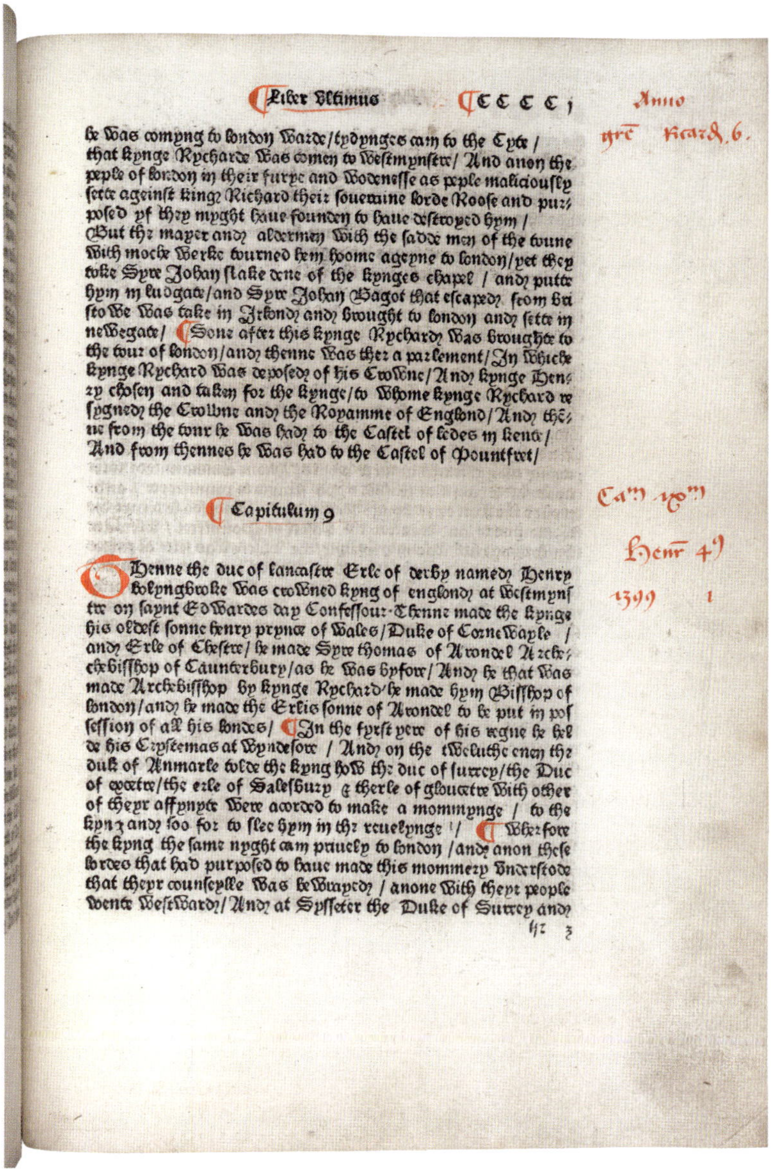

Liber ultimus CCCCi

he was comyng to london warde/tydynges cam to the Cyte/ that kynge Rycharde was comen to westmynster/ And anon the peple of london in their furye and woodnesse as peple maliciously sette ageinst kinge Richard their soueraine lorde roose and purposed yf they myght haue founden to haue destroyed hym/ But the mayer and aldermen with the sadde men of the towne with moche werke tourned hem hoome ageyne to london/yet they toke Syre Johan slake dene of the kynges chapel / and putte hym in ludgate/and Syre Johan Bagot that escaped from Bristowe was take in Irlond and brought to london and sette in newegate/ Sone after this kynge Rychard was broughte to the tour of london/and thenne was ther a parlement/In whiche kynge Rychard was deposed of his Crowne/And kynge Henry chosen and taken for the kynge/to whome kynge Rychard resygned the Crowne and the Royamme of Englond/And thenne from the tour he was had to the Castel of ledes in kente/ And from thennes he was had to the Castel of Pountfret/

Capitulum 9

Thenne the duc of lancastre Erle of derby named Henry bolyngbroke was crowned kyng of englond at westmynster on saynt Edwardes day Confessour. Thenne made the kynge his oldest sonne henry prynce of wales/Duke of Cornewayle / and Erle of Chestre/ he made Syre thomas of Arondel Archebisshop of Caunterbury/as he was byfore/And he that was made Archebisshop by kynge Rychard he made hym Bisshop of london/and he made the Erlis sonne of Arondel to be put in possession of all his londes/ In the fyrst yere of his regne he helde his Crystemas at wyndesore / And on the twelvthe even the duk of Aumarle tolde the kyng how the duc of surrey/the Duc of exetre/the erle of Salesbury & therle of gloucetre with other of theyr affynyte were acorded to make a mommynge / to the kyng and soo for to slee hym in the reuelynge / Wherfore the kyng the same nyght cam priuely to london /and anon these lordes that had purposed to haue made this mommery understode that theyr counseylle was bewrayed / anone with theyr people wente westward/And at Sysseter the Duke of Surrey and

Fig. 31. The *Polychronicon* is a world history, paying prominent attention to the history of Britain. Trevisa's translation was completed in 1387. Caxton brought it up to date to the year 1460 in his 'Liber ultimus', a page of which is shown here. The dates in the margins which guide the reader through the chronicle were added in the printing house with red ink in several distinct hands.

Ranulphus Higden, *Polychronicon*, in the translation by John Trevisa, and extended by William Caxton. Westminster, William Caxton, 1482. London, BL, G. 6012, fol. 52/3.

There are few other works that Caxton published in association with court and aristocracy. In 1481 he completed his translation of *Godfrey of Boloyne*, the history of the First Crusade, and dedicated it to Edward IV, expressing the hope that his two sons would read it. Among the manuscripts written for Edward IV in Bruges was a French version of the text, now complemented by Caxton's translation. In the following year Caxton published the *Polychronicon*, with his own extension of Higden's original to 1460, the first year of Edward IV's reign. He states somewhat ambiguously that he completed it 'under the protection' of Edward IV, but this does not mean that he dedicated the work to him.

The same expression 'sub protectione Serenissimi regis anglorum Edwardi quarti' is found in the colophon of Caxton's edition, published in 1480, of the lectures on Latin rhetoric given in 1478 at the University of Cambridge by the Italian Franciscan Lorenzo Traversagni, a humanist scholar from Savona, on the Ligurian coast. Known as the *Margarita eloquentiae*, or *Rhetorica nova*, its royal protection appears to apply to the presentation of the lectures, rather than to their appearance in print. Caxton printed in the same year a related work by the same author, the *Epitome*, a collection of diplomatic letters presented by Traversagni at the Sorbonne 'sub serenissimo rege franchorum lodovico'. Someone must have commissioned the printing of the lectures, which are remote from Caxton's usual subject matter. We may perhaps think of Pietro Carmeliano, another Italian scholar and poet, who appears several times in print himself in dedicatory verse in publications of Theodericus Rood in Oxford. The only time his name is attached to a book printed by Caxton is at the end of a rather odd collection of letters regarding a conflict between the Venetian senate and the Pope. Caxton printed Sixtus IV, *Sex elegantissime epistolae*, in 1484, and yet again we see him straying far outside his normal publishing programme. Since Carmeliano fostered his relations with the successive kings, we may infer that there is here a connection with the court, or at least its periphery.

A final link with the court of Edward IV was Caxton's translation and publication of a treatise on the upbringing of daughters, Geoffrey de la Tour Landry, *Knight of the Tower*. In his prologue Caxton declares that the work was translated from French at the request of 'a noble lady which hath brought forth many noble and fayr doughters' – an allusion to Elizabeth Woodville, consort of Edward IV and mother of five daughters, who probably commissioned the translation when she was still queen. But when printing was completed, on 31 January 1484, she could no longer be openly declared to be the patron, for by then she was widowed, her brother-in-law Richard crowned as king, and she herself in sanctuary in Westminster Abbey.

This is approximately the time when Caxton's largest enterprise, in translation as well as publication, was brought to completion. *The golden legend* is a compilation of lives of the saints, all more or less arranged in sequences according to the temporal and fixed feast days of the liturgical calendar. Caxton acknowledged in his prologue the support of William Fitz Alan, 11th Earl of Arundel, who undertook to 'take a resonable quantyte' of this enormous book, as well as promising 'a bucke in sommer and a doo in wynter'. How much this helped in the very large investment required for publishing *The golden legend* is a moot point. The book is a large folio, its almost 900 pages printed on larger paper than he used elsewhere, amply illustrated with woodcuts. For his translation Caxton used primarily a recent edition that had appeared in French, printed by an anonymous workshop in Flanders. He supplemented its contents with lives of saints belong-

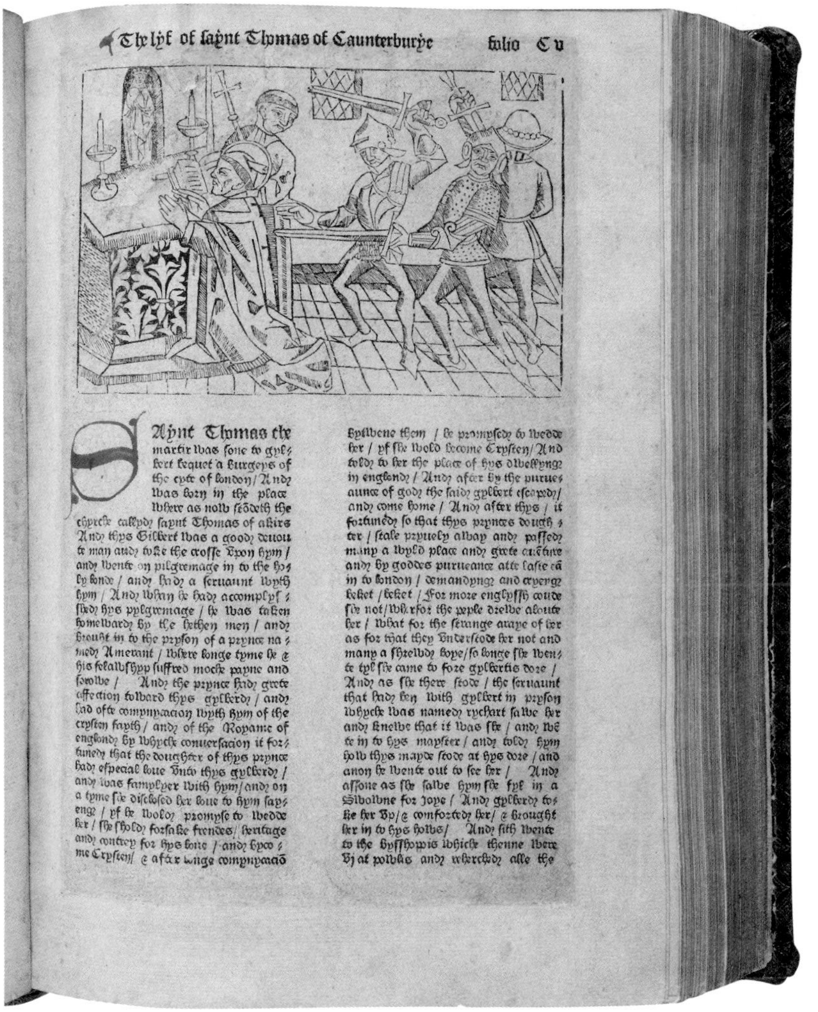

Fig. 32. De Voragine's compilation of lives of the saints had a long tradition in manuscripts and also appeared many times in print. Caxton added lives of English saints to his translation. Each chapter was preceded by a woodcut, 69 in all. One woodcut often served to illustrate different saints, but the scene of the murder of Thomas Becket had to be unique. After the Reformation it was often torn out of the book or defaced. The red initials in this copy were added in the printing house.

Jacobus de Voragine, *The golden legend*, translated from the French version of the *Legenda aurea* by Jean de Vignay, edited and augmented by William Caxton. Westminster, William Caxton [1483–4]. London, BL, C. 11.d.8, fol. n8 recto.

ing to the English liturgies and traditions for which he had to rely on other sources. He also departed from tradition by preceding the work with a section containing 'Stories of the Bible'. Ever since the suppression of the Lollards early in the fifteenth century, dissemination of the text of the Bible in a vernacular language had been forbidden in England, but Caxton ingeniously circumvented this interdict with a paraphrase of the text of the Scriptures, his 'Stories', which could be fitted in the cycle of the liturgical year. As a compilation his *Golden legend* was inventive and original. There can be little doubt that he took a considerable financial risk in producing it, despite the support of his noble patron. The printing history of the book is complicated, but from it we can deduce that Caxton first completed only part of the total print run; the unfinished copies (lacking more than half of the book) were completed probably only a short time later, the sections that had first been printed in a smaller number of copies now printed in a new type-setting and on a new supply of paper. This may have been a matter of financing: possibly copies had to be sold before he could continue. Also, because he seems to have added new legends as printing went on, the book may have turned out to be larger than he had originally calculated, and he could foresee that the original supply of paper would run out before he could complete the whole run. Or it may simply have been that the large paper was in short supply, and he was forced to reduce the print run not quite halfway through completion of the work.

These complications allow us glimpses of Caxton's workshop going full tilt, in a period of sustained creativity and productivity that began once he was fully established in Westminster, about the year 1478, and continued to the end of 1485.

From 1478 Caxton no longer referred exclusively to noble patrons in his prologues, but might allude to an anonymous backer as a 'singuler frende and gossib of myne' – as in Chaucer's translation of *Boethius* in 1478 – or would occasionally name a fellow merchant who had commissioned a translation or advised him on the choice of a text – as in *The royal book*, the translation finished in September 1484. His productivity as a printer was partly fuelled by his industry as translator and editor, and it has to be remembered that Caxton became more famous among his contemporaries as an author than as a printer. Several patrons commissioned translations from him, possibly to be copied in presentation manuscripts, and as a spin-off Caxton would publish the translation in the more modest form of print. This was probably the case with one of the best-known books he printed in this period, *The mirrour of the world*, a medieval cosmology by Gossuin of Metz that traditionally was illustrated with schematic representations of the universe and the earth's place in it. A prominent Londoner, Hugh Bryce, Prime Warden of the Goldsmiths' Company and a governor of the Mint, commissioned in 1481 the translation for presentation to William, Lord Hastings, a collector of manuscripts who was at the time Master of the Mint of the Tower. Caxton's French source for the translation and for his illustrations was closely related to two fine French manuscripts, one written for Loys de Gruuthuse, the other for Edward IV. Bryce's plan probably was to present Lord Hastings with an equally splendid manuscript with the English version, but if so, no such manuscript survives. Caxton's edition (also of 1481) reflects the glory of his model in his lively translation, and in the crude but charming woodcuts and diagrams, the first time he ventured into printed illustrations.

In another, slightly earlier case the fortunes of survival had the opposite effect. Caxton's translation of the *Ovide moralisé*, completed on 22 April 1480, is not quite as long as *The golden legend*, but still substantial. The text is a version of Ovid's *Metamorphoses* with extensive moralizing glosses that became popular in the fifteenth century.

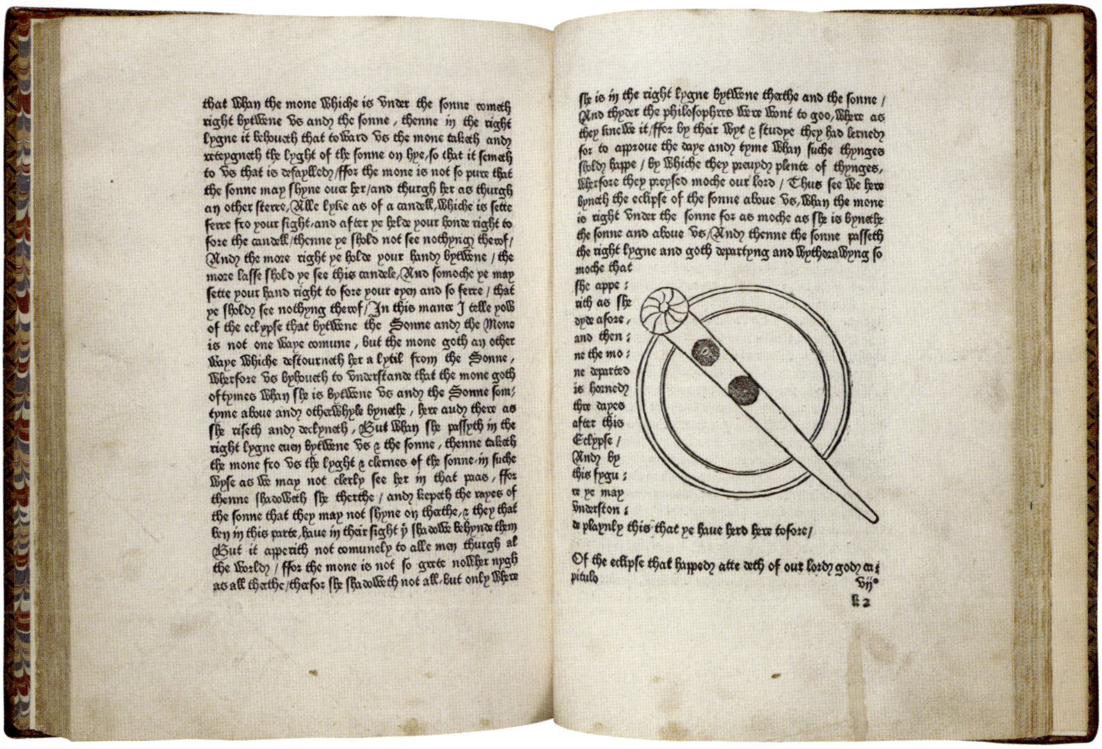

Fig. 33. Caxton's edition of *The mirrour of the world* included illustrations in the tradition of manuscripts of this medieval cosmology, including diagrams of positions of celestial bodies. Depicted here is an eclipse of the sun.

Gossuin de Metz, *The mirrour of the world*, translated from the French *L'image du monde* by William Caxton. Westminster, William Caxton, 1481. London, BL, IB. 55040, fol. k1 verso, k2 recto.

Caxton's translation is known only in a beautiful two-volume manuscript in a sophisticated Flemish style that fits in with some of the manuscripts produced for Edward IV at this time. As with *The mirrour of the world*, Edward IV's library included a manuscript of this work in French, related to a manuscript in the Gruuthuse library. The Ovid translation was probably commissioned by a patron who wished to emulate the two manuscripts in French, and there is some evidence that likewise Caxton's version took one of these as his model, via an intermediate manuscript copy. The patron remains unknown. An early inscription in one of the volumes reveals the name 'Audley Seeley', and the interesting suggestion has been made that in 1538 Thomas, Lord Audley of Walden, married a great-grandniece of Earl Rivers. If not exactly a pointer to former ownership by Caxton's patron, this is at least an indication of the kind of milieu that had the means and interest to commission such an extensive translation, presented as a luxurious manuscript. The work was executed by professional scribes, who indulged in sometimes exuberantly ornamental script forms. When one of the two volumes came to light in the 1960s (the two volumes were then reunited in Magdalene College, Cambridge), it was generally assumed that the manuscript had been commissioned by Caxton himself, as well as three of its four miniatures, which were therefore – rather misleadingly – ascribed to 'the Caxton Master'. It seems now more likely that the writing of the manuscript and the illustrations were two different commissions, by the patron rather than by Caxton. Only four of the fifteen large spaces left blank by the scribes for miniatures were used. The spaces heading the first three books were filled in by mainly grey drawings executed by a skilful artist, the fourth by a different artist using water-colours. This part of the commission was clearly left unfinished.

Caxton's translation has not survived in print. It cannot be ruled out that a printed version once existed, but books of that size tend not to disappear entirely without trace. It seems more probable that Caxton never published it – and we can merely guess at the reasons, since everything about the background of this manuscript has so far remained unknown.

A few years later, in 1484, Caxton published his translation of another text from antiquity, the fables of Aesop combined with similar fables by later authors, and concluding with two tales by himself. He worked from an edition in French printed in Lyon in 1482 by Jehan Rousset, known as 'The Printer of the Abusé en Cour', and illustrated in the tradition of earlier versions of the text. Caxton followed this model, and invested in 185 woodcuts. The translation was a success, and although no reprint by Caxton himself is known, his translation was reprinted many times, even as late as 1634. The Aesop may give us an impression of what an amply illustrated printed edition of *Ovid moralized* might have looked like.

Lyon, a great mercantile centre, was from early on the focal point for printing in French, in contrast to the Latin orientation of the early printers in Paris. Lyonnese printers catered for a readership of merchants, especially in the textile industries of the city, similar to the public that Caxton could count on among his clients. It should therefore be noted that Caxton translated several texts that were available to him in versions printed in Lyon, although we can merely speculate on the nature of any contacts with printers in that city. His translation of the *Disticha* of Cato, extended with paraphrases and examples and published in 1484 shortly before the Aesop, was based on the version printed *circa* 1480 in Lyon by Martin Huss; the two books printed in rapid succession in December 1485, *Charles the Great* and *The history of Paris and Vienne* were likewise based on versions printed in Lyon by Guillaume le Roy in 1484–5 and 1480, respectively. Later, in 1490, a similar combination of Lyonnese sources occurred with the publication of the *Four sons of Aymon* and the *Eneydos*, both again probably based on editions by Guillaume le Roy.

The intense activity of the decade 1476–86 was concluded with *The royal book*, Caxton's own translation of the French *Somme le Roi* that he had completed in September 1484 'at the requeste of a worshipful marchaunt and mercer of London ... for the wele of alle them that shal rede or here it', since it 'may dyrecte a persone to everlastyng blysse'. It was a handbook to the virtuous life, written at the end of the

Fig. 34. Aesop reduces the lady of the house to tears. The woodcut illustrations are a prominent feature in the many printed editions of the fables of Aesop in Latin and in translations. Although the pictures of animals look appealing, this scene of domestic discord shows that this should not be mistaken for a children's book.

Aesop, *Vita et fabulae*, translated from a French version into English by William Caxton. Westminster, William Caxton, 1484. London, BL, C.11.c.17, fol. b2 recto.

¶ Folio x

On a tyme whan the scolyers had ben in the audytorye with Exantus/one of the scolers arayed precious me-tes for the souper/ And whanne they were at souper/ they toke of the most best metes & put them in a plater/ & exantus sayd to Esope/go bere this to her that loueth me best/and Esope thought in hym self/ now is hit tyme to auenge me of my maystresse/ & whan he cam home in to the halle he said to his maystresse/Madame/beware that ye ete not of this mete/And his lady said/ I wote wel/ that thou arte alwey a grete fole And Esope sayd to her/Exantus hath not commaunded me to gyue it to the/But to her that loueth hym best/Thenne esope pre-sented the plater to a lytel hound/ whiche was alwaye in the hows/sayenge to the hound my lord hath sente to the this me-te whiche is precious / & the wyf of Exantus wente in to her chambre/ & began to wepe/ & after Esope retorned to exantus / & he asked how his loue ferd/ & he said ryght wel my lord/ & al the mete that I haue sette to fore her/she hath eten it/ & exantus

b ii

thirteenth century for the French King Philippe III ('le Hardi') by the Dominican Frère Laurent d'Orléans. It treats of the Ten Commandments, the Twelve Articles of the Faith, the Seven Deadly Sins, 'and many other holy thynges and maters good and prouffytable for the wele of mannes soule'. Caxton does not name the Mercer and friend here, but it was probably William Pratt, who in 1487 was named when Caxton printed in his friend's memory his translation of the equally pious *Book of good manners*. Paper and type indicate that *The royal book* was not printed immediately after completion of the translation, but later than the dated works of 1485. Pratt died in July 1486, and if the guess is correct that it was he who commissioned the translation of the work, printing must have been completed before his death. Caxton's formulation in his prologue, that it was the patron's wish that the book should be for the benefit of all who will read or hear it, makes it clear that his colleague was fully convinced that the printed word could reach a long way.

9
Printing in Oxford

For a few years Caxton was the only printer in the British Isles, printing mainly in English, but it did not take long for the need for printed books in Latin to be felt by scholars in the two English universities, Oxford and Cambridge. In centuries to come Latin books of learning and for teaching were mostly imported from the Continent, from centres that routinely produced such materials. But in Oxford two presses operated successively between 1478 and 1483, both for only a short time, almost as an experiment to establish whether it might be economical to print books locally, as demand arose or opportunities were offered, rather than to ship in quantities of the finished product on a speculative basis. In Cambridge, a similar short-lived experiment in book production took place much later, between 1520 and 1524, when the printer Johann Siberch, who came from the Cologne area, produced a dozen small humanist books and a few broadsides with some support from the university.

The two presses in Oxford may have deliberately tried to bypass the wholesale trade, and in particular the duties that were levied on imported goods. Both printers originated from Cologne. The first press owed its existence to Gerard ten Raem, an enterprising merchant, who in 1477–8 had financed a few small books printed in Cologne by a printer whose name remains unknown. Perhaps the same man was sent to Oxford, equipped with the fount of type he had used in Cologne and not much else. Only three small books were printed by this printer, and only the final one was a text taught at the university, a Latin translation of Aristotle's *Ethica ad Nicomachum*, a humanist version of a text that was printed many times in many different places.

The two earlier Oxford books had no connection with the university curriculum. The first is a short treatise on the Apostolic Creed written in the fourth century by Tyrannius Rufinus, famous for his disputes with St Jerome; the text is usually found in collections of St Jerome's letters. The choice of this text would have remained an enigma but for the survival of the small manuscript from which it was copied by the printer. This can be linked to James Goldwell, who in the 1460s and early 1470s, before he became Bishop of Norwich (in 1472), had travelled on diplomatic missions to Hamburg, Italy, and Flanders, and had not missed opportunities to acquire manuscripts and printed books. Goldwell probably acquired the Rufinus manuscript in Florence, where it had been written for the famous bookseller Vespasiano da Bisticci. Its opening page was decorated with a minia-

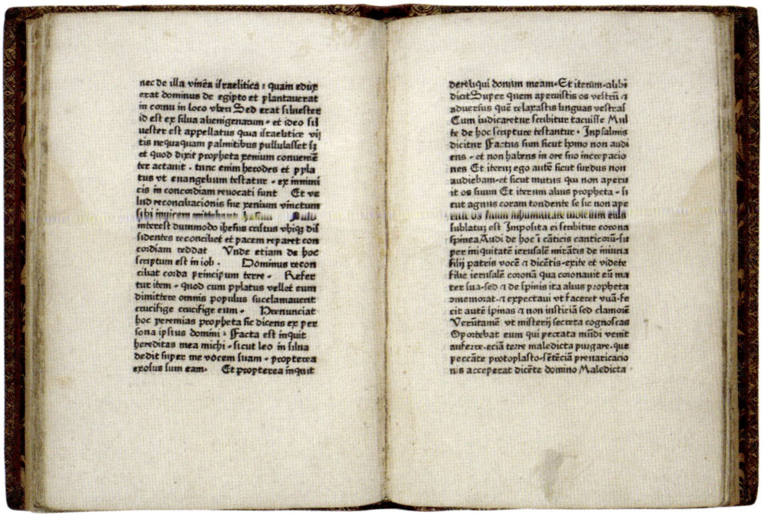

Figs 35, 36. A manuscript written in Florence served as printer's copy for the first book printed in Oxford. The regular script of the expert scribe contrasts with the gaps on the verso page and compression on the recto in the typeseting by the anonymous Oxford printer.

Tyrannius Rufinus Aquileiensis, *Expositio in symbolum apostolorum*. London, BL, Ms Sloane 1579, fol. 2 verso, 3 recto, and Oxford, [Printer of Rufinus], 17 December 14[7]8. BL, 167.b.26, fol. c4 verso, 5 recto.

ture depicting St Jerome in a Tuscan-looking landscape, faced by an Italian-style border with a coat of arms at the bottom, later erased. How a connection was made in Oxford with the printer who, probably newly arrived from Cologne, proceeded to convert the manuscript into print, remains unknown. But the connection undoubtedly existed, for the copy of the printed book in Cambridge University Library includes a painted image of the miniature and decoration of the manuscript, now including Goldwell's coat of arms. The best guess is that a friend of Goldwell in Oxford had intervened, possibly Robert Thompson, at the time bursar of Magdalen Hall, who wrote his initials in the manuscript.

The printer treated the manuscript with care, counting lines in preparation for printing, and marking with discreet little dots the places where pages should begin according to his counting. The typesetting was far from expert, leaving gaps or compressing text where the counting had failed to produce a realistic estimate. Experienced compositors know how to avoid such irregularities. Moreover, this poor printer had to work with a press of unusually small dimensions, capable of printing only one small page at a time, not much more than a table-top toy. It is perhaps not too surprising that after toiling through eighty-two pages he committed an error, missing out an x in the date in roman figures, which therefore reads '17 December 1468' instead of '1478'. For a long time this was taken to be correct, and it was thought that Oxford should be ranked among the earliest places of European printing, even before Venice, and well before Caxton. But even the most argumentative of historians favouring Oxford's priority were silenced in the course of the eighteenth century, for there are many ways to prove that the book could not have been printed before 1478.

A similar-sized book followed three months later, a thirteenth-century treatise on original sin written by Aegidius Columna, its subject matter akin to that of the first book. It has no connection with the university and was perhaps also initiated by Bishop Goldwell, or by Robert Thompson – there is no way of telling. During the printing of his third and last book the printer acquired a better press, and could print two small pages (a half-sheet of paper) at a time. Although with his Aristotle text he was now meeting the requirements of the university curriculum, he did not continue, and disappeared for good. Surviving copies of the three books suggest that they were mainly bought by scholars in Oxford.

Two years later, in 1481, another printer appeared, announcing his origin in his colophon as 'de Colonia'. This time it may not have been a merchant but a printer in Cologne who wished to establish an outstation for his business in a major university. The new printer, who in Oxford went by the name of Theodericus (or Theoderic) Rood, had also the skills of a goldsmith, for he is documented in the proctors' accounts of the university as having repaired a beadle's staff. He was probably capable of modifying and casting type, creating his own variations on a theme. His printing types – he had an assortment of five sets – were stylistically closely related (but not identical) to those of the Cologne printer Arnold ther Hoernen. The kinship of the printing types offers a clue to an equally loose family relationship. Arnold ther Hoernen was married to a widow, Gertrude Molner. After Ther

Hoernen's death in 1482/3 his stepson, Theodericus Molner, continued from 1485 the business together with a Konrad Welker, whom his mother had married in the same year. Theodericus and his new stepfather produced books for the university of Cologne at the late Arnold ther Hoernen's address.

The Theodericus who printed in Oxford did not use the surname 'Molner', but at this time a family name was less stable than a baptismal name, especially when changing countries and background. We shall encounter more cases where surnames show mystifying variations whereas the combination of a baptismal name and printing types seems to leave a less dubious trail. The name 'Rood' may have been an alias or a nickname, 'Rood' signifying 'red' as well as 'rude' and 'cross'. There is no proof, but there is a lot to suggest that the family relations of a stepson with typographical abilities determined the brief career of the second Oxford printer: first to establish a branch of his stepfather Ther Hoernen's Cologne printing house in Oxford, then, upon his death, recalled by his mother to ensure the continuation of the business in Cologne on her behalf.

Whatever the family relations, in the few years that Theodericus Rood operated in Oxford, he was, unlike his enigmatic predecessor, soon well established in the university. His enterprise had many of the characteristics of other early university presses (most of them equally short lived): housed in premises in a central position, and welcomed by some dons who promoted the printing of particular texts. Rood's printing house was situated in the High Street at the present site of Queen's College; it was rented from Magdalen College and round the corner from Cat Street, where booksellers and bookbinders traditionally had their shops. Further down the High Street was the establishment of Thomas Hunt, the university's stationarius (or official book dealer), with whom Rood had a business association and published at least one book.

He first completed two substantial works. In 1481 he began with a commentary on Aristotle's *De anima*. It was probably written by Alexander de Alexandria, general of the Franciscans (*d.* 1314), who has no connection with England, but until recently it was *thought* to have been written by Alexander de Ales, or Hales, in Gloucestershire (*d.* 1245), who had been a canon of St Paul's in London before joining the Franciscan order. This was followed a year later by a commentary on Jeremiah, written in the first half of the fourteenth century by John Lathbury, an English friar. There was undoubtedly a preference for Latin works by Englishmen, and there is some unusual evidence that their publication was supported by several fellows of All Souls and of University College, as well as by Thomas Hunt. A few de luxe copies of both works were printed on vellum, and a few copies were decorated with a large woodcut border with a pattern of boughs and birds fluttering among them surrounding the text (fig. 38). Three vellum copies of the Lathbury, in the libraries of All Souls and Balliol Colleges in Oxford, and in Westminster Abbey, bear in the lower margins signatures, or the remains of signatures, of which five can be identified as belonging to fellows of All Souls, and two to fellows of University College; almost half of all the vellum sheets are signed with the monogram 'TH', known to belong to Thomas Hunt. Confirming the significance of these signatures is an entry in an account book of All Souls that records the expenses for printing the Lathbury and the purchase of vellum 'pro lathbury super libros trenorum imprimendo et emendo pargameno'. Rood had engaged the interest, and with it the active cooperation, of a small community of scholars in the university.

Thomas Hunt appeared once in a colophon with Rood, probably in 1481, the first year of Rood's residence in Oxford. It is in an edition of the *Epistolae* of the pseudo-classical author Phalaris, in a version of the text prepared by the humanist scholar Francesco Griffolini. The colophon had the form of a complicated poem by another humanist scholar, Pietro Carmeliano, who had arrived in London shortly before. It was therefore a modern presentation of a pseudo-classical text that was probably intended for teaching in the newly established Magdalen School. One of its masters, John Anwykyll, prepared several texts to be printed by Rood, a small grammar that was based on the work of the Italian humanist scholars Niccolò Perotti and Lorenzo Valla, as well as a selection of phrases from plays by Terence with English translations, the *Vulgaria*. Cicero's *Oratio pro Milone* was the only truly classical text that was printed by Rood, probably also used for teaching. Other schoolbooks were an elementary grammatical work, the *Parvula*, and the perennial *Doctrinale* of Alexander de Villa Dei, a metrical Latin grammar taught at schools as well as universities. Despite the support of Oxford dons that was manifest in the earliest years, the schoolbooks were probably the bread-and-butter of Rood's press. Short lived as it was, the participation of humanist scholars and teachers meant that it delivered a significant contribution to modernizing education, the prime purpose of any university press.

Its final and by far its largest publication is of a wholly different nature and was undoubtedly printed on commission. It is a huge book containing John Lyndewode's *Constitutiones provinciales*. Two bishops are known to have had some connection with early Oxford printing: James Goldwell, as we have seen above, and William Wayneflete, bishop of Winchester, who was the founder of Magdalen School. Perhaps we may guess that one of them argued that the chance should not be missed to publish in print this volume of the ecclesiastical law as applied in the province of Canterbury, thus producing a uniform instrument for administration. The book, printed on large-format royal paper, survives in many copies.

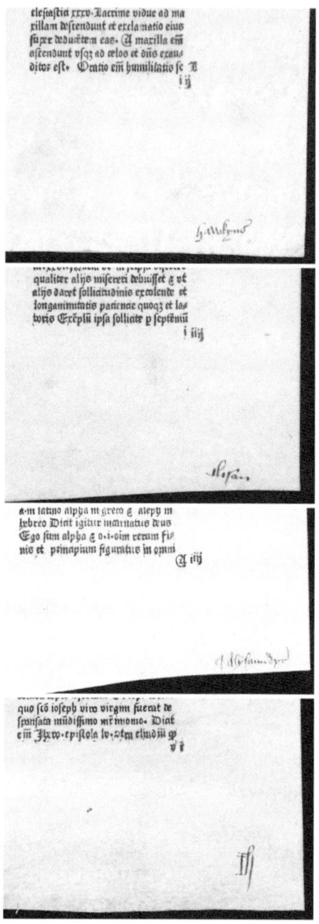

Fig. 37. Several *de luxe* copies of Lathbury were printed on vellum. Sheets in three of these copies still bear names (in faint script) that can be identified as belonging to five fellows of All Souls and two of University College. The monogram TH (found most frequently), can be identified beyond doubt as belonging to Thomas Hunt, the university's stationer. They may all have shared in the cost of printing part of the edition on vellum. Shown above are the marks of Thomas Hunt, Alysaundyr, Alison, and Hawkyns.

John Lathbury, *Liber moralium super threnos Jeremiae*. [Oxford, Theodericus Rood], 31 July 1482. Oxford, All Souls College, The Codrington Library, L. R. 3. g. 15, fol. vi recto, A4 recto, i4 recto, i2 recto (details).

Fig. 38. The opening page of several copies of this sizable book printed by Theodericus Rood, the second printer in Oxford, is embellished with an extensive border consisting of four loose pieces. The type is in a Cologne style that differs from that of the first Oxford printer, and belongs to the family of types used by Arnold ther Hoernen who may have been Rood's stepfather.

John Lathbury, *Liber moralium super threnos Jeremiae*. [Oxford, Theodericus Rood], 31 July 1482. London, BL, IB. 55317a, fol. a2 recto.

There must have been plans for another large book, an edition of the collection of saints' lives known as *The golden legend*. Caxton's publication of his translation of this collection in English in 1483/4 may have dashed expectations of selling another edition of such a large work, even if Rood had planned to publish a version in Latin. Woodcuts were prepared for it, indicating that it would have been a book of the same dimensions as Caxton's *Golden legend* and Rood's own Lyndewode, both printed on royal paper. It is also possible that the commission for the Lyndewode was given priority before fate intervened and Rood left Oxford. One woodcut, probably meant to depict Jacobus de Voragine, the original compiler of *The golden legend*, was used, rather inappropriately, as frontispiece for the Lyndewode. Whatever the causes, the book was not printed, for there is no ground for an assumption that a book of that size would disappear without leaving any trace.

The woodcuts shared the fate of some of Rood's other materials. They were sold on – presumably when he left to return to Cologne.

One of Rood's five founts of type appears in a single book, printed in 1486 or 1487. It is the only book in English to appear in any of Rood's types. The text, John Mirk's *Festial*, was a collection of sermons arranged according to the liturgical year, and turned out to be immensely popular. No English text was printed more often in the fifteenth century, in England as well as in Paris and Rouen. Caxton had published a different version in 1483, but later decided to adopt for reprinting the version published by the purchaser of Rood's type. The eleven woodcuts for the planned *Golden legend* are found here, awkwardly cut down to fit the size of the *Festial*, which was printed in a smaller, standard paper format. The whole book is a specimen of clumsy printing, the result of good intention unsupported by skill.

Its dating, '1486, the day aftir seint Edward the kyng', can be interpreted as either the feast day of St Edward the Confessor, who was usually honoured on the day of his translation, 13 October, in which case the book would have been completed in 1486, or as that of St Edward King and Martyr, whose feast day was on 18 March, and his translation on 18 February. Either of these two dates would fall in the secular year 1487. Not only its dating is problematic. There is no way of telling where it was printed or by whom, although traditionally it is ranged with Oxford printing because of the connection with Rood's printing types.

Fig. 39. Bindings decorated with these tools are associated with Thomas Hunt, Stationer of the University of Oxford. The book, printed in Paris, was presumably imported by him.

Rubbing of a binding on Johannes Nider, *Consolatorium timoratae conscientiae*. Paris, Ulrich Gering, 16 Dec. 1478. London, BL, IA. 39102, lower cover.

Festum sancti ni
colai.
Godd men and
wymmen soch a
day ye shall haue
seint nicolas day the whi
che is moche preysed in
hooly churche and spe-
cially for thre causis. the
furste for his meke le-
uyng The secounde for
his heuenly teching The
thyrde for his grete com-
passion hauyng Furste
he was made lowly Pa
ter eius epiphanius
mater eius iohanna
dicta est. Hit is seyd
that his fadyr highte epi
phanus and his modyr
ione the whiche in theyr
thoughte goto seint nico-
las And whan he was
borne they made her vo-
wes bothe to kepe and to

Fig. 40. The collection of sermons in the *Festial* was one of the most popular English texts of the period. The place of printing of this edition remains uncertain, although its type is a casting of one of the types used in Oxford by Theodericus Rood. The ill-fitting woodcut of St Nicholas, cut down to fit the smaller book, may originally have been intended for an edition of *The golden legend* that was never printed.

John Mirk, *Festial*. [Oxford? Printer of Mirk] 14 October 1486 or 19 March 1487. London, Lambeth Palace Library 1486.9, fol. h5 verso.

10

The first printers in London

Printing in London, the city which was to achieve a place of far greater importance in publishing than any other in the British Isles, began slowly, and in circumstances that raise several questions. As had happened in Oxford, it began with the conjunction of a migrant printer looking for work, and a scholar who took the initiative for a learned text to appear in print, in this instance financed by a London merchant. Rood's first publications were supported by scholars in Oxford, probably because they were works by English authors. The first two works printed in London were likewise connected to English authors, and at least one of them was published on the initiative of its very learned editor. The first book, printed in 1480, was a commentary on Aristotle's *Metaphysica* by the philosopher Antonius Andreae and edited by the Englishman Thomas Penketh, an Augustinian friar who specialized in editing the works of the great philosopher Duns Scotus. Penketh had just returned to England from six years of lecturing on metaphysics and theology at the university of Padua.

Between 1474 and 1480 Penketh edited no fewer than seven editions of works of Duns Scotus, his pupil Antonius Andreae, and St Bonaventure, which all appeared in print in Padua, Venice and Vicenza, published by printing houses as prominent as Nicolas Jenson, Reynaldus de Novimagio, and the firm of Johannes de Colonia and Johannes Manthen in Venice, Albertus de Stendal in Padua, and Hermannus Liechtenstein in Vicenza. The work printed in London had first been printed in Vicenza. In Italy, Penketh had therefore gained experience with as many as five printing houses, and with the quality of the work delivered by some of the most skilled printers of his time. The colophon of the first book printed in London declared that it was printed at the expense of the Draper William Wilcock.

A year later another Latin work appeared in London, again with the financial support of William Wilcock, this time a commentary on the psalter by the fourteenth-century Dominican friar Thomas Waleys. In its colophon the text was mistakenly ascribed to 'Valencius', which may at some point have been a misreading of a Latin form of the name 'Waleys' or 'Wallensis'. We cannot know whether Penketh was involved in the choice.

The printer of the first two London books names himself in the colophons as 'Johannes Lettou'. This name brings with it another of those puzzles of identity that seem to be a characteristic of migrating printers. As elsewhere, the printing type of the two books printed in

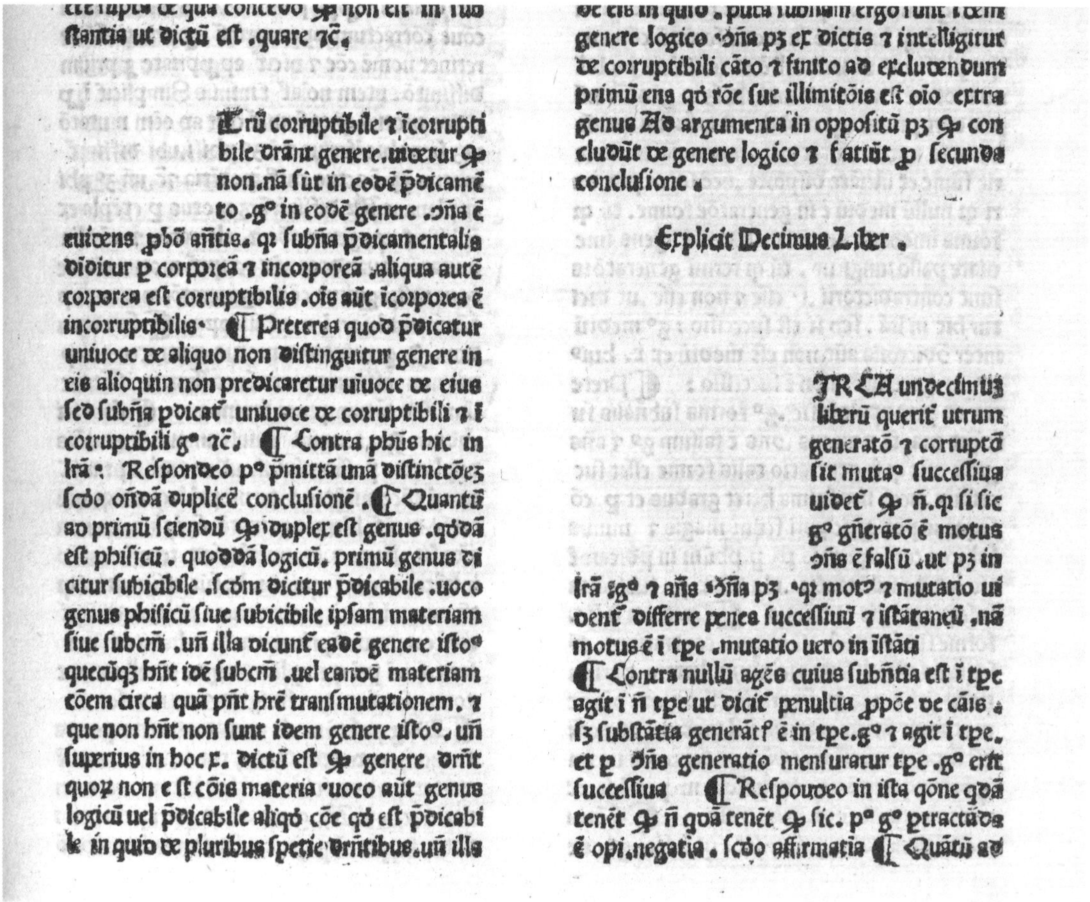

London rather than the name given by their printer provides clues for an identity, and leads to a web of dubious connections spread over a large part of Europe. The fount was first used in Naples in 1476 by Mathias Moravus, an erudite printer who had come from a village near Olomouc (Olmütz) in Moravia, and whose route south can be traced through manuscripts and printed books in northern Italy and Genoa. He reached Naples in 1474. Which local styles may have influenced him on his travels is difficult to unravel, but the printing types he chose to use for his Latin printing were acceptable to the whole world of learning. His narrow and economical text type that appears in the first books printed in London had previously found favour with a printer in Rome, who obtained a casting from Moravus which he used from 1477 to 1479 in some thirty-five mostly small books. He was apparently a skilled printer, who produced mainly works commissioned by the papal Curia. Only rarely did he sign his work, and on those occasions he used the forms 'per Johannem Bullen de Bremis', 'per Magistrum Johannem Bulle de Bremis', or 'per Magistrum Johannem Bremer alias Bulle'. The printer in Rome seems therefore to have hailed from the port of Bremen in north-western

Fig. 41. The first book printed in London was a learned work, printed in a type first seen in Naples, and subsequently in Rome. Its excellent typesetting was the work of an experienced printer, who can probably be identified as having first worked in Rome. Spaces were left open for painting or drawing initials.

Antonius Andreae, *Quaestiones super Metaphysicam Aristotelis*. London, Johannes Lettou, 1480. London, BL, G. 8984, fol. m6 recto (detail).

Germany. The printer in London, with the same baptismal name, and the same fount of type, and equally evident competence in printing, identifies himself as 'Lettou', that is, of Latvian origin. The best guess is that a man named Johannes travelled from the Baltic region via the north coast of Germany to Italy, turning up later in London equipped with the fount of type that had served him well in Rome, and which may have been his most precious possession. But this has to remain a guess.

Like his possible avatar in Rome, he was not in a position to establish an independent printing house: first we see that substantial work was commissioned by William Wilcock; in the same period – and in the same type – he printed some indulgences, which are by definition work on commission. Caxton printed the same indulgences for the papal commissioner Kendale, and he in turn may have ordered additional copies from John Lettou. The next time we find Johannes Lettou in the colophon of a book it is in partnership with a new name, William de Machlinia, 'in the City of London next to the church of All Hallows'. The Alien Subsidy roll of 1483 provides details of their address: it was in Dowgate Ward, and designated as a 'hospicium' held by 'Johannes Letowe Bokeprynter Theotonicus' and also occupied by his wife Elizabeth Northe and by 'William Ravenswalde Theotonicus', four servants, all four 'Theotonici', and two others. The roll records that the servants were employed jointly by Lettou and Ravenswalde, although Lettou, who had married an Englishwoman, was the head of the household. What we therefore see here is the partnership heading the organization of nine persons who lived together, each with a role in the small printing business. The adjoining church can be identified as either All Hallows the Great or All Hallows the Less, both situated on the south side of Thames Street near the Steelyard establishment of the German Hansa merchants.

The name 'William Ravenswalde' for someone who in colophons consistently names himself as 'William de Machlinia' or once 'William Maclyn' poses the same problems of identity as the names of the persons who as printers in England presented themselves as Theodericus Rood and Johannes Lettou. The constant in these names is the baptismal name. 'Ravenswalde' is a German name, rather than Flemish, and he was recorded as 'Theotonicus' (German). Perhaps William de Machlinia originated from Germany and arrived in London via the Low Countries and specifically the city of Mechelen (Malines), north of Brussels.

The partnership did not continue with learned works in Latin, nor did the Neapolitan/Roman type make further appearances. Instead the two printers were discovered by the lawyers of the Inns of Court, and they laid the basis for what was to become one of the specialities of London printing: legal works, and in particular works of the common law. The language for works of the common law was Law-French, which was written with its own traditions of script and abbreviations. For a not particularly convincing approximation of the traditional script the two printers used a rather crude casting of Caxton's smaller text type (Type 4, introduced by him in 1480, see figs 00), and they also had a casting of his large heading type (Type 3). Together they produced five such legal works, undoubtedly on the initiative of lawyers of the Inns of Court. They included three 'Yearbooks', collections of reports of cases brought before the courts of law, which form the basis for case law. They are always identified by the regnal year in which the cases took place, from the first year of the reign of Edward III (1327) until the end of reign of Henry VIII (1547). Yearbooks were to be the mainstay for London printers specializing in legal printing, who over the years, until the 1580s, printed and reprinted hundreds of them.

When the reputation of the two London printers was thus established, it must have been the Court of Chancery that commissioned them in the early months of 1483 to print a legal document, *The promise of matrimony*. This was a record of the Treaty of Picquigny regarding the marriage alliance between the English and French kings, which was repudiated in December 1482 by the Treaty of Arras. This new marriage treaty assured a Franco-Burgundian truce, excluding England, where it was of course regarded as crude betrayal. The printing in 1483 of this document – in English – had a political purpose, for it was intended to persuade members of parliament of the justification of a military campaign against France. It is the first instance of English printing for political and administrative purposes.

During the reign of Richard III the partnership was commissioned by the Court of Chancery to print the statutes of the realm from the time of Edward III, the *Nova statuta*, completed by 1485; it was also in Law-French, but now printed in a new fount of type.

Politicking of a different nature is found in the one publication in Latin that the partnership produced, the controversial *Dialogus de libertate ecclesiastica*, written in Cologne in 1475 by a certain Heinrich Urdemann, who was an office- holder in the Curia of the diocese of Cologne. In it he defended the privileges favouring the clergy in Cologne's urban taxation system. This was much against the interests of the city authorities of Cologne, and when the book was first printed, in 1477, they suppressed it, persecuted the printer, destroyed the copies he had printed and sequestered his type. This is the first recorded case of censorship of a printed book. Printers, however, were not slow to grasp that the arguments might find an enthusiastic reception among clergy elsewhere, and the little book was printed in many places beyond the authority of the Cologne magistrates. The

Fig. 42. Works for the lawyers of the Inns of Court produced by the partnership of Lettou and De Machlinia were the beginning of a long tradition of legal printing in London. Among the earliest was this Yearbook, a report of court cases. Type brought from Rome was now replaced by types obtained either from Caxton (his text-type 4 and formal Type 3 for headings and for the names of the lawyers) or directly from Johan Veldener, who had cut the punches. The coloured manuscript initial is in a style found in many copies of legal works printed by the partners, and must be associated with their printing-house.

Yearbook 36 Henry VI. [London Johannes Lettou and William de Machlinia, 1482–3]. London, BL, IB. 55424, fol. a1 recto.

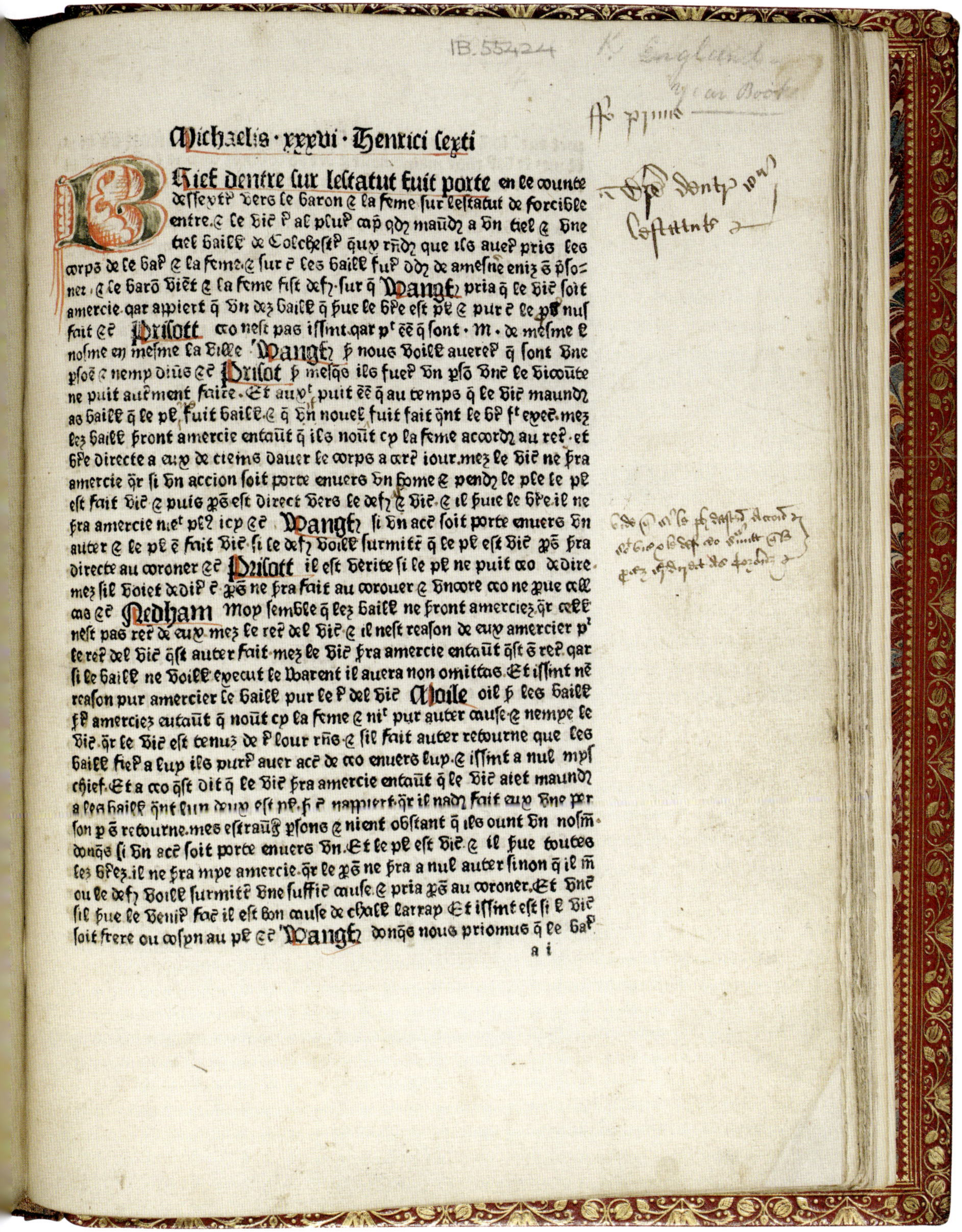
Michaelis · xxxvi · Henrici sexti

B
Rief dentre sur lestatut fuit porte en le counte
dessex vers le baron & la feme sur lestatut de forcible
entre. & le vic r al plus cap qd maund a un tiel & une
tiel baill de Colchest quux rnd que ils auer pris les
corps de le bar & la feme. & sur ceo les baill fur odr de amesne eniz ē pso-
ner . & le baro viet & la feme fist def. sur q Wangf pria q le vic soit
amercie. qar appiert q un dez baill q fue le bre est pl & pur ceo le pl nus
fait &c Prisott ceo nest pas issint. qar pt ee q sont · m · de mesme l
nosme en mesme la ville Wangf nous voill auer q sont une
psoe & nemy dius &c Prisot mesqe ils fuer un pso une le vicoute
ne puit autrement faire. Et aux puit ee q au temps q le vic maund
as baill q le pl fuit baill. & q un nouel fuit fait qnt le br f exec. mez
lez baill front amercie entaunt q ils nount cy la feme accord au ret. et
bre directe a eux de ciems dauer le corps a cert iour. mez le vic ne fra
amercie qr si un accion soit porte enuers un home & pend le ple le pl
est fait vic & puis pces est direct vers le def & vic. & il fue le bre. il ne
fra amercie niet pl icy &c Wangf si un acc soit porte enuers un
auter & le pl e fait vic. si le def voill surmitt q le pl est vic pces fra
directe au coroner &c Prisott il est verite si le pl ne puit ceo dedire.
mez sil voiet dedir e pces ne fra fait au corouer & uncore ceo ne pue cell
cas &c Nedham Moy semble q lez baill ne front amerciez. qr cell
nest pas ret de eux mez le ret del vic & il nest reason de eux amercier p
le ret del vic qst auter fait. mez le vic fra amercie entaunt qst e ret. qar
si le baill ne voill execut le warent il auera non omittas. Et issint ne
reason pur amercier le baill pur le r del vic Moile oil les baill
fr amerciez entaunt q nount cy la feme & nient pur auter cause. & nempe le
vic. qr le vic est tenuz de r lour rns. & sil fait auter retourne que les
baill fier a luy ils pur auer acc de ceo enuers luy. & issint a nul myst
chief. Et a ceo qst dit q le vic fra amercie entaunt q le vic aiet maund
a les baill qnt lun deux est pl. r e nappiert. qr il nad fait eux une per
son p e retourne. mes estraung psons & nient obstant q ils ount un nosm
donqs si un acc soit porte enuers un. Et le pl est vic. & il fue toutes
lez brez. il ne fra mye amercie. qr le pces ne fra a nul auter sinon q il m
ou le def voill surmitt une suffic cause. & pria pces au coroner. Et une
sil fue le venir fac il est bon cause de chall larray Et issint est si l vic
soit frere ou cosyn au pl &c Wangf donqs nous priomus q le bar

a i

edition printed in London was an elegantly revised version of the original text.

After or even during the printing of the *Nova statuta* Johannes Lettou died and the partnership came to an end. An action in Chancery (not later than 1485) allocated his widow Elizabeth a number of copies of the *Statuta*, and it is therefore certain that Lettou had had a stake in its printing. William de Machlinia now became an independent printer, and made a new start by setting up his own establishment at an address at the eastern end of Fleet Street, at Fleet Bridge. Here his contact with lawyers continued, for he printed a few legal works, but he also introduced works of other kinds, albeit on a modest scale. He must have sought to work for schools, for he reprinted twice the *Vulgaria* of Terence, first printed in Oxford; he also printed two devotional texts in English, both probably on commission. The first was the legend of the miraculous appearance of St Nicholas to a monk of Eynsham, followed a year later by the very popular *Speculum Christiani*, which is partly in English verse and partly in Latin prose. The colophon of the latter states that it was printed at the expense of the bookseller Henry Frankenbergh, an alien who is on record as a bookseller in London from 1478.

A small book twice reprinted in rapid succession was highly topical: the text is an English version of a well-known and much-printed treatise on the treatment of the plague, 'the pestilence', and was produced in response to an outbreak of what is known as the 'sweating sickness', a viral infection that raged in London in the summer of 1485.

After not more than two years in Fleet Street William de Machlinia moved out of the City of London to an address in Holborn. It was probably in the immediate vicinity of Gray's Inn, Staple Inn, and Lincoln's Inn, and he may have expected that he might rely more regularly on the clientele or sponsorship of their lawyers. As it was, he spent not much more than a year at this address. In this period he printed only one more Yearbook. For the Court of Chancery he printed the statutes of the first and only parliament of Richard III. In 1486 the Chancery seems to have turned to him to produce printed copies of another document of political importance, the Bull of Pope Innocent VIII issued in March 1486 to declare his dispensation for the marriage of King Henry VII to Elizabeth of York, daughter of Edward IV, which required papal dispensation because they were distant cousins. The King's Council ordered on 13 June 1486 that the Papal Bull should be translated into English and multiplied, and presumably the translation was printed soon after that date. A single large sheet, it is the last of his works that can be dated with certainty.

De Machlinia's career ended on a note of good fortune, with a substantial work in English, printed soon after the Bull. This is the

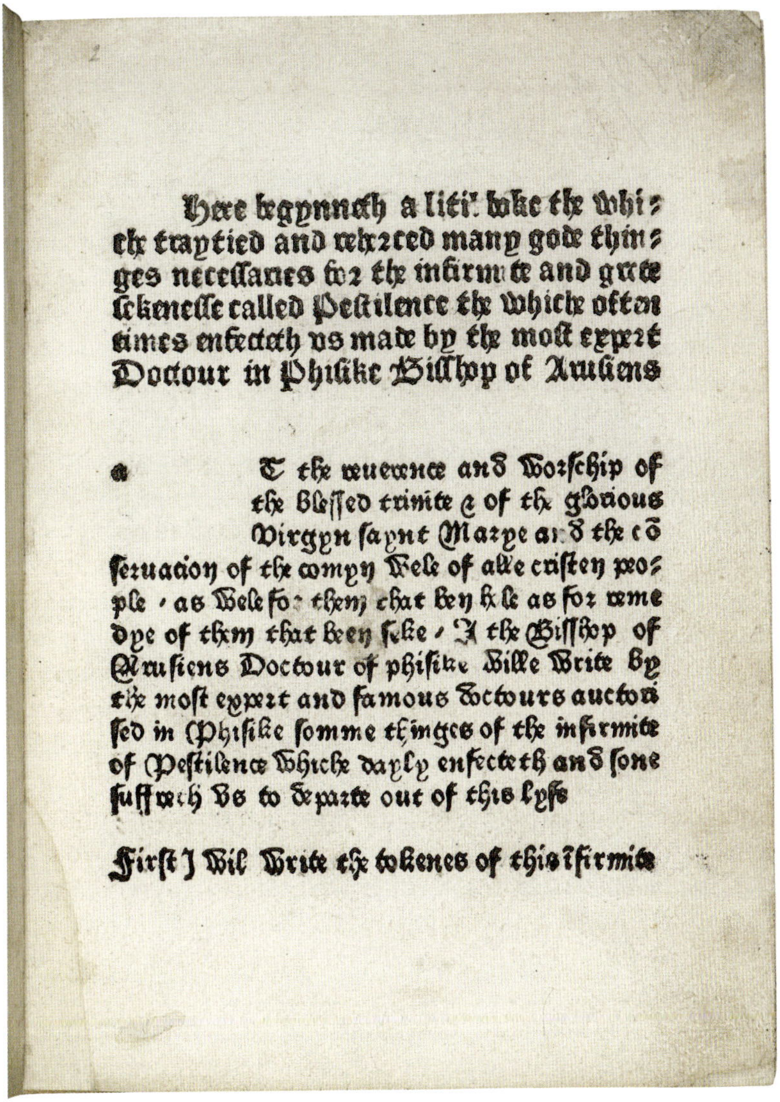

Here begynneth a litil boke the whi-
che traytied and reherced many gode thin-
ges necessaries for the infirmite and grete
sekenesse called Pestilence the whiche often
times enfecteth vs made by the most expert
Doctour in Phisike Bisshop of Arusiens

To the reuerence and worschip of
the blessed trinite & of the glorious
Virgyn saynt Marye and the co-
seruacion of the comyn wele of alle cristen peo-
ple, as wele for them that ben hole as for reme-
dye of them that been seke, I the Bisshop of
Arusiens Doctour of phisike wille write by
the most expert and famous doctours auctori-
sed in Phisike somme thinges of the infirmite
of Pestilence whiche dayly enfecteth and sone
suffreth vs to departe out of this lyfe

First I wil write the tokenes of this infirmite

Fig. 43. A small book with remedies against the bubonic plague became very popular in London when in the summer of 1485 there was an outbreak of the dreaded 'sweating sickness', a viral infection. William de Machlinia, continuing the business alone after Lettou's death, printed several editions in rapid succession. By now he had once again renewed his stock of types; he probably obtained these Flemish-style founts from Johan Veldener.

Regimen contra pestilentiam, in an English translation. [London, William de Machlinia, 1485]. London, BL, IA. 55478, fol. [a]2 recto.

Chronicles of England, reprinted from Caxton's first edition of 1480, a work he apparently undertook at his own expense. It suggests that although he was a printer who throughout his brief career could not afford taking risks, and whose work always looked modest and far from refined, he had found a successful strategy. Catering for a variety of interests seems to have paid off. He printed for the legal profession, for schools, perhaps some clerical contacts, and for the general public. We shall find that a similar spreading of risks was adopted by his first successor in London, Richard Pynson. There is nothing to indicate the circumstances in which he vanished from sight.

11

The Press at St Albans

The abbey of St Albans in Hertfordshire was in the pre-Reformation period for a long time the only religious house in the British Isles to act as an independent printing house. The history of this press and the remains of what it produced are fragmented as no other. A clear distinction can be made between two phases in which printing took place: in the first, *circa* 1479–81, Latin works were produced, in the second, *circa* 1486, English. The printed books surviving from the first phase are all extremely rare, and represent probably less than what was originally printed. In order to understand the nature of at least some of these scarce remnants, it is best to see them as the end of three great traditions for which the abbey was famous. It had for centuries been a centre of learning, particularly strong in historiography, where from the thirteenth century onwards a succession of chroniclers compiled histories; linked to this central activity was a scriptorium, and its library was one of the most important in medieval England. The abbey was very wealthy, and had the status of the premier Benedictine abbey in the British Isles, connected with other abbeys (including Westminster) and with cells dispersed over most of England. The early part of the fifteenth century saw the chronicler Thomas Walsingham continuing the tradition of historiography (in Latin), and scholarship culminated during the two abbacies of John Whethamstede (1420–40, 1452–65), a classical scholar who had visited Italy and stands at the beginning of humanism in England. Whethamstede was an author of some encyclopaedic works on the classics, based on his wide reading, but he is most famous as a collector of books and a generous donor to others, notably to Gloucester College, the Benedictine studium in Oxford, and to Duke Humfrey of Gloucester, who himself was the most important patron of the abbey. Whethamstede directed the rebuilding of the abbey's library and added significantly to its collection, many works being copied for him in the then flourishing scriptorium.

But the history of the abbey is not one of uninterrupted triumph. There were episodes of upheaval and internal conflict. Whethamstede's record as abbot does not match his reputation for scholarship and enthusiasm for rebuilding the library, and his two abbacies were troubled periods for the abbey. His death in 1465 was followed by a long period of steep decline and disorganization, reaching its nadir under the abbacy of William Wallingford (1476–92), who on several occasions was accused of embezzlement, and was said to have led the

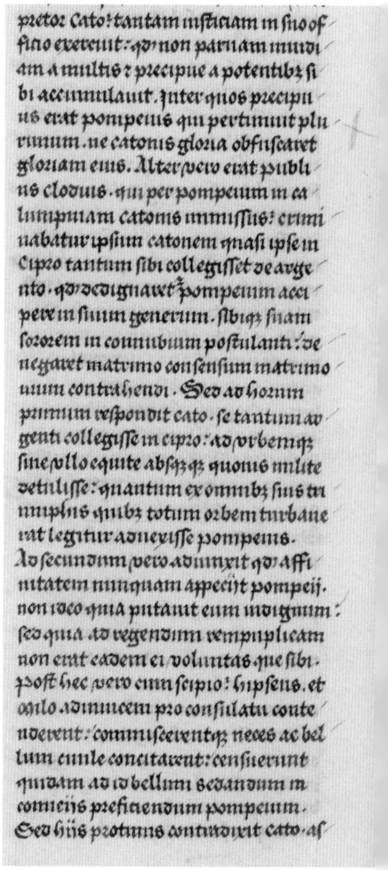

Fig. 44. One of the compilations by abbot John Whethamstede. The style of script is known as 'the St Albans hand'; the printing types used at the abbey in the 1480s have features in common with this hand, see, for example the form of the 'v' (compare with figs 46, l. 12 and 48, l. 8).

John Whethamstede, *Granarium*. Manuscript, Abbey of St Albans, *c.* 1450–55. London, BL, Ms Cotton Nero C.vi, fol. 37 recto (detail).

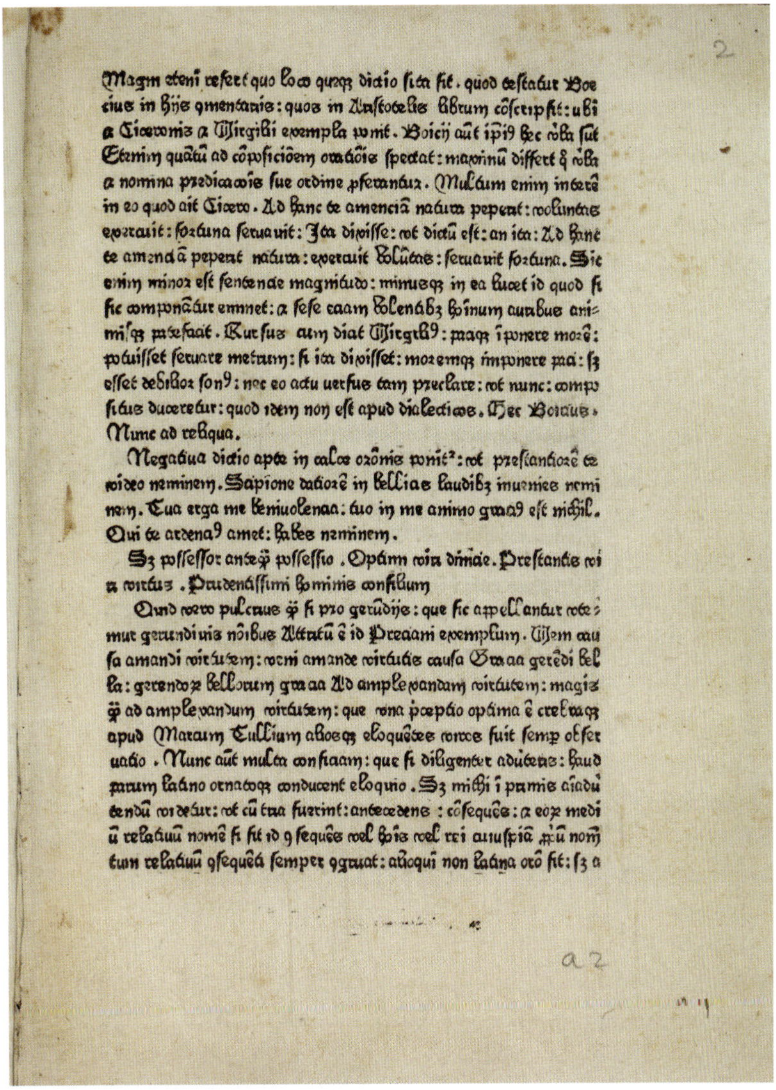

Fig. 45. This is a small type known to have been used only in this book, a schoolbook of eighteen leaves, the first to be printed at the press at St Albans.

Augustinus Datus, *Elegantiolae*. Press at St Albans, [1479]. Cambridge University Library, Oates 4209, fol. [a]2 recto.

monastery into a 'wanton and most dissolute life'. Things came to a head in 1490, when Archbishop John Morton wrote a letter describing in vivid terms the monastery's moral disarray. He threatened a visitation, and the issue was brought before Pope Innocent VIII. The surviving documents give an impression of general disapproval, disrepute and prolonged disorder. We may also imagine that in the preceding years much had gone on to distract attention from what a few monks were quietly doing with a printing press down in the scriptorium.

We know of six Latin works printed at St Albans between 1479 and 1481. Two of them are modern, used for teaching Latin, both with Italian associations. The first, the *Elegantiolae* by the Tuscan author Augustinus Datus, was a small book with excerpts of classical authors, used as an aid to letter writing and composition. It had been

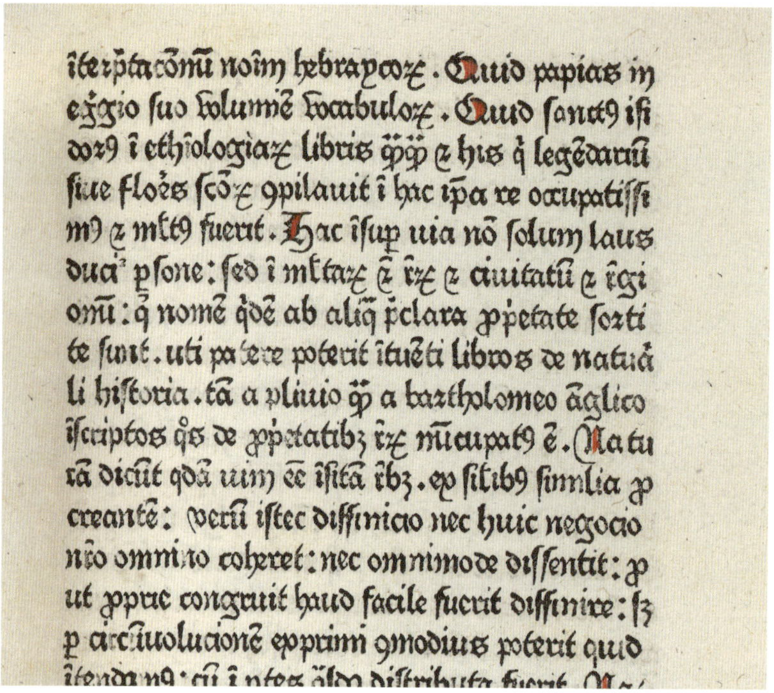

Fig. 46. The lectures of Traversagni, a useful book for teaching, were reprinted from Caxton's edition in a new type that resembles Caxton's Flemish text type Type 2, especially the capitals, but which on closer inspection also has features in common with the St Albans hand.

Laurentius Gulielmus Traversanus de Savona, *Rhetorica nova*. Press at St Albans, 1480. London, BL, C. 11.a.29, fol. n4 recto (detail).

printed many times before it was produced on the press at St Albans, undoubtedly to be used in the abbey's school. The second was a larger and much more ambitious book, a reprint of Caxton's edition of the *Rhetorica nova*, the lectures the Franciscan scholar Traversagni had given at the university of Cambridge in 1478. The edition by the St Albans press, dated 1480, is printed exceptionally well.

The St Albans printer (or printers) then proceeded in 1480 and 1481 to produce four works of greater learning that would have been appropriate for a university. The first was a small book, Thomas de Erfordia's introduction to logic, *De modo significandi*. It was followed by a larger work, the *Exempla sacrae scripturae*, a Bible commentary with exempla written in the late thirteenth century by Nicolaus de Hanapis, Patriarch of Jerusalem, which had already been printed several times in Paris at the Sorbonne press and by Ulrich Gering, as well as in Toulouse by a printer for the university there. Similarly, the commentary by Johannes Canonicus on the *Physica* of Aristotle had already been printed in the university town of Padua in 1475. But the St Albans printer was the only publisher of the scholastic commentaries of Antonius Andreae on a collection of works on logic. These works were produced at the same time as similar works were being printed in Oxford by Theodericus Rood and in London by Johannes Lettou. Briefly, printers in England entertained the ambition to print for universities before the Latin trade from abroad overtook them. But unlike the works produced in Oxford and London at this time, there is at the St Albans press no obvious bias in favour of Latin works with

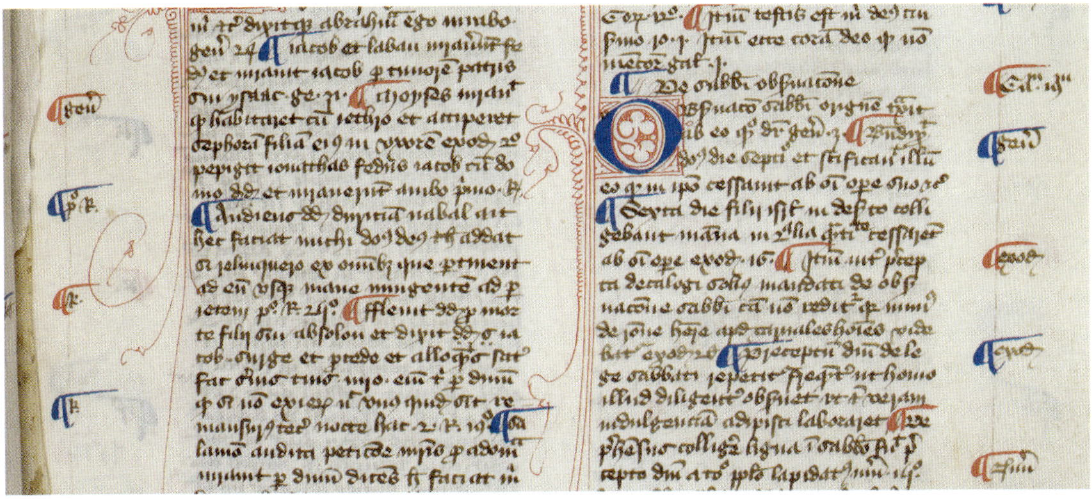

Figs 47, 48. This manuscript was written in the middle of the fifteenth century at St Albans for Dom John Beaver, monk at the abbey, and given by him to the abbey's church with permission granted by abbot John Whethamstede.

The text is a commentary on the Bible, arranged by subjects and extended with *exempla*. Paragraphs are not distinguished with capitals but marked in colour. The marginal notes indicate the Bible books from which each example was taken.

The version of the same text printed at St Albans in 1481 is abbreviated by omitting some exempla and presents them in alphabetical order. This substantial book is set in the third type of the St Albans press, an elaborate fount with numerous abbreviations and contractions. It was also used for three other learned works.

Nicolaus de Hanapis, *Exempla Sacrae Scripturae*. Manuscript written at Abbey of St Albans and book printed at the Press at St Albans. London, BL, Ms Royal 2 F.vii, fol. 14 recto (detail); C. 11.a.24, fol. e3 recto.

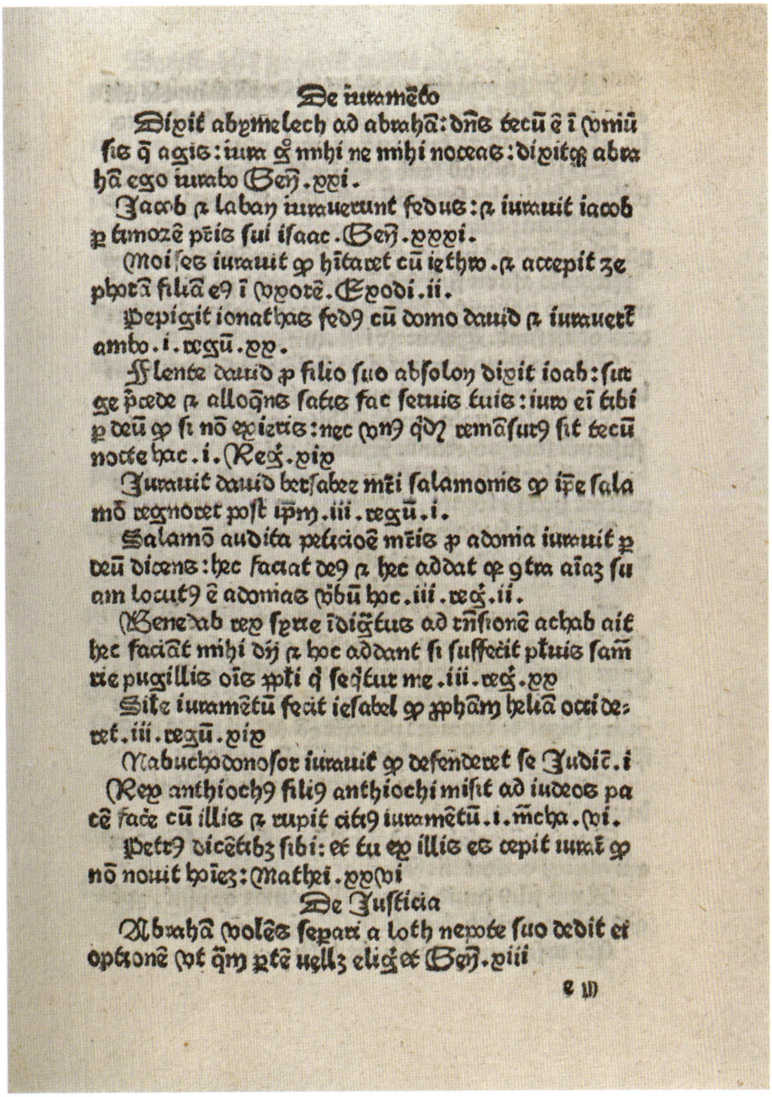

De iuramēto
Dixit abymelech ad abrahā: dñs tecū ē ī omnibus q̄ agis: iura ergo mihi ne mihi noceas: dixitque abrahā ego iurabo Gen. xxi.
Iacob et laban iurauerunt fedus: et iurauit iacob per timorē pris sui isaac. Gen. xxxi.
Moises iurauit quod habitaret cū iethro. et accepit zephorā filiā eius ī uxorē. Exodi. ii.
Pepigit ionathas fedus cū domo dauid et iurauerunt ambo. i. regū. xx.
Flente dauid pro filio suo absolon dixit ioab: surge procede et alloquens satis fac seruis tuis: iuro enī tibi per deū quod si nō exieris: nec unus quidem remansurus sit tecū nocte hac. i. Reg. xix
Iurauit dauid bersabee mři salamonis quod ipse salamō regnaret post ipsum. iii. regū. i.
Salamō audita peticioē mřis pro adonia iurauit per deū dicens: hec faciat deus et hec addat quod contra aīaz suam locutus ē adonias uerbū hoc. iii. reg. ii.
Benedab rex syrie īdignatus ad tēsionē achab ait hec faciāt mihi dii et hoc addant si suffecit pluis samarie pugillis oīs ppli qui sequitur me. iii. reg. xx
Sile iuramētū fecit iesabel quod prophā helia occideret. iii. regū. xix
Nabuchodonosor iurauit quod defenderet se Iudic. i
Rex anthiochus filius anthiochi misit ad iudeos pacē facē cū illis et cepit eis iuramētū. i. macha. vi.
Petrus dicētibus sibi: et tu ex illis es cepit iurare quod nō nouit hoiem: Mathei. xxvi
De Iusticia
Abrahā uolēs separi a loth nepote suo dedit ei optionē ut quam ptē uellz eligeret Gen. xiii
e iii

a connection with English authors. Nor is there an immediate parallel with the works acquired by John Whethamstede for the abbey, of which lists survive. A more extensive version of the *Exempla sacrae scripturae* survives in a codex combined with several other texts, written at the abbey in the middle of the fifteenth century and given to the church.

The press at St Albans may therefore be seen as a final flickering, against a troubled background, of what had been a great scriptorium tradition. Some links to this greater tradition are of a material kind. It should be noted, for example, that in Traversagni's *Rhetorica nova* some sheets of large-size royal paper were used up, the first time this format of paper was used for printing in England. This probably was a remnant of a supply of paper that had been used for the writing of a large codex. Then there is the quite astonishing fact that within a short space of time three founts of type were created in the abbey, an isolated instance of typographical design by an indigenous punch-cutter and typefounder in England, where otherwise printers relied entirely on products originating from overseas, be it Flanders, Cologne, Naples, and in later years Paris and Rouen. Two of the original St Albans designs are typographical representations of English styles of script, in particular of the style developed in the course of the fifteenth century in its own scriptorium, known as 'the St Albans hand', but both also show the influence of Caxton's Flemish types. The earliest was used only once, in the Datus *Elegantiolae*, and it is yet again a cause for wonder why an elaborate and delicate fount was put to so little use – unless we must assume that a large quantity of printed material has vanished. The other design, used in four Latin books printed in 1480–1, is a larger representation of the St Albans hand, but derived many of its capitals from Caxton's Flemish types. The overall effect is, however, very different from Caxton's founts. In between came a fount, used in Latin printing only in the Traversagni of 1480, which was directly modelled on the large bastarda text type Caxton used in Westminster between 1476 and 1484, obtained from Johan Veldener (see fig. 46). It is cast – and cast very well – on a smaller body than Caxton's, and careful comparison reveals that it was produced from a new set of punches, and was not cast from matrices of Caxton's fount; closer inspection shows that it preserved some of the features of the St Albans hand, for example the characteristic form of lower-case v. Nevertheless, its similarity to Caxton Type 2 is striking, especially as it is seen in a reprint of a work that Caxton published not long before.

At this point it may be useful, if still strictly speculative, to recall what happened in the late 1460s at the abbey of St Scolastica in Subiaco, in the mountains south of Rome. The two first printers in Italy, Konrad Sweynheym and Arnold Pannartz, who had introduced

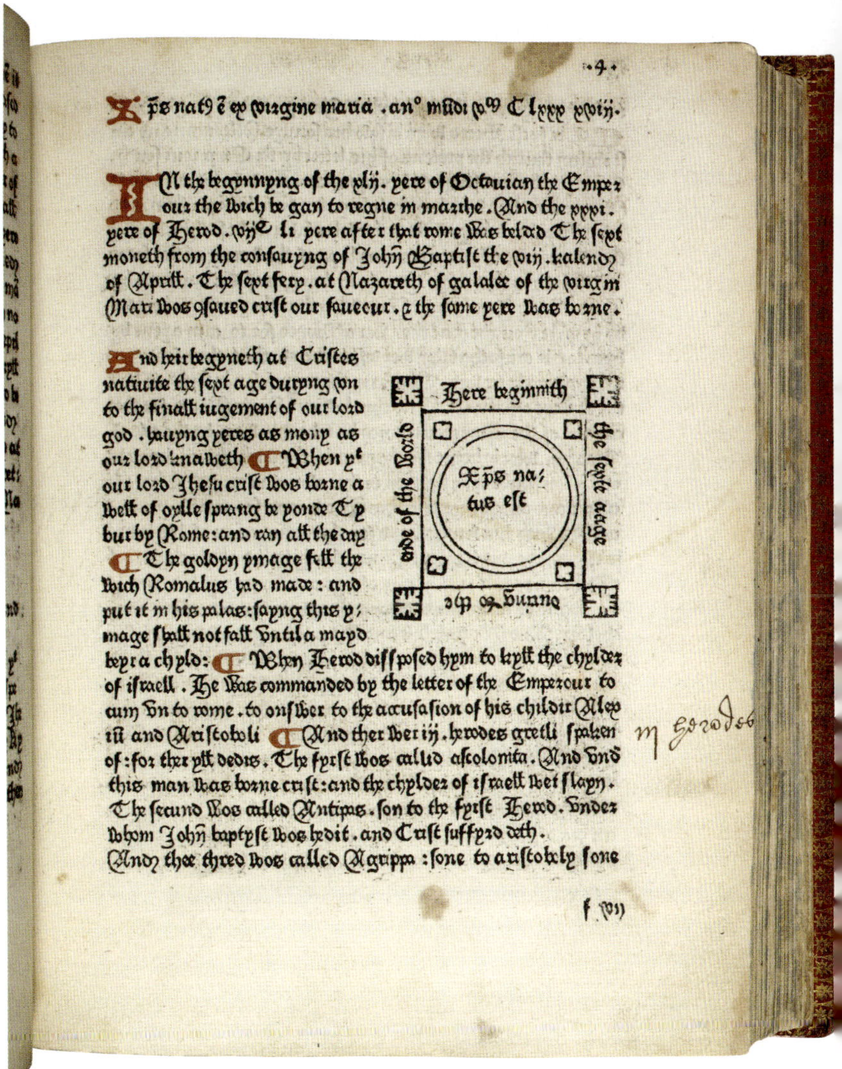

Fig. 49. The St Albans version of the *Chronicles of England* is an extension of Caxton's *Chronicles* printed in 1480 and 1481. It is the first English book printed at the abbey. The printer facilitated consultation of the work by a table of contents with an ingenious reference system based on the quire signatures, which he carefully explained: 'ye must understond that everi leef is markid under with A...' etc.

Three-colour printing (red, blue, and black) was a radical innovation. The type is the Traversagni fount, recast on a slightly larger body, looking much less elegant than in its first version. In addition the printer acquired the use of Caxton's formal Type 3 for headings, and initials similar to a set used by Caxton from 1484.

Chronicles of England, preceded by *Fructus temporum*. Press at St Albans, *c.* 1486. London, BL, C. 11.b.1[illegible], fol. f7 recto.

printing there in 1465, taught at least two monks at the abbey the techniques of printing. They were the compositors of part of an edition of St Augustine's *De civitate Dei*, completed in June 1467. Their work can be recognized by the curious annotation in the manuscript used by them, marking pages as 'Wednesday morning', or 'Saturday afternoon', instead of the usual figures indicating pages within a quire. A few years after the two professional printers had departed for Rome, a monk at the abbey offered to print a breviary since types and presses were available, and – this is the crucial point – monks had been taught to print. Would likewise one or two monks have been taught at Westminster Abbey in Caxton's printing house, and have taken their knowledge to St Albans?

Printing came to a halt after the three large Latin works were produced in 1481. The six books produced in this first phase were, if uncompromising in their severity, all expertly typeset and printed.

When printing was resumed, about five years later, two very different-looking books emerged, and they were in English. The type of the Traversagni was clumsily recast, and now combined with a version of another of Caxton's types, the formal, upright 'textura' style that he had used to contrast with his round bastarda type where contrast was required, for example for chapter headings (see fig. 29). This time the type used at St Albans was cast from Caxton's matrices. Unique for England, there is in these two books colour printing in blue and red for initials and for a printer's device, here seen for the first time, and even some gold and yellow. Again, the printed initials – a new set – seem largely modelled on Caxton's. It is as if after an interval of time a few other monks had strayed into the scriptorium, rediscovered the press, and used what they found as best as they could, apparently with some support from Westminster. They were resourceful and inventive, apparently unhampered by their lack of technical skill.

The two books they decided to print were interesting choices: the *Chronicles of England* and *The book of hawking, hunting and blasing of arms*. The first appears to continue the abbey's great tradition of historiography, except that it departed from the convention of writing in Latin by publishing a chronicle in English. Nor did they publish a translated version of the chronicles written over the centuries at the abbey, but their basis was the version of the *Chronicles* printed by Caxton in 1480 and 1481, edited with some interpolations and preceded by a work on world history, here called the *Fructus temporum*. This was derived from a recently written and widely read Latin work, the *Fasciculus temporum* by Werner Rolevinck, a Carthusian monk in Cologne, which was many times reprinted after its first publication in Cologne in 1474. Caxton translated sections of it in his edition of the *Polychronicon*. The *Fasciculus* made use of complicated diagrams to illustrate what we would call time-lines. They are also found in slightly different form in the English-language *Fructus temporum* of St Albans. The difference between the St Albans *Chronicles* and Caxton's version is substantial enough to speak here of a new compilation, the text of which was completed in 1483, according to its colophon.

When the St Albans version of the *Chronicles* was reprinted in 1497 by Caxton's successor, Wynkyn de Worde, he ended the book with a probably scrambled statement that the work had been 'compiled in a booke and also enprynted by one somtyme scole mayster of saynt Albons'. This evokes an image of a schoolmaster pulling sheets off a press, and since this is an attractive picture, all books printed at St Albans have become known as the work of the 'Schoolmaster Printer'. This, however, has probably no relation to what happened. We may take note of the testimony of another witness, John Bale in his *Illustrium maioris scriptorum ... summarium* published in 1548 as the first bio-bibliography of English authors. Bale states that a history and

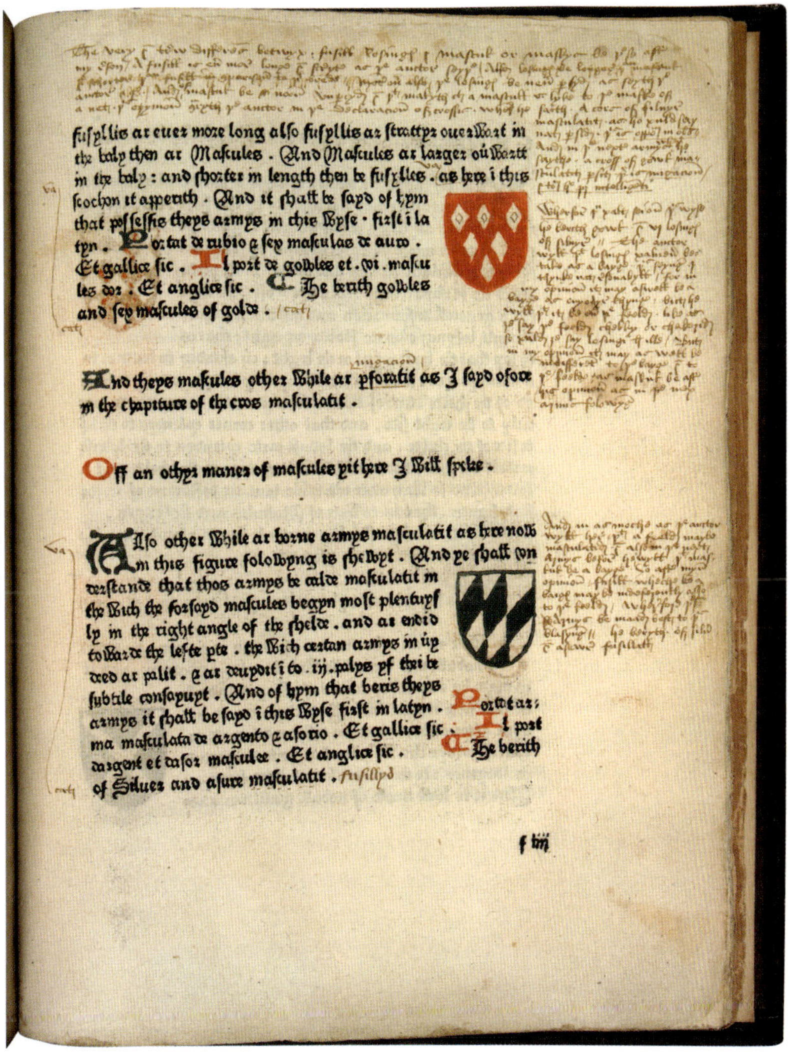
fusyllis ar euer more long also fusyllis ar straytyr ouerthwart in the baly then ar Masculles. And Masculles ar larger ouerthwart in the baly: and shorter in length then be fusylles. as here i this scochon it apperith. And it shall be sayd of hym that possessis theys armys in this wyse. firste i latyn. Portat de rubio & sex masculas de auro. Et gallice sic. Il port de goules et .vi. mascules dor. Et anglice sic. He berith goulles and sex masculles of golde.

And theys masculles other while ar perforatit as I sayd afore in the chapiture of the cros masculatit.

Off an othyr maner of masculles yit here I will speke.

Also other while ar borne armys masculatit as here now in this figure folowyng is shewyt. And ye shall vnderstande that thos armys be calde masculatit in the which the forsayd masculles begyn most plentuysly in the right angle of the shelde. and ar endid towarde the lefte pte. the which certan armys in vp red ar palit. & ar dyuydit i to .iij. palys yf thei be subtile considyryt. And of hym that beris theys armys it shall be sayd i this wyse first in latyn. Portat arma masculata de argento & asorio. Et gallice sic. Il port dargent et dasor masculee. Et anglice sic. He berith of siluer and asure masculatit.

f iiij

Fig. 50. The compilation best known as *The book of St Albans* consists of a number of traditional texts all of interest to country gentlemen. The annotation in this copy shows how well it was used. Heraldry is the subject of the second half of the book, beginning with 'The book of coat armour', followed by 'The book of blasing of arms'. The woodcuts of armorial shields were printed in colour; the three-colour printing of the *Chronicles* was extended with gold. Yellow, where required, is touched in by hand. The typographical material is the same as used for the *Chronicles*.

Book of hawking, hunting, and blasing of arms. Press at St Albans, [c 1486]. London, BL, G. 10547, fol. (2)f4 recto.

description of Britain had been compiled by a certain schoolmaster at St Albans. According to Bale he had died before the work was completed and left the work in loose leaves, which Caxton, 'who was not altogether stupid', preserved and completed from reliable sources. Bale does not offer a source for this statement. If we give it credence, the work of the schoolmaster might primarily have been the translation of the *Fasciculus temporum*. From what we now know of Caxton, it is certainly possible that he continued with editing and revising a work once he had published it. He was particularly interested in historical works, and his own continuations in his historical publications form a clear sequence, and speak for his continuing interest. They can be seen in his successive editions of the *Chronicles of England* in 1480 and 1482, and the editing and extension of the *Polychronicon*, also in 1482, and by his editing and occasional revision of the *Morte Darthur*, partly incorporating sections of his *Chronicles*.

A revision and extension of his *Chronicles* would be in character; the printers at the abbey certainly used a copy of Caxton's edition for setting their edition (preceded by the *Fructus temporum*) and this copy may have been annotated by Caxton himself. Wynkyn de Worde seems to have known more than we do about the St Albans press when he reprinted their two English books. Yet we may improve on his statement that should probably have run: '...compiled in a book by a late schoolmaster at St Albans and also printed at St Albans'. And finally, this opens the possibility that we may see here a confusion with Thomas Walsingham, who was not only the author of the Latin Chronicle of St Albans, but is also recorded as 'precentor' (or cantor) in the abbey as well as a 'scriptorarius'.

The other English book is *The book of hawking, hunting and blasing of arms*, a compilation for country gentlemen in a combination of texts not known from any manuscripts. The St Albans version states at the end of a short poem, 'Explicit Dam Julyans Barnes in her boke of huntyng', and this ascription to Dame Juliana Barnes, prioress of Sopwell (a cell of St Albans and situated not far from the abbey), for which there is no further evidence, has become traditional for the whole work. The compilation includes treatises on caring for hawks, on hunting, on terminology, and useful lists of terms for hunting and of collective nouns, some verse, some page-fillers; it ends with the *Book of coat armour* and the *Book of blasing of arms*, illustrated with 117 woodcuts of armorial shields, printed in red, blue, black, and gold. Dialect forms show that the texts are not of local origin but possibly from Lincolnshire, and early owners of the book can often be traced to East Anglia. It was a book produced for rural users, and the few surviving copies show that it found its way to them.

The compilation was completed in 1486, and printing is assumed to be at about the same date. The *Chronicles* (with the same poor presswork) and the *Book of hawking* are materially closely connected, in their two printing types and their colour printing, and the books are printed on partly the same paper supply. Although its compilation was completed in 1483, the *Chronicles* was therefore probably printed in 1486 shortly before the *Book of hawking*.

Mystery and myth surround the press at St Albans, probably because there was no real continuity: its progress was dependent on the vagaries and incidence of what was a rather irregular monastic community at that time. With other monastic presses, even in untroubled houses, it is often striking that they work in fits and bursts, with major interruptions, and that they usually do not remain active for any length of time. In all likelihood Westminster Abbey had some involvement in the later part of the enterprise, lending expertise and some material; and inevitably, William Caxton must have played some part in this, at the very least by making matrices for one of his types available, and perhaps an annotated copy of his *Chronicles of England* for the preparation of the St Albans version. The few books that remain show that there were several people successively working in the abbey who made good use of their unusual typographical talents and literary gifts and taste.

12

Caxton's final years

No precise line can be drawn linking the end of the activity of printing houses in Oxford, London, St Albans, and the temporary cessation in Westminster that occurred in the mid-1480s. Too much remains uncertain about dating of very rare books and about their rate of survival – or disappearance – to conclude that a single circumstance caused this to happen at more or less the same time. In Oxford, Theoderic Rood had left by the end of 1484; the location of printing and the date (14 October 1486 or 19 March 1486/7) of the single English *Festial* by John Mirk remains mysterious. In London, William de Machlinia's last datable work, the broadsheet Bull of Pope Innocent VIII, was printed in the summer of 1486, followed shortly after by his reprint of the *Chronicles of England*. The printers at the abbey of St Albans produced their final book, *The book of hawking*, in the same year. Thus ended around 1486 a period of considerable diversity in English printing. Political turmoil in the preceding years, the dramatic changes in royal and personal power and influence, not to mention the many executions, as well as the steadily increasing influx of Latin books from overseas, all added to the uncertainties that printing houses were facing. There may have been also circumstances affecting individuals: family obligations for Theoderic Rood, organizational chaos at St Albans, and quite probably death for William de Machlinia.

We do not know if any of this played a role in Caxton's lack of production from the beginning of 1486 to early in 1489. His activity as a printer did not come to a standstill entirely, but there are no works at all dated in Westminster in 1486 and 1488. In 1487 he dated one work, Jacques le Grand, *Livre de bonnes moeurs*, that became in his translation *The book of good manners*. It is a small book, a popular abbreviation of a larger work on moral theology, that Caxton dedicated to the memory of his friend and fellow-Mercer William Pratt, who shortly before his death in 1486 had given him a French manuscript of the text, asking him to translate it. Pratt may have been the friend who several years before had commissioned the translation of the much larger *Royal*

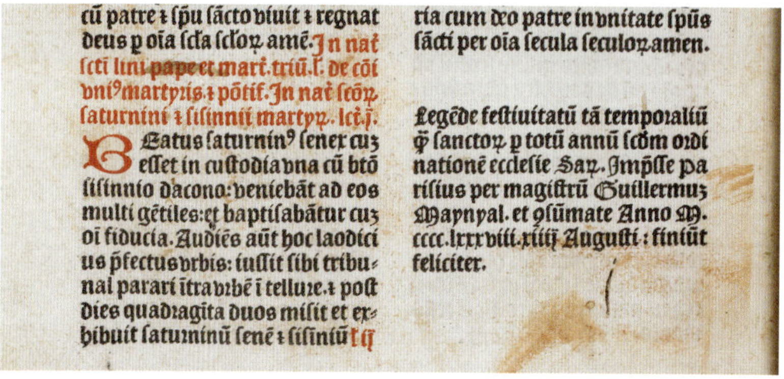

cū patre ꝛ spū sācto viuit ꝛ regnat deus ꝑ oīa scla scloꝝ. amē. In nat scti lini pape et mart. triū. l. de cōi vni9 martyris ꝛ pōtif. In nat scōꝝ saturnini ꝛ sisinnii martyꝝ. lc. j.

B Eatus saturnin9 senex cuȝ esset in custodia vna cū btō sisinnio dacono: veniebāt ad eos multi gētiles: et baptisabātur cuȝ oī fiducia. Audiēs aūt hoc laodici us ꝑfectus vrbis: iussit sibi tribu- nal parari itra vrbē i tellure. ꝛ post dies quadragita duos misit et ex- hibuit saturninū senē ꝛ sisiniū l ij

ria cum deo patre in vnitate spūs sācti per oīa secula seculoꝝ. amen.

Legēde festiuitatū tā temporaliū ꝙ sanctoꝝ ꝑ totū annū scdm ordi natione ecclesie Saꝝ. Impsse pa risius per magistrū Guillermuȝ Maynyal. et ↄsūmate Anno M. cccc. lxxxviii. xiiij Augusti: finiūt feliciter.

book, published by Caxton in 1485 or early in 1486. However unfavourable circumstances may have been in 1487 for the printing business, Caxton brought out the pious *Book of good manners* his friend had requested on his deathbed. For its printing Caxton appears to have used up a supply of paper he had left over from *The royal book*, and he supplemented it with a further supply. This is also found in another small book, a collection of four sermons (known as the *Quattuor sermones*) which later became firmly linked with John Mirk's *Festial*, and was reprinted many times with it. Except for two very difficult-to-date small service books, this sums up the total output of his Westminster press in the years 1486 to 1489.

Perhaps – we can only guess – Caxton was thinking of switching to the trade in books imported from abroad rather than books printed by himself. Such a change of direction had taken place a few years earlier in the career of Peter Schoeffer in Mainz. For Schoeffer, decoration and bindings of books not printed by him are the main source of evidence for that aspect of his trade. For Caxton, little such evidence exists, although a few Latin books printed in Basel, Nuremberg, Cologne, and Venice are known in bindings with blind-tooled stamps that are more often seen on copies of his own publications. He also tells us that on one occasion Margaret Beaufort, mother of Henry VII, had bought a French manuscript from him. These scattered facts are enough to show that Caxton did indeed import books, but on what scale we cannot know.

We do know, however, that 1487 was the year of an innovation. He turned to Paris to commission the printing of a missal for the use of Salisbury, or 'Sarum'. At that time there was nobody in England sufficiently skilled in black-and-red printing to produce a missal. This required specialist skills in two-colour printing, for the two colours would be interlocking, sometimes even in the same line, and therefore required high-quality type and very accurate presswork. The colour printing at St Albans in 1485–6, when their presswork was remarkably poor, fell far short of the standards required for liturgical printing. Yet demand for such a work, necessary at the altar in every

Fig. 51 a & b. Caxton's famous printer's device was first used in Paris in two editions of liturgical works for the use of Salisbury, printed for him by a specialist in this kind of material. They are the *Missale Sarum*, completed on 4 December 1487 and eight months later the *Legenda Sarum*, shown here. Along with the woodcut device Caxton obtained from Paris a new fount of type and a set of initials, all first used in these two works.

From 1489 the device appeared in Caxton's Westminster publications; it was taken over by Wynkyn de Worde who used it until the end of the century.

Legenda Sarum. Paris, Guillaume Maynyal for William Caxton, 14 August 1488. London, BL, IB. 40010, fol. z5 verso, Z4 verso (details).

church or chapel for celebrating the service of the Mass, would be guaranteed.

Almost nothing is known about Guillaume Maynyal, who printed the missal for Caxton, completing it in Paris on 4 December 1487. In 1480 he had been associated with Ulrich Gering, one of the earliest printers in Paris, with whom he produced five works in quick succession. The firm was among the exporters of books to England. In 1489–90 he worked briefly alone, then disappeared from view for good. The missal (of which only one not quite perfect copy survives) is printed in two clear founts of type in the Parisian style, no doubt produced by Ulrich Gering, who was one of the most prolific typefounders of his time. It has red staves for music, the notes to be filled in by hand, and space was left blank for writing in the English text of the Wedding Mass. The work includes large woodcuts of the Crucifixion and the Trinity owned by another Parisian printer, Jean Dupré, who was the first to illustrate books printed in Paris with woodcuts. Caxton's satisfaction with Maynyal is evident, for eight months later the missal was followed by another substantial liturgical work to be used by priests, the *Legenda Sarum*, which contains – in Latin – readings of the Bible, lives of the saints and homilies appropriate to each day of the liturgical calendar. This work, also containing a lot of red printing, was completed for him by Maynyal on 14 August 1488. The *Legenda Sarum* also survives in a single, not quite complete copy, and some scattered fragments. Remarkably, the two remaining copies of both books – each a unique item – were used in the chapels of houses of noble families, neglected over the centuries and in due course rediscovered. When they eventually came to light, in 1874 and *circa* 1956, they caused a sensation: the discovery of a hitherto unknown aspect of Caxton's career.

Obviously, works for Salisbury use could only be sold in England, and Caxton had to transport all the copies printed in Paris by ship, which meant they had to pass through customs at the port where they were landed. Native Englishmen paid tax on imported goods, known as the subsidy or poundage, at a lower rate (one shilling per pound in value, or 5 per cent) than that paid by foreigners. From the years of Caxton's activity in Westminster, 1476 to 1492, only a few subsidy rolls survive of the Port of London, one of them for Michaelmas (29 September) 1487–8, which includes two entries recording Caxton's importation of printed books, in all 261 copies. In view of the dates (25 February and 25 April), it is very likely that these books were copies of the missal. Goods transported in barrels, chests, sacks, or baskets, whatever their nature, were traditionally marked with merchants' marks. It was in the interest of an English merchant, particularly in a mixed cargo, to mark his goods very clearly, in order not to pay the much higher tax levied on a foreigner. It can therefore hardly be a coincidence that we see at the end of the missal for the first time a large rectangular woodcut including Caxton's initials and his merchants' mark. The block is much larger than the printer's devices that are seen below colophons of many printing houses from the 1460s on, in the early years often consisting of shields with merchant's marks or other symbols. Caxton's woodcut device is rather coarse, with borders of crude ornaments, and even in the missal, its earliest use in a book, the lower rim of the block shows breaks that in later use became progressively worse. Its exceptional form, and its first use in imported books, may well indicate that the already battered block originally served to mark Caxton's other merchandise, and may even have been in use when he sent goods in sacks from Flanders to England. After using it for the two books printed in Paris, the missal and the *Legenda Sarum*, it became a regular feature of his books printed in Westminster, and was later taken over by his successor Wynkyn de Worde, no longer as the mark representing Caxton's person, but as the logo of the firm.

Around this time, other materials for his printing business were transported for Caxton across the Channel. Cargoes from France must have contained the matrices or cast type for a new fount, the same as found in the missal and the *Legenda Sarum*. Caxton apparently liked the printing types of the two liturgical works printed for him, and he decided that it was time to update his style, which until then showed its Flemish origins, lightly adapted for use in England. With these and related founts Gering's typefoundry was initiating a style that would dominate printing in Paris and Rouen for decades to come. Caxton introduced it into England, where the 'characteres parisiaci' became the 'black letter' of most English printing of the sixteenth century and later. Along with the fount came a set of initials that had been used by Maynyal, and of course the woodblock with the device. Caxton, who first printed with the new fount in 1489, made only sparse use of it, but, in conjunction with a smaller Parisian text type, it became one of Wynkyn de Worde's most useful resources when he took over Caxton's material.

In 1489 Caxton made a new beginning. This time the roles were reversed: the initiative came from the king, as far as we can tell without any approaches, supplications or hints on Caxton's part. By 1489 Henry VII had fully grasped the political potential of the press. Caxton was by then the only printer still active in England, and remained so until shortly before his death, early in 1492. In 1489, Henry started preparations for a military campaign in France, and wished to set out rules for the conduct of his army. In his epilogue to his translation of Christine de Pisan's *Livre des faits d'armes et de chevalerie*, a work that in English became the *Fayts of arms*, Caxton relates the sequence of events: on 23 January 1489 the Earl of Oxford handed Caxton, on

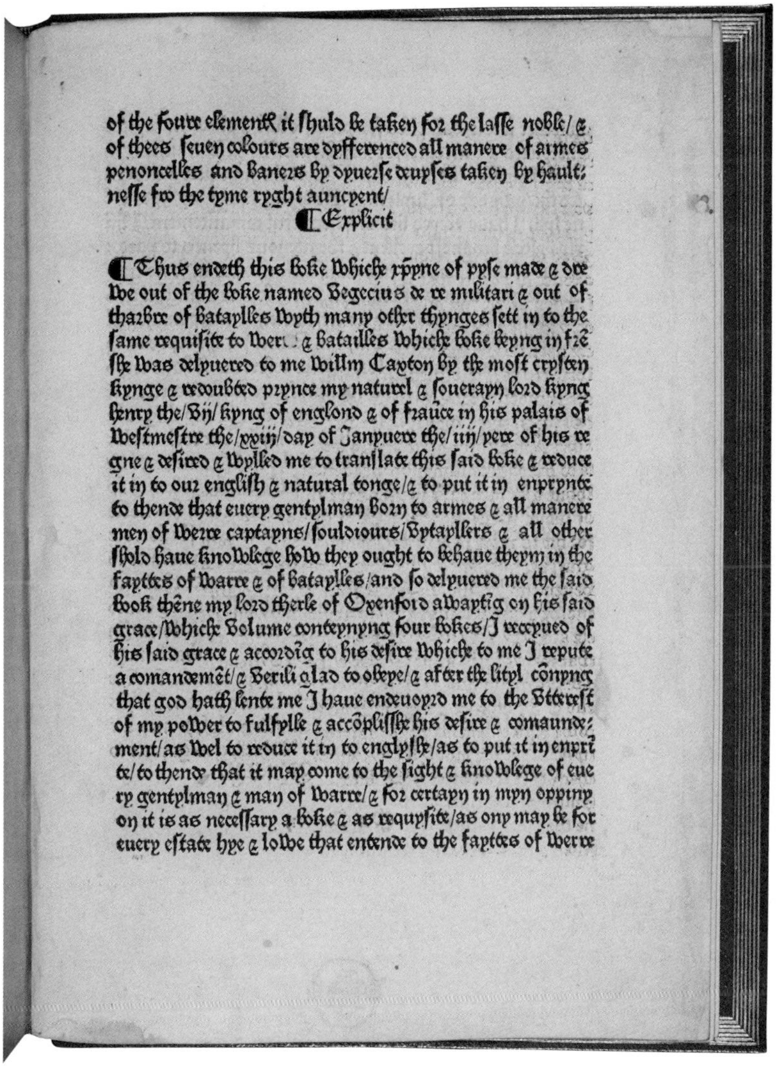

of the fourre elementk it shuld be taken for the lasse noble/ &
of thees seuen colours are dyfferenced all manere of armes
penoncelles and baners by dyuerse deuyses taken by hault;
nesse fro the tyme ryght auncyent/
¶ Explicit
¶ Thus endeth this boke whiche xpyne of pyse made & dre
we out of the boke named Vegecius de re militari & out of
tharbre of batayles wyth many other thynges sett in to the
same requisite to werr & batailles whiche boke beyng in frē
she was delyuered to me William Caxton by the most crysten
kynge & redoubted prynce my naturel & souerayn lord kyng
henry the/vij/ kyng of englond & of fraūce in his palais of
westmestre the/xxiij/ day of Ianyuere the/iiij/ yere of his re
gne & desired & wylled me to translate this said boke & reduce
it in to our englisshe & natural tonge/& to put it in enprynte
to thende that euery gentylman born to armes & all manere
men of werre captayns/souldiours/vytaillers & all other
sholde haue knowlege how they ought to behaue theym in the
faytes of warre & of batayles/and so delyuered me the said
book thene my lord therle of Oxenford awaytyng on his said
grace/whiche volume conteynyng four bokes/I receyued of
his said grace & accordyng to his desire whiche to me I repute
a comandemēt/& verili glad to obeye/& after the lityl cōnyng
that god hath lente me I haue endeuoyrd me to the vtterest
of my power to fulfylle & accōplisshe his desire & comaunde;
ment/as wel to reduce it in to englysshe/as to put it in enprī
te/ to thende that it may come to the syght & knowlege of eue
ry gentylman & man of warre/& for certayn in myn oppinyon
it is as necessary a boke & as requysite/as ony may be for
euery estate hye & lowe that entende to the faytes of werre

Fig. 52. In his epilogue to the *Fayts of arms* Caxton explains the circumstances of Henry VII's request for a translation of this substantial work: in print the text comprises 286 pages. The whole commission was executed within six months. Caxton states that he completed the translation on 8 July, six days before printing was finished. He must have worked in a hurry in order to stay ahead of his printers.

The type was a new fount (Type 6), modelled on the Flemish fount cut by Veldener, but more economical in use.

Christine de Pisan, *Livre des faits d'armes*, translated by William Caxton with the title *Fayts of armes*. Westminster, William Caxton, 14 July 1489. London, BL, G. 10546, fol. s5 recto.

behalf of the king, a manuscript of the French text of *Faits d'armes*, with the request that it be translated and printed. The printing of the *Fayts of arms* started while the translation was still in progress, and, with a haste that left permanent traces, was completed on 14 July 1489. The book had a military and organizational purpose: 'every gentylman born to armes and all manere men of werre, captayns, souldiours vytayllers and all other shold have knowledge how they ought to behave theym in the fayttes of warre and of bataylles'. These words anticipate those in the *Statutes of war* of spring 1492, an official document that set out the rules of conduct of the king's army and was used for the indenture of officers in preparation for another campaign in France. This was printed by Richard Pynson, since in the months following Caxton's death he was the only printer available.

The notion of making all concerned fully aware of the rules of law, first expressed in the epilogue to the *Fayts of arms*, became fully

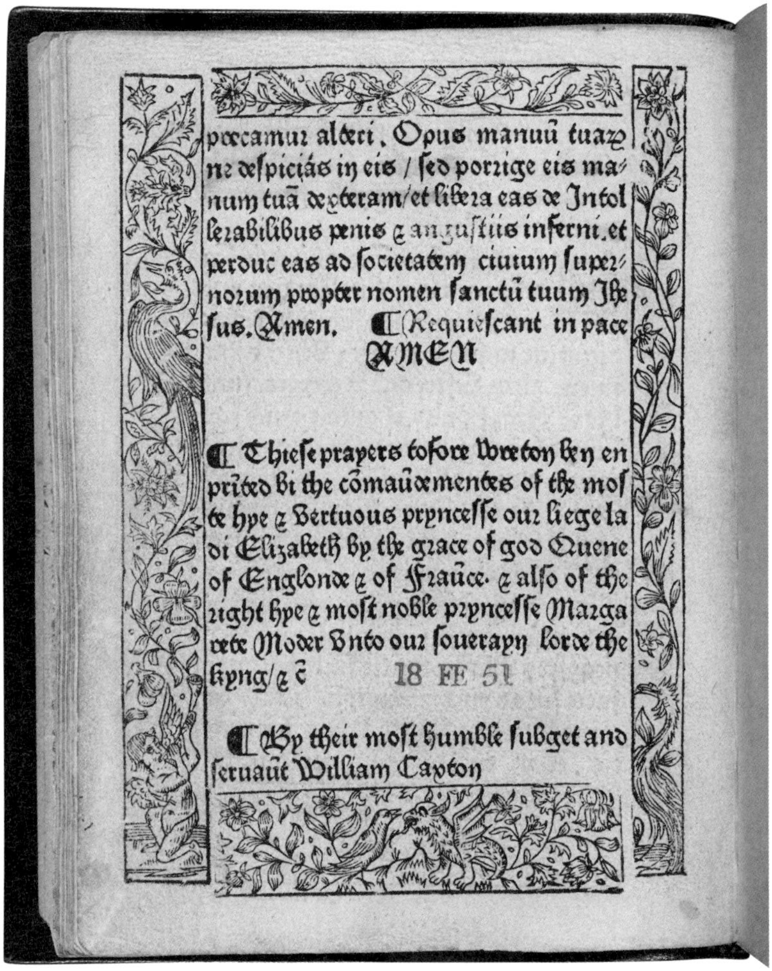
precamur alteri. Opus manuum tuarum
ne despiciás in eis / sed porrige eis ma-
num tuā dexteram/et libera eas de Intol
lerabilibus penis & angustiis inferni. et
perduc eas ad societatem ciuium super-
norum propter nomen sanctū tuum Ihe
sus. Amen. ¶ Requiescant in pace
AMEN

¶ Thiese prayers tofore wreton ben en
prited bi the cōmaūdementes of the mos
te hye & vertuous pryncesse our liege la
di Elizabeth by the grace of god Quene
of Englonde & of Fraūce. & also of the
right hye & most noble pryncesse Marga
rete Moder vnto our souerayn lorde the
kyng/ &c

18 FE 51

¶ By their most humble subget and
seruaūt William Caxton

Fig. 53. In the colophon to this collection of prayers Caxton writes that Elizabeth of York, Henry VII's consort, and his mother Margaret Beaufort, sponsored its publication. They were probably intended as a supplement to an edition of the Sarum Hours of which no copy survives, for that is how they appear in later editions by Wynkyn de Worde. Each of the fifteen prayers begins with the exclamation 'O'.

The fifteen Oes and other prayers. Westminster, William Caxton, [1491]. London, BL, IA. 55144, fol. c6 verso.

implemented in Henry VII's decision, taken in 1490, to have the statutes of the first three parliaments of his reign printed in English instead of Law-French, thus promulgating parliamentary law 'to alle Englissmen'. This was a step beyond Richard III's decision to make the statutes of his first parliament generally available by having them printed, since their language was still the traditional Law-French. (See below, fig. 57.)

Printing official publications for the king was one thing, convincing him of the attraction of printed literature for edification or entertainment another. As a confirmation of the royal patronage, Caxton dedicated in 1490 his translation of a French version of the *Eneydos* to Arthur, Prince of Wales, then still a toddler. In the area of belles lettres, however, Caxton was hardly more successful with Henry VII than he had been with Edward IV. Henry's personal taste was largely for works in French, both manuscripts and printed versions obtained from Flanders and Paris. He contributed significantly to the royal library, where among the printed books that were acquired for him are copies of the Parisian printer Antoine Vérard's richly illustrated books, some of them printed for the French king and adapted for Henry by a few neat manuscript corrections and colourful over-painting of the woodcuts. But, like Earl Rivers before him, the Earl of Oxford proved to be more amenable to making use of Caxton's skills. He commissioned for himself the translation of the romance of *The four sons of Aymon*, which Caxton completed and printed not long after the *Eneydos*. Caxton claims in his prologue to *The four sons* to have also translated for him the life of one of his ancestors, 'Robert Earl of Oxford' from a French version, but no trace of this work, either in manuscript or print, remains.

Henry's mother, Lady Margaret Beaufort, used the printing press in a different way. Until her death in 1509 the queen mother was inspired by her intense and lasting contacts with the Bridgettines at Syon Abbey, the Carthusians at Sheen and other religious houses to sponsor or support the publication in print of devotional works in English in order to make them known to a wider circle of lay readers. We may see here a parallel with her son's wish to make the law accessible to all English speakers. Shortly after Henry commissioned Caxton to translate and print the *Fayts of arms*, Lady Margaret began what amounted to a sustained campaign of disseminating vernacular texts of theology and piety. The first printed work with which she is explicitly associated is, however, a romance. She had bought a manuscript of the French *Blancandin* from Caxton some years before she asked him to translate it. A statement to this effect in Caxton's prologue to *Blanchardyn and Eglantine* allows us a glimpse of him as a dealer in material other than his own printed books. Caxton produced the translation and printed it *circa* 1490. The first time Lady Margaret is mentioned as supporting the publication of a devotional text is about a year later, in the collection of prayers known as *The fifteen Oes*, in which she is named as sponsor together with her daughter-in-law Elizabeth of York, Henry's queen. One of Caxton's last publications, probably completed in 1491, is a collection of three small tracts known as *The book of diverse ghostly* [i.e. spiritual] *matters*. It is clearly intended for use in women's convents, and, although this is not explicitly stated, it too may well have a connection with Lady Margaret Beaufort. The few devotional publications at the very end of Caxton's life foreshadow a turning point in the publishing of religious texts for lay readers.

The final years of Caxton's career as a printer were deeply influenced by the first Tudors, mother and son, and by the new impulse towards private devotion. The production of these years is considerable, for he reprinted no fewer than six of his most successful works of the earlier period, *The mirrour of the world*, the pseudo-Bonaventura *Mirrour of the life of Christ*, *Dicts of the philosophers*, and his one translation

Capitulum/xxv Die Iouis/ Quarta pars/

Incipit Quarta pars pro die Iouis

Item Bernardus de abstinencia in Epistola ad Fratres de monte dei quantum ad religiosos. Itē in sermone iij/ de circumcisione domini.

Of the fedynge of the grete peple wyth brede multyplyed/ Capitulum. xxv

Two tymes the gospel telleth that oure lord Jhesus multyplyed a fewe loues of brede: & therewyth fedde many thousandes of men to the fyl In the whyche processe takynge hede to the wordes and the dedes of oure lord Jhesu as the Gospel openly telleth. We may see to oure edyfycacyon ghostly many goode sterynges to loue hym and thanke hym & worshype hym soueraynly. And specyally we maye see in thys processe that our lorde Jhesus was mercyful and curteys and kynde & discrete & circūspecte First that he was merciful shewen hys wordes he sayd thus I haue pyte and mercy vpon the people / soo that mercy styred hym & drouz hym to helpe hem and fede hem at her nede for as dauyd witnesseth. Alle the erthe is ful of hys mercy. also he shewed hys grete curtosy and wonderful kyndenesse in the cause that he assigned after sayeng thus. For lo now these thre dayes they abyden and suffren and heren me fastyng: & they haue not wherof to ete. as though he were bounden to them for her

Jhesus misericors

Jhesus curialis.

Fig. 54. The translation by Nicholas Love of the *Meditationes Vitae Christi* was very popular until the Reformation. The work is divided in sections for every day of the week. After wide dissemination in manuscript it was printed at least nine times. This is Caxton's second edition, printed with a new text type (Type 5). A set of woodcuts, perhaps obtained from Flanders or France, was used in both editions. Shown here is Christ feeding the multitude.

Pseudo-Bonaventura, *Myrrour of the Life of Christ*. Westminster, William Caxton, [c. 1489-90]. London, BL, C.10.b.15, fol. h7 recto.

from the Dutch, *Reynard the fox*. When he printed John Mirk's *Festial* again it was in an improved version, based on the version printed in 1486–7 in the Oxford types, now combined with the *Quattuor sermones*. But there were also some new titles, signalling that he was aware of old age and the approaching end: *The governayle of health*, a sheet of Deathbed prayers, *The art of dying*, and finally *Ars moriendi*. The accounts of St Margaret's Church, Westminster, where he was buried, show that he died in 1491/2, and it is thought that this must have been in the early months of 1492.

13
'Standing abasshed' – between patrons and readers

In a timespan of only ten years, between 1476 and 1486, Caxton created a new demand for texts in English, whether literary, historical or devotional. He successfully expanded the existing reading culture into new strata of society, not only 'lordes and prelates gostly and worldly, but also emonge marchantes and other comone people' (as he put it *circa* 1481–2 in his prologue to his translation of *Reynard the fox*). 'Common people' is a designation that can easily lead to misunderstanding, and is perhaps best interpreted as comprising the landed gentry (but not the nobility), the administrative classes, members of Parliament, judges and lawyers, together with an urban elite of prosperous merchants. Among those known to have owned books printed by Caxton are Sir Thomas Lovell, Speaker of the House of Commons and Chancellor of the Exchequer, and Sir Anthony Browne, a judge. Women owners, some of them belonging to religious orders, can often be identified as members of families of high standing, linked by friendship. For such people book ownership was probably not a novelty. But Caxton's books soon penetrated beyond these very privileged and often interrelated circles. Early owners' notes in Caxton's books reveal the names of other merchants and members of livery companies, mainly in the City of London: Thomas Stretton, Skinner, living in the Poultry in the City of London; Richard Story, Fishmonger; one Hobert, Draper; M. Umfray, Goldsmith of Cheapside; Robert Spensar, Leatherseller, of London, who later became a hermit at Charing Cross, and also Peter Stowghton, merchant of Kent living in Dartford. Of these people, not much more is known than that they wrote their names and professional status in their books. But such inscriptions are enough to tell us a tale of dissemination, that works which had originated at courts in England, France, and Flanders were now being bought and read by a new class of readers.

Success may create its own difficulties, and in Caxton's case he found he had a stylistic problem in addressing the new audience created through the new medium of print. In his earliest translations he had been inspired by the lofty French of courtly authors, who wrote for the worldly and spiritual leaders associated with the Burgundian court. That this was not a style in which he naturally expressed himself was made clear to him at the very beginning of his career as translator, when, in his tentative first sheets of translation of the

Recueil des histoires de Troies, Margaret of York found 'a defaute in myn englishh whiche sche comanded me to amende'. Was his use of English not up to the standards of 'high style' expected by the court?

The authors and translators he published at Westminster are far beyond such doubt, and it should be noted that in his early years in England they dominated his publishing programme: Chaucer, Lydgate, Gower, Earl Rivers, and the Earl of Worcester all had impeccable courtly credentials. He particularly admired John Lydgate's resonant style to the point that he felt 'not worthy to bere his penner and ynke horne after hym', an expression taken directly from Lydgate's own praise of Chaucer. Other telling phrases used by Caxton, such as his many terms of apologetic modesty, are also borrowed from Lydgate.

In *The Canterbury tales*, Chaucer had revelled in showing the colourful variety in the language that is collectively still 'our Englyssh'. No doubt Caxton fully appreciated Chaucer's mimicry. However in 1483, in the epilogue to *The house of fame*, he gave expansive praise to Chaucer on different grounds, stating that 'he excellyth in myn oppynyon alle other wryters in our Englyssh. For he wrytteth no voyde wordes, but alle hys mater is ful of hye and quycke sentence', recognizing stylistic economy as a quality that is superior to courtly ornamentation. This realization runs parallel to the development of his own prose.

Caxton was no mimic himself. Throughout his career as author and translator, he stressed in his prologues the plainness of his own language, referring to himself as a 'symple persone' and thereby implying that his style reflected his own nature. He frequently used the words 'simple', 'ignorant', 'rude', and 'imperfect' to beg the reader's indulgence for his prose. Such expressions of humility are commonplace when authors present their work, but in Caxton's case they also highlight his lack of pretentiousness. Perhaps it was his many years as expatriate – in a bilingual environment – that heightened his awareness that language is an infallible social indicator, not only of the writer or speaker, but also of the addressee. As his readership evidently expanded, and books associated with court and aristocracy were taken up by merchants and other 'common people', his own output of prose grew at an astounding rate. He wrote in a metropolitan form of English, apparently – in spite of his protestations – unhindered by undue social reservations. From 1481, when he first published his translation of the *Mirrour of the world* at the request of Hugh Bryce, citizen and alderman of London, his own translations began to comprise an increasing proportion of his publishing programme.

The impression that his prose grew less ornate and 'courtly' over the years is worth investigating. The most obvious stylistic elaboration that characterizes his early work was 'doubling', using two near-

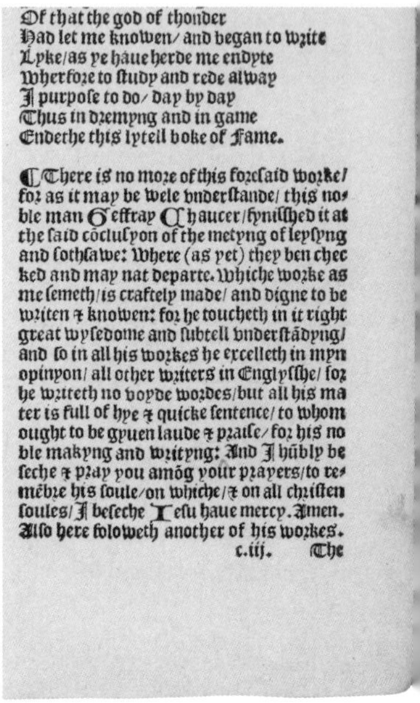
Of that the god of thonder
Had let me knowen/ and began to write
Lyke/as ye haue herde me endyte
Wherfore to ſtudy and rede alway
I purpoſe to do/ day by day
Thus in dremyng and in game
Endethe this lytell boke of Fame.

There is no more of this forſaid worke/ for as it may be wele vnderſtande/ this noble man Geffray Chaucer/fyniſſhed it at the ſaid cóclusyon of the metyng of leyſyng and ſothſawe: Where (as yet) they ben chec ked and may nat departe. Whiche worke as me ſemeth/is craftely made/ and digne to be writen ⁊ knowen: for he toucheth in it right great wyſedome and ſubtell vnderſtādyng/ and ſo in all his workes he excelleth in myn opinyon/ all other writers in Englyſſhe/ for he writeth no voyde wordes/but all his ma ter is full of hye ⁊ quicke ſentence/ to whom ought to be gyuen laude ⁊ praiſe/ for his noble makyng and writyng: And I hūbly beſeche ⁊ pray you amōg your prayers/to remēbre his ſoule/on whiche/⁊ on all chriſten ſoules/ I beſeche Jeſu haue mercy. Amen. Also here foloweth another of his workes.

c.iij. The

Fig. 55. 'In myn opinyon': when after 43 years Pynson reprinted *The house of fame* from Caxton's edition of *c.* 1483, he also reprinted (with slight modernization) Caxton's praise of Chaucer's language, without clarifying who expressed this opinion.

Geoffrey Chaucer, *Collected works*. London, Richard Pynson, 1526. G. 11584/2, fol. c3 recto (detail) synonyms in harness. To look no further than the beginning of his prologue to the *Recuyell*, we find, for example, 'slouthe and ydlenes', 'ocupacion and besynesse', 'pleasyr and delyte'. Such embellishments seem to be rarer in his later works. For a while we hear also a bit less of his 'simpleness' when he translated and published books at the request of fellow-merchants, to return only towards the end of his life when addressing the king, Lady Margaret Beaufort, or the Earl of Oxford, all of whom had commissioned translations. But we may suspect that such expressions of self-doubt were by then formulaic rather than sincere.

Indeed, we may perceive increasing self-confidence in his comments about his own use of language gained in the early years in Westminster. This is manifest in his editorial work, where he did not hesitate to interfere with the text of others. In 1480 Caxton probably added a substantial section to the *Chronicles of England*, and the 'Liber Ultimus' of the *Polychronicon* of 1482 is certainly from his hand. For the earlier books of the *Polychronicon* Caxton states that he had 'somewhat chaunged the rude and old englysh that is to wete certayn wordes'. Similar changes in spelling and vocabulary can be found between the two successive editions of the *Chronicles*, of 1480 and 1482, one reprinted from the other; but despite Caxton's words regarding spelling and vocabulary in the *Polychronicon*, we cannot know where his own influence ended and that of his compositors began. Compositors at that time were entitled to their own views regarding spelling, unlike compositors of later days, and when they thought fit they might replace archaic or dialectal forms with forms that they regarded as more current or appropriate. The master printer might have given general instructions, either giving the compositors a more or less free hand, or demanding that such rules as he issued were enforced. Strictness might vary from printing house to printing house, or even from text to text, and the attentiveness of compositors was equally variable.

Style, however, is more than the sum of its parts, among them spelling and vocabulary. In matters of rhetorical style, it was certainly Caxton's intention to treat the works of his authors with respect, but respect did not exclude the occasional updating of their language, especially in prose. Here judgement and discretion came into play. He was not reluctant to interfere in the historical works, or pseudo-historical fiction such as Malory's *Morte Darthur*, making sure that the text could function for his contemporaries as a fluent communication. But Caxton's two editions of Nicholas Love's early fifteenth-century translation of the *Mirrour of the life of Christ* include archaic and regional words and spellings that were not ironed out until later editions by his successors.

Caxton as publisher and as author of a substantial body of prose

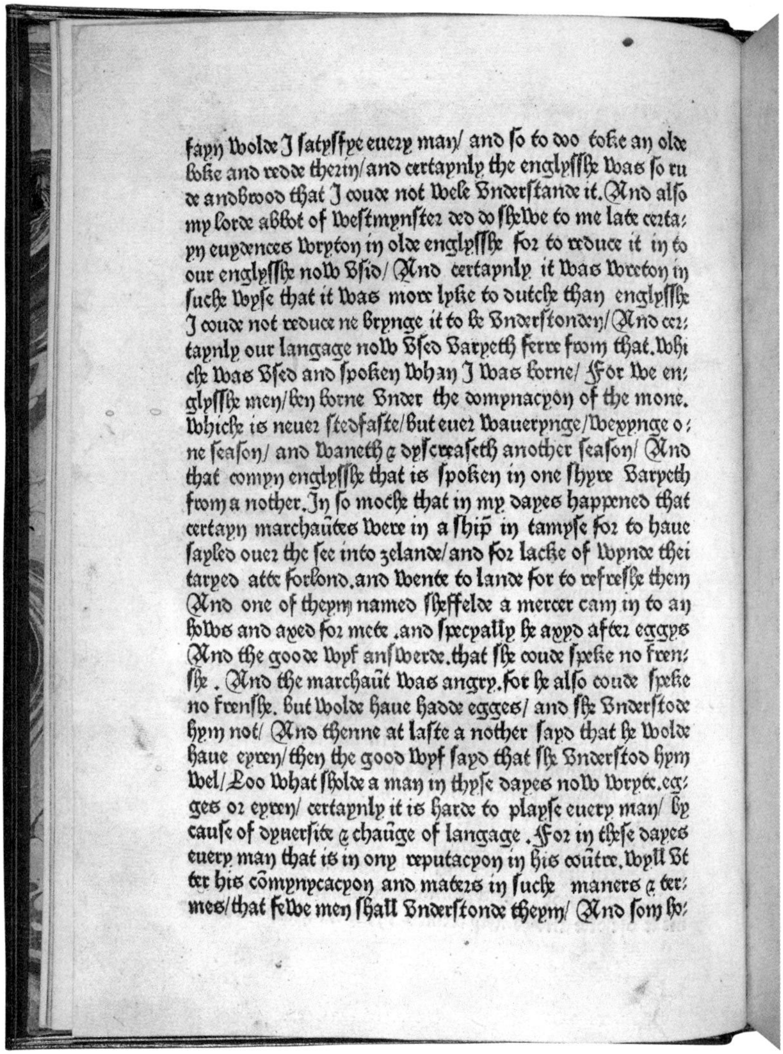
fayn wolde I satysfye euery man/ and so to doo toke an olde
boke and redde therin/ and certaynly the englysshe was so ru
de and brood that I coude not wele vnderstande it. And also
my lorde abbot of westmynster ded do shewe to me late certa-
yn euydences wryton in olde englysshe for to reduce it in to
our englysshe now vsid/ And certaynly it was wreton in
suche wyse that it was more lyke to dutche than englysshe
I coude not reduce ne brynge it to be vnderstonden/ And cer-
taynly our langage now vsed varyeth ferre from that. whi
che was vsed and spoken whan I was borne/ For we en-
glysshe men/ ben borne vnder the domynacyon of the mone.
whiche is neuer stedfaste/ but euer wauerynge/ wexynge o-
ne season/ and waneth & dyscreaseth another season/ And
that comyn englysshe that is spoken in one shyre varyeth
from a nother. In so moche that in my dayes happened that
certayn marchau͂tes were in a ship in tamyse for to haue
sayled ouer the see into zelande/ and for lacke of wynde thei
taryed atte forlond. and wente to lande for to refreshe them
And one of theym named sheffelde a mercer cam in to an
hows and axed for mete. and specyally he axyd after eggys
And the goode wyf answerde. that she coude speke no fren-
she. And the marchau͂t was angry. for he also coude speke
no frenshe. but wolde haue hadde egges/ and she vnderstode
hym not/ And thenne at laste a nother sayd that he wolde
haue eyren/ then the good wyf sayd that she vnderstod hym
wel/ Loo what sholde a man in thyse dayes now wryte. eg-
ges or eyren/ certaynly it is harde to playse euery man/ by
cause of dyuersite & chau͂ge of langage. For in these dayes
euery man that is in ony reputacyon in his coũtre. wyll vt
ter his cõmynycacyon and maters in suche maners & ter-
mes/ that fewe men shall vnderstonde theym/ And som ho-

Fig. 56. 'It is hard to please every man because of diversity and change of language' (ll. 27–28). With the experience of many translations behind him, Caxton closed the circle with Virgil's sequel to the histories of Troy. In his lengthy prologue he ponders on the diversity of the English language, and declares in the end that he expects his book to be read by educated readers: 'clerks and gentlemen that understand gentleness and science'. He dedicated the work to another Prince of Wales, Arthur, the elder son of Henry VII.

Publius Virgilius Maro, *Livre des Enéides* (a French prose adaptation of the *Aeneid*), translated by William Caxton with the title *The Book of Eneydos*. Westminster, William Caxton, [c. 1490]. London, BL, C. 10.b.12, fol. A2 verso.

seems to have been constantly preoccupied with seeking ways to satisfy a growing number of unknown readers. Once he seriously began publishing on a commercial basis, he first relied on the quality and talent of well-known and well-proven authors. When publishing proved to be successful, he began to seek for his own prose the correct tone to address the great variety of readers that could now be reached through the medium of print. Instead of the high-flown rhetoric of a royal court, proclaiming itself as if from a platform, it was an intimate tone that he made his own, always implying that his position was not among the great of this world, and that language and what can be created by it are there to be shared. At his best he seems to address each reader individually.

In the prologue to one of his last translations, the *Eneydos*, he meditated on the dilemma that he had faced throughout his career as writer in trying to find his way through the instability and diversity of the language written and spoken in England. The anecdote he quotes – the merchant who is not understood when he tries to buy eggs on the Foreland of the Thames estuary – is one about the problems of dialect; he notes historical development and the difficulty of understanding ancient or obsolete language forms. But then he continues by addressing the issue of seeking a balance between the plain English that served him so well in making his meaning clear to different echelons of society, and the more contrived forms of 'high' or 'curious' style that signal sophistication in communication, and hence exclusivity. 'Fayn wolde I satisfye every man – certaynly it is harde to playse every man bycause of dyversite and chaunge of langage'. And he concludes, famously: 'And thus bytwene playn rude and curyous I stande abasshed'.

He wrote this in 1490. Abashed Caxton may have been many times in the preceding years, but abashed he was no longer. By then he had found his level and felt at ease with it, a form of English that was suited for communication in the medium of print. The new medium had stimulated the beginning of a notion of a 'received' form of the language that would appeal to many. His prologue to the *Eneydos*, in which he was able to formulate so clearly the nature of the diversity of English usage, also provides a justification for his preference for forms of language that are common to many, at least to the readers he might expect to address. As did every publisher after him, he had to guess the potential readership of his books, and how best to please them.

In the fifteenth century, the arrival of printing had a similar effect on other vernacular languages, but the proportion of English printing in England (72 per cent) was far higher than of vernacular printing in all other countries. (The closest rival was the Czech language, with thirty-two out of fifty-five titles printed in Czech in the relevant area.) In continental Europe, printing in Latin far exceeded that in vernacular languages, a balance that began to shift in the first half of the sixteenth century. In England, printing, and specifically Caxton's large share of printing in English, with his good judgement in finding the right style to address a widening range of people, had, therefore, an unusually high impact on the development of the English language as a means of communication in print.

It had also an enduring impact on governance, a direct result of Caxton's success in reaching a wider spectrum of society, although this process was more gradual. It was not until 1489 that Henry VII was ready to exploit the potential of the press to the full. We have already seen that in that year the king started to use the press in preparation for a military campaign in France, and ordered the translation and printing of Christine de Pisan's *Faits d'armes* in order to communicate rules of conduct to his entire army. In the *Statutes of war*,

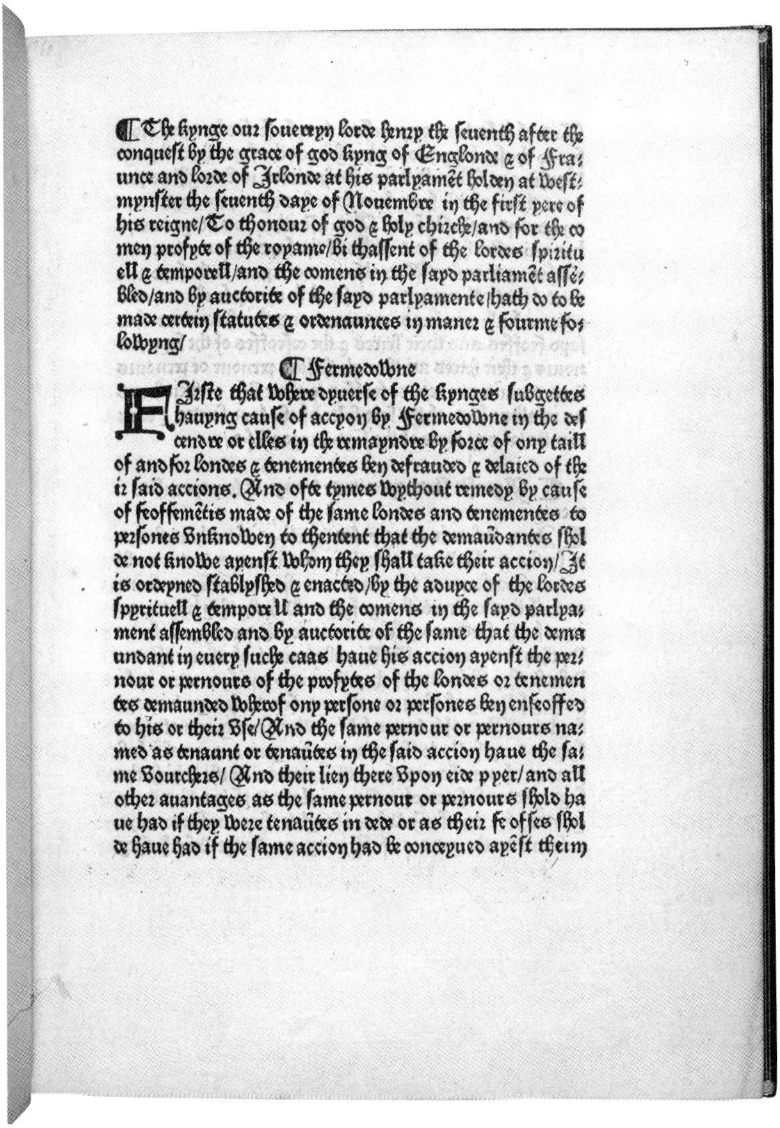
The kynge our souereyn lorde Henry the seuenth after the conquest by the grace of god kyng of Englonde & of Fraunce and lorde of Irlonde at his parlyamēt holden at Westmynster the seuenth daye of Nouembre in the first yere of his reigne/ To thonour of god & holy chirche/and for the comen profyte of the royame/ bi thassent of the lordes spirituell & temporell/and the comens in the sayd parliamēt assēbled/and by auctorite of the sayd parlyamente/hath do to be made certein statutes & ordenaunces in maner & fourme folowyng/

Fermedowne

Firste that where dyuerse of the kynges subgettes hauyng cause of accyon by Fermedowne in the descendre or elles in the remayndre by force of ony taill of and for londes & tenementes ben defrauded & delaied of their said accions. And ofte tymes wythout remedy by cause of feoffemētis made of the same londes and tenementes to persones vnknowen to thentent that the demaūdantes shold not knowe ayenst whom they shall take their accion/ It is ordeyned stablysshed & enacted/by the aduyce of the lordes spyrituell & temporell and the comens in the sayd parlyament assembled and by auctorite of the same that the demaundant in euery suche caas haue his accion ayenst the pernour or pernours of the profytes of the londes or tenementes demaunded wherof ony persone or persones ben enfeoffed to his or their vse/ And the same pernour or pernours named as tenaunt or tenaūtes in the said accion haue the same vouchers/ And their lien there vpon eide p yer/ and all other auantages as the same pernour or pernours shold haue had if they were tenaūtes in dede or as their feoffes shold haue had if the same accion had be conceyued ayēst theim

Fig. 57. This is Caxton's only official publication. Henry VII ordered the statutes of his first parliaments to be printed in English, a precedent that was followed thereafter.

Statutes 1, 3, 4, Henry VII. [Westminster, William Caxton, c. 1490-91]. London, BL, G. 6002, fol. a2 recto.

a document printed by Richard Pynson in the spring of 1492, the rules of conduct of the king's army were formally set out as a condition of joining. The two pieces of printing, the book and the document, are a remarkable testimony to the faith the king put in the printed word, in English, and in the literacy of his army, which comprised not only gentlemen but also 'all manner of men' who from now on, since conditions and prescriptions for conduct were widely available, were expected to be acquainted with them. It is a precursor of the constitutional principle that every citizen is expected to know the law of the land. This principle can also be found in the king's next decision regarding printing. In the course of 1490 he took the important decision not only to have the statutes of the first three years of his reign printed, but to have them printed in English, thus promulgating parliamentary law 'to alle Englissmen', and removing the language barrier that had existed with Law-French. With this decision, publication of the parliamentary statutes in English became standard practice. However, the works on which the practice of the legal professionals was based, the Yearbooks and other texts of the common law, remained firmly fixed in the arcane legal language until far into the seventeenth century.

Caxton's influence on future generations goes beyond the considerable corpus of the 111 items he published in print and the twenty-four works he translated. He also bequeathed to future generations something more abstract, the notion that the English language could be adapted to suit the new medium destined to reach an ever widening audience. The development of English continued in the medium of print. Caxton's immediate successors, however, none of them native-born English speakers, slowed this process. For this reason, Caxton's contribution stands out as marking a unique phase in the long evolution of the English language.

14
Richard Pynson: the canny entrepreneur

When Caxton died early in 1492, two printers were there to take his place. Wynkyn de Worde, who by then may have worked for many years in Caxton's own workshop, and a newcomer in London, Richard Pynson. De Worde was not in a position to continue Caxton's business immediately, for there were formalities to be fulfilled, arrangements with the legal heirs to be agreed, before he could begin to make use of the materials that Caxton had left behind, let alone set up an independent firm. Richard Pynson, however, had already made a beginning before the year 1491 was out, giving him the advantages of a head start and for a short time of a monopoly on printing in England.

The two firms, however, soon fell into step, and maintained their businesses for almost forty years until the two masters died within a few years of each other. Usually they worked independently, occasionally cooperating, seldom entirely overlapping, and each maintaining a distinct character. After both had moved to Fleet Street at the turn of the century, competition between them was sharpened by proximity, and an edition by one was often promptly followed by a reprint by the other. Yet the rivalry was obviously not entirely hostile, for they also produced some joint imprints; in short, they behaved like neighbours. Peter Blayney, the most recent historian of the Stationers'

Company, has argued that it is likely that with their moves to Fleet Street, and their establishment within the City of London, both became Stationers and were allowed to purchase the freedom of London. This would have enabled them to have apprentices, and to retail bound books.

Neither Pynson nor De Worde had the literary creativity that was the driving force behind Caxton's career as printer, and, unlike Caxton, neither was given to revealing much of his purposes and motivation, or indeed of his personality. As with so many other printers of their time, if they gave their works an imprint at all, it was in the formulaic terms such as had by the 1490s become well established: 'Enprynted at westmestre by wynkyn de worde', or 'Per me Ricardum pinson'. Yet from the oeuvre that each left and that survives to the present day – an estimated 500 editions in the case of Pynson and about 750 of De Worde – it is possible to construct images of their preferences, their diverse ways of operating, their contacts, and what they represented in print, and therefore obtain at least some insight into the kind of people they were. From Caxton's self-explanatory prose a personal portrait emerges from the inside out; for Pynson and De Worde we have to rely on the abundant remains of their work as publisher-printers, as we attempt to assemble their portraits from the outside in.

Pynson's area of specialism, in which for a long time he held a virtual monopoly, was legal printing in Law-French; the Crown appointed him King's Printer in 1506, but he had printed several official publications in English before that date; he had also a reliable client base in schools, for which he printed textbooks at all levels. Initially he reprinted some of Caxton's successes, but soon left that field largely to Wynkyn de Worde. On and off, alternating with his colleague, Margaret Beaufort gave him commissions in both Latin and English, including her own translations, and devotional texts add up to a significant proportion of his output. This quite distinct section of his oeuvre is interwoven with the production of the same or similar texts by Wynkyn de Worde, which together reflected a radical change in attitudes to religious observance, and the two are treated together in chapter 17. In the meantime, we may consider Pynson's more secular output.

Fig. 58. Pynson started his career as a glover, and remained interested in the trade in leather goods. Bindings that can be ascribed to him feature the monogram that is also part of his printer's devices (see figs 59 and 63).

Binding by or for Richard Pynson (rubbing) on *Abbreviamentum statutorum*. London, Richard Pynson, [1499]. London, BL, IA. 55514, upper cover.

Pynson was born in Normandy, and may have been born before 1451 while Normandy was still paying obeisance to the king of England, a circumstance that would have allowed him the privileges of an English subject. He may have studied in Paris, and had settled in the early 1480s on the outskirts of London, in the parish of St Clement Danes just outside Temple Bar, where he was recorded as a glover and 'pouchmaker', and where he remained until 1502. In that year he moved to Fleet Street within the boundaries of the City, to an address named 'The George' on the corner of Chancery Lane, facing the Temple. His way into the book trade may have been via bookbinding as a branch of the trade in leather goods. There are several bindings decorated with a panel with a design including his monogram that Pynson used as printer's device, and other panels and tools are associated with him.

At the time in the early 1480s when Johannes Lettou and William de Machlinia were printing for a clientele of lawyers, Pynson's first address 'withoute Tempill Barr' was in the vicinity of the Inns of Court. After the disappearance of De Machlinia's business, there was for a while no printer capable of dealing with Law-French. Pynson may eventually have perceived that here was a need to be met, but this was not an immediate response to De Machlinia's absence. There is, in fact, no continuity in printing materials except for one small decorative border and a few scraps of waste paper found in one of his bindings, and several years passed before Pynson began to print legal works for De Machlinia's old customers.

Fig. 59. The first of Pynson's devices, here used in *The Canterbury tales* of 1491–2; it remained in use until after 1500. Later and more elaborate devices all included the monogram, that after his death was taken over by Robert Redman.

London, BL, G. 11588, fol. K5 verso (detail).

Before Pynson began printing himself he commissioned in 1490 two legal works in Law-French from Guillaume le Talleur in Rouen, who, as his name indicates, was a punchcutter as well as a printer. Pynson's earliest printing types, first used in 1491, were probably procured from Le Talleur. Once the founts were taken into use there was a good deal of tinkering before they settled into a permanent form some two or three years later. The slight variations help in establishing the chronology of Pynson's production in the early years, and also suggest perhaps that a member of Le Talleur's team worked for a few years with Pynson in London. Pynson's native language may have helped him in dealing with the legal works in Law-French, which remained one of the pillars of his business; the style of his printing types and ornaments were also French, for the works he printed in English and Latin not less than for those in French. There is an unsubstantiated record (now lost), indicating that at some point in these early years he was granted denization, as De Worde was in 1496, thus ensuring that he would have rights as a foreign-born resident to establish a household from which to conduct a business, should Richard III's statute granting these rights to aliens in the book trade be changed. This would undermine the equally unsubstantiated assumption that he was Norman, born before 1451 and could thus claim to be an Englishman.

Pynson's earliest printing for which a date can be established is an indulgence, in English, printed for the Crutched Friars of Tower Hill whose convent had been hit by lightning and burned down on Midsummer Eve of 1491. The indulgence, issued by their prior to support the rebuilding, bears the date 1491, and was therefore printed before the end of the year. In 1492 Pynson published a great variety of works,

Prologue

A cristofer on his brest of siluer shene
An horne he baar the bawdryk was of grene
A foster was he sothly as I gesse

Ther was also a nonne a prioresse
t That of her smylyng was symple and coy
Her grettest othe was by seint loy
And she was cleppyd dame Eglentyn
Fulle wele she songe the seruice dyuine
Entoyned in her voyce fulle semely
And frenche she spake fulle fetously
After the scole of stratford at the bowe
For frenshe of Paris was to her vnknowe
At mete wele taught was she with alle
She lete no morsel fro her lyppes falle
Ne wette her fyngers in her sauce depe
Wele coude she carye a morselle of mete
That no drope fel vpon her breest

Fig. 60. The third edition of the *Canterbury tales* was published early in Pynson's career as printer. It was reprinted from Caxton's second, revised edition, from which the woodcut illustrations were copied. Shown here is the General prologue with the Prioress. Pynson used two founts of type, a heavy bastarda type (Type 1) for verse, and for the prose section a much more refined bastarda (Type 2), which remained in use for many years. (see fig. 65) Both were probably obtained in Rouen from Guillaume le Talleur.

Geoffrey Chaucer, *The Canterbury tales*. London, Richard Pynson, [1491–2]. London, BL, G. 11588, fol. a4 verso.

for which it is not possible to establish in what order they appeared. There was in April an official document, the *Statutes of war*, printed at the behest of the king, as already noted. It was an elegant piece of printing, preceded by a woodcut with the royal coat of arms (displaying the shields of both France and England) that the printer had instructions to deliver with precisely specified colouring. There was a popular schoolbook for the elementary teaching of Latin, and a Book of Hours. And for legal clients there was a first set of eight Yearbooks; from then on Pynson published several of these every year, over eighty in the course of his lifetime. Also for the particular entertainment of lawyers Pynson reprinted Caxton's translation of *Reynard the fox*, a medieval courtroom drama transposed to the animal world. By far the largest and most ambitious enterprise of his first year was the reprinting of *The Canterbury tales* from Caxton's second, revised edition. There was no attempt at improving Caxton's version (as De Worde later did), and in fact quite a few new errors were introduced. Pynson had copies made of the woodcut illustrations that gave Caxton's second edition such a distinct character. Their stylistic effect is different from Caxton's; they are heavier, surrounded by thick borders, and some of the pilgrims bear scrolls with the name of the character they represent; other scrolls remained empty, perhaps for the names to be filled in by hand. It is impossible to decide whether this reprint was made just before or just after Caxton's death. In an adaptation of Caxton's prologue, Pynson refers to him as 'my worshipful master', a term that can be interpreted in a variety of ways, and does not prove whether Caxton was still alive.

From this miscellany, on typographical evidence all printed between late 1491 and November 1492, when he published a dated edition of a schoolbook (the *Doctrinale* of Alexander de Villa Dei), we can infer that Pynson intended from the beginning to work for more than one specific group of clients: lawyers (in Law-French), schools (in Latin), and in English the odd official publication that came his way, as well as works for the kind of public that Caxton had so successfully persuaded to buy literary texts in English. He would later extend this with a significant clientele for Latin works specifically intended for the clergy.

Of the three main printers in England in the first fifty years of printing, Caxton, De Worde and Pynson, the last-named was the most entrepreneurial. Throughout his entire career he strove to maintain a balance between groups of clients, partly reflected in the languages in which he printed. A calculation on the basis of surviving material from the first ten years of his business shows that 18 per cent of his production was for lawyers, 17 per cent for schools, 15 per cent was for clergy, and 8.5 per cent were official publications, but 40 per cent were English texts for 'laymen', literary as well as devotional. Of the total production of this period his output in English was 39 per cent, in Latin 36 per cent, and in Law-French 25 per cent (including the statutes from Edward III, the *Statuta nova*, counted as an official publication). In the later years he probably increased the proportion of legal printing, for not a year passed without the production of a substantial number of legal works, Yearbooks, and works by the main authors on the common law, often edited and revised by lawyers at the Inns of Court. In 1493–4 he printed, for example, the *Old tenures* 'at the instaunce of my maisters of the company of stronde Inne [the Strand Inn]'. For many years legal printing was practically his monopoly, but from 1514 he had competitors in this particular field in John Rastell, Robert Redman and occasionally Wynkyn de Worde, Redman very actively trying to undercut him. Yet Pynson had created

Fig. 61. As the king's printer Pynson was not restricted to official publications. Henry VIII requested Pynson to print Lydgate's version of the history of Troy when he was preparing a campaign in France. Troy remained an enduring model of the varying fortunes in war, contemplated in this woodcut by the author.

John Lydgate, *The hystorye, siege and dystruccyon of Troye* (in verse). London, Richard Pynson, 1513. London, BL, G. 11607, fol. E4 recto (detail).

a solid if unexciting business model on which he played variations as the opportunity arose; he could produce books that stood out as major publications, and others that were witnesses to interesting connections in the world of contemporary learning.

Pynson's most prominent role was as King's Printer. Enduring connections with the Chancery eventually led to his appointment in 1506. Henry VII had early on recognized the usefulness of the printing press as an aid to the distribution of documents that would give legitimacy to his reign, impose uniformity in conduct in his army, and disseminate the parliamentary statutes in English. With the *Statutes of war* in 1492, Pynson had established an early connection with court and Chancery, and Henry VII turned to him intermittently, although it was William Faques who was first formally appointed as King's Printer in 1504. It seems that at first the rights this title gave were uncertain. Until 1513 other printers printed statutes and proclamations, but from 1513 Pynson had secured exclusive rights, and printed all documents and propaganda relating to the preparation of wars with France and with Scotland. These included in 1512 *The gardyners passetaunce touchyng the outrage of Fraunce*, a popular justification of the war with France in verse, and in 1513 a grand illustrated folio edition of Lydgate's *The historye, siege and dystruccyon of Troye*, a story of war printed at Henry VIII's express command – his coat of arms appears on the title page.

From 1521 Pynson's press was the vehicle for Henry VIII's campaign against the heresy of Martin Luther. Pynson printed in 1521 the tract *Assertio septem sacramentorum adversus M. Lutherum*, partly written by Henry himself. A fine manuscript copy (now in the Vatican Library)

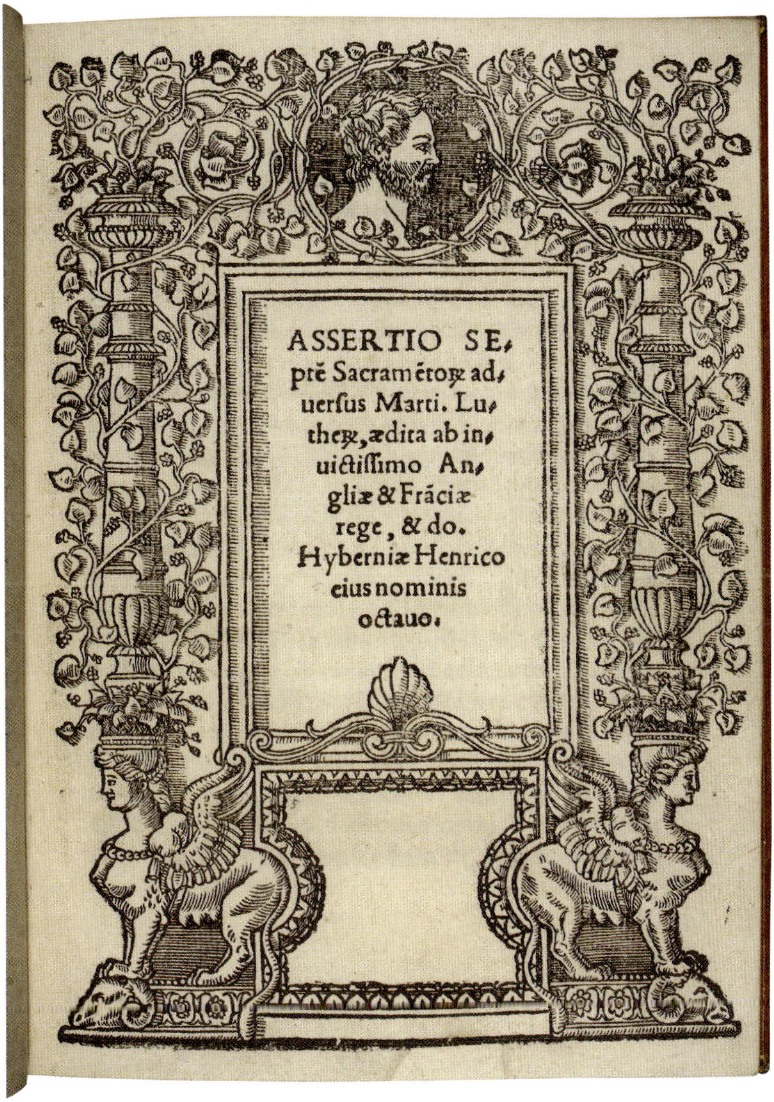
ASSERTIO SE,
ptẽ Sacramẽtorꝝ ad,
uersus Marti. Lu,
therꝝ, ædita ab in,
uictissimo An,
gliæ & Frãciæ
rege, & do.
Hyberniæ Henrico
eius nominis
octauo.

Fig. 62. Pope Leo X rewarded Henry VIII with the title 'Fidei Defensor' in 1521 after the publication by Pynson of his tract against Luther. The tract was reprinted a few months later in Rome, in full Renaissance glory, as a further signal of the Pope's approval. Printing was completed shortly after the Pope's death.

Henry VIII, *Assertio septem sacramentorum adversus Martinum Lutherum*. Rome, Stephan Guillereti, December 1521. London, BL, G. 1210, fol. 5 recto.

had been presented to the Pope, but copies of the tract, preceded by a title-page with elegant woodcut border, were printed on vellum for presentation to sovereigns, cardinals and universities. Luther's response was followed by a further *Epistola regia* from Henry, and by tracts by scholars who were encouraged to join in. Late in 1526 Pynson printed another response by Henry to a letter sent by Luther. Among the last items printed by Pynson as King's Printer was in 1526 a proclamation forbidding the importation of heretical texts printed in Germany and the Low Countries. By 1529 Luther's heresy had become a matter for official suppression.

His employment as King's Printer, although of lasting renown, was not Pynson's only source of income, nor even in all likelihood his main one. From the beginning Pynson recognized that schoolbooks could be relied on to provide steady business, and throughout his

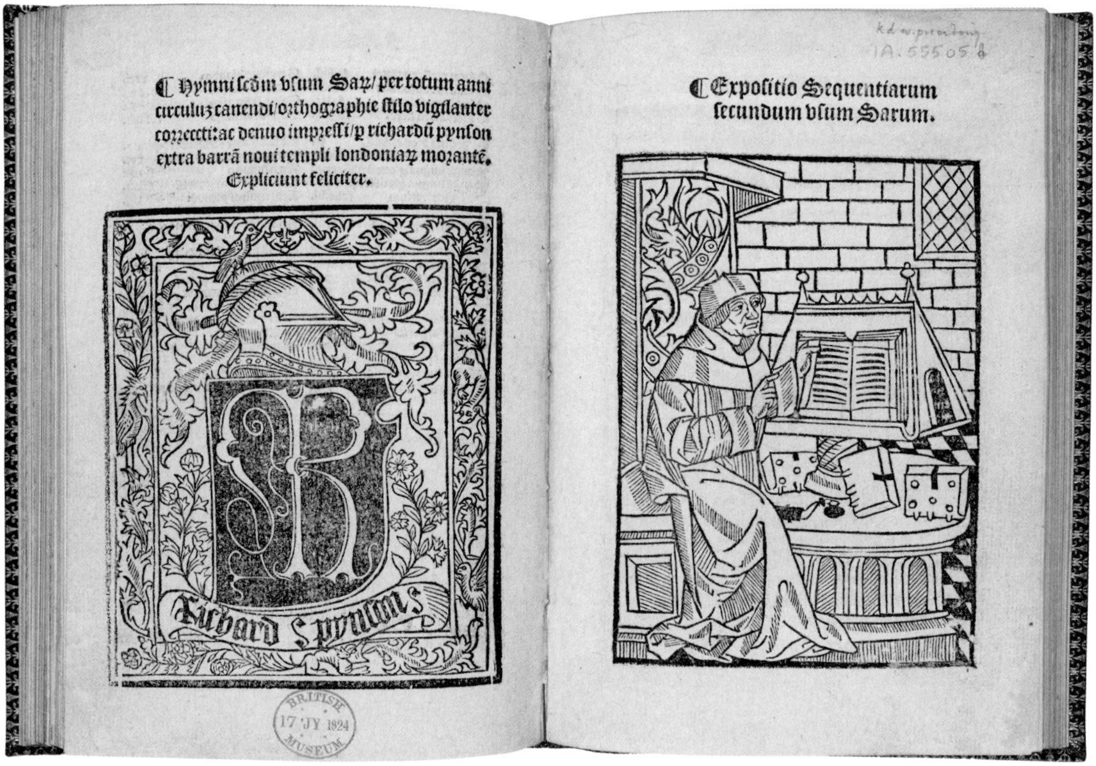

Fig. 63. The two *Expositio* texts, usually issued together (as they were here), were popular reading material in schools. At the end of the *Expositio hymnorum* Pynson printed below the colophon with his address his second printer's device, his monogram now surrounded by elaborate decorations. In this edition it shows a crack in the upper right-hand corner. In later editions this section had splintered off.

Expositio hymnorum, *Expositio sequentiarum*, *secundum usum Sarum*. London, Richard Pynson, 1497. London, BL, IA. 55505a, fol. M4 verso, IA. 55505b, fol. A1 recto.

career he produced them competently and regularly, undoubtedly at the request of various schools and their teachers, and probably with their support. He included texts that had been popular in schools on the Continent, the *Expositio hymnorum et sequentiarum*, a text used for teaching that had often been printed in Cologne and to which he added some new material, and Sulpizio, *De arte grammatices*, probably intending to undercut the importation of such texts from specialist printers overseas. But he also initiated the printing of more original works: from as early as 1493 we find the *Dialogus linguae et ventris*, signed in print with the initials 'W.H.', which may be those of the Eton master and vice-provost William Horman. The text was later reprinted in Paris and Poitiers. The works of Johannes de Garlandia and John Stanbridge, John Anwykyll's successor at Magdalen College School in Oxford, were regular fixtures in his list of publications, and from 1512 he occasionally reprinted Wynkyn de Worde's editions of the grammatical works of Robert Whittinton. In 1499 he printed for Frederic Egmondt and Petrus post Pascha, who at that time were booksellers in London, the earliest English–Latin dictionary, the *Promptorium parvulorum*, reprinted several times by De Worde. Most delightful are his editions of the comedies of Terence, fitfully printed and reprinted and therefore probably ordered by a school for reading and perhaps for periodically planned performances. The one identifiable note of ownership in a copy is of a pupil at Eton.

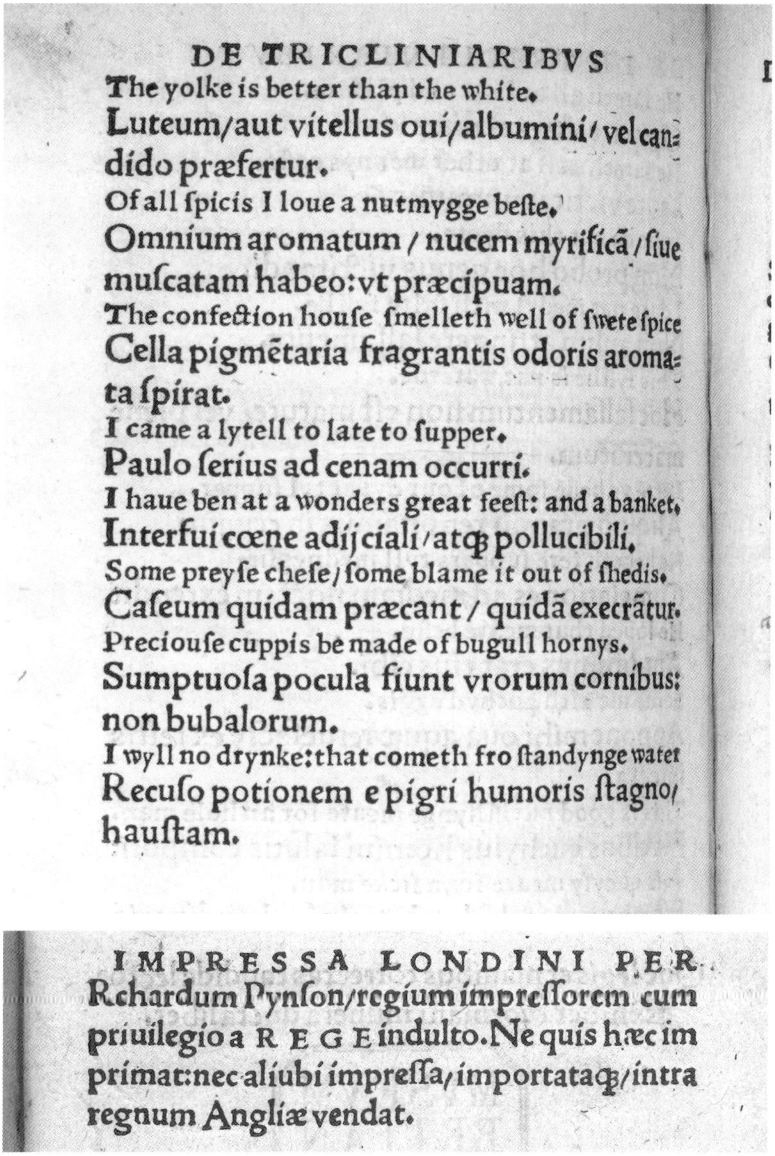
DE TRICLINIARIBVS
The yolke is better than the white.
Luteum/aut vitellus oui/albumini/ vel can=
dido præfertur.
Of all ſpicis I loue a nutmygge beſte.
Omnium aromatum / nucem myriſticā / ſiue
muſcatam habeo: vt præcipuam.
The confection houſe ſmelleth well of ſwete ſpice
Cella pigmētaria fragrantis odoris aroma=
ta ſpirat.
I came a lytell to late to ſupper.
Paulo ſerius ad cenam occurri.
I haue ben at a wonders great feeſt: and a banket.
Interfui cœne adijciali / atq; pollucibili.
Some preyſe cheſe / ſome blame it out of ſhedis.
Caſeum quidam præcant / quidā execrātur.
Preciouſe cuppis be made of bugull hornys.
Sumptuoſa pocula fiunt vrorum cornibus:
non bubalorum.
I wyll no drynke: that cometh fro ſtandynge water
Recuſo potionem e pigri humoris ſtagno/
hauſtam.

IMPRESSA LONDINI PER
Richardum Pynſon/regium impreſſorem cum
priuilegio a R E G E indulto. Ne quis hæc im
primat: nec aliubi impreſſa/importataq;/intra
regnum Angliæ vendat.

Fig. 64 a & b. 'De tricliniaribus' – about the dinner table: Horman, headmaster of Eton, used homely sentences, 'vulgaria', for teaching children Latin. The conversational coverage of subjects amply demonstrates the point: Latin can be useful in numerous situations. The book is set in roman type, introduced ten years earlier by Pynson for scholarly Latin works (see fig. 70). It is the first time it was deemed suitable for children's reading matter.

The book was published with royal privilege. In the colophon Pynson, stating his function as king's printer, sets out what this means: within the king's jurisdiction (England) nobody should reprint it, nor should anyone sell a copy if it was printed elsewhere and imported.

William Horman, *Vulgaria*. London, Richard Pynson, 1519. London, BL, C. 33.i.5, fol. d2 verso, ee3 recto (detail).

In the sixteenth century his particular strength became the works of humanist renewers of the teaching of Latin: from abroad Jodocus Badius and Joannes Despauterius, and in England William Horman, William Lily, high master of St Paul's School (assisted by Erasmus), and John Colet, Dean of St Paul's, who drew up the statutes for the teaching at the school; all occur in the list of Pynson's publications. St Paul's is probably one of the schools with which Pynson had a regular and strong connection. In 1519 he printed at the expense of William Horman 800 copies of his *Vulgaria*, a collection of sentences in English and Latin introduced by Lily for which the contract is still extant. This work was the *casus belli* for what is known as the 'Grammarians' War' which raged between 1519 and 1521 between Lily,

Horman and Whittinton, in which Pynson loyally printed the defences of his own authors. In the sixteenth century his production of school-books was considerably lower than that of Wynkyn de Worde. They were no longer such a significant part of his income as they had been before 1500. They may seem modest books, but they point to a productive interaction between the printer and the most learned and ultimately influential teachers of his time.

Pynson's printing of substantial English works occurred only intermittently. In the early years he reprinted after *The Canterbury tales* several other of Caxton's successes, among them Caxton's translation of Aesop, for which he obtained the use of Caxton's woodcuts. He reprinted the same text in 1500 with more than 150 woodcuts, this time copied from the original. In 1494 Pynson reprinted from Caxton the *Mirrour of the life of Christ* (twice printed by Caxton) for which he had copies made of Caxton's thirty woodcuts. He reprinted several times Caxton's editions of John Mirk's *Festial* and the *Quattuor sermones*, this in competition with many others, including De Worde. Of other English texts Pynson was the first printer. In a lawsuit he claimed that his edition of *Dives and Pauper*, a treatise on holy poverty and the Ten Commandments which is among texts that were suppressed by censorship during much of the fifteenth century, had been supported by John Russhe, a London merchant who had undertaken to pay half of the cost of printing and undertook part of the marketing of this and other books. Later, in a protracted case lasting from 1506 to 1510, Pynson met the heirs of John Russhe in successive courts of law when the two parties failed to resolve a dispute about payment. One of the documents submitted in the case is a schedule of the number of copies printed, showing that at that time Pynson printed editions of 600 copies. Also allegedly underwritten by Russhe were editions of Mirk, and, most important of all, *The fall of princes*, published in January 1494. This is John Lydgate's adaptation from the French version by Laurent de Premierfait of Boccaccio's *De casibus virorum illustrium*. Pynson, who referred to it as his 'bocas', turned it into a beautiful book, printed on the larger than standard-size paper called 'median', and he had procured nine large woodcuts from the Parisian printer Jean Dupré which were placed one at the head of each chapter. Dupré's own edition of the text in French had obviously been the model.

These were the large English books of the early years, to which he did not return until well into the sixteenth century. As late as 1526 he reprinted a compilation of Chaucer's works, *The Canterbury tales*, *The house of Fame*, and *Troilus and Creseyde* with other poems. Instead of large works, Pynson steadily produced during most of his career smaller texts of more popular nature, later known as chapbooks: saints' lives, popular romances in verse, historical or pseudo-historical works, and even verse with such appealing titles as *The smith that*

Fig. 65. The many manuscripts of Lydgate's long poem based on Boccaccio show that it was popular; Pynson printed 600 copies, as revealed in a legal dispute with the heirs of the merchant John Russhe. The manuscript used in the printing house is still extant (now in the John Rylands University Library). The appearance of Pynson's book was, however, modelled on the French version published in Paris by Jean Dupré in 1484, and he used the same woodcuts. The type for the verse is a bastarda fount probably obtained from Rouen. Pynson used it for many years.

Giovanni Boccaccio, *De casibus virorum illustrium*, in an English verse adaptation by John Lydgate of the French version by Laurent le Premierfait, entitled *The fall of princes*. London, Richard Pynson, 1494. London, BL, IB. 55497, fol. f4 recto.

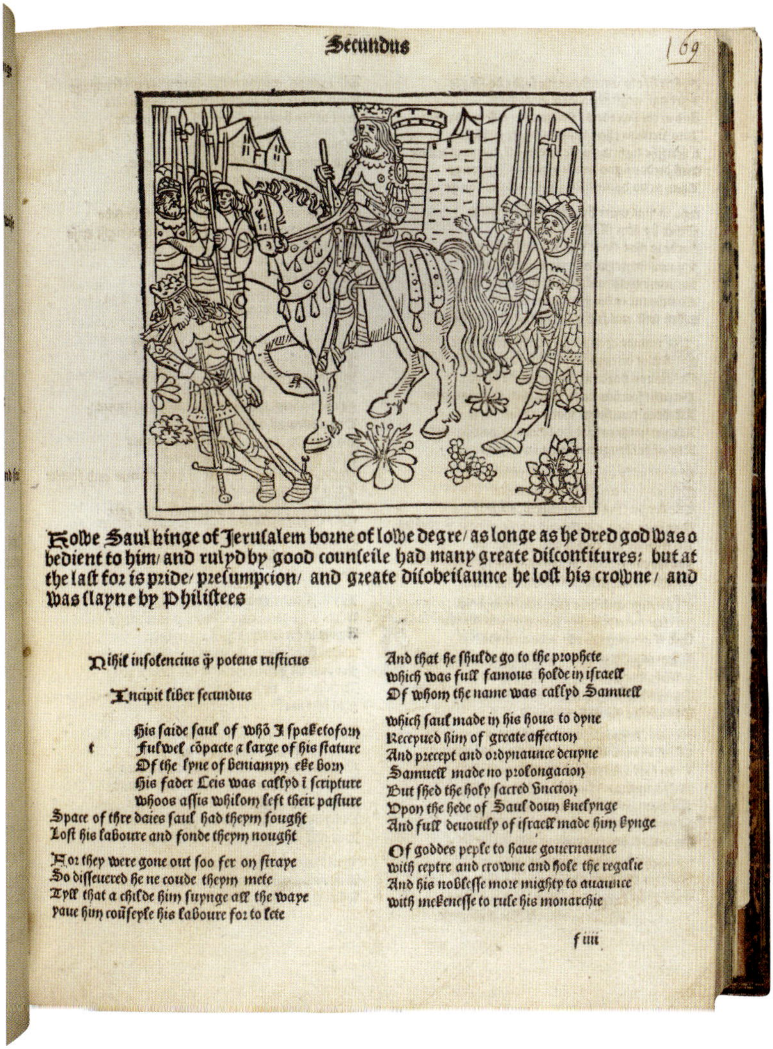

Secundus 169

Howe Saul kinge of Jerusalem borne of lowe degre/ as longe as he dred god was obedient to him/ and rulyd by good counseile had many greate disconfitures: but at the last for is pride/ presumpcion/ and greate disobeisaunce he lost his crowne/ and was slayne by Philistees

Nihil insolencius q̈ potens rusticus

Incipit liber secundus

This saide saul of whō I spake tofore
Ful wel cōpacte & large of his stature
Of the lyne of beniamyn eke born
His fader Ceis was callyd i scripture
Whoos assis whilom left their pasture
Space of thre daies saul had theym sought
Lost his laboure and fonde theym nought

For they were gone out soo fer on straye
So disseuered he ne coude theym mete
Tyll that a childe him sayngė all the waye
Yaue him counseyle his laboure for to lete
And that he shulde go to the prophete
Which was full famous holde in israell
Of whom the name was callyd Samuell

Which saul made in his hous to dyne
Receyued him of greate affection
And precept and ordynaunce deuyne
Samuell made no prolongacion
But shed the holy sacred Unccion
Upon the hede of Saul down knelynge
And full deuoutly of israell made him kynge

Of goddes peple to haue gouernaunce
With ceptre and crowne and hole the regalie
And his noblesse more mighty to auaunce
With mekenesse to rule his monarchie

f iiii

forged him a new dame. Since many of these survive only as fragments, we may assume that much of his production of that kind has been lost.

Pynson's editions of major English texts show no traces of editorial interference or development; unlike Caxton and Wynkyn de Worde, he had neither ambitions in that respect, nor advisers encouraging him to tread that path. But for the works of common law he relied on expertise provided by the lawyers themselves. He published a great variety of titles, for which manuscripts must have been provided by members of the Inns of Court. They were probably also often employed in proofreading and correcting texts; there is some direct evidence for such an arrangement that must have been a quite common exchange of skills, a lawsuit in 1506 between Pynson and three gentlemen of the Middle Temple who were to proofread an edition of the *Abbreviamentum statutorum* (printed twice in 1499) and would receive against payment 419 bound copies of the book. Pynson's frequent

The assemble of foules.

The lyfe so short/y craft so long to lerne
Thassay so harde/ so sharpe the cōqueryng
The slydder ioye/y alway slydde so yerne
All this meane I by loue/that my felyng
Astonyeth so/ with a dredefull workyng
So sore iwys/that whan I on him thynke
Nat wote I well/ wheder I wake or wynke

For albeit that I/ knowe nat loue in dede
Ne wote/ howe he quyteth folke her hyre
yet happeth me/in bokes ofte to rede
Of his myracles/and of his cruell yre
There rede I well/he wyll be lorde & syre
Dare I nat say/ his strokes ben so sore
But god saue suche a lorde/I can no more

Of vsage/ what for lust/ what for lore
On bokes rede I ofte/as I you tolde
But why that I spoke all this nat yore
A gone: it happed me for to beholde
Upon a boke / was writte with letters olde
And ther vpon/a certayne thyng to lerne
The long day I reed/full fast and yerne

For out of olde feldes/ as men sayth
Cometh all this newe corne fro yere to yere
And out of olde bokes/in good faythe
Cometh all this newe science/that men lere
But nowe to purpose/of my fyrst matere
To rede forthe/gan me so delyte
That all the day/thought me but a lyte.

This

Fig. 66. Pynson reprinted not only Chaucer's substantial works, but placed shorter poems in between, such as here the *Parliament of fowls*, following on *The house of fame*. He reprinted these texts from Caxton without editorial intervention, but he improved their presentation with some large woodcuts.

Geoffrey Chaucer, *Collected works*. London, Richard Pynson, 1526. London, BL, G. 11584/2, fol. c4 recto

appearances in the law courts, either challenged by others or pursuing litigation of his own, may have been due to not only the fact that his lawyer clients could act as advisers and were always near at hand, but also that lack of venture capital forced him into entering into quite complicated deals with financial backers, as is evident from the case with the Russhe heirs.

Yet there may also have been something provocative, perhaps even devious, in Pynson's character, as emerges from the many occasions when he became involved with the legal system – far more often than any of his contemporaries. As early as 1492 he was sued for having seized a man named James Borbyke and imprisoning him for six days, and at the end of his life the printer John Rastell accused him of reneging on an obligation to support his daughter, the widow of Pynson's son Richard. There are extensive records of a complaint by Pynson

Fig. 67. The opportunity to exploit John Alcock's name was not missed: in the title of this sermon, and in the woodcut frontispiece. No large initial was required at the beginning of the text, and another cockerel fills in the space mistakenly left open. John Alcock, bishop of Ely, preached this sermon for the curates of his diocese. His face in the woodcut may well be a realistic portrait.

John Alcock, *Gallicantus*. London, Richard Pynson, [1498]. Oxford, Bodleian Library, Auct. Q1.5.33, fol. A1 verso, A2 recto.

after an assault by a street gang on members of his family, friends, and himself, one evening in April 1500. This happened in the parish of St Clements, outside Temple Bar. A few days later the same gang again accosted his 'servants' (apprentices or journeymen), this time in Fleet Street. According to Pynson the gang members had taken an oath that 'there shall nother ffrenshman nor flemmyng dwell nor abide wythyn the seid parish of Saint Clements'. The alleged leader of the gang gave a different version of the course of events – and we are not to know who spoke the truth. Pynson's complaint that he was prevented from carrying out his business since his workmen were afraid to go out was tried in the Star Chamber. The outcome is unknown. But whether justified by any kind of misbehaviour or not, such sentiments among one's neighbours are a clear incentive to move house.

His relations with backers among the clergy were apparently trouble free. He produced a succession of editions of such indispensable works for which no special backers were required as Maydestone's *Directorium sacerdotum*, Lyndewode's *Constitutiones provinciales*, Guido de Monte Rochen's *Manipulus curatorum*, and the *Stella clericorum*, all in small formats. He regularly printed indulgences, most of which are probably lost. But he extended his connections with clerics to more direct associations. In 1498 he took over from De Worde the

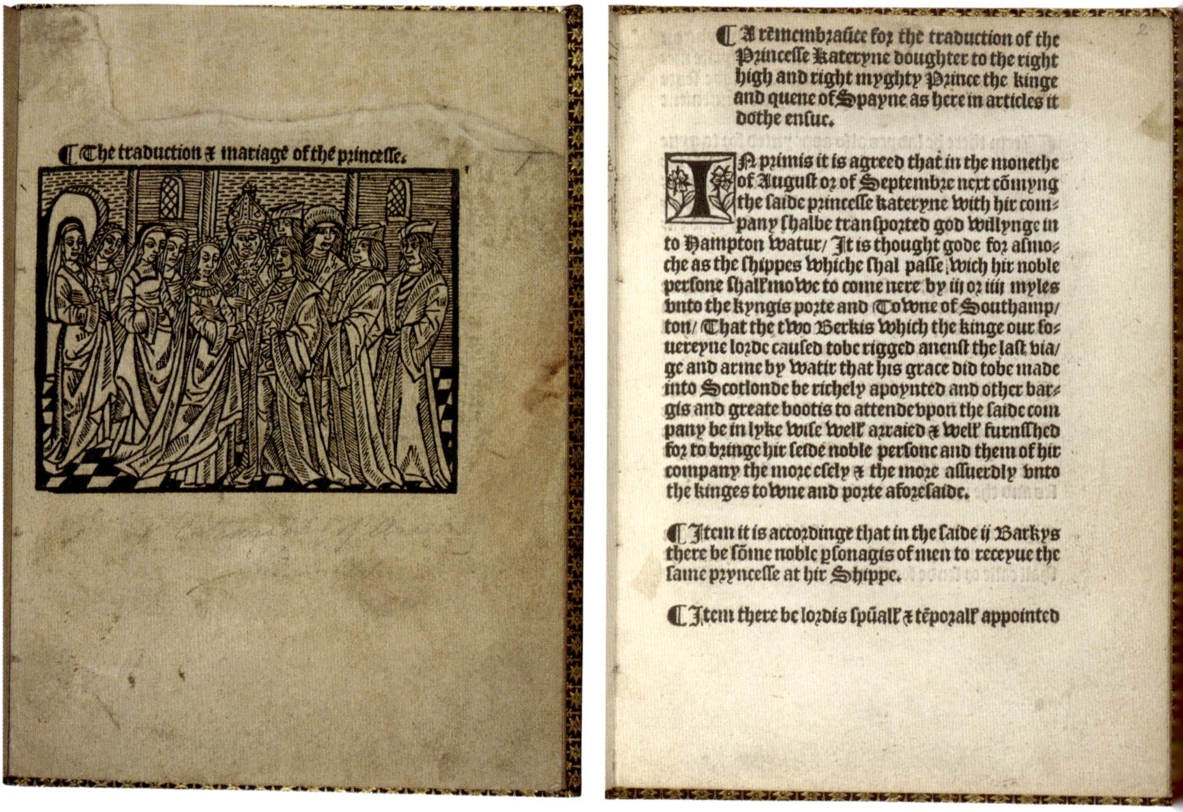

The traduction & mariage of the princesse.

A remembraũce for the traduction of the Princesse Kateryne doughter to the right high and right myghty Prince the kinge and quene of Spayne as here in articles it dothe ensue.

IN primis it is agreed that in the monethe of August or of Septembre next cõmyng the saide princesse katerine with hir company shalbe transported god willynge in to Hampton watur/ It is thought gode for asmoche as the shippes whiche shal passe with hir noble persone shall mowe to come nere by iij or iiij myles vnto the kyngis porte and Towne of Southamp/ ton/ That the two Berkis which the kinge our so/ uereyne lorde caused tobe rigged anenst the last via/ ge and arme by watir that his grace did tobe made into Scotlonde be richely apoynted and other bar/ gis and greate bootis to attende vpon the saide com pany be in lyke wise well arraied & well furnished for to bringe hir seide noble persone and them of hir company the more esely & the more assuerdly vnto the kinges towne and porte aforesaide.

Item it is accordinge that in the saide ij Barkys there be some noble psonagis of men to receyue the same pryncesse at hir Shippe.

Item there be lordis spũall & tẽporall appointed

Fig. 68 a & b. This official publication is a memorandum addressed to officials who were to prepare and attend all stages of the ceremonies to welcome Catherine of Aragon, the bride of Arthur, Prince of Wales, from her arrival in Southampton to her entrance into the City of London; it concludes with instructions for the wedding itself. The woodcut anticipates the event.

The traduction and marriage of the Princesse Katherine of Aragon. [London, Richard Pynson, 1500, before June]. London, BL, IA. 55528, fol. [a]1 recto, 2 recto.

publishing of short works by John Alcock, Bishop of Ely, reprinted one of them and gave to the first edition of a Latin sermon with the punning title *Gallicantus* ('the cockerel's song') a woodcut frontispiece with a portrait of the author delivering a sermon, and a cockerel pictured at the beginning of the text. At that time he must have found an excellent artist, whose hand can also be recognized in a large commission Pynson landed, to print a missal for the Cardinal Archbishop John Morton. Printers in England were late to tackle missals; Caxton was the first to commission one in Paris, as we have seen, and his was followed by missals for Salisbury use printed in Basel, Speyer, Rouen, Venice, again in Paris (including one commissioned by De Worde), until De Worde had one printed in London in 1498 by the French printer Julian Notary and his associates. The missal completed by Pynson in January 1500 is by far the most splendid in this sequence, adorned with brand-new initials, a fine woodcut frontispiece with John Morton's coat of arms, and a rebus of his name, also found in the woodcut borders and some of the initials. This and other decorative material used in the missal must have been the property of Cardinal Morton himself, who died in September of the same year, for it was never used again. Morton's missal must have impressed Henry VII, who commissioned the printing of another one in 1504. The brilliant

Fig. 69. The missal Archbishop John Morton commissioned Pynson to print was lavishly executed with extensive red printing, and with many decorative initials and borders. They include a rebus of the Archbishop's name: the monogram M O R within a tun (i.e. a barrel).

Missale ad usum Sarum. London, Richard Pynson, 1500. Manchester, John Rylands University Library, 16904, fol. A2 recto.

red printing which is also found in a *Processionale* printed for Richard Fox, Bishop of Durham and Lord Privy Seal, is a remarkable feature of Pynson's books in these years, and he must have engaged a printer who was an expert in the technique of two-colour liturgical printing.

In the same years, around the turn of the century, he completed a splendid edition of the *Nova statuta* (beginning with the parliament of Edward III), undoubtedly with the support of the Court of Chancery, that was to remain the authoritative version until the great edition of the *Statutes of the realm* of 1810. A more modest but hardly less interesting official publication of the same time is a pamphlet issued by the royal court with instructions for the arrangements for the reception of Catherine of Aragon on her arrival from Spain. It was to be

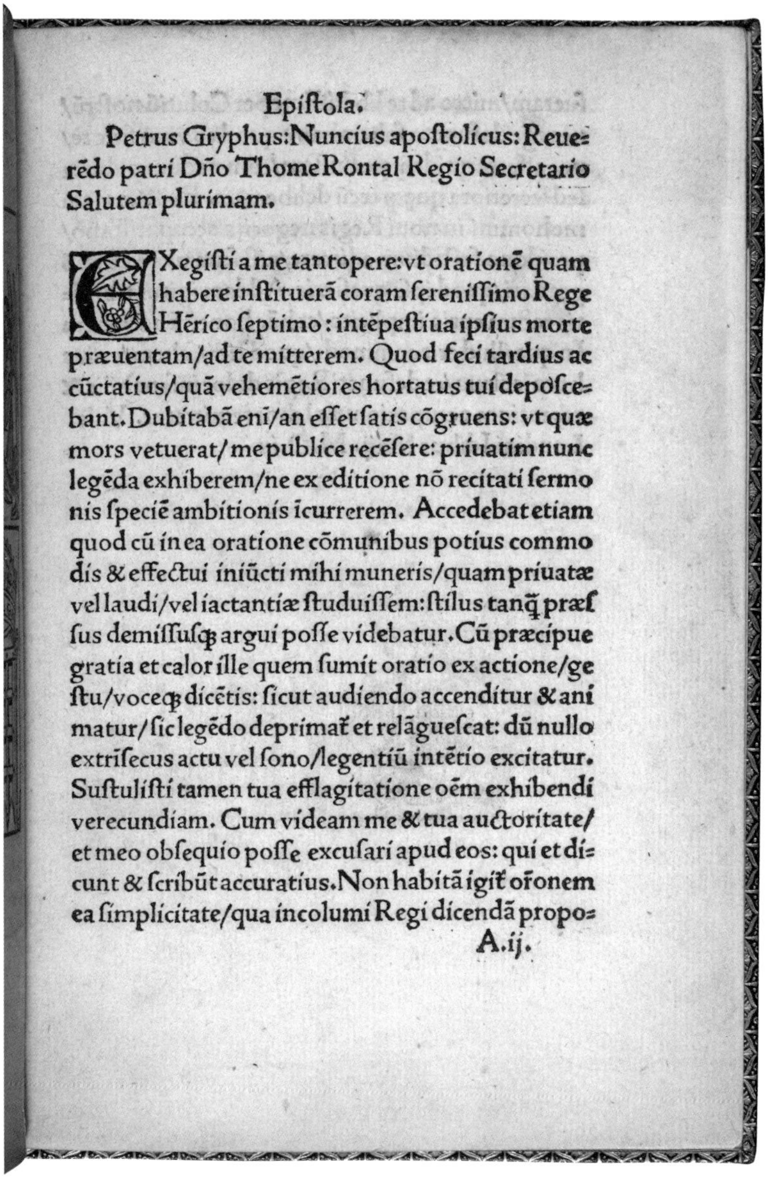
Epistola.

Petrus Gryphus:Nuncius apostolicus: Reuerēdo patri Dño Thome Rontal Regio Secretario Salutem plurimam.

EXegisti a me tantopere: vt orationē quam habere instituerā coram serenissimo Rege Hērico septimo: intēpestiua ipsius morte præuentam/ad te mitterem. Quod feci tardius ac cūctatius/quā vehemētiores hortatus tui deposcebant. Dubitabā eni/an esset satis cōgruens: vt quæ mors vetuerat/ me publice recēsere: priuatim nunc legēda exhiberem/ne ex editione nō recitati sermonis speciē ambitionis īcurrerem. Accedebat etiam quod cū in ea oratione cōmunibus potius commodis & effectui iniūcti mihi muneris/quam priuatæ vel laudi/vel iactantiæ studuissem: stilus tanq̄ præssus demissusq; argui posse videbatur. Cū præcipue gratia et calor ille quem sumit oratio ex actione/gestu/voceq; dicētis: sicut audiendo accenditur & animatur/ sic legēdo deprimat̄ et relāguescat: dū nullo extrīsecus actu vel sono/legentiū intētio excitatur. Sustulisti tamen tua efflagitatione oēm exhibendi verecundiam. Cum videam me & tua auctoritate/ et meo obsequio posse excusari apud eos: qui et dicunt & scribūt accuratius. Non habitā igit̄ orōnem ea simplicitate/qua incolumi Regi dicendā propo=

A.ij.

Fig. 70. Pynson's first use of a roman type – and the first use of roman type in England – is in the Latin oration that the papal collector Pietro Griffo had intended to present to Henry VII. The king's death meant that the oration could not be delivered, and instead the author presented his text to the late king's secretary.

Pietro Griffo, *Oratio ad Henricum VII Anglie regem*. London, Richard Pynson, 1509. London, BL, G. 1203, fol. A2 recto.

issued to all officials concerned, and includes lists of all who were to meet her at various points of her progress, from her landing in Southampton to London, and those who were to attend her wedding to Arthur, Prince of Wales. The *Book of cookery*, published at this time, may also have had the purpose of providing formal instructions for the feasts held in her honour. It is an example of the kind of early use of the press for a practical, organizational purpose that survives only rarely.

The presentation of the *Nova statuta* is a model of typographical restraint. With the new century – or the move to Fleet Street – came some renewal in Pynson's typographical repertoire. From then on he tended to embellish, even overburden, his small books in English

¶ AD ILLVSTRISSIMVM ARcturum Cornubiæ Valliæq; Principem Thomæ Linacri Angli in Procli Diadochi Spęram præfatio.

CVm ſtatuiſſē Arcture princeps illuſtriſſime: & totius ęui tui dec⁹: pro mea incredibili erga te pietate: ſummaq; obſeruātia: mearum lucubrationum monumentum aliquid: tibi nuncupare: ſuccurrebat in primis Procli Sphęra. dignum ni fallor opus: cui tu preſertim aliquam partem ſtudiorum tuorū impertias. Quippe qui ſecundus ex omni maiorum numero extitiſti: qui gētili ſyderis nomine vocarere: huc accedit quod nō parū adiumenti præſtabit. vel ad poetarum lectionem (cui te incumbere miro iam ſucceſſu cœpiſſe intelligo) vel ad celebrium locorum ſitus: naturæq; cognitionē: quæ reliquam quoq; ætatem, poſt publicas ſolicitudines iucūdiſſima voluptate: recreet atq; reficiat. Neq; eni ea cognitio alia ratione: parabilis eſt preſertim tibi: cui per occupationes regni: peragrare orbem minime licebit: q ex iis libris: qui prorſus intelligi ſine ſphęræ notitia non poſſunt. Id quod firmiſſimis rationi

a.ij.

Fig. 71. This short didactic tract on features of the planet earth, with a concluding section on the stars, belonged to the education of a prince. Linacre dedicated his translation to Arthur, Prince of Wales, who died in April 1502. In Pynson's edition printed about twenty years later at a time when he published more of Linacre's translations, the text is ascribed to the fifth-century neo-Platonist philosopher and mathematician Proclus. It is, however, not known as an authentic work by him.

Pseudo-Proclus, *Sphaera*. translated from the Greek into Latin by Thomas Linacre. London, Richard Pynson, c. 1522. London, BL, C.132.i.25, fol. a1 verso, a2 recto.

with heavy borders, and any blank space would be covered with ornamental fillers. These features can be seen, for example, in the books Margaret Beaufort commissioned, which are discussed below with the other devotional texts in English published by Pynson and De Worde. Such decoration seems to stress deliberately the vernacular character of the book. In contrast, Latin works were executed in sober style. At the end of the decade, in 1509, Pynson emphasized his identity as a printer of modern learning by introducing a roman type, the first in England, in a posthumously published oration for Henry VII by the humanist scholar and papal collector Pietro Griffo, and a sermon by Savonarola.

Outstanding works of history were, in the following decade, *Chronicles of England* (the St Albans–De Worde version) in 1510, Fabyan's *The chronicles of England and France* in 1516, followed in 1518 by *The chronicles of the kings of England*, and later, in 1523–5 by Froissart's *Chronicles*. In the last decade of his life, several illustrious names appear, among harbingers of future events in which the printing press would play a crucial role. As King's Printer Pynson published Henry VIII's *Assertio* and following tracts, as already noted, as well as tracts by Thomas

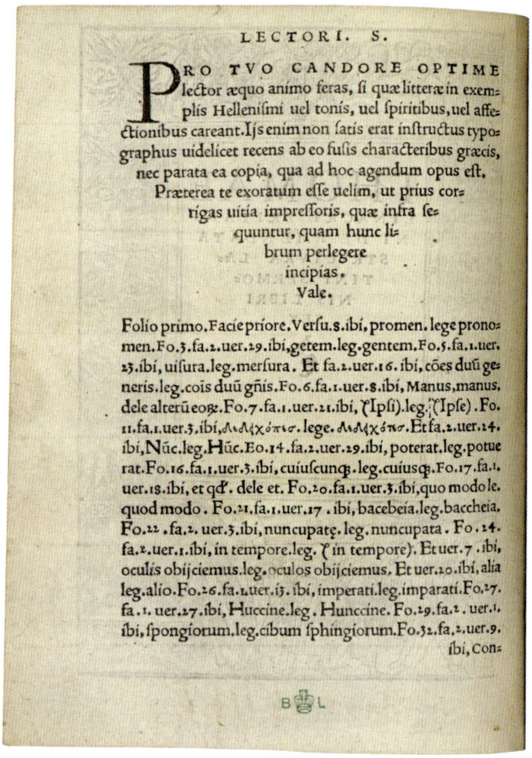
LECTORI. S.

PRO TVO CANDORE OPTIME lector æquo animo feras, si quæ litteræ in exemplis Hellenismi uel tonis, uel spiritibus, uel affectionibus careant. Ijs enim non satis erat instructus typographus uidelicet recens ab eo fusis characteribus græcis, nec parata ea copia, qua ad hoc agendum opus est. Præterea te exoratum esse uelim, ut prius corrigas uitia impressoris, quæ infra sequuntur, quam hunc librum perlegere incipias.
Vale.

Folio primo. Facie priore. Versu. 8. ibi, promen. lege pronomen. Fo. 3. fa. 2. uer. 29. ibi, getem. leg. gentem. Fo. 5. fa. 1. uer. 23. ibi, uisura. leg. mersura. Et fa. 2. uer. 16. ibi, cões duũ generis. leg. cois duũ gñis. Fo. 6. fa. 1. uer. 8. ibi, Manus, manus, dele alterũ eorum. Fo. 7. fa. 1. uer. 21. ibi, (Ipsi). leg. (Ipse). Fo. 11. fa. 1. uer. 3. ibi, ἀλλαχόπισ. lege. ἀλλαχόπισ. Et fa. 2. uer. 24. ibi, Nũc. leg. Hũc. Fo. 14. fa. 2. uer. 29. ibi, poterat. leg. potuerat. Fo. 16. fa. 1. uer. 3. ibi, cuiuscunque. leg. cuiusque. Fo. 17. fa. 1. uer. 18. ibi, et quod. dele et. Fo. 20. fa. 1. uer. 3. ibi, quo modo le. quod modo. Fo. 21. fa. 1. uer. 17. ibi, bacebeia. leg. baccheia. Fo. 22. fa. 2. uer. 3. ibi, nuncupatę. leg. nuncupata. Fo. 24. fa. 2. uer. 1. ibi, in tempore. leg. (in tempore). Et uer. 7. ibi, oculis obijciemus. leg. oculos obijciemus. Et uer. 20. ibi, alia leg. alio. Fo. 26. fa. 1. uer. 13. ibi, imperati. leg. imparati. Fo. 27. fa. 1. uer. 27. ibi, Huccine. leg. Hunccine. Fo. 29. fa. 2. uer. 1. ibi, spongiorum. leg. cibum sphingiorum. Fo. 32. fa. 2. uer. 9. ibi, Con-

More, Edward Powell, Alphonsus de Villa Sancta, and verse by Skelton. Erasmus, who was printed many times in England, appears only in a short translation of Lactantius, reprinted from De Worde. Between 1522 and 1525 Pynson published a sequence of the great scholar Thomas Linacre's Greek-Latin translations of the medical works of Galen and a small primer on geography ascribed to the philosopher Proclus, presented with fine borders and initials. None include Greek, but in 1524 Pynson acquired a Greek fount that he used in one of Linacre's grammatical works, *De emendata structura Latini sermonis*, the typesetting giving rise to a long list of corrigenda.

Although Pynson did not die until the end of 1529, his production dwindled to almost nothing in that year, showing that he had indeed been the active centre of his business, and that without him it could not operate. His wife and only son had predeceased him, leaving him a daughter and her children. He left some property, but there are only small bequests to two apprentices. Despite bad relations in the past, his business was largely taken over by Robert Redman.

Fig. 72 a & b. In 1524 Pynson acquired a Greek fount of type, and used it in one of Linacre's grammatical works that included a good deal of Greek. Its typesetting was not trouble free. In a long list of errata in the prelims the printer begs the reader to correct the misprints before using the book, partly blaming the author's manuscript. The border of the title-page, copied from a design by Hans Holbein for Froben in Basel, shows the story of Mucius Scaevola and king Lars Porsenna.

Thomas Linacre, *De emendata structura Latini sermonis Libri sex.* London, Richard Pynson, 1524. London, BL, G. 7599, fol. 1 recto, 1 verso.

15
Wynkyn de Worde: taking over Caxton's firm

There are only a few documents relating to Wynkyn de Worde's life before 1494, the year when his name appears for the first time in a colophon. Out of this scarcity several biographical edifices have been built, only to be demolished. When as the successor in Caxton's printing firm he began to acquire a public face, a few more biographical facts followed, from which it is possible to construct – retrospectively – a little more of his earlier life. His rich heritage in the form of almost 750 books (large and small) that he published and which are still extant helps to fill in some of the many gaps and to build an image of his personality. At the end of his long and active life he left an elaborate will that shows him as a well-established printer in Fleet Street, a devout man, caring for those with whom he had shared his work.

The earliest document relating to Wynkyn de Worde (in Latin, Wynandus) is in the muniments of Westminster Abbey and it records the lease of a house inherited in 1479 by Elizabeth, wife of Wynkyn de Worde, probably from John Dardan, a saddler, who may have been her father. The couple arranged to let the house to someone else after renewing the lease, and may either have lived outside the abbey, or, if De Worde was in Caxton's service, in one of his tenements in the abbey precincts. In 1480–2 Wynkyn de Worde is recorded in the archives of the Churchwardens of St Margaret's, the church adjoining the abbey, as paying for a pew for his wife. In December 1498 her burial in St Margaret's is recorded in the same accounts. He remarried about a year later, only to bury his second wife, Juliane, in the same church in July 1500, at a time when the plague raged in London. There is no other record of his family.

The abbey's sacrist rolls record that in the year Caxton died (1491/2) De Worde took over the rent of the various premises Caxton had occupied; until then there is no record of rents paid by him. It has always been assumed from the fact that De Worde printed with Caxton's materials at 'Caxton's House' in Westminster (as he put it in some colophons), that he had had an active and even prominent role in Caxton's printing business during his lifetime; most biographers assert that he was Caxton's 'foreman'. This is indeed a possible interpretation of the relationship between the two, but it must be remembered that there is not a scrap of documentation or other evidence to support this.

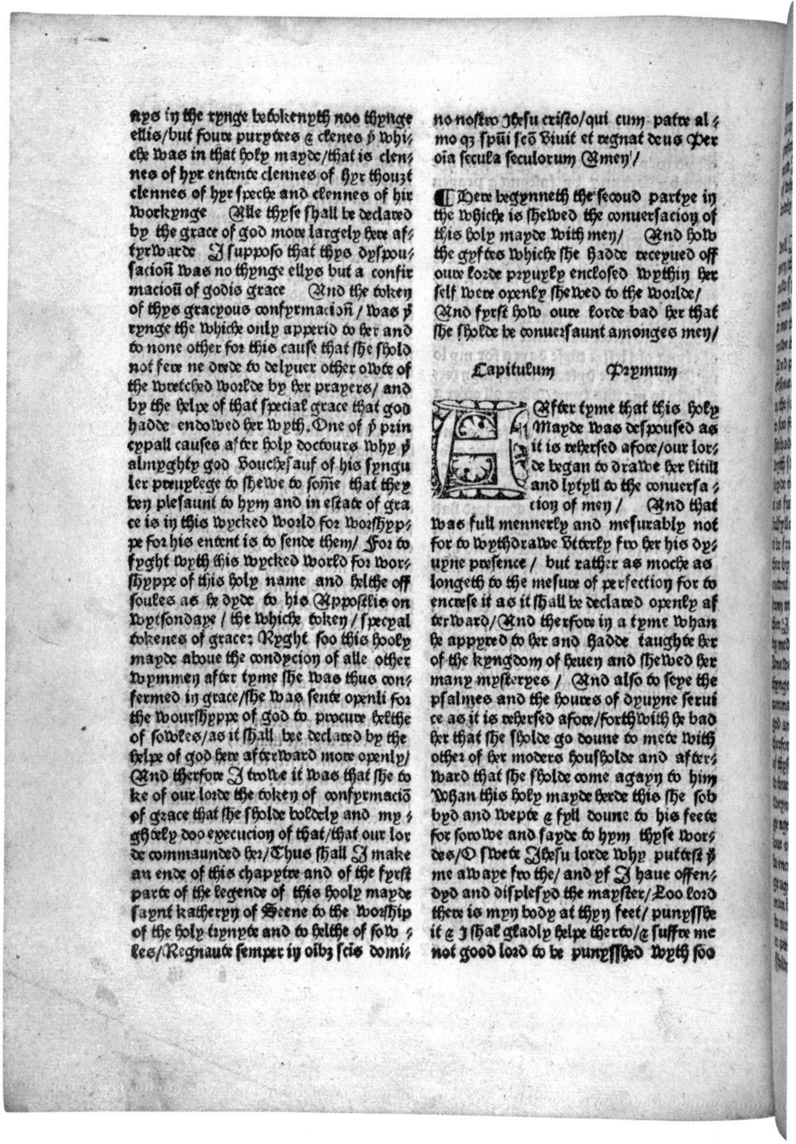

teys in the rynge betokenyth noo thynge ellis/but foure purytees & clenes þ whiche was in that holy mayde/that is clennes of hyr entente clennes of hyr thouzt clennes of hyr speche and clennes of hir workynge Alle thyse shall be declared by the grace of god more largely here aftyrwarde I suppose that thys dyspousacion was no thynge ellys but a confirmacion of godis grace And the token of thys gracyous confyrmacion / was þ rynge the whiche only apperid to her and to none other for this cause that she shold not fere ne drede to delyuer other owte of the wretched worlde by her prayers/ and by the helpe of that special grace that god hadde endowed her wyth. One of þ principall causes after holy doctours why þ almyghty god vouchesauf of his synguler preuylege to shewe to somme that they ben plesaunt to hym and in estate of grace is in this wycked world for worshyppe for his entent is to sende them/ For to fyght wyth this wycked world for worshyppe of this holy name and helthe off soules as he dyde to his Appostlis on Whytsondaye / the whiche token / specyal tokenes of grace; Ryght soo this hooly mayde aboue the condycion of alle other wymmen after tyme she was thus confermed in grace/she was sente openli for the wourshyppe of god to procure helthe of sowles/as it shall bee declared by the helpe of god here afterward more openly/ And therfore I trowe it was that she take of our lorde the token of confyrmacio of grace that she sholde boldely and myghtely doo execucion of that/that our lorde commaunded her/Thus shall I make an ende of this chapytre and of the fyrst parte of the legende of this hooly mayde saynt katheryn of Seene to the worship of the holy trynyte and to helthe of sowles/Regnaunte semper in oibz scis domino nostro Jhesu cristo/qui cum patre almo qz spui sco viuit et regnat deus Per oia secula seculorum Amen/

¶ Here begynneth the secound partye in the whiche is shewed the conuersacion of this holy mayde with men/ And how the gyftes whiche she hadde receyued off oure lorde pryuyly enclosed wythin her self were openly shewed to the worlde/ And fyrst how oure lorde bad her that she sholde be conuersaunt amonges men/

Capitulum Prymum

After tyme that this holy Mayde was despoused as it is reherced afore/our lorde began to drawe her litill and lytyll to the conuersacion of men / And that was full mennerly and mesurably not for to wythdrawe vtterly fro her his dyuyne presence / but rather as moche as longeth to the mesure of perfection for to encrese it as it shall be declared openly afterward/And therfore in a tyme whan he appyred to her and hadde taughte her of the kyngdom of heuen and shewed her many mysteryes / And also to seye the psalmes and the houres of dyuyne seruice as it is reherced afore/forthwith he bad her that she sholde go doune to mete with other of her moders housholde and afterward that she sholde come agayn to him Whan this holy mayde herde this she sobbyd and wepte & fyll doune to his feete for sorowe and sayde to hym thyse wordes/O swete Jhesu lorde why puttest þ me awaye fro the/ and yf I haue offendyd and displesyd the mayster/Loo lord there is myn body at thyn feet/ punysshe it & I shal gladly helpe therto/& suffre me not good lord to be punysshed wyth soo

Fig. 73. The *Life of St Catherine* is one of the first works De Worde printed when he took over Caxton's printing house. Although his recast version of Caxton's worn-out Type 4 gave it a fresh look, he used it for only two books. He introduced here a fine set of initials that had first been used in Gouda in Holland.

Raimundus de Vineis, *Life of St Catherine of Siena* in an English translation. Westminster, Wynkyn de Worde, [1492–3]. London, BL, G. 10542, fol. e3 verso.

Regular payments of rents can be followed in the Westminster accounts until late in 1500, when De Worde moved to a large house in Fleet Street just west of Shoe Lane, in St Bride's parish, that he leased from Ankerwyke Priory in Buckinghamshire. The house had until then been known as 'The Falcon', but De Worde chose to rename it 'In the Sign of the Sonne', and from that time on a radiant sun in his printer's device may signal to us that he had emerged at last from Caxton's shadow. For him it was perhaps a long play on his name – 'Verbum Dei ... Lux Vera'. The beginning of the Gospel of St John is never far from a printer's mind.

The years 1492–6 before his move to Fleet Street were indeed overshadowed by the circumstances of Caxton's bequest, a prolonged soap-opera of disturbed family relations which cannot have left De

Worde unaffected, although, once again, there is no document that shows what his position was in the developing drama, and the printing house managed to remain productive. It is evident that De Worde continued Caxton's printing business after an interval of less than a year, but nothing is known about the conditions that allowed him to do so. Was it an outright sale by the heirs? Or, as seems more likely, was at least some of the work of the early years carried out on behalf of the heirs as a steward, until such time as he could become the outright owner? The conflict among the heirs may have made any such position difficult, although he seems to have had a free hand in the conduct of the business. De Worde's first publication to bear a date – 20 May 1493 – is a reprint of Caxton's *Golden legend* (omitting the 'Stories of the Bible'), startlingly stating in the colophon 'By me wyllyam Caxton'. This formulation suggests that the work was printed at the behest of the heirs. We shall see that it was preceded by several smaller works, editions of devotional texts, which far from being reprints are an immediate departure from Caxton's taste and practice. They are discussed separately below in chapter 17.

The formal situation remains as obscure as all the other circumstances surrounding Caxton's estate after his death. His will, if there was one, has not been found, and there is no way of verifying the validity of the various claims and counter-claims made against each another by his heirs, his daughter Elizabeth and her husband Gerard Crop, a tailor. On separate occasions both spouses were imprisoned as a result of their claims and accusations; both issued petitions to be released and demanded justice. This was meted out in May 1496 when they both appeared before two of the king's most distinguished councillors, Richard Fitzjames and Sir Richard Hatton, then Henry VII's chaplains, who granted them a legal separation and settled the claims. Crop received twenty copies of *The golden legend*, and Caxton's executors then at last honoured his bequest of printed books, including copies of the *Legenda Sarum*, to the Churchwardens of St Margaret's Westminster and the wardens of one of the fraternities based there.

By 1496, when the conflicts around Caxton's estate were finally settled, De Worde may have been in a position to become the outright owner of the printing house. It may be in this connection that he took the step of seeking 'denization', that is, to apply for the status that allows an alien to establish a household, resembling the modern notion of granting a residence permit. The record of this procedure is both revealing and misleading. It is a copy of the letter in which on 20 April 1496 (just less than three weeks before the court appearance of Gerard Crop and his wife, and its consequences) such rights were granted, copied at a later date onto the Patent Roll. The need for such a procedure reveals, of course, that De Worde was not born

Thus endeth the legēde named in latyn legenda aurea / that is to say in englisshe the golden legēde For lyke as passeth golde in valewe al other metallis / soo thys Legende excedeth all other bokes / wherin ben conteyned alle the hyghe and grete festys of our lorde The festys of our blessyd lady / The lyues passiōs & myracles of many other saintes hystoryes & actes / as all alonge here afore is made mencyon / whiche werke I dyde accomplisshed at the commaundemēte and requeste of the noble and puyssaunte erle & my specyal good lord Wyllyam erle of Arondel / And now haue renewed & fynysshed it at westmestre the xx day of May / The yere of our lord M CCCC lxxxxiiii / And in the viii yere of the reygne of kynge Henry the vii /
By me Wyllyam Caxton /

Fig. 74. The reprint of Caxton's *Golden legend*, his largest book (abbreviated by omitting 'The stories of the Bible') was set in the same economical type as the *Life of St Catherine* (fig. 73), but for distinguishing headlines and the colophon (shown here) De Worde used the fount Caxton had acquired in Paris. The spectacular woodcut initial T occurs only here. The woodcut of the crucifixion was first used by Caxton.

Jacobus de Voragine, *The golden legend*, reprinted from Caxton's edition. Westminster, Wynkyn de Worde, 1494. London, BL, IB. 55161, fol. gg4 verso.

an Englishman – as his name clearly indicates – but the document's statement of his place of origin, 'de ducatu Lotharingie oriundo', appears misleading, until we realize that 'Dux Lotharingie' was one of the main titles of the Burgundian dukes, a title with a very complicated political rather than a territorial background. Either in 1496, or perhaps later when the original letter was copied onto the Patent Roll, any formal document shown by De Worde to the authorities, for example a safe conduct issued on behalf of the Duke of Burgundy giving his customary titles as 'Dux Burgundie, Lotharingie, Brabantie etc.', might have been misunderstood by English officials, all the more probable since Burgundian rule was by then a thing of the past, having virtually ended in 1477. There is, however, a great deal of circumstantial evidence that De Worde's name indicates his or his family's origins in the town of Woerden in Holland, not far from

Leiden and Gouda, in a county under Burgundian rule until the end of the dynasty. The name 'Wynandus' and its vernacular diminutive 'Wynkyn' belongs to the north-west of the Low Countries, and not at all to the German-speaking region of Alsace-Lorraine, as was formerly believed. But the main evidence is circumstantial, and is found in the Dutch origin of materials De Worde used: woodcut initials, woodcut illustrations, a fount of type – and there are some indications that he knew Dutch-language books. Taken together, they suggest that he remained in touch with printers in the north-west of the Low Countries.

The letter of denization is significant as the only documentary key to De Worde's non-English background. It is probably no coincidence that De Worde obtained his denization at the same time as the settlement of Caxton's will was completed: he may have found it prudent to secure his rights to conduct an independent printing business, even though Richard III's statute of 1484 granted him those rights as a foreigner. One never knows when circumstances might change, as indeed they did thirty years later in 1534, around the time of De Worde's death, when the 1484 law was repealed.

There is one more set of circumstances strongly indicating that De Worde maintained connections with Holland. Soon after Caxton's death, De Worde must have started planning to overhaul the material that was left by the late printer. This may suggest that he was indeed familiar with it, but if this was so, its styles and state did not enjoy his approval. In the workshop he found four complete and usable founts of text type, as well as a complete fount of a large display type useful for headings or running titles in combination with smaller type (see figs 25, 29). This large fount as well as three of the text founts were left unchanged. One of them, the Parisian type that Caxton had obtained from Maynyal and had hardly used, was as good as new, and De Worde was to use it frequently for many years to come without noticeable changes (see figs 74, 75). A fount of very small type had been very sparingly used by Caxton, mainly for indulgences, and appears even less often in De Worde's work. In 1489 Caxton's mood of new beginning was signalled by the introduction of a text type (Type 6) that was a copy of the larger of his two main text types of the period 1476–85, in the same 'Flemish' style, but cast on a smaller body (see figs 52, 56). De Worde used it unchanged, apparently as a transitional measure, for his first two books, *The chastising of God's children*, and a small *Book of courtesy* that survives only as a trial sheet. He then discarded the fount, obviously not wishing to continue what had been Caxton's signature style. He temporarily overcame his aversion and used Caxton's smaller text type (Type 4) for his reprint of *The golden legend*, preceded by the much shorter *Life of St Catherine*. This was the small-scale version of the Flemish style that had proved a very economical medium for large books. It had been in use by Caxton since 1480, inexpertly recast in 1483 and looking irregular, but the recasting shows that Caxton owned matrices. De Worde had the fount recast again, this time very expertly, resulting in a much refreshed aspect of what by then was an aging fount, in a style that in De Worde's view had had its time. After May 1493, when *The golden legend* was completed, it was seen no more, except a few of its capitals (K, W, and a flourished I) which were brought in to supplement a fine new fount he had purchased from Paris, in what in England was to become the 'black letter' style. These few elements from Caxton's old fount helped to give the books an English aspect. This new Parisian fount was for many years De Worde's main text type, sometimes used in conjunction with the other Parisian fount for contrast, and ensured that his books had no resemblance whatever to Caxton's style (see fig. 76).

Who was the gifted typefounder who managed to resuscitate Caxton's old fount? There is an indication that leads into another of those mazes of identity of migratory workers, where names change with new environments. De Worde illustrated *The golden legend* with the woodcuts that had first appeared in Caxton's edition, but at the end he added a very large and spectacular woodcut initial T. The *Life of St Catherine* and *The golden legend* include a complete alphabet of smaller woodcut initials undoubtedly cut by the same hand, a few of which are found in his earliest book, *The chastising of God's children*. This set of initials had been used in Gouda in Holland at a much earlier date, in 1486, in a Latin schoolbook whose printer named himself 'Gotfridus de Os'. One of the unsolved problems in the history of printing in the Low Countries is whether Gotfridus de Os is the same man who in a vernacular context called himself 'Godevaert van Ghemen', or later in Copenhagen 'Godefridus de ghemen' and 'Gotfred af Ghemen'. Govert or Godevaert (which are vernacular equivalents of 'Gotfridus') certainly used this set of initials in Holland, when he printed in Dutch at several times between 1486 and 1505 in Gouda and Leiden, and when he printed in Copenhagen in Danish between 1505 and 1510, but not when he printed Latin textbooks for the University of Copenhagen in 1493. In the 1490s, it would seem, the set was in Westminster.

In the history of printing types in the Low Countries Gotfridus/Govert is equated with 'the Gouda typecutter', the originator of a printing type that was used from 1486 in successive castings by many printers in the Netherlands (in Deventer, Haarlem, Gouda, Leiden, and Schiedam). In Copenhagen it was Gotfred af Ghemen's only fount of type. In 1496 a version of the type, recast and adapted for English-language printing, was used by Wynkyn de Worde for his reprint of the St Albans *Book of hawking*, for which he may have judged

Fig. 75. De Worde's editions of books of hours, printed in rapid succession in his early years, include some very fine woodcuts. The meeting of the three living hunters and the dead is placed at the beginning of the Vigiliae mortuorum. Their story is related by a hermit, seated in the foreground. The floral border-pieces are used throughout the work.

Horae ad usum Sarum. [Westminster, Wynkyn de Worde, 1493?]. London, BL, IA. 55169, fol. l6 verso, l7 recto.

its angular and perhaps rather archaic and rustic appearance (compared with his Parisian type) to be appropriate (see fig. 78). He never used it again. Finally, at least two woodcuts that had earlier appeared in the work of Gotfridus/Govert turned up in De Worde's books. There are several major gaps and uncertainties in the patchy story of Govert van Ghemen's peripatetic life. One or more periods of useful work helping Wynkyn de Worde to give his business a distinctive appearance would fit in very well.

The publication of the *Book of hawking* in 1496 with its unique use of this slightly out-of-place type is one of several signs that at about this time De Worde was taking over the printing house with a new sense of control. Although there may be some over-simplification in this observation, it should be noted that before that year he published more works that were straight reprints from Caxton than thereafter: in 1493 *The golden legend*, followed by the *Festial* and *Quattuor sermones*, some of Lydgate's short poems, the *Mirrour of the life of Christ*, Earl Rivers's translation of the *Cordiale*, and in 1495 the *Polychronicon* and Maydestone's *Directorium sacerdotum*. In 1495 he published Caxton's own translation of the *Vitas patrum* or *Lives of the Fathers*, the very popular work on the lives of the early Christian hermits in the Egyptian desert during the third century that he had completed on the last day of his life. De Worde illustrated this with a large number of new woodcuts, whereas for previous books he had used the stock of

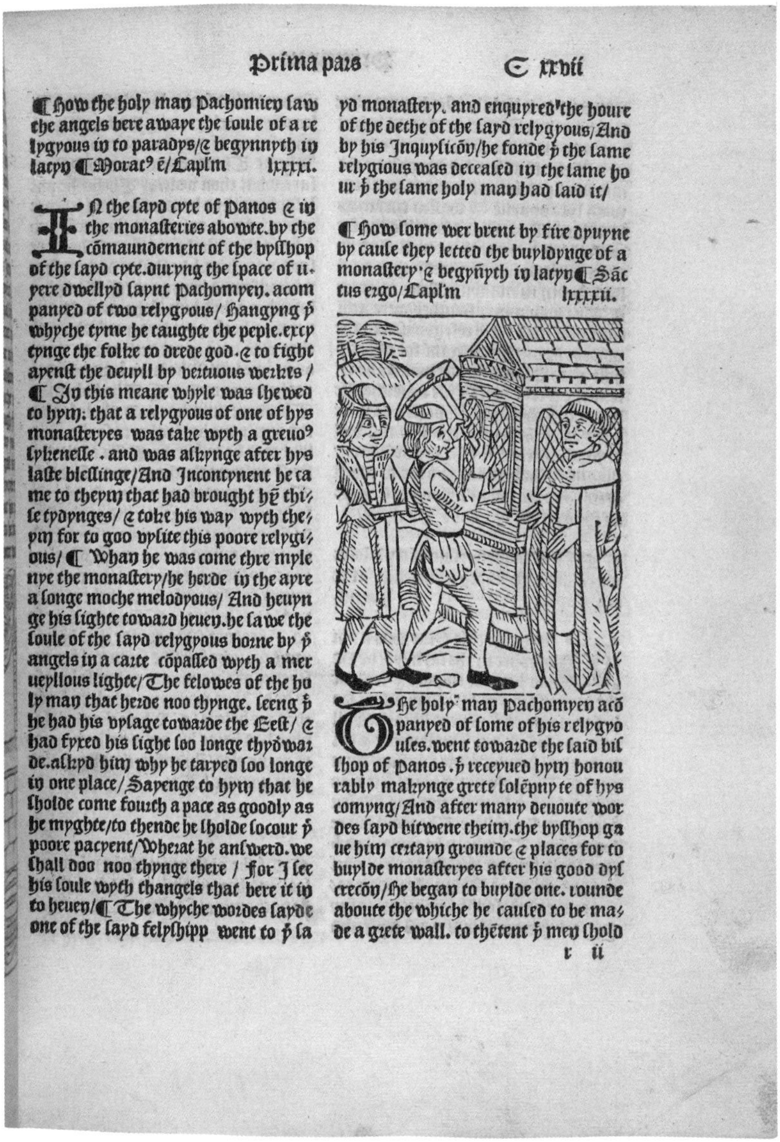

Prima pars ℭ xxvii

¶ How the holy man Pachomien saw the angels bere awaye the soule of a re lygyous in to paradys/& begynnyth in latyn ¶ Morat⁹ ē/Capl'm lxxxi.

In the sayd cyte of Panos & in the monasteries abowte.by the cōmaundement of the bysshop of the sayd cyte.durynge the space of ii. yere dwellyd saynt Pachompen.acom panyed of two relygyous/ hangyng ẏ whyche tyme he taughte the peple.excep tynge the folke to drede god.& to fight ayenst the deuyll by vertuous werkes/ ¶ In this meane whyle was shewed to hym: that a relygyous of one of hys monasteryes was take wyth a greuo⁹ syknesse. and was askynge after hys laste blessinge/And Incontynent he ca me to theym that had brought hȳ thi- se tydynges/ & toke his way wyth the- ym for to goo vysite this poore relygi- ous/ ¶ Whan he was come thre myle nye the monasterye/he herde in the ayre a songe moche melodyous/ And heuyn ge his syghte toward heuen.he sawe the soule of the sayd relygyous borne by ẏ angels in a carte cōpassed wyth a mer ueyllous lyghte/The felowes of the ho ly man that herde noo thynge. seeng ẏ he had his vysage towarde the Eest/ & had fyxed his sight soo longe thydōwar de.asked hym why he taryed soo longe in one place/Sayenge to hym that he sholde come fourth a pace as goodly as he myghte/to thende he sholde socour ẏ poore pacyent/Wherat he answerd.we shall doo noo thynge there / For I see his soule wyth thangels that bere it in to heuen/¶ The whyche wordes sayde one of the sayd felyshipp went to ẏ sa yd monasterye. and enquyred the houre of the dethe of the sayd relygyous/And by his Inquysicōn/he fonde ẏ the same relygious was deceased in the same ho ur ẏ the same holy man had said it/

¶ How some wer brent by fire dyuyne by cause they letted the byldynge of a monasterye·& begynnyth in latyn ¶ Sāc tus ergo/Capl'm lxxxii.

The holy man Pachompen acō panyed of some of his relygyo uses.went towarde the said bis shop of Panos.ẏ receyued hym honou rably makynge grete solēpnyte of hys comyng/And after many deuoute wor des sayd bitwene theim.the bysshop ga ue him certayn grounde & places for to bylde monasteryes after his good dys crecōn/he began to bylde one.rounde aboute the whiche he caused to be ma- de a grete wall. to thētent ẏ men shold

r ii

Fig. 76. Caxton's final substantial translation was a work of hagiography, the lives of the hermits who lived in the Egyptian desert, their stories told as *exempla*. Caxton, the colophon tells us, 'fynysshed it at the laste daye of his lyff'. De Worde printed it in the 'black letter' text type he had obtained in 1493 from Paris, and he ordered 40 small woodcuts representing the fathers, many repeated, one even fifteen times.

The lives of the Fathers. Translated from a French version of the *Vitas sanctorum patrum* by William Caxton. Westminster, Wynkyn de Worde, 1495. London, BL, C. 11.b.3, fol. r2 recto.

woodcuts found among Caxton's materials. These works, continuing a tradition, were interspersed with the devotional texts which were among the first books he printed, following his own inclinations and initiatives, but also under new influences from outside what had been Caxton's ambience.

16
Wynkyn de Worde's career as independent publisher

Over the more than forty years through which we can follow De Worde's long career as a printer, from 1492 to his death in 1535, the nature of his enterprise changed. He remained productive to the end, but when we compare his production in the 1490s, in which major devotional and literary works stand out, with that of the last decade of his life, dominated by small books, and especially elementary schoolbooks that were endlessly reprinted, we see two very different landscapes. In the early years his only possible competitor was Richard Pynson, and at that time they seem to have left each other alone. This gave freedom to both, and De Worde in particular made the most of it. In the course of the sixteenth century, a steadily increasing number of printers began to work in and beyond London, and ever more books (mainly in Latin) reached the English market from abroad and were sold by their printers' agents and by booksellers. The world of books had indeed changed. With some of his colleagues De Worde had links of business and friendship, and they even formed a kind of literary coterie, but with others he was in open and at times virulent competition. Under new pressures it may have been impossible for him to continue with the high standards and originality of the early part of his career, and he may have been obliged to match conviction, taste and enthusiasm with risk-free work that is distinctly less appealing to posterity. There are no clear demarcation lines to mark the shifts in the nature of his business, no single events, but a gradual development that makes his output progressively less interesting.

Yet there are also constants that distinguish him from his contemporaries. He gave much attention to textual presentation and accuracy, most famously in 1498 in a drastic revision of *The Canterbury tales*. He not only published, like Caxton, poetry from the canon of English literature, Chaucer and Lydgate, but also the poetry of his contemporaries, John Skelton, Robert Copland, Alexander Barclay, Stephen Hawes, William Walter, Thomas Feylde, William Neville, and Christopher Goodwyn. There were anonymous poems, religious verse (e.g. *The parlyament of devylles*, *The life of St Ursula*, *The remorse of conscience*, *The example of evyll tongues*), and verse romances (e.g. *Merlin*, *King Richard Coeur de Lyon*). Andrew Chertsey translated French prose for him, as did his apprentices, Henry Watson and John Gough, who later became independent printers. By the second quarter of the sixteenth century there was even a small network of printers who had formerly been his assistants, and many show his influence in their taste and practice.

Another constant is his care for illustration. This had been a distinct weakness in Caxton's work; with the exception of a set of woodcuts he acquired to illustrate the *Mirrour of the life of Christ*, and the set he had made for the second edition of *The Canterbury tales*, Caxton's illustrations can nowadays only charm by their naive clumsiness. De Worde used a few very fine woodcuts in his early editions of books of hours (fig. 75) – it is possible that Caxton had already obtained them for now-lost editions of the hours printed towards the end of his life. In 1495 De Worde began to commission new woodcuts in earnest for the *Lives of the Fathers*, which opens with a full-page illustration depicting St Jerome surrounded by the whole heavenly host, followed by as many as 160 small woodcuts in the text (fig. 76). From that date on he illustrated his works lavishly, and began to present title pages with large woodcuts and woodcut titles. He illustrated romances, starting with a reprint of Caxton's edition of Malory's *Morte Darthur* and amassed a large quantity of religious cuts. In all some 950 woodcuts are recorded as having been used by him. They are a strong characteristic of his publications. They were also a considerable investment in material, and often were used again and again, not always appropriately. (See, for example, below, figs 74–6, his adaptation of the woodcut depicting successive royal funerals in 1509.)

Once Wynkyn de Worde was entirely settled, had overhauled the material in Caxton's printing house and had fulfilled possible commitments to the heirs, he hit his stride; in his publishing career, no period equals the years between 1496 and 1499, if not in quantity, then in originality of the books he brought out in rapid succession, with hardly a schoolbook in sight. His books were well produced, aimed at the English readership created by Caxton, but he did not reprint many of Caxton's works. Evidently he did not share Caxton's love of prose romances, for not one of his translations of such texts was reprinted by him until the early years of the sixteenth century. De Worde's great books of this period were interspersed with smaller quartos of religious texts in English, including some by living authors, John Alcock and Richard Fitzjames, which are discussed in chapter 17.

The sequence of books published in this productive period begins in 1496 with the English translation by John Trevisa of what was by then already a classic, Bartholomaeus Anglicus, *De proprietatibus rerum*, a medieval natural history that had already been printed many times in Latin and French; Dutch and Spanish versions had also appeared in print. It was the first book Caxton had printed (in Latin) in Cologne. The very large manuscript that De Worde used in the

Liber ·xij·

Incipit liber·xij· de Auib9 in generali et ſpeciacili· Ca· J

For the treatiſe is ended of the proprytees of the ayre and of thȳges that ben gendryd therin/ It is couenable to this preſent volume to treate of ſome thȳges whiche bylonge to the worſhyp & magnyfyſence of god·in whiche thynges the merueyllous & excellent dedes of the Creatour maye be prayſid as of otherſthynges / To the ornamement of the ayre bylongen byrdes & foules as Beda sayth/ And therfore by the helpe of ẏ goodnes of Jhesu Cryſt·som what of them ſhall be treated conſequently in this boke· Not of all·but oonly of ſuche byrdes & foules whiche ben ſpecially ſpo

Fig. 77. The printer's copy used in the printing house is Plimpton ms 263 (New York, Columbia University) but De Worde modelled the layout of the English version of this popular text on editions in French and Dutch from which he copied the illustrations. The woodcut heading the chapter on birds is copied from the Dutch version.

Bartholomaeus Anglicus, *De proprietatibus rerum*, in the English translation of John Trevisa. Westminster, Wynkyn de Worde, c. 1496. London, BL, G.10565, fol. (2) A1 recto.

printing house is still extant. At that time it belonged to Sir Henry Willoughby, an influential courtier of Henry VII. Splendid as it is, De Worde improved on it by introducing each of the nineteen divisions of the book with a large woodcut illustrating its subject: the Creation, the ages of man, fishes, birds, animals, landscapes, precious stones and metals, and so on. He found models for the woodcuts in two of the vernacular editions of the text, a French one printed in 1482 in Lyon, and a Dutch one printed in Haarlem in 1485. His models were very different in style, the Dutch woodcuts delicate images of plants and animals, the Lyonnese including vivid representations of human activities such as mining in the mountains. The book was printed 'at prayer and desyre of Roger Thorney mercer'. The year before, Thorney had financed the reprint of the *Polychronicon*, and in 1494 he provided a manuscript for De Worde's edition of Lydgate's *The siege of Thebes* (a poem not printed by Caxton). Thorney owned manuscripts and printed books, and was obviously interested in their texts. Although not an author himself, some of his literary inclinations

Here begynnyth the treatyse of fysshynge wyth an Angle.

Salamon in his parablys sayth that a good spyryte
makyth a flourynge aege/ that is a fayre aege & a
longe. And syth it is soo: I aske this questyon/. Whi
che ben the meanes & the causes that enduce a man
in to a mery spyryte.: Truly to my beste dyscrecōn
it semeth good dysportes & honest gamys in whom a man Joy
eth wythout ony repentaunce after. Thenne folowyth it ỷ go
de dysportes & honest games ben cause of mannys fayr aege &
longe life. And therfore now woll I chose of foure good dispor
tes & honeste gamys/ that is to wyte: of huntynge: hawkynge:
fysshynge: & foulynge. The beste to my symple dyscrecōn why
che is fysshynge: callyd Anglynge wyth a rodde: and a lyne

Fig. 78. The treatise De Worde added to his reprint of the St Albans *The book of hawking* begins with an image of an angler catching a fish in the river Ver. The building complex in the background is Sopwell Priory, where Dame Juliana Barnes, the putative author of part of the *Book of hawking*, once was prioress. The text is set in a Dutch type, used by De Worde only here, but owned by Govert van Ghemen, a printer who moved between Gouda and Leiden in Holland, and Copenhagen. De Worde may have deemed its style appropriate for a rustic text.

Treatise of fishing, a section of *The book of hawking, hunting, fishing, and blasing of arms.* Westminster, Wynkyn de Worde, 1496. London, BL, C. 11.b.5, fol. g3 verso.

are comparable to those of Caxton, but instead of actively producing books, he preferred the role of financial backer, probably shared in profits, and may have taken part in marketing. In that respect his role was similar to that of the merchant John Russhe, who had a share in the finance and marketing of Pynson's firm. Yet another Mercer, John Tate, probably also had a financial stake in the Bartholomaeus Anglicus edition and several of the other major books De Worde printed in these years. They were printed on paper produced by Tate's paper mill in Hertfordshire, the first in England, and his praises, along with Roger Thorney's, were sung in the long introductory poem that also relates (as quoted earlier) that Caxton had printed the book in Latin in Cologne:

> '...and Iohn Tate the yonger Ioye mote he broke
> which late hathe in Englond, doo make this paper thynne
> That now in our englyssh this boke is prynted Inne.'

There are two earlier such poems in De Worde's publications by an anonymous rhymer, all three very similar in tone. The first is in Hylton's *Scala perfectionis* of 1494, revealing Margaret Beaufort as patron, the second in the *Polychronicon*:

> which Roger Thorney Mercer / hath exhorted
> Wynken de worde / of vertuous entent
> Well to correcte / and greatly hym comforted
> This specyall boke / to make and sette in prent...
>
> That it may fynnyshe / parteless of all blame
> The prynter restynge / ever in good name.

The poems have the same function as Caxton's prologues and epilogues, acknowledgement of support, an explanation of the usefulness of the text, and devout blessings. After the Bartholomaeus Anglicus, poems in this style do not recur.

Only seldom did De Worde interpose himself between text and reader. On the rare occasions he did, his words are interesting and pragmatic, his eye on the job in hand, rather than a meditation in Caxton's mode on the contents of the work. One such short text explains why he added a treatise on fishing with a rod when he reprinted in 1496 the *Book of hawking, hunting, and blasing of arms* from the version printed at St Albans in 1486. In his reprint he inserted between two distinct sections of text the *Treatise of fishing*, preceded by a woodcut of a cheerful angler, fishing in a river that has been identified as the Ver, near St Albans. De Worde obviously knew a good deal about the St Albans background of the original publication, and it is remarkable that in 1496–7 he reprinted in rapid succession the two English works, *The book of hawking* and the *Chronicles of England* printed at St Albans ten years earlier, stressing their origin at the abbey with the woodcut and in the colophon of the *Chronicles*. He ended the *Treatise of fishing* with a note leaving us in no doubt for whom the book was intended; clearly we should not impute to him any anachronistic notions of the democratic values of the spread of printing. His ecological concerns show him centuries in advance of his time:

> And for by cause that thys present treatyse sholde not come to the hondys [hands] of eche ydle persone whyche wolde desire it yf it were empryntyd allone by itself and put in a lytyll plaunflet therfore I haue compylyd it in a greter volume of dyverse bokys concernynge to gentyll and noble men. To the entent that the forsayd ydle persones whyche sholde have but lytyll mesure in the sayd dysporte of fysshyng sholde not by this meane utterly dystroye it.

Fig. 79. In preparation for reprinting *The book of hawking* a copy of the first edition was annotated with instructions for the design and colouring of the armorial shields. In the opening shown here the notes read: 'the rondes most be yolo', 'this end most be as the other is, the cros gold', 'the cros gold', 'put in lityll blake or none'.

The book of hawking, hunting, and blasing of arms. The press at St Albans, 1486. Printer's copy, used by Wynkyn de Worde, 1496. London, BL, IB. 55712, fol. (2)c3 verso, c4 recto.

The *Book of hawking* was intended to be read by noblemen and gentlemen, but that should not be taken to mean that generally his public was meant to be limited to this social layer. The contents of the book, a combination of hunting, husbandry, and heraldry, was always bound to be directed at landed nobility and gentry. The real interest in this declaration is that he expects a 'pamphlet', being cheaper, to get into the hands of the lower orders, who might fish not for sport but for gain, 'for theyr dayly encrease of goodes'. About a year later he printed a veterinary text which has indeed the format of a 'pamphlet', a quarto of eighteen leaves. *The proprytees and medicynes of hors*, full of good advice about horses and treatment of their infirmities, is intended, as he writes in the colophon, to be 'necessarye to be knowen to gentyll men and men of honour' but also to 'servysable and rustyk people' – publishing it as a pamphlet, much lower in price than a volume such as *The book of hawking*, would make it accessible to lower ranks in the social order.

As it happens, a section of the St Albans version of *The book of hawking* used in De Worde's printing house survives, with annotations by an editor or master printer and the compositors, showing that great pains were taken to modernize regional vocabulary and spelling by turning them into metropolitan usage, and to introduce some textual corrections. The surviving document is the section with the 'blasing of arms', and the annotations also include numerous amendments

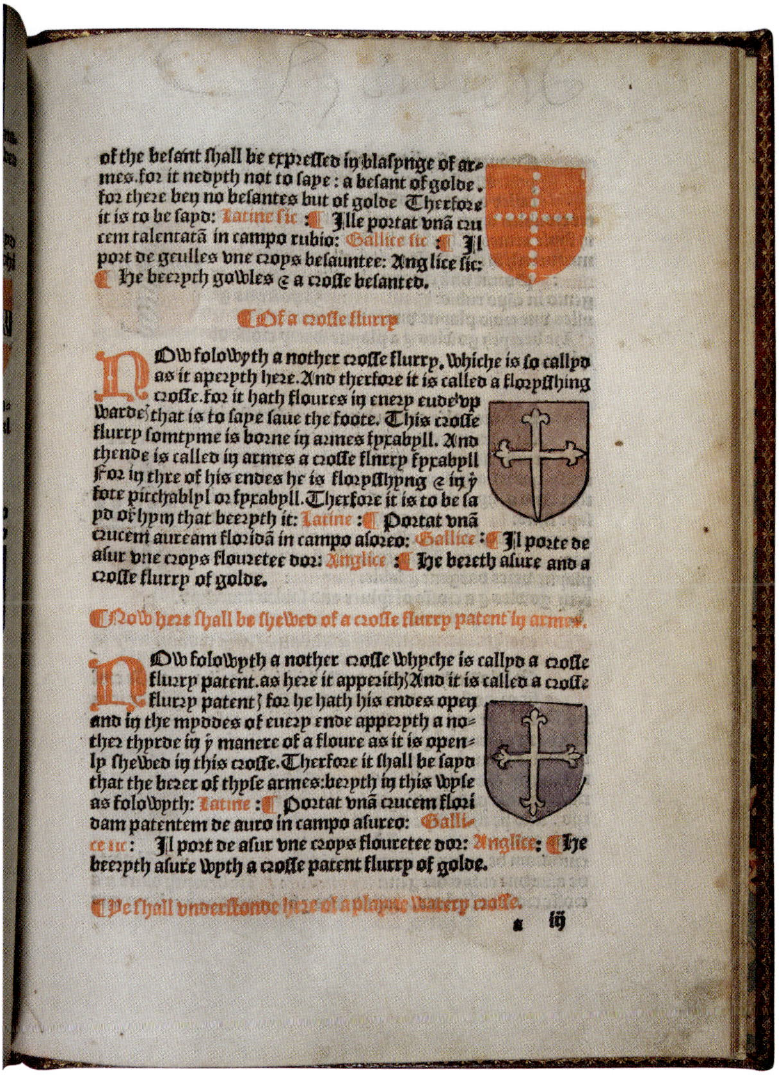
of the besant shall be expressed in blasynge of armes.for it nedyth not to saye : a besant of golde. for there ben no besantes but of golde Therfore it is to be sayd: Latine sic : Ille portat vnā crucem talentatā in campo rubio: Gallice sic : Il port de geulles vne crops besauntee: Anglice sic: He berith gowles ⁊ a crosse besanted.

Of a crosse flurry

Now foloweth a nother crosse flurry, whiche is so callyd as it apperyth here. And therfore it is called a florysshing crosse. for it hath floures in every ende vp warde/ that is to saye saue the foote. This crosse flurry somtyme is borne in armes fytchabyll. And thenne is called in armes a crosse flurry fytchabyll For in thre of his endes he is florysshyng ⁊ in ẏ fote pitchabyl or fytchabyll. Therfore it is to be sayd of hym that berith it: Latine : Portat vnā crucem auream floridā in campo asoreo: Gallice : Il porte de asur vne crops flouretee dor: Anglice : He berith asure and a crosse flurry of golde.

Now here shall be shewed of a crosse flurry patent in armes.

Now foloweth a nother crosse whyche is callyd a crosse flurry patent. as here it apperith/ And it is called a crosse flurry patent/ for he hath his endes open and in the myddes of every ende apperyth a nother thyrde in ẏ manere of a floure as it is openly shewed in this crosse. Therfore it shall be sayd that the berer of thyse armes: berith in this wyse as foloweth: Latine : Portat vnā crucem floridam patentem de auro in campo asureo: Gallice sic : Il port de asur vne crops flouretee dor: Anglice : He berith asure wyth a crosse patent flurry of golde.

Ye shall vnderstonde here of a playne watery crosse.

a iij

Fig. 80. The corresponding page in De Worde's edition of 1496. The instructions were not always carried out, but for these shields they were.

London, BL, C. 11.b.5, fol. (2)a3 recto.

for the colouring and design of the many small armorial illustrations that form part of this section.

Similar treatment was given to the *Chronicles of England*, which a year later he chose to reprint from the St Albans version in preference to Caxton's two editions. The St Albans version, as we have already seen, extended the form in which Caxton had published the text. In this case we are not so fortunate as to have the actual printer's copy with its annotations, but comparison of the two editions shows that De Worde's version is indeed an accurate reprint, but updated with consistent spelling amendments and modernization of the language. At the end of the colophon of the *Chronicles* is the well-known sentence naming the schoolmaster of St Albans as compiler of the work, as well as stating that the work was first printed at St Albans (as discussed above, p. 96). The *Chronicles* were followed in 1498 by Ranulph Higden's *Description of Britain*, the text with which Caxton combined his editions

The prologe of the prioresse

To telle a story I woll do my labour
Not that I maye encrese her honour
For she herself is honour and the rote
Of bounte nexte her sonne and soulis bote

O moder mayde o mayde and moder fre
O busshe unbrent brennynge in moyses syght
That rauesshedist downe from the deyte
Thruh thyn hūblynes the ghost þ in the alyзt
Of whose vertue whan he thin herte lyghte
Conceyued was the faders sapyence
Helpe me to telle it in thy reuerence

Lady thy bounte thy magnyfycence
Thy vertue and thy grete humylyte
Ther may no tunge expresse in no scyence
For somtyme lady or men praye the
Thou ghost beforn of thy benygnyte
And getyst us the lyght of thy prayer
To gyden us unto thy sone so deer

My cunnynge is so weke o blysfull quene
For to declare thyn hyghe worthynesse
That I ne may the weyght sustene
But as a chylde of twelfmonth olde or lesse
That can unnethe ony worde expresse
Ryght so fare I and therfore I you praye
Gydeth my songe as I shall you saye

Here endyth the prioresse prologue

And here begynneth her tale

Ther was in asye in a grete cyte
Amonge cristen folke a Jurye
Susteyned by a lorde of that countre
For fowle usure and lucre of vylonye
Hatefull to cryst and to his companye
And thorouh this strete men might ryde & wen
For it was fre and open at euery ende

Fig. 81. For the fourth edition of *The Canterbury tales* De Worde made sparing use of the set of woodcuts that had illustrated Caxton's second edition, printing only one woodcut for each prologue and tale combined. Typographically his edition was superior to Caxton's, the Parisian text type refreshed by recasting.

Geoffrey Chaucer, *The Canterbury tales*. Westminster, Wynkyn de Worde, 1498. London, BL, G.11587/1, fol. q6 verso.

of the *Chronicles*, and De Worde followed his version, placing a woodcut from the Bartholomaeus Anglicus on the title page.

The *Chronicles* and *Description* were followed immediately by two literary texts, Chaucer's *Canterbury tales* and the anonymous *Assembly of gods*, completed early in 1498. The *Assembly*, which De Worde had already printed in 1494 in a small quarto edition, was now printed more generously in the same layout as the folio *Canterbury tales*, and the two books were undoubtedly meant to be sold together. De Worde used for his new edition of *The Canterbury tales* partly Caxton's second edition (revised from the first), but he or his editor also compared Caxton's new version with manuscripts of the text, and in consequence made drastic changes. The order of the tales was once again changed, and within the tales, the 'Monk's Tale' was revised by shifting the order of the strophes. 'Sir Thopas', 'The Parson's Tale' and probably the whole later section of the book were printed from a manuscript. There are small corrections in many of the tales compared with the text of the second edition, the result of the editor consulting more than one manuscript: at the abrupt end of the 'The Squire's Tale' the note is printed: 'There can be founde no more of this forsayd tale, whyche I have ryght dilygently serchyd in many dyvers scopy' [i.e. manuscript copies of the text]. Who 'I' is remains undisclosed, but whoever he was, he showed great care in providing a version as good and fresh as the sources available to him allowed. We see here and in the reprinting of the St Albans books a principle of editing and presentation at work that should be well understood: the text should be intact, and as complete as the author intended, but it should not be perceived as an antiquarian relict, rather allowed to be read in the reader's own time, as if it had been written recently.

The last and much larger literary publication of this period, following immediately on *The Canterbury tales* and completed on 25 March 1498, is Thomas Malory's *Morte Darthur*, reprinted from Caxton's edition of 1485, but now improved by fine oblong woodcuts placed at the head of each of the twenty-one books into which the text is divided, and also with textual amendments. Many of the woodcuts are strongly reminiscent of those appearing in Haarlem in Jacob Bellaert's editions in Dutch and French of Raoul Lefevre's *Jason* and *Recueil* of *circa* 1485–6, and we may wonder whether De Worde had once again taken Haarlem woodcuts as models for his woodcutter, as he had done two years earlier with the Bartholomaeus Anglicus. The Haarlem woodcutter had probably migrated to Antwerp after 1486, where until 1492 he worked for Gheraert Leeu, who had his own connections with the English market. New woodcuts in this style were to appear for several more years in De Worde's books.

The last major work printed by De Worde in Westminster is a reprint of *The golden legend*, this time including again the 'Stories of the Bible' and printed on the larger-size 'median' paper, still using many of the woodcuts of the saints that had first appeared in Caxton's edition. Meanwhile there was a constant stream of smaller publications, mainly devotional texts; they include two editions of the *Meditations* ascribed to St Bernard translated by 'a devoute student of the University of Cambridge', recent sermons by Bishop John Alcock and Bishop Richard Fitzjames, a charming guide for pilgrims to Jerusalem, and at the request of Bishop Richard Foxe, William Touris, *The contemplation of sinners*. For the Church he printed indulgences and Papal Bulls. There were several editions of annual parliamentary statutes, for which he remained the main printer until Pynson obtained the monopoly. In 1499 De Worde printed the first of his editions of contemporary poets, John Skelton's *The bowge of court*. Only a few schoolbooks appeared before his move to Fleet Street. His most important schoolbook at that time was a Latin–English dictionary, the

Fig. 82. How Hercules was enamoured of Yole the daughter of king Prycus. Almost thirty years after the first edition by Caxton, Wynkyn de Worde reprinted his translation of the Trojan histories. This time it was illustrated with many sometimes crude and ill-fitting woodcuts.

Raoul Lefevre, *Recueil des histoires de Troies*, in the translation by William Caxton entitled *Recuyell of the histories of Troy*. London, Wynkyn de Worde, 1502. London, BL, G. 10509, fol. Z1 verso (detail).

Ortus vocabulorum, which after the first edition of 1500 he was to reprint several times. Its title is a play on 'hortus' (garden) and 'ortus' (origin). It complements the *Promptorium parvulorum*, the English–Latin dictionary printed by Pynson in 1499, reprinted later by De Worde.

Amid all this activity De Worde sought to expand production by commissioning work from others. In January 1497 the printing of a missal for Salisbury use was completed for him in Paris by the firm of Ulrich Gering and Bertold Rembolt; two other printer-publishers, Michael Morin and Pierre Levet, shared in the venture. About two years later, at the end of 1498, De Worde entered into an arrangement with two French printers who had moved to London, Julian Notary, a native of Brittany, in partnership with Jean Barbier. In December 1498 they completed for him another missal for Salisbury, at an address in Westminster, with their own type but with large woodcut initials that De Worde had provided. Previously the printing house, with a third partner known only by his initials 'I.H.', had printed in London a Book of Hours and a schoolbook. Notary's rather small-scale establishment continued to be linked with that of De Worde after the latter's move to Fleet Street towards the end of 1500.

By the time he left Westminster, De Worde had developed a personal publishing style, had attracted the beginning of a circle of authors, mainly ecclesiastics, had availed himself of the services of a gifted woodcutter, and found someone who was capable of a critical revision of *The Canterbury tales* and who may also have overseen other texts. He had entered into joint enterprises with printers specializing in liturgical printing in Paris and with Julian Notary and his partners, who were equally expert. His production – and his energy – had been

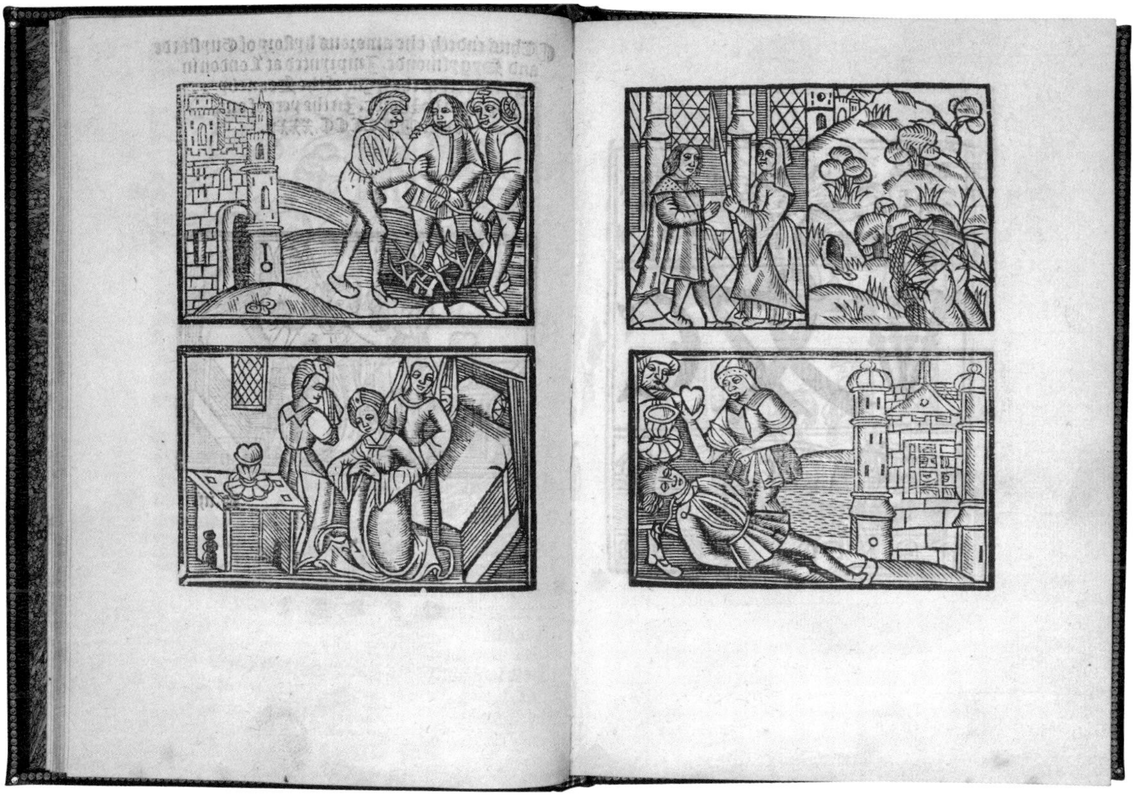

Fig. 83. Robert Copland added many verses to William Walter's translation. Two blank pages at the end of the book were used for summing up Boccaccio's romantic story of love and betrayal by repeating the four woodcuts that illustrate it.

Guystarde and Sygysmonde. London, Wynkyn de Worde, 1532. London, BL, C. 132.i.42, fol. D3 verso, D4 recto.

constant. Once installed at his new address in Fleet Street, 'In the Sign of the Sonne', his activity did not diminish, but it was not long before his production apparently lost some of its originality. The first year saw business as before, with the publication of Savonarola's *Expositio* on the Psalm 'In te domine speravi', the mystic Margery Kempe's *Treatise on contemplation*, another reprint of *The golden legend*, and the edifying story of *Robert the devil*, translated from French verse. In 1502 he published several major books, including once again the *Chronicles of England*, but also titles that were new for De Worde, such as an English translation of the popular *Gesta Romanorum*, a collection of exempla based on ancient narrative themes. He also reprinted Caxton's *Recuyell of the histories of Troy*, this time illustrated with woodcuts, some of which had earlier been used in the *Morte Darthur*. In the subsequent years a new pattern took hold: a few very interesting new titles among which poetry by Stephen Hawes, Robert Copland and translations by Andrew Chertsey stand out, among increasing numbers of reprints of his own and also Pynson's publications, and soon a rising tide of schoolbooks. From Caxton he reprinted in 1505 the romances of *The four sons of Aymon* and *Paris and Vienne*, and in 1506 *The governayle of health*. From 1507 we see him occasionally reprinting law books, which until then had been Pynson's exclusive territory: the *Carta feodi*, the *Modus tenendi Curiam Baronis* and *Modus tenendi unum*

Hundredum, the *Book of Justices of the Peace*, and in 1510 a small cluster of Yearbooks. It is precisely in 1507 that De Worde and Pynson published, with joint imprints, *The royal book* (in Caxton's translation) and *The golden legend*. The great edition of Sir Anthony Fitzherbert, *La graunde abbregement de le ley*, in three volumes (1516–17), was the combined enterprise of John Rastell and Wynkyn de Worde, in which Pynson may also have had a small share. It is therefore impossible to decide whether De Worde's reprinting of Pynson's legal books meant that he was trying to steal his customers (who were now also his own near-neighbours) or that he was helping Pynson in meeting a demand.

De Worde maintained his association with the Parisian printer Michel Morin, publishing with him a Breviarium in 1506, and sharing Parisian imprints in 1507 and 1509. In 1511 Morin printed a missal for him in Rouen, other printers or booksellers in France joining in the imprint, and De Worde and William Faques offered it for sale in London at St Paul's Churchyard. It should be noted that from 1503 Wynkyn de Worde is on record as a great importer of books. Paul Christianson, who has analysed the Customs Rolls for this period, found that De Worde was charged in the years between 1503 and 1532 for no fewer than twenty-nine shipments of books (averaging one per year), to the value of £147 10s. Pynson does not appear at all, but his absence from the Customs Rolls may be explained if he had argued that as an Englishman he was exempt from aliens' duties, being born in Normandy when it was still under obeisance to the King of England.

Christianson also notes that in this period there was a great influx of aliens in the book trade, booksellers as well as printers. Competition began to bite. These circumstances may have led De Worde to be less inclined to take risks, and instead balance new titles with reprints of proven successes, both his own and others', in particular Pynson's. Whereas Pynson managed to secure his income with his work as King's Printer and his legal clientele, and may therefore have been in a position to be more discriminating and attract more interesting authors, De Worde increasingly took recourse to the publishing of schoolbooks for the elementary teaching of Latin. In the 1490s Pynson had been the main supplier of such books, and only a sprinkling was produced by De Worde. From the early years of the sixteenth century demand for schoolbooks rose rapidly, as schools began to take advantage of the uniformity that textbooks printed in their preferred versions could provide. At the same time, De Worde's output increased to rival and eventually overtake that of Pynson. Until about 1510 the leading English author of schoolbooks for teaching Latin had been John Stanbridge, successor of John Anwykyll, who continued Anwykyll's tradition of teaching influenced by the methods of the Italian humanists Sulpizio and Perotti. Stanbridge died in 1510, but some of his texts remained in print until well into the seventeenth

Fig. 84. Two of Whittinton's popular grammatical works, bound together. Shown here is the final page of the first, with De Worde's most elaborate printer's device, and the title-page of the second. The device includes Caxton's monogram, and also a sun, for The Sign of the Sonne, the name of De Worde's house in Fleet Street.

Robert Whittinton, *De nominibus generibus* and *De nominum declinatione*. London, Wynkyn de Worde, 1524, 1523. London, BL, G. 7551/1 and 2, fol. C4 verso, A1 recto.

century. In 1511 another author began to be published, one educated in the same tradition and for whose work there was immediately great demand. Robert Whittinton, who had edited one of Stanbridge's texts, was published fifty times by De Worde in the decade 1511 to 1520 (and reprinted thirteen times by Pynson). Overall there are 167 Whittinton editions by De Worde on record, against only thirty-three by Pynson. They are all small books, each dealing with a particular subject, that generally sold for a penny. Stanbridge was printed by more different printers than Whittinton, but here De Worde leads too, with overall eighty-six editions recorded in the sixteenth century, against Pynson's twenty. The demand was undoubtedly led by individual schools or schoolmasters who either became the printers' clients or could order multiple copies of specific texts through a bookseller. Whittinton was very much De Worde's author, and it is thought that they had been closely associated in preparing the little books. Whittinton's works were undoubtedly a publishing success; on the strength of this he may have persuaded De Worde to publish a collection of Latin epigrams, the first such publication of humanist poetry in England. Whittinton's *Epigrammata* is a collection full of flattery of Henry VIII (who had succeeded to the throne in 1509), John Skelton, and especially Cardinal Wolsey, and its author was striving for their attention in a very public manner.

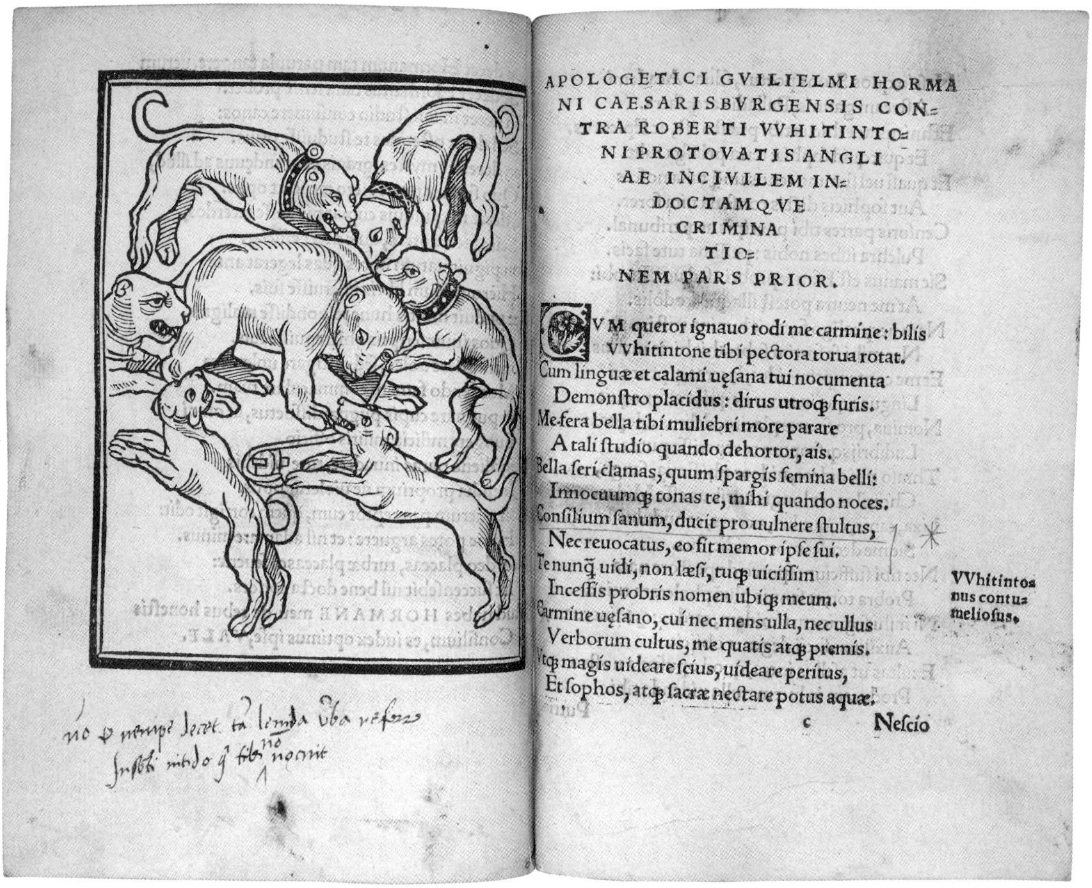

The popularity of Whittinton's grammatical works may not have been entirely welcomed by William Horman, headmaster of Eton, and William Lily, high master of St Paul's School, both published authors of grammatical works, and both men of greater learning than Whittinton (although their principles of teaching were similar to his). Horman had over the years been published by Pynson, and in 1519 Pynson published his *Vulgaria*, a large collection of everyday sentences in English and Latin, introduced with Latin verse by Lily (see fig. 64). Whittinton chose to ridicule this publication in derogatory verse which he posted on the door of St Paul's school, a self-promoting stunt that deliberately provoked what has come to be known as the Grammarians' War. Escalation came in the form of a published response by Lily and Horman in Latin verse, entitled *Antibossicon*, printed – by Pynson – in 1521. Whittinton and De Worde responded in kind by publishing in the same year Whittinton's *Antilycon*, and the aggrieved author persisted with some further attacks in some of his small grammars that continued to be published by the score. He also achieved what may well have been the ultimate purpose of his self-promotion: he was appointed at court as schoolmaster of the royal pages or 'henchmen'.

Fig. 85. The Grammarians at war. Whittinton, operating under the pseudonym 'Bossus', had ridiculed Horman's *Vulgaria* (see fig. 64). Horman's verse against Whittinton's rude and ignorant 'criminatio' (calumny) is more restrained than the image of scholarly dispute that accompanies it.

William Horman and William Lily, *Antibossicon*. London, Richard Pynson, 1521. London, BL, C. 70.e.16/2, fol. b4 verso, c1 recto.

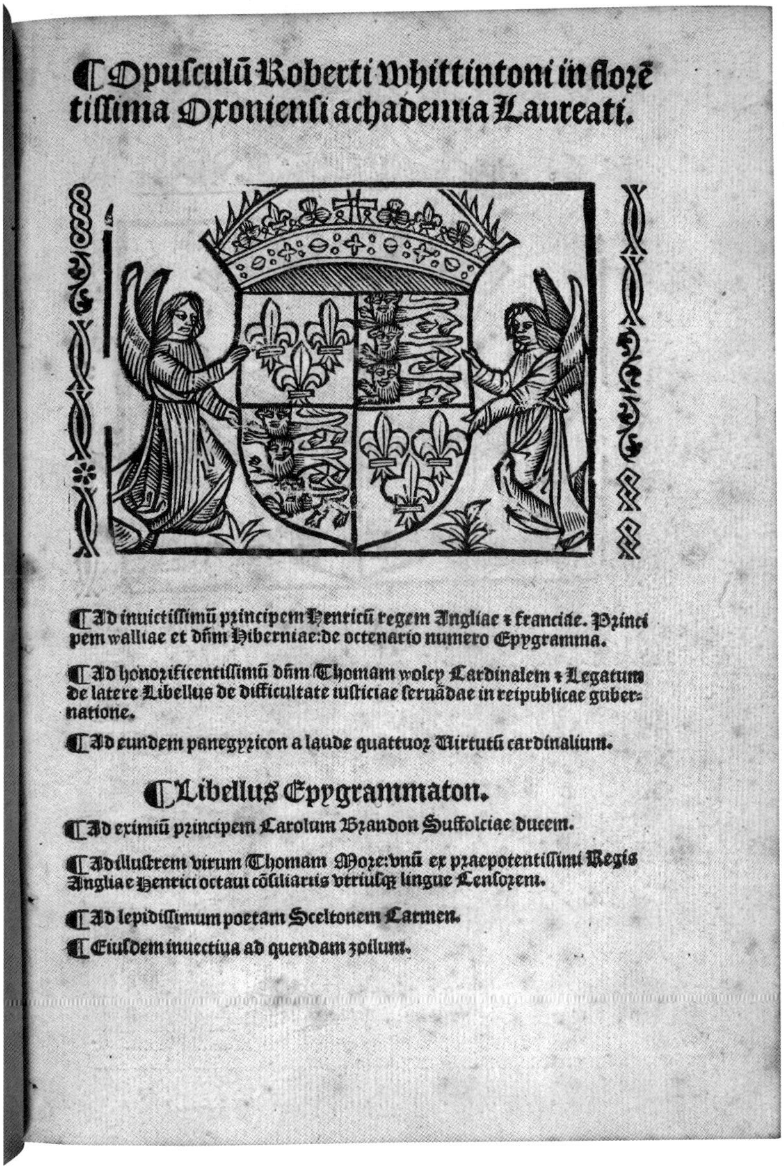

Opusculū Roberti Whittintoni in florētissima Oxoniensi achademia Laureati.

Ad inuictissimū principem Henricū regem Angliae & franciae. Principem walliae et dñm Hiberniae: de octenario numero Epygramma.

Ad honorificentissimū dñm Thomam wolcy Cardinalem & Legatum de latere Libellus de difficultate iusticiae seruādae in reipublicae gubernatione.

Ad eundem panegyricon a laude quattuor Uirtutū cardinalium.

Libellus Epygrammaton.

Ad eximiū principem Carolum Brandon Suffolciae ducem.

Ad illustrem virum Thomam More: vnū ex praepotentissimi Regis Angliae Henrici octaui cōsiliariis vtriusq; linguae Censorem.

Ad lepidissimum poetam Sceltonem Carmen.

Eiusdem inuectiua ad quendam zoilum.

Fig. 86. The collection of Latin epigrams, dedicated to the king by the highly ambitious Whittinton, was published in order to seek the attention of the royal court and flatter other scholars. It was also copied in a beautifully executed manuscript for presentation to Cardinal Wolsey. It may have irked Whittinton's more learned colleagues Lily and Horman.

Robert Whittinton, *Libellus epigrammaton*. London, Wynkyn de Worde, 1519. London, BL, C.132.i.36, fol. A1 recto.

In the episode of the Grammarians' War De Worde and Pynson found themselves in opposing camps, and each loyally helped to defend the authors in whom they had a vested interest, De Worde especially so. His publishing of grammars continued, and in the last fifteen years of his life they formed a very significant proportion of his total output. This cash crop enabled him to indulge his other tastes, if on a modest scale: new English poetry, devotional texts, many reprinted and some new, a few romances, including two editions of *The life of Ipomydon* and William Walter's translation of a tale by Boccaccio, *Guystarde and Sygysmonde*. In between there are surprises: humanist authors, Badius Ascensius, the first English translation of the *Colloquia* of Erasmus and of his *Enchiridion militis Christiani*, and

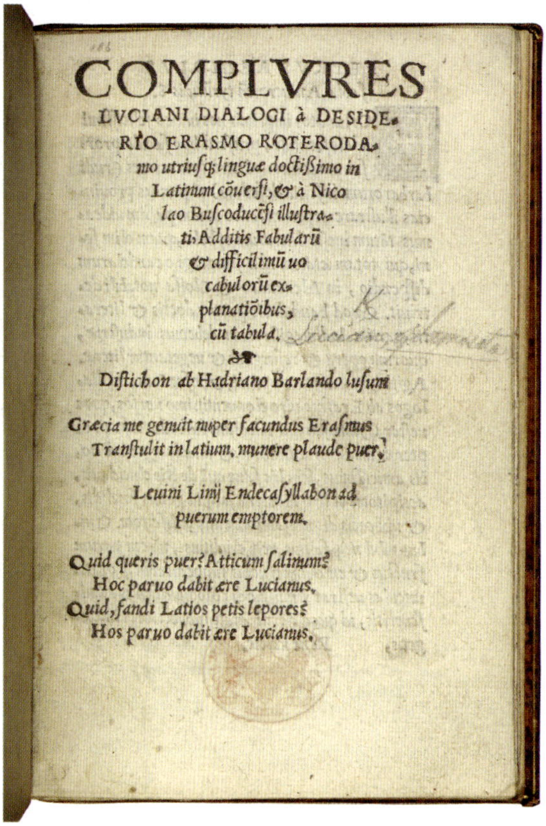

COMPLVRES
LVCIANI DIALOGI à DESIDE-
RIO ERASMO ROTERODA-
mo utriusq; linguæ doctißimo in
Latinum cōuersi, & à Nico
lao Buscoducēsi illustra-
ti: Additis Fabularū
& difficilimū uo
cabulorū ex-
planatiōibus,
cū tabula.

Distichon ab Hadriano Barlando lusum

Græcia me genuit nuper facundus Erasmus
Transtulit in latium, munere plaude puer.

Leuini Linij Endecasyllabon ad
puerum emptorem.

Quid queris puer? Atticum salinum?
Hoc paruo dabit ære Lucianus.
Quid, fandi Latios petis lepores?
Hos paruo dabit ære Lucianus.

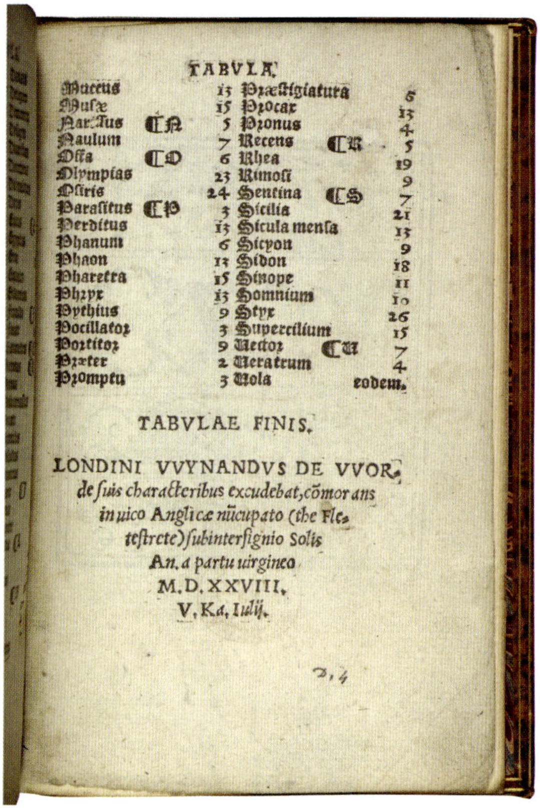

TABVLA.

Muccus		13	Præstigiatura		6
Musæ		15	Procax		13
Nar. Tus	C N	5	Pronus		4
Naulum		7	Recens	C R	5
Offa	C O	6	Rhea		19
Olympias		23	Rimosi		9
Osiris		24	Sentina	C S	7
Parasitus	C P	3	Sicilia		21
Perditus		13	Sicula mensa		13
Phanum		6	Sicyon		9
Phaon		13	Sidon		18
Pharetra		15	Sinope		11
Phryx		13	Somnium		10
Pythius		9	Styx		26
Pocillator		3	Supercilium		15
Portitor		9	Vector	C V	7
Præter		2	Veratrum		4
Prompetu		3	Vola		eodem.

TABVLAE FINIS.

LONDINI VVYNANDVS DE VVOR-
de suis charactteribus excudebat, cōmorans
in uico Anglicæ nūcupato (the Fle-
testrete) sub interfignio Solis
An. a partu uirgineo
M.D.XXVIII.
V. Ka. Iulij.

Erasmus' own translation of Lucian; even more unexpected are works by the humanist Despauterus from Louvain and the Dutch grammarian Murmellius. Woodcut insertions (rather than type) in Robert Wakefield's *Oratio de laudibus trium linguarum* of 1528 mark the first attempts in England to represent Hebrew and Arabic script; in 1519 an anonymous text, *A lytell treatyse of the turkes lawe called Alcaron*, also shows that he did not fear the exotic. He had no truck with new developments in religious thinking, though in 1525 he was summoned to the Consistorial Court of the Bishop of London, and upbraided for having published John Gough's translation of *The ymage of love*, apparently forgetful of the newly introduced censorship measures.

This incident apart, Wynkyn de Worde's work seems entirely unaffected by the religious and political upheaval that was taking place place around him. He died early in 1535, six years after Pynson. In June 1534 he had prepared a will 'being hole of mynde and body ... knowing nothing so certayne as death and nothing so uncerteyne as how where and when'. His will in all its carefully set out detail reveals more about his personality and his outlook on life than any of the other scarce documents that recorded some of his life's events. In a recent analysis of this document Mary Erler has traced the extensive network of connections of the many people mentioned in the list of bequests and dispositions. They show him, in her words, 'as an equal

Fig. 87 a & b. Works by Erasmus, first printed on the Continent, were often reprinted in England. De Worde introduced for Erasmus's translation of this classical text an italic fount to which he draws attention in an elegant colophon in Latin at the end of the work.

Lucianus Samosatensis, *Complures dialogi*, translated from the Greek into Latin by Desiderius Erasmus. London, Wynkyn de Worde, 1528. London, BL, C. 48.b.1, fol. a1 recto, d4 recto.

FOr to knowe and to here some newe ty-
dynges for to refresshe ẏ mēnes wyttes
and understandynge. So wyll I som-
what wryte of ẏ turkes lawes/whiche
lawe in many poyntes accordeth to our
lawe & is ẏ lawe of Machomet/ẏ whi-
che in his lawe used a worde (occidite. That is to saye
kylle. So all them ẏ wyll not byleue in theyr lawe they
slee them. And ẏ is agaynst ẏ lawe of oure lorde Jhesu
cryst/for he byddeth ẏ we shall loue them ẏ loue not us
and praye for oure enemys. And ẏ turkes ben charged
to theyr byleue. But the crysten people be not soo/but
amyably lerned & teched. And whan ẏ the predycante
or prechour shal go to preche theyr fals byleue he hath
a naked swerde in his hande as longe as his sermon
shall endure & last. Or elles he putteth ẏ sayd swerde in
a hyghe place wher as euery body may beholde it ẏ is
there for to fere and threten them therwithall. And we
crysten people putteth a crucyfyxe in the myddes of ẏ
chyrche on hyghe for humylyte & not for fere or threte-
nynge lyke as the turkes do the forsayd swerde. And so
forthe I wyll procede and wryte of theyr lawes and bo-
ke the whiche is named comenly Alcaron. And some
men dothe call it the boke of Mesaap and some of them
be of dyuers langages and in lyke wyse of dyuers coū-
trees ẏ whiche boke Machamet made and gaue it un-
to them. In the whiche boke this fals nygromancer
Machamet wrote amōge other thynges as many one
hathe redde and sene here before that they the whiche
ben good shall go unto paradyse and they the whiche
ben euyll to helle/and that byleueth all the sarasyns/
Alca. A.ii.

Fig. 88. The treatise, including a woodcut of a preacher addressing an audience of men and women in the open air, compares the laws of the Koran with Christian doctrine. It comprises only six leaves. The initial at the beginning of the text belongs to a set first used by Caxton in 1484.

Treatise of the Turkes lawe called Alcaron. London, Wynkyn de Worde, 1519 (?) London, BL, C. 25.k.13, fol. A1 verso, A2 recto.

in a group of well-connected, substantial, and prosperous contemporaries', centred on his own household, his apprentices, journeymen and domestic servants, and on his neighbours in the parish of St Bride, among whom were several former apprentices, now fellow-printers in Fleet Street. His testamentary executors were three independent printers: Henry Pepwell, John Gough (or 'Gowghe') and Robert Copland; witnesses to the will were men of good standing in the parish and the disposition for requiem masses and distribution of money to the poor was entrusted to two churchwardens of St Bride's. He made a small bequest to the fraternity of Our Lady based at the church, and wished to be buried in front of the altar of St Katherine. His financial bequests are precise. He made two in cash to servants, to a total of £6, but his largest single legacy was £10 for the upkeep of the child of a pouchmaker in Shoe Lane. He forgave four debts, including one to Robert Woodward in Bristol, who was probably a stationer. Most of his cash he seems to have reserved for his various arrangements with St Bride's. To fourteen named legatees, servants, printers, stationers and bookbinders he left printed books to a total value of £48, and in addition he bequeathed printed books to the value of £3 to 'each of my apprentices' – not specifying their number. Clearly, his most valuable asset was his stock. His legatees must have disposed of great bundles of Whittinton's works.

17
Printing devotional texts in English

In the years before 1535, the work of the two main printers in England of the period, Richard Pynson and Wynkyn de Worde, was hardly touched by the Reformation, although the printing press was to be a powerful instrument for both sides during the 1520s. Pynson published several anti-Lutheran tracts, some partly written by Henry VIII, but since these were published by him in his function of King's Printer, we cannot infer from them his personal position in matters of religion. Wynkyn de Worde seems to have been entirely averse to the new doctrine and remained faithful to the tradition of contemplative, private devotion that is expressed in so many of the works he published. But, because of the enormous significance of the Reformation and its consequences, we risk overlooking another, less dramatic evolutionary development that took place in the Church in England from the early 1490s on, in which De Worde's publishing programme with a range of devotional texts was in the vanguard.

The few devotional publications in English which in the last year of Caxton's life were sponsored by Margaret Beaufort and her daughter-in-law Elizabeth of York, Henry VII's queen, foreshadow a turning point in the publishing of religious texts for lay readers. During most of the fifteenth century the dissemination of religious texts in the vernacular had been inhibited by the movement in the Church that sought to counter heresy, specifically Lollardry, formalized in 1409 by the promulgation of Archbishop Arundel's Constitutions. Lollards had put much emphasis on contemplation and private devotion, and to this purpose on the reading of religious texts in English, the language of lay people. The Constitutions forbade not only the circulation of translations of the Scriptures, directed against Wycliffe's Bible translation, but also suppressed texts in English that were not approved as orthodox. Possession of such texts without explicit approval of Church authorities could lead to prosecution. In the application of these laws there was a strong element of social distinction: the aristocracy and other elites were allowed to own English-language religious texts, even the Wycliffe Bible. But the authorities feared that, in the 'wrong' hands, devotional texts printed in English would lead to unorthodox beliefs, and so prohibited the 'common people' access to them. Works by authors such as Walter Hylton, the anonymous authors of *Dives and Pauper* and the *Chastising of God's children* had therefore in the fifteenth century very limited circulation. Even *The Canterbury tales* might be perceived – by a zealous prosecutor – as a precedent for socially diverse lay devotion, as happened in 1464 in the Chilterns, when unfortunate members of the sect of the Free Spirit, suspected of heresy, were prosecuted for possessing it. Nevertheless, the success of the attempts at censorship remains debatable.

Caxton steered clear of the issue, and he may even have been directed by advice of his landlords at Westminster Abbey. When he published his editions of *The Canterbury tales* there is no hint of any objection by the Church, which would have expected the book – as did Caxton – to be bought by his fellow merchants and other urban elites. None of the originally English religious texts he published were under suspicion of heresy. Nicholas Love's translation of the *Mirrour of the life of Christ* had been approved for dissemination by Archbishop Arundel himself, his words of approval printed by Caxton in his edition. For *The golden legend* Caxton evaded the issue by adding a paraphrase of selections from the Scriptures to be read at the appropriate times in the liturgical year, along with the saints' feast days. There may even be some particular significance in the patronage and encouragement of the 11th Earl of Arundel (a great-nephew of the Archbishop), circumstantially related in Caxton's prologue. John Mirk's *Festial*, written in the 1380s at a time when many of the Lollard texts were produced, was explicitly anti-Lollard. John Lydgate's works were beyond suspicion of heresy. The other religious texts Caxton published before 1490 were all translations by himself, e.g. the *Royal book* and the *Book of good manners*, and as such had not been disputed at the time, earlier in the century, when censorship was most acutely observed. *The fifteen Oes* and the *Book of diverse ghostly matter* therefore represent a distinct departure from his previous practice, initiated by his new patrons, the two royal ladies. (See fig. 53).

What had started tentatively and uncontroversially just within Caxton's lifetime became a significant movement during that of his two successors, Wynkyn de Worde and Richard Pynson. With all their differences – Pynson always the clever businessman, judiciously spreading his risks between areas of interest and categories of clients, De Worde, especially in the early years, showing independence and originality in every aspect of publishing – they have one important element in common: both were instrumental in bringing about the abundance of printed editions of English texts for lay devotion that is characteristic of the two decades that followed Caxton's death. By the first decade of the sixteenth century the Arundel Constitutions were disregarded, though they would be re-invoked in the 1520s when heresy became a new and much more serious issue. The causes of the sea change in the 1490s are complex: the influence and patronage of

Margaret Beaufort and her religious advisers, the individual religious inclination of the printers, especially of Wynkyn de Worde, and possibly the realization among some religious orders, in particular Bridgettines and Carthusians, that the success of the introduction of printing gave new opportunities for the dissemination of texts in English, and also that this medium might be difficult for the secular authorities to control.

During the short time in 1492 when, after his death, Caxton's printing house could not operate, Margaret Beaufort may have commissioned at least one work from Pynson although she is not named explicitly as patron. This is the *Officium* for the Feast of the Name of Jesus, celebrated on 7 August, one of the three Nova Festa that were introduced in the 1480s by the Convocation of Canterbury. Lady Margaret is known to have been particularly attached to this devotion, and in 1494 she was recognized by the Pope as chief promoter of the feast in England. That Pynson printed at about the same time a *Life of St Margaret*, in verse, is probably no coincidence. In the following year he printed the offices for all three Nova Festa, the Name of Jesus, the Transfiguration and the Visitation.

Thereafter she seems to have favoured Wynkyn de Worde, who did name her twice as patron, but more of whose publications may be due to her interventions with religious houses, encouraging them to disseminate texts in print. Among the first, although not the earliest of his publications is *The lyf of St Jerome*, a work that is also associated with Margaret Beaufort. This English version of the *Vita et transitus Sancti Hieronymi* had been commissioned in the 1440s by Margaret, Duchess of Clarence, Margaret Beaufort's grandmother, from Symon Wynter of Syon Abbey with the purpose of disseminating copies. The version printed by De Worde contains additional Bridgettine material, and the manuscript from which he worked was probably provided by Syon Abbey, either prompted by the Lady Margaret or proffered by the abbey for further dissemination, this time in print, as a compliment to her.

The first books printed by De Worde in 1492/3 are quite unlike Caxton's choices, and reveal a taste for the kind of lay devotion that had been so problematic in England since Archbishop Arundel had issued his Constitutions. The very first volume he produced, *The chastising of God's children*, is a text written late in the fourteenth century and partly derived via a Latin translation from the visionary work of the Dutch mystic Johan Ruusbroec. It was one of the texts that could not be owned without permission, and was therefore circulated mainly in religious houses and among people of rank. De Worde combined it with William Flete's *Remedy against the troubles of temptations*, which had a wider distribution in manuscript. It was followed by an edition of the *Treatise of love* and an English translation of the *Life of St Catherine* combined with the *Life of St Elizabeth* (see fig. 73). These are all texts of the kind that may be associated with Syon Abbey or Margaret Beaufort, but no sponsor or source is mentioned in them. *The golden legend* (completed in May 1493, and probably printed on behalf of Caxton's heirs) was followed later in the year by books of hours in two formats, several times reprinted, that are almost indistinguishable from two editions printed by Caxton (or possibly De Worde) of which offsets on printer's waste are all that remain. In the complete copies of De Worde's reprints of the larger format, the colophons reveal that they were printed 'by the commaundementys of the moost hye and vertuous pryncesse our lyege lady Elyzabeth by the grace of god quene of englond and of fraunce and also of the ryght hye and moost noble pryncesse Margarete moder to our soverayn lord the kyng'. Equally uncontroversial were the reprints at about the same time of Mirk's *Festial* and the *Quattuor sermones*. But in 1494 De Worde printed another work that in the preceding years had been heavily restricted by censorship, Walter Hylton's *Scale of perfection*, and this time it was left in no doubt who had taken the initiative. The colophon, in verse, includes lines mentioning De Worde for the first time in print, and reveals the commission by Margaret Beaufort:

> Infynite laude wyth thankynges many folde
> I yelde to god me socouryng wyth his grace
> This boke to finysshe whiche that ye beholde
> Scale of perfeccion calde in euery place
> Whereof thauctor walter Hilton was
> And wynkyn de worde this hath sett in prynt
> In willyam Caxstons hows so fyll the case
> God rest his soule. In Ioy ther mot it stynt
>
> This heuenly boke more precyous than golde
> Was late direct wyth great humylyte
> For godly plesur. Theron to beholde
> Vnto the right noble Margaret as ye see
> The kyngis moder of excellent bounte
> Herry the seventh that Ihesu hym preserve
> This myghty pryncesse hath commaunded me
> Temprynt this boke her grace for to deserve.

At the beginning of the book appears a woodcut of the Virgin Mary with the Christ child, including a text which is an indulgence related to the veneration of the Name of Jesus. The same woodcut is present in the last of the controversial works printed by De Worde in the early years of his career, *Dives and Pauper* (1496). This is a dialogue between a rich and a poor man about the Ten Commandments in which the simple life is commended; it was probably written early in the fifteenth century and was considered to be dangerously close to Lollard views. Pynson had printed it in 1493, preceding De Worde's edition by three years, the only text of this nature that he produced in those early years. In Pynson's case we know that it was partly financed by the merchant John Russhe, and that 600 copies were printed, of which as many as thirty-one still survive. Once in print, the text obviously enjoyed much popularity, and it may in this form have attracted Lady Margaret's attention, for the presence of the woodcut relating to the Name of Jesus in De Worde's reprint would suggest a connection with her.

In recent literature the early phase of anti-Lollardry and the suppression of any discussion of theological issues in the vernacular, and hence the censoring of devotional texts in English, has been amply highlighted, but less attention has been paid to the phenomenon of their dissemination in print in the 1490s. More than one factor may have brought about a real change which set these texts before a larger public. Would Margaret Beaufort's influence have been decisive, without the connections she had with religious houses, in particular the Bridgettines at Syon Abbey, the Carthusians at Mountgrace, at Sheen, and in London? These houses all enjoyed royal protection, as did the Charterhouse of St Anne in Coventry, which is explicitly acknowledged in 1497 by De Worde in his edition of John Alcock's *Mons perfectionis* (which is an English text). Did Lady Margaret encourage the connections of these houses with the printer? Or was the generation of clerics and prelates who came to prominence in these years and who were associated with the courts of her son and herself – John Alcock, Richard Fitzjames, John Morton, Richard Fox, and John Fisher – less censorious? The English sermons of Alcock, Fitzjames and Fisher began to appear in print only a few years later. Was there perhaps generally a tendency to employ the medium of print for dissemination of religious texts in the English language, similar to Henry VII's decision that the statutes should be printed in English? And if so, did the authorities at that time foresee the scale of dissemination, the impact a text in print might have when freely available in hundreds of copies, not within the controlled confines of a religious house or a well-defined social class but at the unpredictable whim of market forces? Censorship of printed texts began only in the mid-1520s, in response to the Reformation. Margaret Beaufort's household accounts amply document her intense involvement with publishing and printing in the early years of the sixteenth century, until her death in 1509. For the years between 1490 and 1500 it is harder to unravel distinctions between her influence and the initiatives of others.

Touching inscriptions survive in printed devotional books as testimony of the way they were passed on as gifts among women in religious orders and high-ranking ladies. Notes and messages in such

Fig. 89 a & b. When De Worde reprinted this work from Pynson he added an attractive title-page showing the rich and the poor man in discussion. The text on the scroll in the woodcut printed at the end of the book reads: O in eterno memento do', and underneath is the only partly legible woodcut text of the indulgence for the Name of Jesus. The presence of this woodcut suggests that Margaret Beaufort may have encouraged this edition.

Dives and Pauper. Westminster, Wynkyn de Worde, 1496. London, BL, IB. 55197, fol. A1 recto, z6 recto.

devotional books indicate that among women the social pattern of ownership remained static for a long time. It is among readers in the high echelons of female society, in Syon Abbey and in Carthusian houses, that Margaret Beaufort's influence was most immediate, but her direct contact with the two main printers of the period, offering protection and stimulating their work, had a more enduring effect on much broader layers of society as a rapidly rising number of devotional works in English – not only formerly suppressed ones – began to circulate in the wider world. Works that were first published under the direct influence of either Margaret Beaufort or the religious houses were reprinted many times.

As for the two printers, Pynson and De Worde, as non-natives they may have been less sensitive than Caxton had been to the risks that publishing or owning these texts used to incur. Countering the movement towards private forms of devotion was unknown in the Low Countries and France in the fifteenth century. De Worde gave a clear indication where his preference lay by printing the *Chastising of God's children*, a formerly prohibited text, before he undertook anything else, and following this with other devotional works. The mysticism and the simplicity of faith that characterize the texts he first printed in the fifteenth century were similar to those of the Devotio Moderna in the Low Countries, which in Holland would have been at the root of his education. Another quite different manifestation of independence in religious views is De Worde's publication of Savonarola's unfinished sermon on the psalm *In te Domine speravi*, written in his prison cell just before his execution on 23 May 1498. It was probably one of the first works De Worde produced at his new address in Fleet Street, in the autumn of 1500, reprinting an edition published in Pavia in 1499. The question of where the initiative and incentive for particular publications should be sought can only be answered speculatively, but what seems beyond doubt is that Wynkyn de Worde was driven to publishing these works by genuine devotion, as before him Caxton had been driven by his love of translation and his own literary talent.

If few of such publications before the end of the fifteenth century were openly sponsored, this changed in the early years of the sixteenth. In 1503 Margaret Beaufort commissioned Pynson to print the first three books of Thomas a Kempis's *Imitatio Christi* in the translation of William Atkinson, and in the following year she had herself written a translation of the little-known fourth book of the *Imitatio*, which was then also printed by Pynson. In 1506 he also published her own translation of the Carthusian Jacobus de Gruytrode's *The mirroure of golde for the synfulle soule*. In those years Margaret Beaufort also commissioned (perhaps for the second time) the printing of offices of the Nova Festa, and in 1507 Pynson printed a Sarum breviary with her

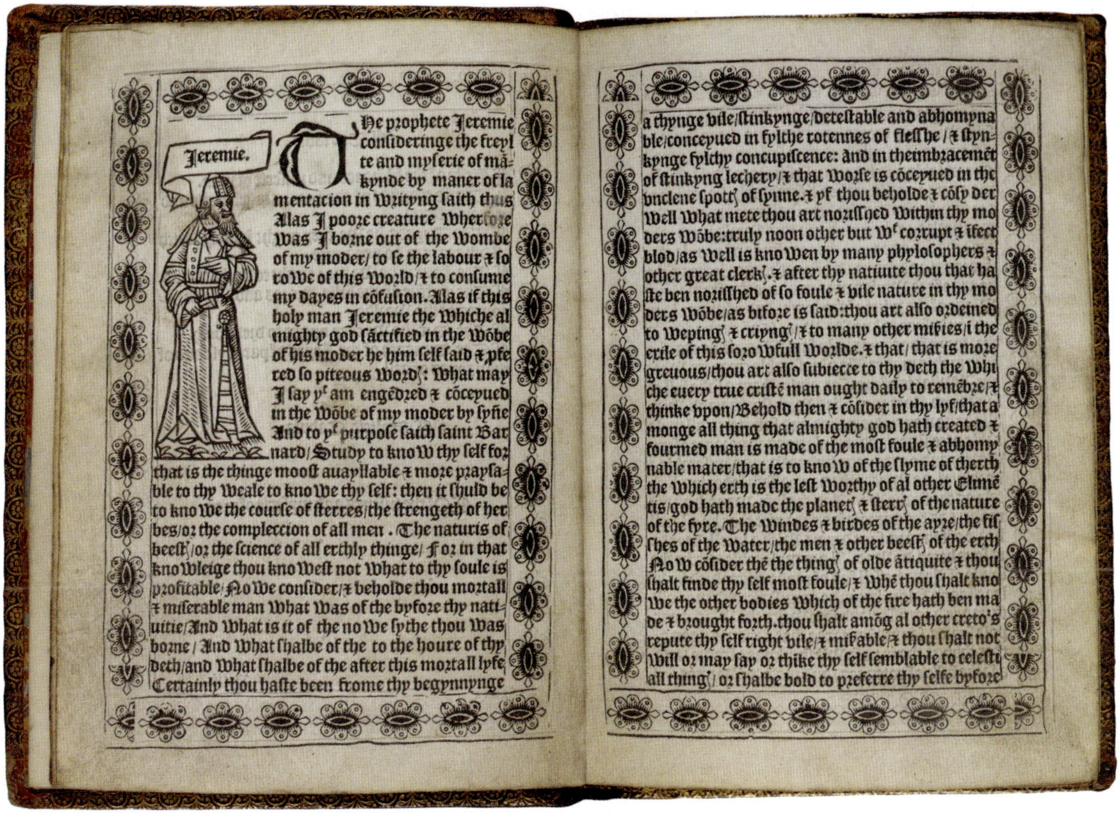

Fig. 90. A mirror for the soul. This devout treatise, originally in Latin, was translated from a French version into English by Margaret Beaufort. The text is divided into seven days of the week, every chapter presenting a new mirror in which to scrutinize the face of one's soul. Pynson framed the beginning of the text in ornate style, here reproduced from a copy printed on vellum.

Jacobus de Gruytrode, *Mirroure of golde for the synfull soule.* London, Richard Pynson, c. 1505. London, BL, C. 175.l.14, fol. B3 verso, B4 recto.

financial support. Her household accounts show that she bought books in large numbers from Pynson, sometimes in many copies, and that he was a frequent visitor to her palaces, laden with volumes she had ordered.

In 1508 and 1509, at the end of her life, she turned to De Worde for commissioned work, although she continued to buy books from Pynson. In colophons De Worde styles himself in those two years 'prynter unto the moost excellent pryncesse my lady the kynges moder', and after her son's death once 'prynter unto ... the kynges graundame'. In those few years De Worde printed for her translations of Sebastian Brant's *The shyppe of fooles* and of *The lyf of St Ursula*, as well as two editions of John Fisher's sermons on the penitential psalms and his funeral oration for her son, whose death preceded her own by two months. Some other works printed and frequently reprinted by him at this time, and which are aimed at a lay audience, are sometimes thought to have been instigated by her: *The parlyament of devils*, *Nychodemus Gospell*, and a different version of William Flete's *The remedy ayenst the troubles of temptacyon* from that published in 1499. But here it becomes more difficult to distinguish between her direct commissions, those of patrons she had influenced, and the demands of the widened audience she and the printers had succeeded in creating which encouraged printers to publish on their own account.

Dieu et mon droit.

This treatise concernynge the fruytfull saynges of Dauyd the kynge & prophete in the seuen penytencyall psalmes. Deuyded in seuen sermons was made and compyled by the ryght reuerente fader in god Iohan fyssher doctour of dyuynyte and bysshop of Rochester at the exortacion and sterynge of the moost excellente pryncesse Margarete countesse of Rychemount & Derby / & moder to our souerayne lorde kynge Henry the. vii.

Domine ne in furore.

Rendes this day I shall not declare to you ony parte of the epystle or gospelle / whiche perauenture ye abyde to here atte this tyme. But at the desire & instaunce of them (whome I may not contrary in ony thynge whiche is bothe accordynge to my dute and also to theyr soules helth). I haue taken vpon me shortely to declare the fyrst penytencyall psalme. Wherin I beseche almyghty god for his grete mercy and pyte so to helpe me this daye by his grace that whatsoeuer I shall say may fyrst be to his pleasure to the profyte of myn owne wretched soule / and also for the holsome comforte to all synners whiche be repentaunte for theyr synnes & hath tourned themselfe with al theyr hole herte & mynde vnto god / the way of wyckednes & synne vtterly forsaken. But or we go to the declaracyon of this psalme / it shall be profitable & conuenyent to shewe who dyde wryte this psalme / for what occasyon he wrote it / and what fruyte / profyte / & helpe he obteyned by the same Dauyd the sone of Iesse a man syngularly chosen of almyghty god / & endued with many grete benefytes / afterwarde he synned greuously ayenst god and his lawe / & for the occasyon of his grete offence / he made this holy

aa.ii.

Fig. 91 a & b. Reflections on the penitential psalms. John Fisher was from the mid-1490s in the service of Margaret Beaufort and became her spiritual director. His treatise, divided into seven sermons for daily reading, was compiled and presumably published 'at her exhortation'. Her portcullis badge on the title-page, and the initial at the beginning of the text with the same badge, emphasize her connection with the publication. The scene in the small woodcut is David spying on Bathsheba. This copy was printed on vellum.

John Fisher, *The fruytfull saynges of Davyd in the seven penytencyall psalmes*. London, Wynkyn de Worde, 1508. London, BL, G. 12026, fol. aa1 recto, aa2 recto.

In the fifteenth century (the period for which a more detailed calculation has been carried out than for the later years) more than half of De Worde's surviving production (57 per cent) is of devotional texts in English. Some were explicitly sponsored by prominent prelates. He printed and reprinted between 1496 and 1498 John Alcock's *Mons perfectionis* and several of his sermons; other texts by Alcock, then Bishop of Ely and councillor of the king, were later published by Pynson; Richard Fox, Bishop of Durham and Lord Privy Seal, commissioned De Worde in 1499 to print William de Touris's *Contemplation of sinners*. In 1501 he was also the sponsor of a liturgical work, a *Processionale ad usum Sarum*.

Yet many devotional texts show no sign of having been sponsored. The four editions of the allegorical *Charter* and *Abbey of the Holy Ghost* (1496, 1497, 1500, 1501), the *Meditations* of (pseudo-) St Bernard, translated by an anonymous 'scholar of the University of Cambridge' and printed three times (1496, 1498–9, 1525), *The three kings of Coleyne* (1499), reprinted at least once (1511), Margery Kempe's *Treatise of contemplation* (1501) and the reprint of Caxton's translation of Jacques le Grand, *The book of good manners* (1507), were apparently published on a commercial basis, even if some of them were perhaps prompted by De Worde's connections in religious houses. The risk of publishing a later edition of the very large *Golden legend* was shared with

Fig. 92. Reportage of a funeral. The scene in the woodcut is precisely as the title says: King Henry VII's body lying in state in St Paul's Cathedral as Bishop John Fisher holds the funeral oration.

Henry had died on 21 April 1509, and was given a state funeral on 10 May. First among the mourners at the Requiem Mass in St Paul's is Henry VIII, newly proclaimed successor to the throne; this is the earliest portrayal of him as king. The female figure by his right-hand side has to be identified as his grandmother, Margaret Beaufort, mourning her only child. The sermon was printed 'at [her] specyall request'.

John Fisher, *Sermon: The sermon ... sayd in the Cathedrall chyrche of saynt Poule ... the body beynge present of ... kynge Henry the .vij. the .x.* day of Maye ... M. CCCCC. IX. London, Wynkyn de Worde, May 1509. London, BL, G. 1201, fol. A1 recto.

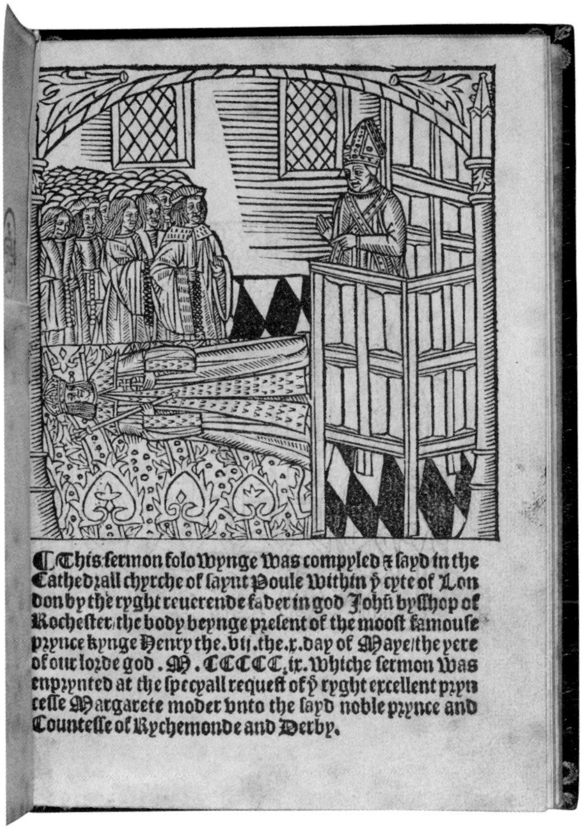

This sermon folowynge was compyled & sayd in the Cathedrall chyrche of saynt Poule within ŷ cyte of London by the ryght reuerende fader in god Iohñ bysshop of Rochester/the body beynge present of the moost famouse prynce kynge Henry the.vij.the.x.day of Maye/the yere of our lorde god. M. CCCCC.ix. whiche sermon was enprynted at the specyall requeest of ŷ ryght excellent pryncesse Margarete moder vnto the sayd noble prynce and Countesse of Rychemonde and Derby.

Fig. 93. Margaret Beaufort survived her son for just over two months, and died on 29 June 1509. Bishop John Fisher officiated at her 'moneth mynde', the Requiem Mass a month after her death.

Wynkyn de Worde printed Fisher's eulogy, and frugally adapted the woodcut that had depicted Henry VII's funeral by cutting out the king's body and replacing it with a bier with candles. The mourners remained the same, the female figure flanking king Henry now representing his spouse, Catherine of Aragon, whom he had married on 11 June.

John Fisher, *A mornynge remembraunce had at the moneth mynde of Margarete countesse of Rychemonde*. London, Wynkyn de Worde, July 1509. London, BL, G. 1202, fol. A1 recto.

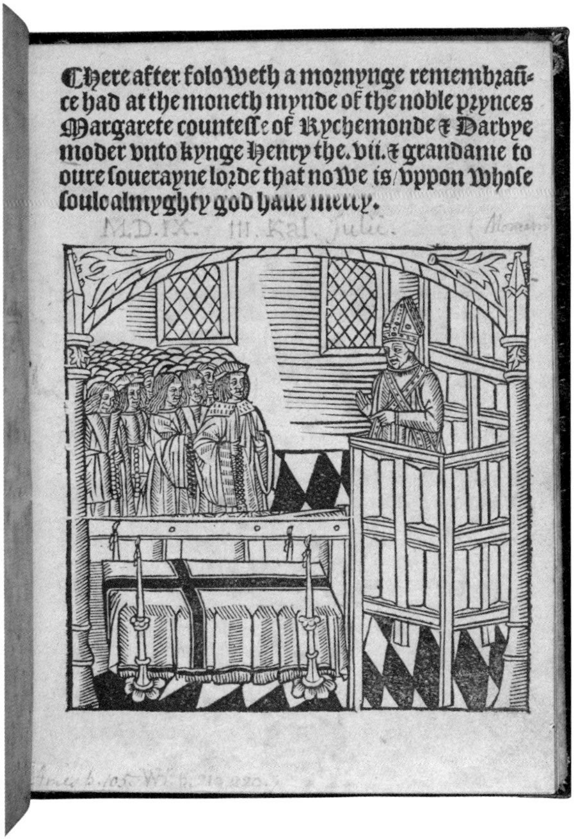

Here after foloweth a mornynge remembrãce had at the moneth mynde of the noble prynces Margarete countesse of Rychemonde & Darbye moder vnto kynge Henry the.vii.& grandame to oure souerayne lorde that now is/vppon whose soule almyghty god haue mercy.

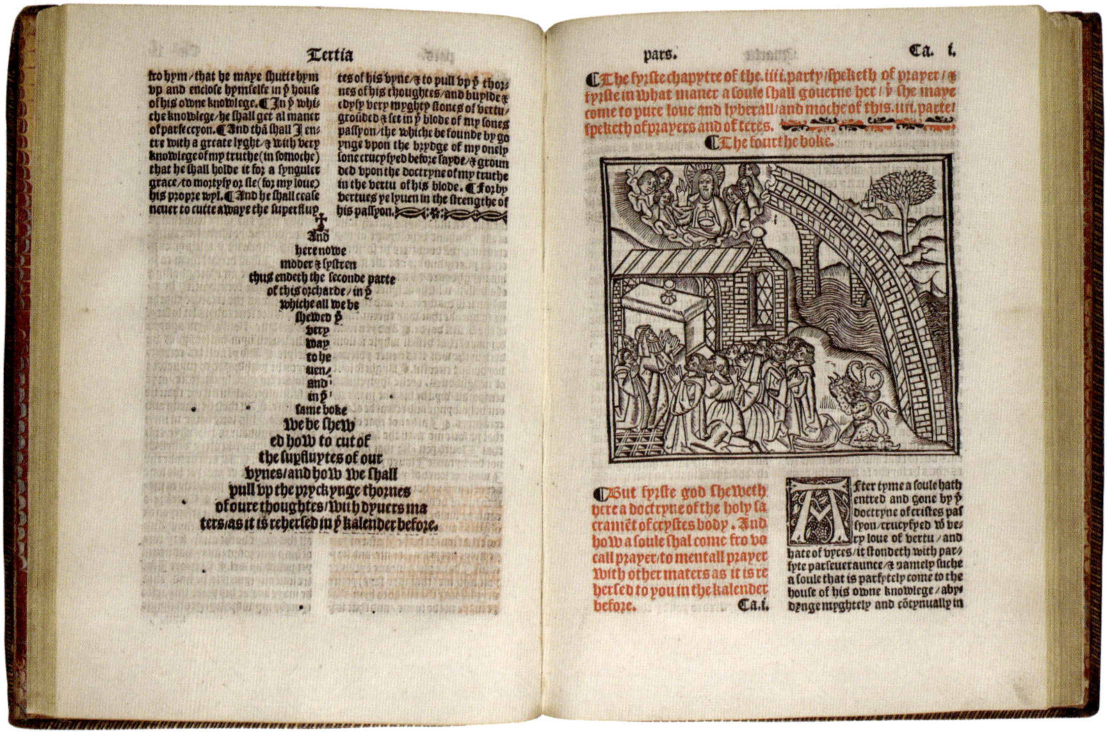

Fig. 94. In the middle of the fifteenth century, the mystical vision of Catherine of Siena (d. 1380), known as the *Dialogo della divina providenza*, was translated for the nuns of Syon from a Latin version into English. The translation was given an allegorical framework of paths though an orchard, all leading to a bridge to heaven.

After the English text was rediscovered at Syon and the decision was made to publish it in print, the allegory was the inspiration for eight elaborate woodcuts. No effort was spared in the printing-house: the woodcuts, red printing, and fine initials, are complemented by the typesetting which expresses in its own way the narrowness of the bridge.

The Orcharde of Syon. London, Wynkyn de Worde, 1519. London, BL, C. 11.b.6, fol. i4 verso, i5 recto.

Pynson in 1507, but six other editions were at De Worde's sole expense (1493, 1499, 1503, 1512, 1521, 1527). Pynson eagerly reprinted several of the devotional books, where De Worde usually led.

Connections with the Bridgettines at Syon Abbey recurred until the end of De Worde's life. Thomas Betson was a monk, scribe, and probably a librarian at the abbey, and his *Profytable treatyse to dyspose men to be vertuously occupied*, published in 1500, ends abruptly with the exhortation 'Lerne to kepe your bokes clene'. In 1519 Richard Sutton, founder of Brasenose College in Oxford and steward of Syon Abbey since 1513, paid for De Worde's printing of *The orcherd of Syon*, a translation of the revelations of St Catherine of Siena, from a manuscript he had found forgotten in a corner at the abbey. The book was splendidly printed with much use of red, and illustrated with spectacular woodcuts. It was followed in 1520 by a more modest publication connected with Syon, the *Dyetary of ghostly helthe*.

Syon was a source for much religious printing, some of it not connected with named authors. Richard Faques, a bookseller who was probably a relative of William, the first King's Printer and who used some of his material, published in 1530 the anonymous *The mirrour of Our Lady*, 'imprynted at the desyre and instaunce of the worshypfull and devoute lady Abbesse of the worshypfull Monastery of Syon. And the reverende fader in god. Generall confessoure of the same'.

Several men of great learning had joined the abbey and maintained contacts with the London printers, among them William Bonde and

Richard Whitford. Bonde's very large *Pylgrimage of perfection* was first printed by Pynson in 1526, and an extended version by De Worde in 1531. Richard Whitford, who was an impassioned opponent of the Reformation, was the most prolific of the authors at Syon. His *A werke for householders*, first published by Robert Redman in 1530, became a bestseller and was reprinted at least six times before 1538. It was followed in 1532 by his *Pype or tonne of the life of perfection*, also printed by Robert Redman, which was almost equally successful. In his much reprinted *Dayly exercyse and experyence of dethe* he observed, 'Bycause that wrytynge unto me is very tedyous I thought better to put it in print'. That in these years the monks at Syon encouraged the printing of texts for lay readers appears also from the publication of *The pomander of prayer*, written by a Carthusian at Sheen, and published by Robert Copland in 1528 and 1530 with a preface written anonymously by a brother at Syon.

When we compare the publishing of devotional works in the three successive decades between 1480 and 1510, we can observe an unmistakable development.

Caxton seems to have been intent on avoiding risks, and the prohibitions of the Arundel Constitutions still loomed large. Most of the English devotional texts he printed were his own translations from the French, and had thus not been subject to the debates and suppression that had continued from 1409. Caxton's main ecclesiastical connection was with the Benedictine Order at Westminster Abbey. When at the end of his life he printed two texts with a Bridgettine slant, they were commissioned by Henry VII's wife and mother.

In the 1490s Margaret Beaufort's influence on printing intensified, as she initially employed both Pynson and De Worde. After a radical start with a formerly suppressed text, De Worde, partly supported by Margaret Beaufort but increasingly by other high-ranking patrons, published in this decade more than forty devotional works, large books, but also sermons and other small works that were often sold (and now preserved in bindings) several at a time as compilations. He was apparently untroubled by censorship, and succeeded in mediating to a wider lay public works that had formerly been confined mainly to the closed orders of the Carthusians and the Bridgettines. Several were rapidly reprinted. Obviously, there was a high demand for newly available texts of a contemplative, devotional nature. Meanwhile, the public's desire to own Mirk's *Festial* and the *Quattuor sermones* was apparently insatiable, and De Worde contributed his share of the twenty-three known editions of this work.

The third decade, from 1500, is a period of intensification of the publishing of devotional works by Pynson and De Worde. In 1507 they shared the cost of printing two major works, *The golden legend* and the *Royal book* – both translations by Caxton and originally published by him. Margaret Beaufort enthusiastically promoted the dissemination of texts in English, including a translation of the *Imitatio Christi* which she bought in bulk to give away. She herself contributed two important translations. Apart from sponsored publications, both printers published devotional works in English at their own risk, in response to increasing demands of a new reading public. Apparently, discussion by laymen of the theological principles expounded in these works, and private devotion as opposed to formal and public celebration, were in practice no longer prohibited by the Church. In other words, the leaders of the Church in England had responded to the new medium of print, not only by accepting it but also by actively using it. As long as no new heterodox ideas were disseminated through the press, as they later were in response to Martin Luther's words, the Church in England acquiesced, and even modernized itself, taking in the new tendency towards personal piety.

The acceptance of once banned texts that had developed between 1490 and 1510 continued for another decade, by which time they had become popular and were frequently reprinted. The first intimations of Lutheranism to reach England brought a halt to this process. In the 1520s the authorities rapidly recognized that the medium of print would be the principal conduit for heresy to spread. But the two printers who had been instrumental in bringing devotional literature to a larger readership were by the 1520s in their old age, and did not show signs of changing course in response to the events that were now taking place. In October 1524 the Bishop of London, Cuthbert Tunstall, summoned the booksellers of London and warned them against importing Lutheran books, or selling any they had in stock. New imports were to be submitted for approval to the Archbishop of Canterbury, the Bishop of London or the Bishop of Rochester. Apparently, the same censorship applied to books printed in England, in any case of texts translated into English, which were seen as another form of importation of foreign material.

Wynkyn de Worde, who for over thirty years had grown used to printing English devotional texts as he saw fit, fell foul of the new measures. He and John Gough, his former apprentice who had translated the work in question, were summoned a year later to the Consistory Court to be admonished for printing an unorthodox text, *The ymage of love*, without permission. The author of the original Latin version is revealed in the later edition (of 1532) as John Ryckes, 'an observant fryre', who can be identified as belonging to the Observant Franciscan house at Greenwich. He was a learned man, who was from 1503 a Fellow of Corpus Christi College in Cambridge, and who was twice appointed university preacher, in 1511 and 1515, before taking orders. In *The ymage of love* he contested the veneration of statues and images, quoting many patristic sources. Thomas More discussed and rejected its arguments in the second edition (1530) of his *Dialogue concerning heresies*, possibly adding this to his first version at the request of church authorities, who distrusted the implications of the evangelical stance of the book.

Gough, who was an ardent evangelist, addressed his translation to 'good ladyes ... spouses of Christ', apparently referring to the nuns at Syon. The report of the court case is still extant, which allows us a glimpse into the circumstances of this publication. Gough confessed that he had obtained the text from a certain Edward Lockwood, of the parish of St Bride's, and that immediately after publication (in October 1525) he had donated a copy to each of the sixty nuns at Syon abbey. De Worde declared that he had sold as many, and the court ordered him to retrieve those, as well as copies sent (on commission?) to the universities of Oxford and Cambridge. The two got off with a warning, which did not prevent them from publishing the work again some seven years later, this time even protected by royal privilege, despite More's arguments.

Of a different dimension in the history of the English Reformation is Bishop Tunstall's refusal in 1523/4 to support William Tyndale's translation of the New Testament from the Greek. His work was influenced by Erasmus's edition of the Greek New Testament as well as his new translation into Latin, and also Luther's German translation; the reformatory nature of Tyndale's translation was beyond doubt. Upon Tunstall's refusal, Tyndale first went to Cologne, where Peter Quentell began to print a version of the translation until he was stopped by the local authorities. A few sheets of this unfinished work may have reached England. Tyndale then fled with his work to Worms, where the printer Peter Schoeffer (a son of the great printer in Mainz) printed a smaller version, without expository notes, and completed it in 1526. Thousands of copies were shipped to England, where the Arundel Constitution was invoked to seize and burn them. Bishop Tunstall himself warned the booksellers again, and in October 1526 arranged a public burning of the books at St Paul's Cross. The fact that of the thousands of copies that once reached England only two survive (one other complete copy, now in Stuttgart, was never in England) shows that suppression was indeed wholly effective.

Several short tracts by Tyndale were subsequently printed on the Continent, one in Worms, but most in Antwerp, where their printers were soon prosecuted under the edicts of the Emperor Charles V. Despite the risk of severe punishment, reprints of the New Testament were followed by Tyndale's translation from the Hebrew of the Pentateuch, also printed in Antwerp with a false address. Suppressed like the New Testament, its survival is equally rare.

In 1529 the first royal proclamation against the spread of heresy appeared, including the prohibition of heretical books. But the Church changed its standpoint on English translations of the Scriptures, and the Convocation of Canterbury petitioned the Crown for an English version, without immediate result. Yet an English version that owed much to Tyndale, the Coverdale Bible, printed in Cologne in 1535, was imported without suppression, followed by editions printed in Antwerp. The printing of the Bible known as 'the Great Bible', the version eventually authorized in 1541 by Henry VIII for use in every church in England, was begun in Paris, but completed in London in 1539. Until then the linchpin of the English Reformation – the Bible made accessible by its translation into English – had been entirely the work and the risk of printers on the Continent.

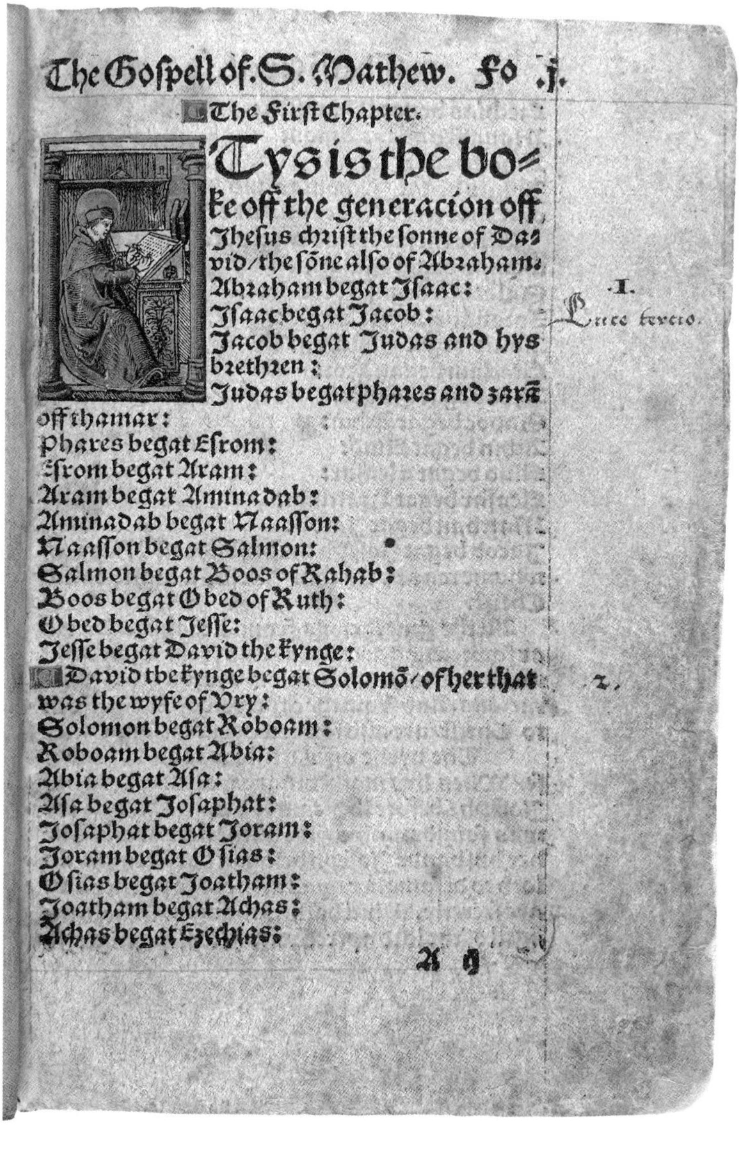

The Gospell of S. Mathew. Fo .j.
The First Chapter.
Tys is the boke off the generacion off
Jhesus christ the sonne of Da=
vid/the sõne also of Abraham.
Abraham begat Isaac: I.
Isaac begat Jacob: Luce tercio.
Jacob begat Judas and hys
brethren:
Judas begat phares and zarã
off thamar:
Phares begat Esrom:
Esrom begat Aram:
Aram begat Aminadab:
Aminadab begat Naasson:
Naasson begat Salmon:
Salmon begat Boos of Rahab:
Boos begat Obed of Ruth:
Obed begat Jesse:
Jesse begat David the kynge:
David the kynge begat Solomõ/of her that 2.
was the wyfe of Ury:
Solomon begat Roboam:
Roboam begat Abia:
Abia begat Asa:
Asa begat Josaphat:
Josaphat begat Joram:
Joram begat Osias:
Osias begat Joatham:
Joatham begat Achas:
Achas begat Ezechias:
A ij

Fig. 95. One of only two copies of Tyndale's Bible translation that reached England but escaped public burning is now in the British Library. The other (of which a fragment survives) is at St Paul's Cathedral

Bible, New testament. In the translation into English of William Tyndale. Worms, Peter Schoeffer the Younger, 1526. London, BL, C. 188.a.17, fol. A2 recto.

18

Contemporaries outside the mainstream

In 1534, the twenty-fifth year of Henry VIII's reign, the statute of 1484 exempting alien traders in all branches of the book trade from protective restrictions imposed on all other trades was declared void by Parliament in a new statute. This, its preamble says, was in response to the fact that, since the issuing of the former act, 'many of this Realme being the Kynges naturall subjectes have geven theyme soo dylygently to lerne and exercyse the seid craft of pryntyng that at this day there be within this Realme a greate nombre connyng and expert in the seid science or craft of pryntyng as abyll to exercyse the seid craft in all poyntes as any Stranger in any other Realme or Countre'. The Act did indeed respond to a changed balance in the trade, for distinctions that had persisted during the main periods of activity of the first and second generations of printers in England had diminished when the third generation had grown up to take over. When we read the will Wynkyn de Worde drew up in the summer of 1534, the year the new statute was promulgated, we can see for ourselves the changes referred to in it. De Worde, an alien (denizened since 1496 but nonetheless an alien), had by the end of his life formed a household with apprentices, journeymen, and servants almost all of whom were English, and enjoyed friendships with neighbours and with a circle of native-born colleagues who had also been apprentices and journeymen. There are only two Dutch names among the many beneficiaries named in his will. Robert Maas, who received a modest bequest, appears to have been a domestic servant. The bequest to Hercules Diricke, the pouchmaker's son referred to earlier, was apparently an act of charity unconnected with De Worde's professional contacts. His will reflects, in the words of Paul Christianson, who has extensively studied the London book trade of the time, 'the successful merging of commercial interests on the part of the London stationers and of foreign bookmen. By 1534 that merger was already well in place.'

The process of the rise of distinct communities of bookmen in London and the eventual integration of their national identities took sixty years. From early in the fifteenth century the greatest concentration of the book trade in England was in the City of London, located round St Paul's Cathedral. Here a community of scribes, illuminators (or 'limners'), binders and booksellers had consolidated and had begun to regulate itself as a 'mistery' or small guild. They were located near the sites where the literate customers for books worked and lived: schoolmasters and lawyers. The profession of 'stationer', already traditional in universities, became dominant and united the various functions of book production and book selling, their oversight in the hands of the guild. Much later, in 1557, their organization in London was to receive the royal charter of incorporation as 'The Stationers' Company'.

Until the arrival of printing, the professions of the book in London were largely in the hands of Englishmen. This changed with the gradual introduction of printed books. We know that the first printed books to arrive in England were bought overseas by travelling prelates and diplomats, such as John Russell and Bishop James Goldwell. The two Gutenberg Bibles that were decorated in London, probably within a decade of their printing (see fig. 1), may have been brought in as items in the baggage of a Benedictine or Carthusian visitor. But such individual events cannot be classified as trade. Trade in books printed abroad began at approximately the same time as Caxton began to print English books. An anonymous printer, probably in the southern Netherlands, produced *circa* 1475 a one-off breviary for Salisbury use; apart from Caxton's books it is the first book printed overseas for the market in England. In terms of the book trade, Caxton is well recognized as a pioneer, but he was also an eccentric: by locating himself outside the City of London, by apparently having nothing or very little to do with the book trade established there, by printing only few English texts for which demand was already well established in manuscript, and by preferring instead new translations by several others and above all by himself.

There was, however, a demand for printed books which grew as the medium became better known in England and which Caxton's production could not meet, in particular a demand for Latin works of learning, teaching, and liturgy. There was more than one way to meet such demand and further stimulate the market for the new product. We have already seen that two printing firms in Cologne successively (in 1478 and 1481) decided to open a branch in Oxford to produce books on the spot in response to local demand instead of shipping them in from overseas. There is good evidence that in Oxford they interacted quite successfully with the local community of scholars, and the second enterprise, that of Theodericus Rood, even published once in partnership with Oxford University's Stationarius, Thomas Hunt. But these enterprises did not last long. The pattern was briefly repeated in Oxford by John Scolar in 1517–18 and in Cambridge by Johannes Siberch in 1520–23.

We have also seen that in the City of London a Draper, William Wilcock, engaged in 1480 a printer from Rome, Johannes Lettou, to print two learned Latin books. Lettou then continued as a small printing house in the City in partnership with another alien, William de Machlinia, specializing in books for which the demand was strictly local, books of the common law and Statutes in Law-French.

Enterprising printers in some of the great centres of printing on the Continent sensed there was a business opportunity in England, but until the 1490s the number of named continental printers who produced books for use in England – liturgies for Salisbury use and Latin schoolbooks with a few words in English – was limited to no more than six: single liturgical works in Venice, Paris and Basel, a few schoolbooks in Louvain, Antwerp and Deventer. In the 1490s missals for Salisbury use were printed in Paris, and in Speyer by the liturgical specialist Peter Drach, but from that time printing for the English market concentrated in Paris and the seaboard of the Narrow Seas from Normandy to Antwerp. Before 1500, printers in Paris and Rouen printed books of hours and missals for Salisbury use, and several editions of the English *Festial*. In Antwerp, Gheraert Leeu, who printed some books for the English market from 1486, reprinted after Caxton's death two of his titles, the *History of Jason* and the *Chronicles of England*, a venture that ended following his own accidental death in 1493. But in the period 1500–35 the number of books printed exclusively for the English market – either on commission or speculatively – grew to thirty-eight printed in Paris and eighteen in Rouen, a far greater variety of titles than before. Stationers in London (including Pynson and De Worde) and a few in the provinces, relied on the specialist skills of printers in these great continental centres, who at other times were undoubtedly considered to be competitors.

In the first three decades of the sixteenth century no fewer than fourteen printers in Antwerp printed in English or for England, a trade that changed in character with the Reformation when for a while they became the main support for the dissemination of prohibited Protestant texts, including English Bible translations. As we have already seen, the most famous and influential Bible translation, Tyndale's of the New Testament, was printed in Worms in 1526. But the dramatic story of English Bible translations and the printing of heterodox texts on the Continent falls outside the scope of the present book.

Books printed for the English market were imported along with many Latin books which were in demand throughout the Latin-reading world. They all came in through the ports, printers operating a system of agents who took care of distribution of the works in England, and at times acted as publishers and financial backers. The career-path of one such publisher/agent can be followed, beginning with a series of eight service books (breviaries, missals and a Book of Hours) for the use of the diocese of York as well as of Salisbury, printed between 1493 and 1495 in Venice by Johannes Hertzog de Landoia for Frederick Egmondt and Gerardus Barrevelt. The two Dutchmen worked in association, and Egmondt was the London agent. He is also named in 1499 as the backer of Pynson's dictionary, the *Promptorium parvulorum*, this time with an otherwise unknown associate named Petrus Post Pascha. In 1502 the dedicatory letter to a Paris edition of Johannes de Garlandia's *Equivoca*, a textbook for which there was enduring demand, reveals that the book was to be sold in the shop of Frederick Egmondt, 'the most reliable bookseller in your most excellent land of England'. Some of the books he sold can be recognized by fine panel bindings that bear his name. As publisher, agent and bookseller, Egmondt knew how to establish contacts in many different worlds.

Fig. 96. A panel binding for Frederick Egmondt includes green men holding a shield with his device. His name appears in full at the bottom of the panel.

London, BL, C. 188.a.15, rubbing of part of binding.

Although the number of books printed specifically for the English market in Paris and Rouen grew very significantly from the 1490s on, and continued to grow in the sixteenth century, their numbers are dwarfed by the importation of Latin books produced in Venice, Strasbourg, Cologne, Basel, Paris, and Lyon, the great centres of publishing for the world of learning. Their publishing strategy was aimed at the whole world of learning, including England. Books were imported into England by agents, middlemen who were usually aliens, their transactions known through the record of the import duties they had to pay, which survives more completely than the records of the importation by native Englishmen such as Caxton. In 1478 an importer recorded as 'John of Acon', identified as Johannes de Westfalia, from 1474 to 1500 the greatest printer in the university town of Louvain, first appears in the Petty Customs Rolls of the Port of London, and he continued to pay import duties until 1491. A document dated 1483 survives in which Thomas Hunt, the stationer of the University of Oxford, records his imports from John of Acon in association with Petrus Actors, who was in this period the greatest importer of books. He, a Savoyard, imported between 1478 and 1491 more than 1,300 books, mainly for the University of Oxford. In 1485 he became Royal Stationer to Henry VII, which gave him the advantage of freedom from import duties.

In 1483 another name recorded on the rolls is Henry Frankenbergh. He continued until 1485 with a large number of books. With a Bernard van Stondo, of Utrecht, Frankenbergh established in 1482 a household with five servants in Langbourne Ward in the City, and *circa* 1485 his name appears in the colophon of the *Speculum Christiani* as having financed this publication, printed by William de Machlinia at his nearby address at Fleet Bridge.

The London trade in printed books was for a long time dominated by aliens, by 1484 already so well established that Richard III's statute that gave them freedom to operate can be understood as recognition that they were an irreplaceable link to the publishing industry that had sprung up on the Continent. The sole disadvantage for the aliens was the high duties they had to pay. Caxton, a native Englishman who

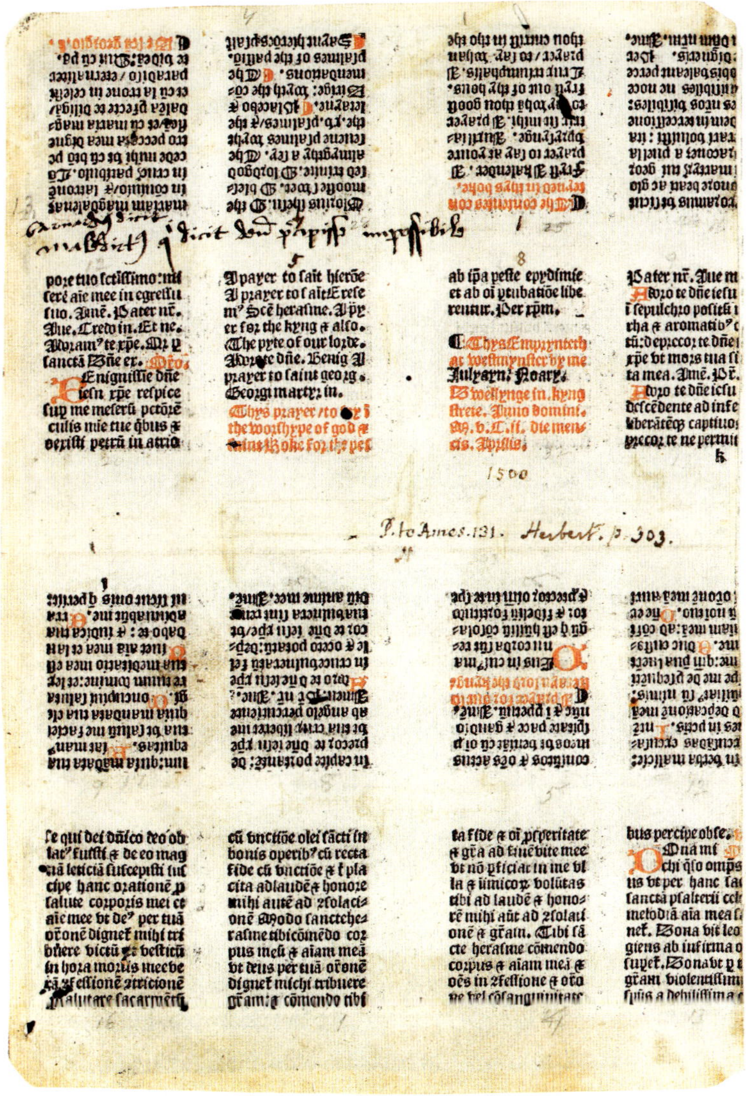

Fig. 97. Julian Notary was a printer with specialist skills. Two-colour printing was one of them, and here he tried his hand at the extremely small format of 64°, meaning that the full sheet would be folded six times in all. Notary had the very small fount of type required to bring this off, but the imposition of this format was complicated and unfamiliar. Several pages in the present half-sheet are in the wrong place. It is a rough proof, marked up in the printing house, and survived as printer's waste.

Horae ad usum Sarum. Westminster, Julian Notary, 1500. Trial sheet for quire k. Melbourne, State Library of Victoria.

undoubtedly imported more books than are shown on the defective record, had to pay less.

Frankenbergh's household is similar to that of Lettou and De Machlinia in that they were all aliens, living together, with servants of the same nationality as their own, reflecting on a small scale the 'nations' of merchants in the great trading cities. Paul Christianson has identified several other such households of aliens in the same area. They all lived close to the Hanseatic settlement of German merchants at the Steelyard. As these aliens and their alien trade settled, the old trade round St Paul's Cathedral continued as before. The scribes, limners and bookbinders seem not to have objected to the newcomers, and only one lone voice is recorded as grumbling about the arrival of print. Print also brought new business to the auxiliary trades of decorating, binding, and retailing. We see therefore in a

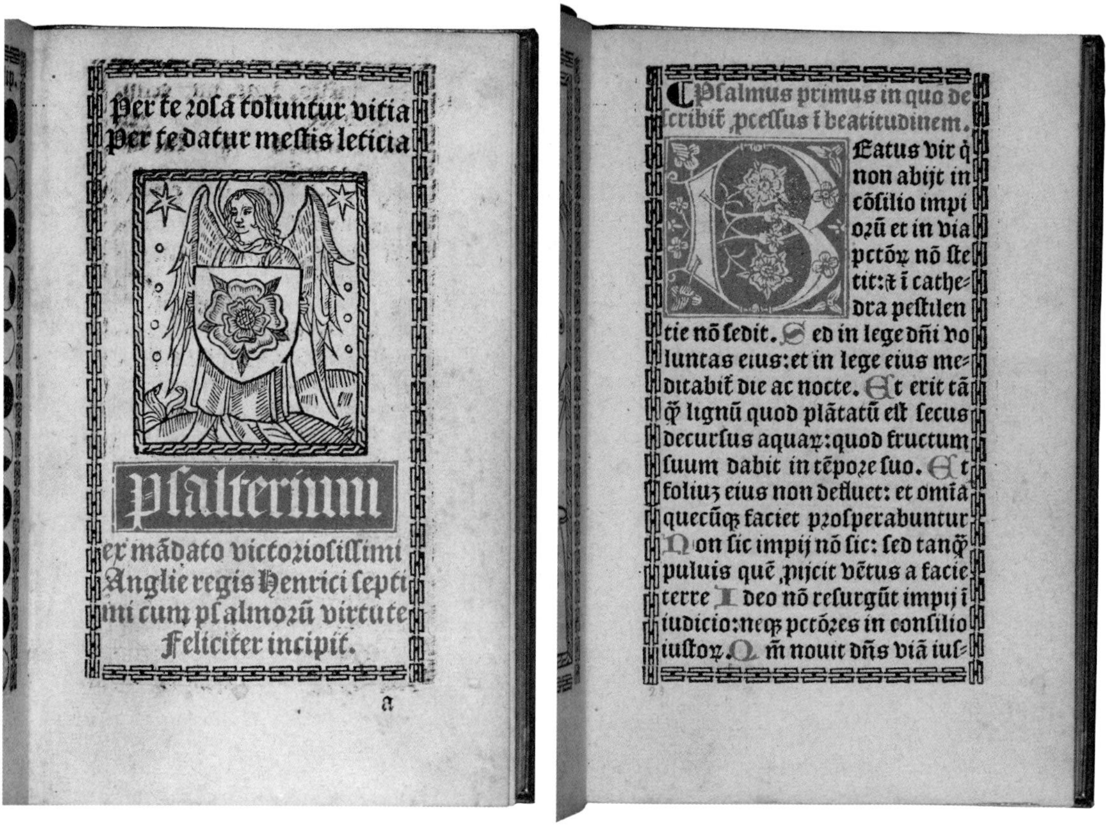

Fig. 98 a & b. The psalter which Henry VII commissioned from William Faques, then king's printer, is executed with skilful two-colour printing and with fine woodcuts and initials.

Psalterium. London, William Faques, 1504. London, BL, G. 12150, fol. a1 recto, a2 recto.

limited space four communities largely leaving one another alone in the manner characteristic for a metropolis: in the City of London the old established stationers, the newcomer importers of printed books, and the printers, the last two very occasionally interacting, and lastly, in Westminster Caxton's idiosyncratic business, succeeded for a while by Wynkyn de Worde. Oxford and St Albans were remote from this small but cosmopolitan community.

While in the 1490s De Worde and Pynson held a monopoly in printing in England, this changed at the turn of the century when they no longer worked in isolation, and the change was partly of their own making. Their moves to Fleet Street are a clear signal that they, literally, no longer wished to distance themselves from the central location of the book trade at St Paul's Churchyard.

A few new printers were beginning to appear on the scene. First Julian Notary and his associates arrived from France. In 1497 they were engaged by De Worde, who provided them with some material and made use of their special skill in red printing by commissioning a Book of Hours and, in 1498, a missal for Salisbury use. Notary, a native of Vannes in Brittany, continued until 1520 partly as an independent, printing in all some thirty-five books; his work remained closely linked with that of De Worde, but he was also a major importer of books.

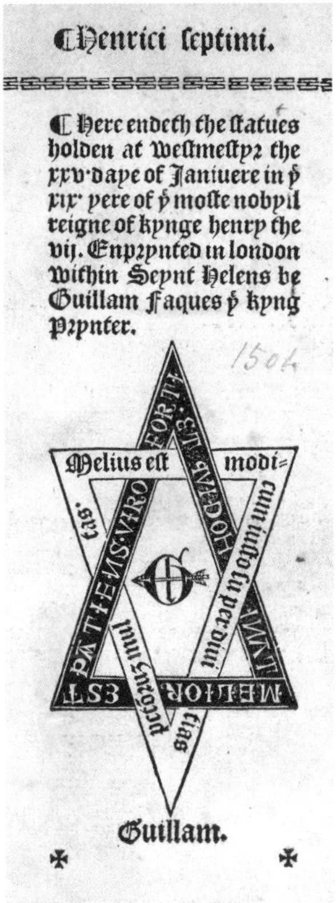

Fig. 99 a & b. One of the few official publications by Faques in the newly created function of king's printer was produced in highly ornamental fashion. The woodcut calligraphic S on the title-page is in a style associated with chanceries, and emphasizes the authority of the statutes, even when presented in print. In the colophon Faques identified himself as King's Printer.

Statutes of Parliament of the nineteenth year of the reign of Henry VII. London, William Faques, *c.* 1504. London, BL, C. 122.f.9, fol. A1 recto (title), C8 recto (device, detail).

William Faques, a native of Normandy, produced a few school-books before he became King's Printer in 1504, a newly instituted title. In this capacity he printed a proclamation and the statutes of Henry VII's last parliament. Since the position was new, the rights attached were unclear, and both official publications were soon reprinted by others. His most significant publication is a beautiful psalter, printed in 1504 'ex mandato ... regis Henrici septimi'. After Pynson succeeded him as King's printer in 1506/7 William Faques did not continue in the business (he became the king's librarian), and we hear no more of him.

A master printer always works with a team, compositors and press-men, a corrector who perhaps may also be the supervisor or foreman, in a hierarchy of journeymen and apprentices whose interdependent actions ideally slot together like clockwork. A printing house that

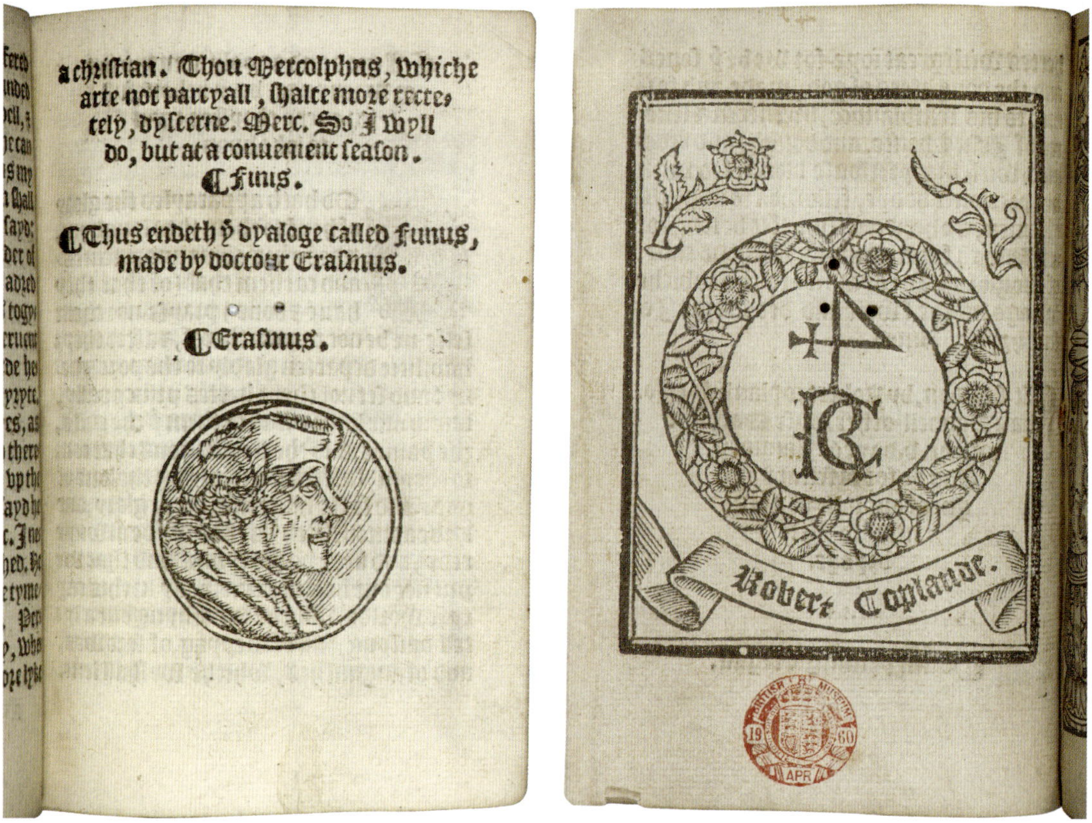

conforms to this common pattern, whether regulated by a guild or not, brings forth a new generation of professionals. The two printing houses that were dominant between 1491 and 1535, Pynson's and De Worde's, employed English journeymen, some of whom became independent printers. One might therefore expect the process described in the Act of 1534, the gradual transition to a new generation of independent printers who had been brought up by working in the two dominant printing houses – whether formally as apprentices and journeymen or not – to have taken effect not later than 1505–10. Indeed, several Englishmen known to have worked with De Worde set up as independent printers, but none of them produced an oeuvre in any way comparable to his.

The best known of De Worde's apprentices is Robert Copland, whom he nominated to be one of the executors of his will in 1534. Copland is best remembered for his translations of French light poetry and romances which were published by De Worde from 1505. In 1514 Copland printed two books under his own name at De Worde's press, and a year later he opened his own printing house in Fleet Street, named The Rose Garland in defiance of the smells of the nearby River Fleet. Copland seems to have been more preoccupied with his translations than with publishing and printing. Until his

Fig. 100 a & b. The translation of Erasmus's satirical dialogue *Funus* ('Last rites') is anonymous. The text is anti-clerical, and especially directed against parish priests and the mendicant orders preying on the rich. It survives as the first in a collection of three short anti-clerical texts by or associated with Erasmus. The medallion printed at the end of the text is a copy of Hans Holbein's engraving first published by Froben in Basel. The book ends with Copland's printer's device, a garland of roses surrounding his merchant's mark.

Desiderius Erasmus, Colloquium *Funus*, translated into English. London, Robert Copland for John Byddell, 1534. London, BL, C. 108.bb.29/1, fol. D2 recto, D4 verso

¶ The dialoge be-
twene Julius the
seconde / Ge-
nius / and saynt
Peter.
¶ Reader, refrayne
from laughynge.

¶ A dyaloge made by a certayne fa-
mous lerned man, pleasaunt & fru-
tefull, shewyng how Julius the
second, a grete bisshop of Rome
knockyng after his dethe at ye
gates of heuen, coude not be
suffred to come in. Saynt
Peter beynge ye porter,
albeit yt in his lyfe ty
me he was called
moost holy, yea
& by the name
of holynesse
it selfe / &
therto
a grete cõ-
querour in ma
ny batayls / wher
by he supposed hĩselfe
also to be ye lorde of heuen.

¶ Spekers in this dyaloge ben these
Julius. Genius and Petrus.

¶ Julius

Fig. 101 a & b. 'Reader, refrain from laughing.' The anti-papal satire *Julius exclusus*, or *Pope Julius barred from Heaven*, has generally been ascribed to Erasmus, although he denied authorship. It is now thought to be the work of the humanist and diplomat Richard Pace. This is the first edition of an anonymous translation into English, after which the text became popular. It survives in a unique copy together with the translation of Erasmus's *Funus*.

The dialogue between Julius II, Genius and St Peter. London, Robert Copland for John Byddell, c. 1534. London, BL, C. 108.bb.29/3, fol. [a]1 recto, [a]1 verso.

death in 1547 he published some thirty-five substantial works, while he produced a constant stream of translations which ranged from the early *Complaynt of them that be to soone maryed* (in verse) to a dancing manual, a navigational route book entitled *The rutter of the see*, his own translation of a *Colloquium* of Erasmus, and a treatise on the art of memory. When in his translation of the prose romance *Kynge Appolyn of Thyre* he declared he was following the trail of 'his mayster' Caxton, he may have alluded to him as translator from the French rather than as a printer.

In his will De Worde appointed apart from Copland four other executors: three printers who must have been old and trusted friends, Henry Watson, Henry Pepwell, and John Gough, and a younger one, John Gaver. All except Gaver were native Englishmen. Henry Watson, who had been an apprentice of De Worde, briefly worked in his own printing house at Charing Cross in partnership with Hugo Goes, but the enterprise did not last, and no more than two titles were produced. Goes, whose name is Dutch, had worked between 1506 and 1509 at York with a fount of type that De Worde had discarded. Henry Pepwell, a native Englishman who had a shop in St Paul's Churchyard, printed only twelve books between 1518 and 1531, among them Erasmus's translation in Latin verse of a tract by John Colet. He was high ranking among the booksellers, and De Worde did not call him a former servant. John Gough had been in De Worde's service and from 1523 was a stationer. Gough was the translator of John Ryckes's *The ymage of love*, discussed above, which he published again in 1532, printed for him by De Worde. Other publications by Gough appeared occasionally until 1546. James Gaver continued in De Worde's business at The Sign of the Sonne in partnership with John Byddell. Gaver was a bookbinder and bookseller of Dutch descent, and issued in 1539 the only book, a Stanbridge *Accidence*, to bear his name. Two other beneficiaries of De Worde's will, John Butler and John Byddell, had apparently been more recently in his service. John Butler was a bookseller in Fleet Street, who published nine books between 1528 and 1531. Byddell was a stationer and bookseller, who did not begin to print until 1533, and printed some thirty books at The Sign of the Sonne between 1535 and 1544, apparently working initially under the protection of Thomas Cromwell.

During De Worde's lifetime the independent production of the printers who were in one way or other associated with him was invariably small. This can partly be explained by the status of the profession of 'stationer'. A good example of such a career is offered by John Reynes, a bookseller and bookbinder who originated from the Netherlands. He was granted letters of denization in 1510, is regularly recorded as an importer of books between 1514 and 1535, and had a shop in St Paul's Churchyard. In 1527 he financed a well-illustrated reprint of Higden's *Polychronicon*, printed for him by Peter Treveris in Southwark. Also in 1527, a magnificent *Graduale* for the use of Salisbury was published by Reynes in partnership with De Worde, printed for them in Paris by Nicolas Prevost. Reynes continued occasionally to finance books sold in his shop until his death in 1544. Bookselling and binding featured much more prominently in his business than involvement with printing, and this business pattern may have been repeated many times: importing and selling books was for most book-men more important than producing them.

Wynkyn de Worde would have disagreed, although he was an importer himself. He and Pynson seem jealously to have guarded their position as the two most prolific printers in the land. De Worde was greatly upset when in 1530 Peter Treveris began to print works by his own cherished author Robert Whittinton, and directed invective at him in print. Treveris, who presumably originated from Trier, was one of the few aliens who for a short period deployed considerable activity, usually in association with other printers. Between 1525 and 1532 he shared imprints with Laurence Andrewe, John Rastell, John Reynes, and De Worde. In 1529 he produced *The great herbal*, partly for Laurence Andrewe, who owned the blocks for the very fine woodcut illustrations.

vnder the plate shall be made foure wyn-de holes/ for to let the smoke out/ and the plate shall be enoynted as the barrys be fore specyfyed well thycke/ and aboue the plate the fornays shall be reysed all moste halfe a stone thycknesse and in the myddest of the fornays a hole shall be lefte euen iust aboue the hole of the plate where the coles be cast through. Upon the sayd plate shall be lefte foure brode pyt-tys accordynge to the quantyte of your helmys In the whiche pytys ye shall put or strewe fyne syfted asshes or sande of two ynches hye/ in the whiche ye shall sette your pannys of erth/ coper/ or lede but the leden pannys may not well a by de by the fyre without meltyng/ excepte ye make very small fyre vnder it/ vpon suche pānis be set the styllatoryes named helmettys or rose garlandys here before reherced and fygured. And to euery smo-ke hole ye shal make a plogge or tappe to gouerne your fyre with/ great or smal as it is nedefull.

Fig. 102. Laurence Andrewe, the printer, was himself able to translate the *Kleines Destillierbuch* from the original German. Obviously it was a success, for it was reprinted twice within three years. Andrewe's interest was in science, and his illustrations of the processes of the distillation of herbs and flowers gave him the opportunity to show how science was applied.

Hieronymus Brunschwig, *The vertuose boke of distyllacyon*. Translated from the German by Laurence Andrewe. London, Laurence Andrewe, 1528. London, BL, 448.g.1, fol. a6 recto.

Laurence Andrewe is another alien printer who in the short time he was active in London, between 1527 and 1530 'at the sygne of the golden crosse' in Fleet Street, produced a few very interesting books. Born in Calais, he was able to translate from French and German. In 1527, before crossing over to England, he had produced an English translation for the Antwerp printer Jan van Doesborch of a German version of the *Hortus sanitatis*, a natural history that had been popular in Germany since the 1480s. He was obviously interested in science and its applications, and published in London between 1527 and 1530 three editions of his own translation – from the German again – of Hieronymus Brunschwig's manual for the distillation of herbs, richly

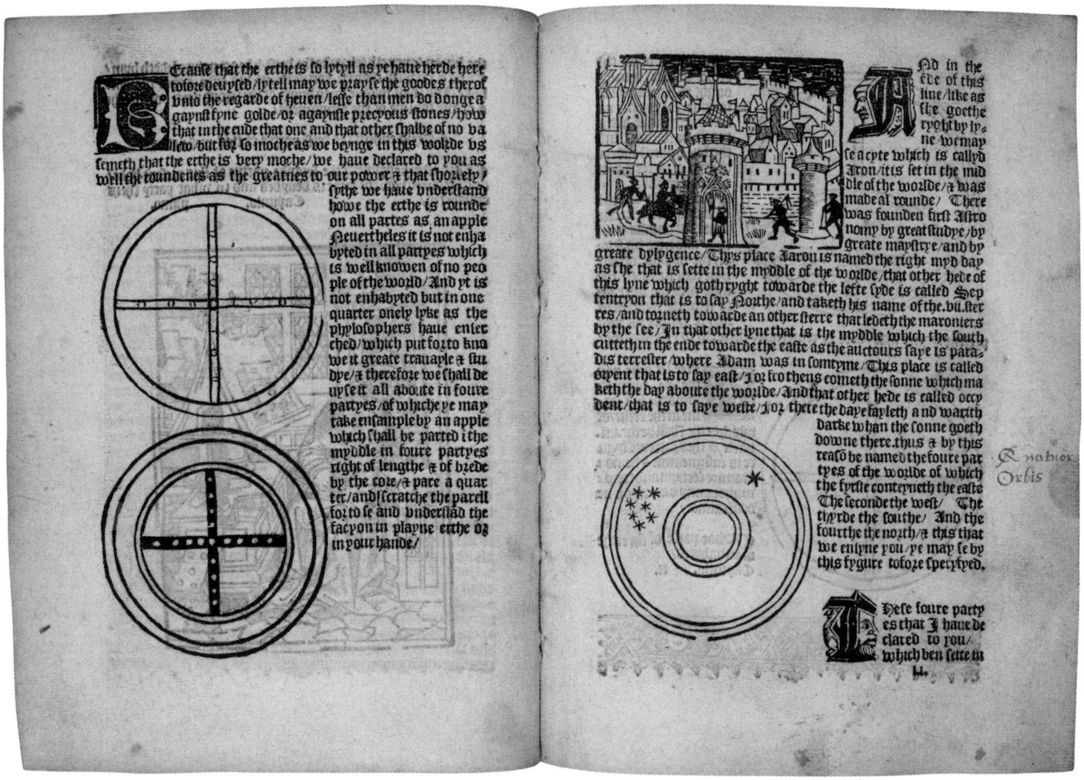

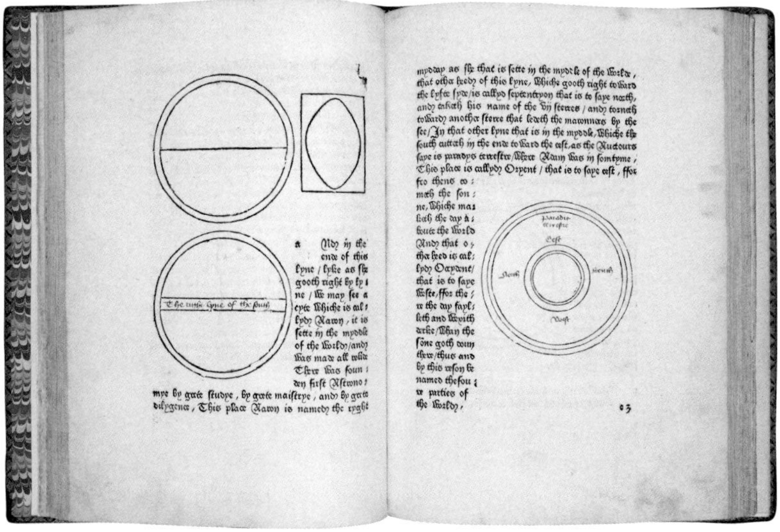

Fig. 103. Andrewe's text follows Caxton's version of *The mirrour of the world* (1481), including the traditional medieval representation of the earth and the cosmos. But Andrewe inserted extensive sections with more up-to-date science, on measuring, arithmetic, and 'the most pleasant science of music'.

Gossuin de Metz, *L'image du monde*, translated from the French by William Caxton entitled *Mirrour of the world*, and augmented by Laurence Andrewe. London, Laurence Andrewe, *c.* 1527. London, BL, C. 11.b.13, fol. H4 verso, H5 recto.

Fig. 104. Map of the earth and a diagram of the cosmos in Caxton's edition of 1481. The manuscript captions were written in the printing house.

Mirrour of the world. [Westminster, William Caxton, 1481. London, BL, IB. 55040, fol. e2 verso, e3 recto.

illustrated with images of furnaces and retorts, as well as of the herbs that also appeared in *The great herbal*. In a new edition of Caxton's translation of the *Mirrour of the world* (*circa* 1527), Andrewe reprinted Caxton's text faithfully with extensive interpolations of his own on mathematics, and with many new illustrations.

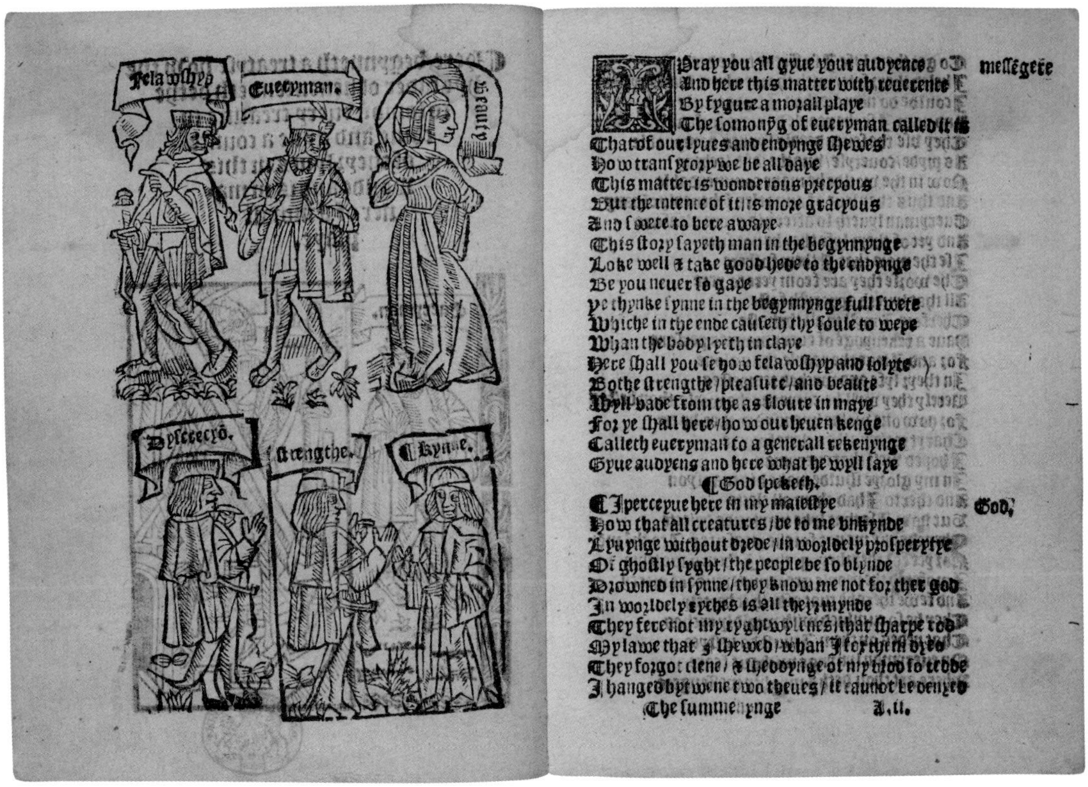

I Pray you all gyue your audyence
And here this matter with reuerence
By fygure a morall playe
The somonyg of eueryman called it is
That of our lyues and endynge shewes
How transytory we be all daye
This matter is wonderous precyous
But the intente of it is more gracyous
And swete to bere awaye
This story sayeth man in the begynnynge
Loke well & take good hede to the endynge
Be you neuer so gaye
ye thynke synne in the begynnynge full swete
Whiche in the ende causeth thy soule to wepe
Whan the body lyeth in claye
Here shall you se how felawshyp and iolyte
Bothe strengthe/pleasure/and beaute
Wyll vade from the as floure in maye
For ye shall here/how our heuen kenge
Calleth eueryman to a generall rekenynge
Gyue audyens and here what he wyll saye
¶ God speketh.
¶ I perceyue here in my maiestye
How that all creatures/be to me vnkynde
Lyuynge without drede/in worldely prosperytye
Of ghostly syght/the people be so blynde
Drowned in synne/they know me not for ther god
In worldely ryches is all theyr mynde
They fere not my ryghtwysnes/that sharpe rod
My lawe that I shewed/whan I for them dyed
They forgot clene/& shedynge of my blod so redde
I hanged bytwene two theues/it cannot be denyed
The summenynge A.ii.

messegere
God.

Fig. 105. Pynson had printed the morality play *Everyman* several times in an anonymous translation from the Dutch. Skot added illustrations to his reprint, and used the opening page to introduce the characters with their images, as an early form of the list of *dramatis personae* that later became the traditional beginning of plays.

Everyman. London, John Skot, c. 1535. London, BL, Huth 32, fol. A1 verso, A2 recto.

In the years between 1500 and 1535 the individual production of De Worde and Pynson, the two long-established printers, far exceeded that of any of the other printers. As they grew older, both appear to have sought to retain what they may have considered their virtual monopoly – as it had been before 1500. They may have encouraged and even supported their former servants, as long as they knew their limits. Others may have been competitors, albeit on a small scale. John Skot, who was active in London between 1521 and 1537, produced every year a few items that seem to mirror De Worde's preference for popular devotion. His most remarkable work is an illustrated edition of *Everyman*.

Pynson stoutly defended the territory that had exclusively been his: legal printing. His main competitors in the area were John Rastell and Robert Redman. John Rastell, who began printing in 1508/9, had the advantage over Pynson that he was a barrister of the Middle Temple, and was able to make important contributions by editing texts and providing translations where Pynson had been dependent on the expertise of others. He was a brother-in-law of Thomas More, and published some of his works, a family duty taken over by Rastell's son William from about 1530. But John Rastell's interests were many sided. He printed several of his own plays and interludes, and pioneered single-impression music printing from movable type. His

Fig. 106. Rastell printed music for one of his interludes, the right-hand page showing the score for three voices of the line 'Tyme to pas with goodly sport our spryts to...'. On the following page the song continues: 'revyne and comfort to pipe to singe to daunce to spring with plesure and delyte folowing sensual appetyte'.

John Rastell, *A new interlude and a mery of the nature of the .iiij. elements*. London, John Rastell c. 1520. London, BL, C. 39.b.17, fol. E4 verso, E5 recto.

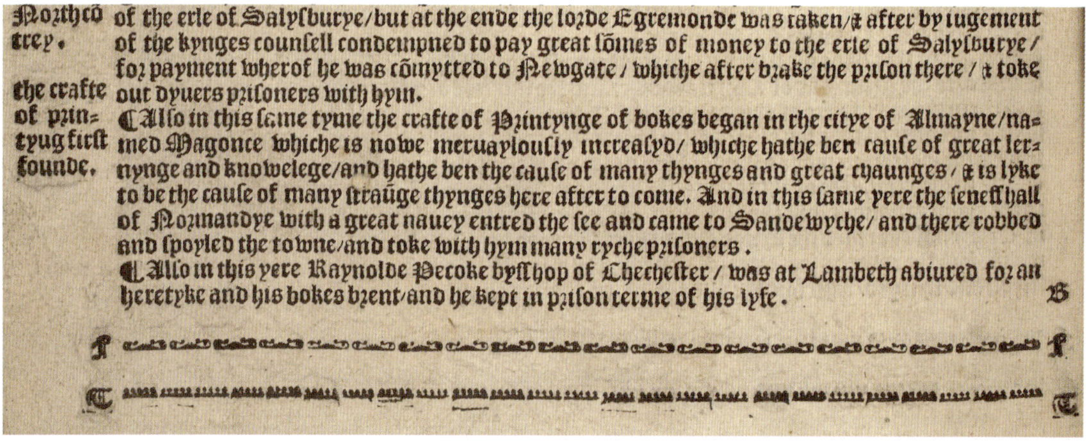
Northcon trey. of the erle of Salysburye/but at the ende the lorde Egremonde was taken/& after by iugement of the kynges counsell condempned to pay great somes of money to the erle of Salysburye/ for payment wherof he was cōmytted to Newgate/whiche after brake the prison there/& toke out dyuers prisoners with hym.

The crafte of printyng first founde. Also in this same tyme the crafte of Printynge of bokes began in the citye of Almayne/named Magonce whiche is nowe meruaylously increasyd/ whiche hathe ben cause of great lernynge and knowelege/and hathe ben the cause of many thynges and great chaunges/& is lyke to be the cause of many straūge thynges here after to come. And in this same yere the seneshall of Normandye with a great nauey entred the see and came to Sandewyche/ and there robbed and spoyled the towne/and toke with hym many ryche prisoners.

Also in this yere Raynolde Pecoke bysshop of Chechester/was at Lambeth abiured for an heretyke and his bokes brent/and he kept in prison terme of his lyfe. B

Fig. 107. Rastell made his great chronicle visually interesting with large portraits, but the typesetting was cramped. He included a passage in praise of the invention of printing, immediately followed by relating an incident of the burning of books.

John Rastell, *The pastyme of people*. London, John Rastell, c. 1530. London, BL, G. 6030, fol. (2) E6 verso (detail).

typographical style is inventive. In 1529/30 he published *The pastyme of people*, a chronicle adapted from Fabyan's, with large portraits of the English monarchs from William I. Printing was no more than a sideline for Rastell, to serve his many interests, and his publishing activities were not a real threat to Pynson. Robert Redman, however, was a piratical rival. From 1523 he printed over 200 mainly legal works previously printed by Pynson, at two addresses, both, like Pynson's own, misleadingly named 'The George', and he imitated Pynson's printer's device. Pynson retaliated by reprinting Redman, and both unsuccessfully tried to thwart the other by obtaining privileges preventing the reprinting of their work. Like Rastell, Redman was a thorough editor and sometimes produced better versions than Pynson's. This did not prevent Pynson from calling him publicly 'Rudeman', and attacking him in print as incompetent.

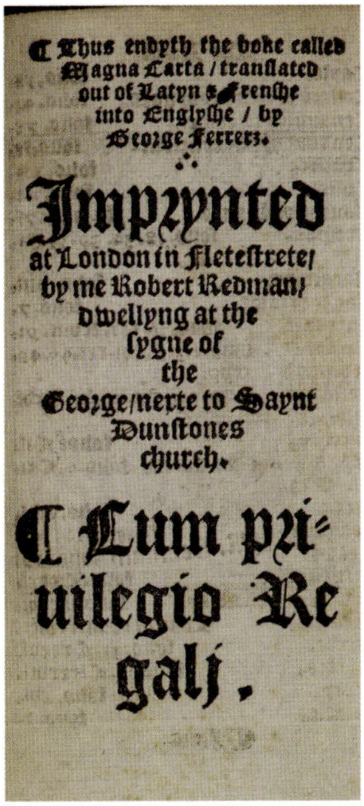
¶ Thus endyth the boke called Magna Carta / translated out of Latyn & Frenshe into Englyshe / by George Ferrers.

Imprynted at London in Fletestrete / by me Robert Redman / dwellyng at the sygne of the George / nexte to Saynt Dunstones church.

¶ Cum privilegio Regali.

Fig. 108. Redman, the expert in legal printing, published a translation of *Magna Carta* in a handsome small format. Although Pynson was no longer alive to compete with him, Redman made his address abundantly clear.

Magna Carta, translated out of Latin and French by George Ferrers. London, Robert Redman, 1534. London, BL, C. 112.a.6, fol. BB8 recto.

Thomas Berthelet, who was in Pynson's service around 1520, became one of the most distinguished and prolific printers in England in the sixteenth century. His first independent publication is dated 1524, but it was not until 1530 or 1531 that he began to publish in any quantity. By then Pynson had died, and in 1530 Berthelet was appointed his successor as King's Printer. His career as an independent printer took off just before the end of De Worde's, and there was not enough overlap to pose a threat to the old printer. He continued a very successful printing career until his death in 1555. Berthelet seems therefore to have followed the pattern of Pynson and De Worde by making printing – partly of official publications – his main business. In style, and in his choice of texts, he did not follow the model of these two predecessors, but radically modernized printing in England.

The two editions that appeared in 1532 of Chaucer and Gower show a clear generational distinction from the practices of Berthelet's predecessor and old master. Here we may observe that modernization can entail a consciously critical view of texts with a long history. Berthelet, who published Gower's *Confessio amantis* in that year, may also have had a stake in the publication of Chaucer's collected works by Thomas Godfray. In the Gower edition he explains in a prefatory note 'to the reader' that there are differences between his sources, Caxton's edition of 1483 and manuscripts. He decided to present both versions in his edition: 'I thought it good to warne the reder that the writen copies do not agre with the prynted. Therfore syr I have prynted here those same lynes that I fynde in the wrytten copies. The whiche alteration ye shall perceyve beganne at the .xxiiij. lyne in the prologue'. He then proceeded to present this section twice, first accurately from Caxton's edition, and then from an unspecified manuscript.

Thomas Godfray is a printer about whom little else is known but that his name appears in books between 1532 and 1537, the most important an edition of works by Chaucer. Duff observed that Godfray used some of Berthelet's material, and surmised that Berthelet may have financed some of his publications. For the Chaucer we know the name of the editor, William Thynne, who was in various functions a courtier to Henry VIII. After his death his son testified that his father had collected some twenty-five manuscripts, and several have recently come to light marked up for use in the printing house. For other sections Caxton's and Pynson's printed editions were used. Thynne went one step beyond the method Berthelet indicated, and made editorial choices where sources seemingly contradicted each other. The two books are early instances of textual criticism applied to vernacular texts; in both instances the early printed sources were used as a framework into which variant readings from manuscripts were intermittently introduced – when noted.

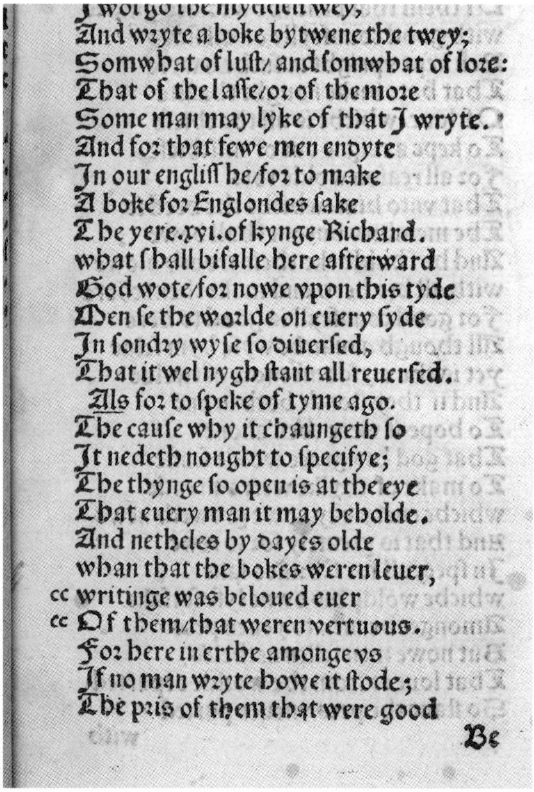

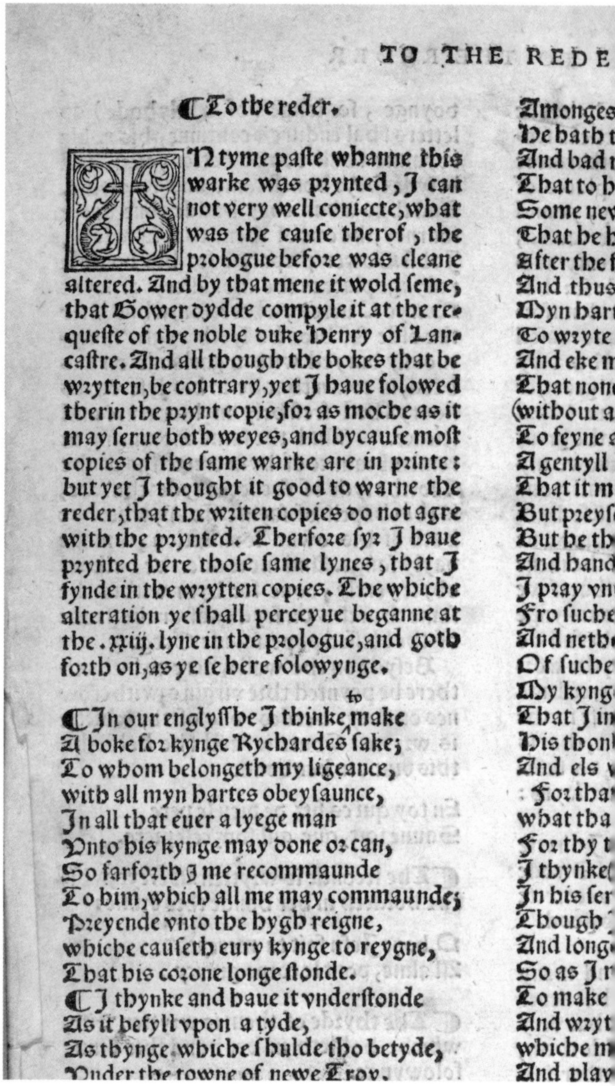

Fig. 109 a, b & c. Thomas Berthelet gave his edition of Gower a fine, modern title-page (fig. 109a). His approach to the sources for an early literary text is critical, and modern by showing a beginning of antiquarian awareness. He warns the reader that in the text of the author's prologue manuscript sources diverge from his printed source, Caxton's edition of 1483. He states 'I have folowed therin the prynt copie', but he precedes this with the variant text from his manuscript source (fig. 109b), before turning to Caxton's text (fig. 109c and fig. 110, col. 1, ll. 1–20). The exceptional style for this time of the fount of type serves also to present the text as 'ancient' – not of the present time – and contrasts with the roman type used for the running titles and for glosses later in the book.

John Gower, *Confessio amantis*. London, Thomas Berthelet, 1532. London, BL, 641.k.3, fol. aa2 recto; aa3 recto, A1 recto (details).

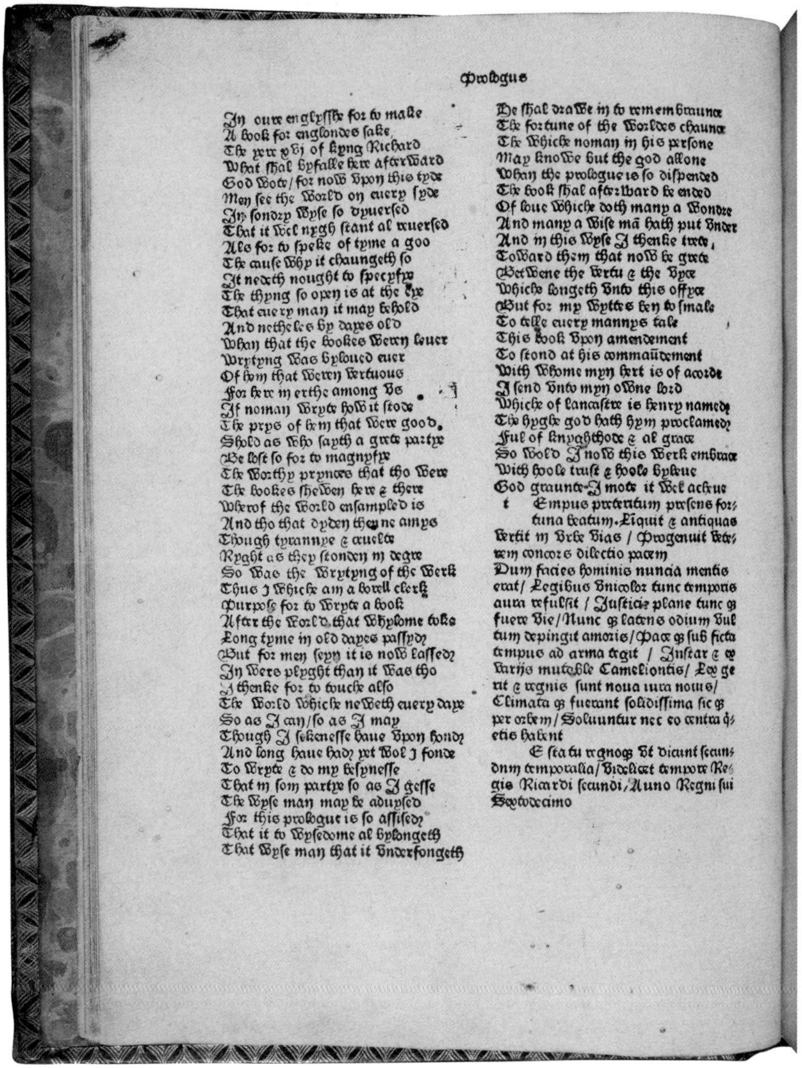

Prologus

In oure englysshe for to make
A book for englondes sake,
The yere xvj of kyng Richard
What shal byfalle here afterward
God woot / for now vpon this tyde
Men see the world on euery syde
In sondry wyse so dyuersed
That it wel nygh stant al reuersed
Als for to speke of tyme a goo
The cause why it chaungeth so
It nedeth nought to specyfye
The thyng so open is at the eye
That euery man it may behold
And netheles by dayes old
Whan that the bookes weren leuer
Wrytyng was bylouid euer
Of hem that weren vertuous
For here in erthe among vs
If noman wryte how it stode
The prys of hem that were good,
Shold as who sayth a grete partye
Be lost so for to magnyfye
The worthy prynces that tho were
The bookes shewen here & there
Wherof the world ensampled is
And tho that dyden thenne amys
Though tyrannye & crueltee
Ryght as they stonden in degre
So was the wrytyng of the werk
Thus I whiche am a borell clerk
Purpose for to wryte a book
After the world that whylome toke
Long tyme in old dayes passyd
But for men seyn it is now lassed
In wers plyght than it was tho
I thenke for to touche also
The world whiche neweth euery daye
So as I can / so as I may
Though I seknesse haue vpon honde
And long haue had yet wol I fonde
To wryte & do my besynesse
That in som partye so as I gesse
The wyse man may be aduysed
For this prologue is so assised
That it to wysedome al bylongeth
That wyse man that it vnderfongeth

He shal drawe in to remembraunce
The fortune of the worldes chaunce
The whiche noman in his persone
May knowe but the god allone
Whan the prologue is so dispended
The book shal afterward be ended
Of loue whiche doth many a wondre
And many a wise mā hath put vnder
And in this wyse I thenke trete,
Toward them that now be grete
Betwene the vertu & the vyce
Whiche longeth vnto this offyce
But for my wyttes ben to smale
To telle euery mannys tale
This book vpon amendement
To stond at his commaūdement
With whome myn herte is of acorde
I send vnto myn owne lord
Whiche of lancastre is henry named
The hyghe god hath hym proclamed
Ful of knyghthode & al grace
So wold I now this werk embrace
With hoole trust & hoole byleue
God graunte I mote it wel acheue

t Empus preteritum presens for-
tuna beatum. Liquit & antiquas
vertit in vrbe vias / Progenuit vete-
rem concors dilectio pacem
Dum facies hominis nuncia mentis
erat / Legibus vnicolor tunc temporis
aurea refulsit / Justicie plane tunc q
fuere vie / Nunc q latens odium vul
tum depingit amoris / Pace q sub ficta
tempus ad arma tegit / Instar & ex
varijs mutabile Cameliontis / Lex ge
rit & regnis sunt noua iura nouis /
Climata q fuerant solidissima sic q
per orbem / Soluuntur nec eo centra q-
etis habent

E statu regnoq vt dicunt secun-
dum temporalia / Videlicet tempore Re-
gis Ricardi secundi / Anno Regni sui
Sextodecimo

Fig. 110. The author's prologue in Caxton's edition which served Thomas Berthelet as printer's copy.

John Gower, *Confessio amantis*. Westminster, William Caxton, 1483. London, BL, IB. 55077, fol. 1.2 verso.

Outside London, and outside the universities, such little printing as there was followed the pattern of the stationers who occasionally printed a small book to meet a local need. The earliest of those provincial stationers whose names appear in colophons is Martin Coeffin, a native of Normandy who settled in Exeter, where his career as a bookbinder and bookseller can be followed from 1505. In that year he commissioned a printer in Rouen to produce a short vocabulary for schoolchildren, *Os, facies, mentum*, and possibly a *Tractatus defectivorum verborum*. He seems to have continued to flourish as an importer and bookbinder until at least the 1530s, but did not have a press himself. Similarly, the presumed stationer in Bristol, Robert Woodward, whose debt De Worde forgave in his will, is not known to have printed at all. In Hereford, Ingelbert Haghe, from Rouen, was active as a stationer about 1510. In 1505 his name had appeared in the

The Marchauntes prologue Fo. xxxiii.

Quod the marchaunt/and so haue other mo
That wedded be/I trowe that it be so
For wel I wote it fareth so by me
I haue a wife/the worst that may be
For though the fende coupled to her were
She wolde him ouermatch I dare well swere
What shulde I reherce in speciall
Her high malyce: she is a shrewe at all
There is a longe and a large difference
Betwyxt Grisyldes great pacience
And of my wife the passyng cruelte
Were I vnbounde/ also mote I the
I wolde neuer efte come in the snare
We wedded men lyue in sorowe and care
Assay who so wol/and he shal fynde
That I say soth/ by saynt Thomas of Inde
As for the more parte/I say nat all
God shelde that it shulde so befall
Ah good sir host/ I haue wedded be
These monethes two/and more nat parde
And yet I trowe he that all his lyfe
Hath wedded be/ though men him rife
In to the hert/ ne couthe in no manere
Tell so moche sorowe/as I nowe here
Coude tell/of my wyues cursednesse
Now qd our host marchant/so god y blesse
Syn ye be so moche knowe of that arte
Full hertely I pray you tell vs parte
Gladly quod he/but of myn owne sore
For sory hert I tell may no more.

Here endeth the marchantes prologue/
and here foloweth his tale.

Whilom there was dwelling in Lõbardy
A worthy knyght/ that borne was at Pauy
In whiche he lyued in great prosperite
And sixty yere a wifeles man was he
And folowed aye his bodely delyte
On women/there as was his appetyte
As don these foles that ben seculeres
And whan that he was past sixty yeres
Were it for holynesse or dotage
I can not sayn/ but suche a great corage
Had this knyght to ben a wedded man
That day and nyght he dothe al that he can
To espy/ where that he wedded myght be
Prayeng our lorde to graunten him that he
Mighten ones knowen of that blyssfull lyfe
That is bitwixt an husbande and his wyfe
H.iii. And

Fig. 111. For the edition of Chaucer's works William Thynne used a mixture of manuscripts and printed editions. The fount chosen for the *Works* is reminiscent of the bastarda type Pynson used for the prose section of the *Tales*, and in many other books (see fig. 65). As with Berthelet's edition of Gower, the text may intentionally have been presented as being of earlier times. The woodcut illustrations are the blocks first used by Caxton in 1483 and by De Worde in 1498.

Geoffrey Chaucer, *Works*, edited by William Thynne. London, Thomas Godfray, 1532. London, BL, G. 11623, fol. h3 recto.

colophon of a breviary for the use of Hereford that was financed by Margaret Beaufort, and printed by a firm in Rouen.

Other provincial stationers indeed did some printing. At Tavistock Abbey, in Devon, Dom Thomas Richard, monk of the abbey, printed John Walton's verse translation of Boethius in 1525 at the request of Robert Langdon, a gentleman from Cornwall, and in 1534 *The statutes of stannary*. In York, Hugo Goes reprinted between 1506 and 1509 several works previously published by De Worde, including the *Ortus vocabulorum* and on a smaller scale *Robin Hood*, using De Worde's old fount of type. De Worde seems to have installed him as a branch of his London printing house, his main activity undoubtedly that of stationer, who printed now and then as the occasion arose. Several

Fig. 112. Printing at the Benedictine abbey at Tavistock in Devon seems to have been an almost one-off event. The Boethius translation by John Walton, completed in 1410, was less well-known than Chaucer's, printed in 1478 by Caxton. The typesetting is competent, and Dom Richard must have been taught by an experienced printer. Four stanzas are added to the text, with at the beginning of lines the names of the patron, Robert Langdon, and of John Walton spelled out in an acrostic.

Boethius, *De consolatione philosophiae*, translated into English by John Walton with the title *The boke of comfort called in laten Boetius*. Tavistock, Dom Thomas Richard, 1525. Manchester, John Rylands University Library, S10600, fol. R7 recto.

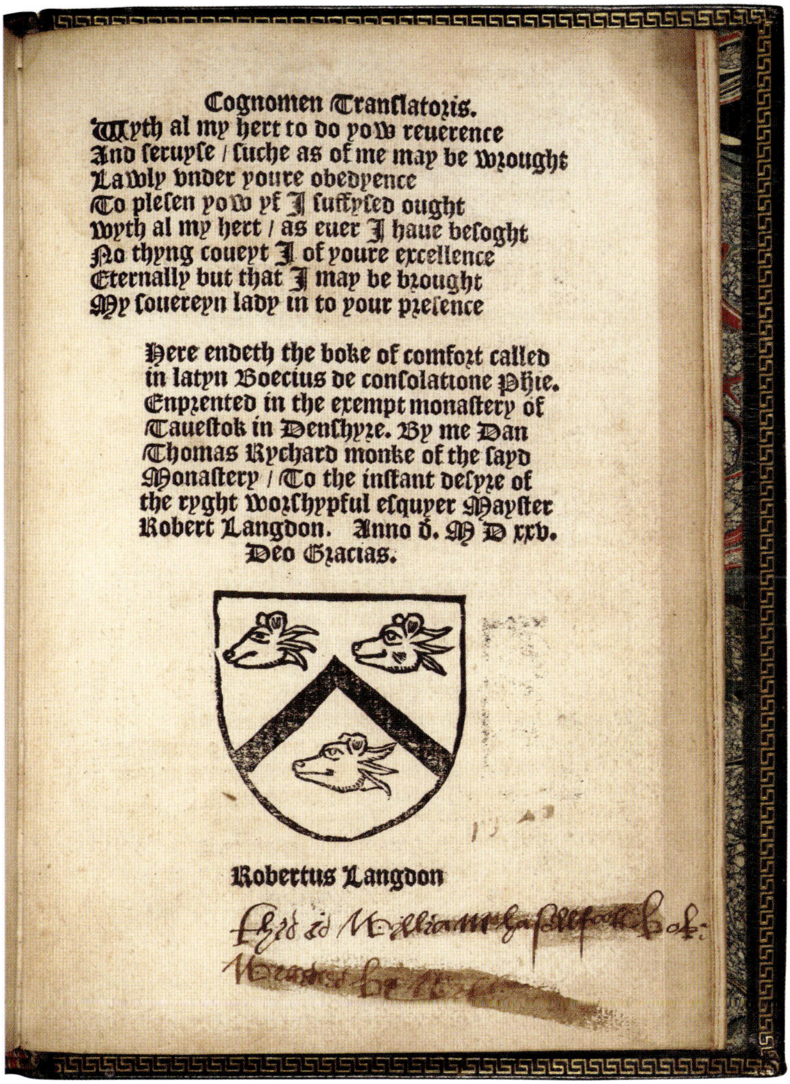

Cognomen Translatoris.
Wyth al my hert to do yow reuerence
And seruyse / suche as of me may be wrought
Lawly vnder youre obedyence
To plesen yow yf I suffysed ought
Wyth al my hert / as euer I haue besoght
No thyng coueyt I of youre excellence
Eternally but that I may be brought
My souereyn lady in to your presence

Here endeth the boke of comfort called in latyn Boecius de consolatione Phie. Enprented in the exempt monastery of Tauestok in Denshyre. By me Dan Thomas Rychard monke of the sayd Monastery / To the instant desyre of the ryght worshypful esquyer Mayster Robert Langdon. Anno d. M D xxv. Deo Gracias.

Robertus Langdon

stationers worked in York in the years between 1506 and 1531, including Ursyn Mylner and John Gashet who occasionally printed a small item, but more usually commissioned items elsewhere, and probably dealt generally in imported books. Gashet had *Manuals* for the use of York printed for him in Paris in 1509 and in 1530, the first partly financed by De Worde.

De Worde also maintained connections with a few stationer/printers in Oxford. From the 1480s scholars in Oxford depended for the supply of books on importation by stationers, even when the printer Theoderic Rood was in residence. Most books came from overseas, but sometimes a book that was apparently not obtainable on this market was printed at the request of an Oxford stationer. In 1508 Pynson printed a tract by Peregrinus de Lugo on the philosophy of Duns Scotus for the Oxford stationer George Chastelayne. The

Questiones
moralissime super li-
bros Ethicorũ eruditissimi
viri Joannis Dedicus artium libe-
ralium triumqꝫ philosophiarum magistri
optime meriti/et in moralibus pre ceteris satis pe-
riti feliciter incipiunt subtilissimis Oxoniensibus in philo-
sophia morali lucubrare cupientibus non magis
utiles q̃ necessarie.

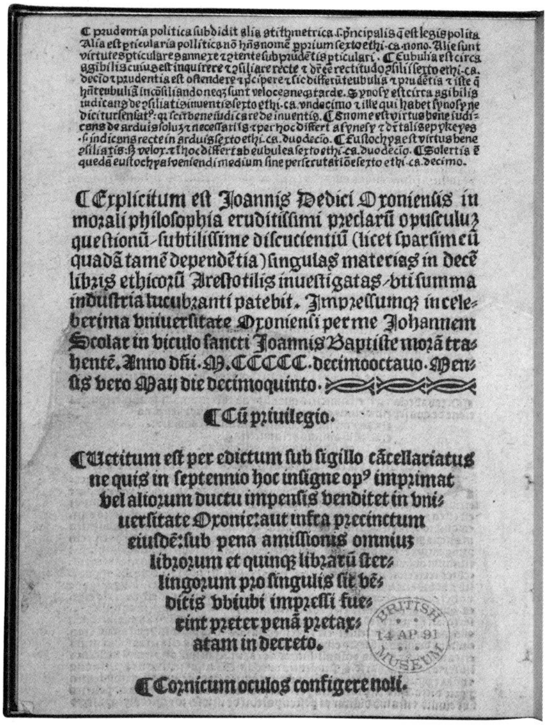
Explicitum est Joannis Dedici Oxoniensis in
morali philosophia eruditissimi preclarũ opusculuꝫ
questionũ subtilissime discucientiũ (licet sparsim cũ
quadã tamẽ dependẽtia) singulas materias in decẽ
libris ethicorũ Arestotilis investigatas/uti summa
industria lucubranti patebit. Impressumqꝫ in cele-
berima universitate Oxoniensi per me Johannem
Scolar in viculo sancti Joannis Baptiste morã tra-
hentẽ. Anno dñi. M.CCCCC. decimooctavo. Men-
sis vero Maii die decimoquinto.

Cũ privilegio.

Vetitum est per edictum sub sigillo cãcellariatus
ne quis in septennio hoc insigne op⁹ imprimat
vel aliorum ductu impensis venditet in uni-
versitate Oxonie: aut infra precinctum
eiusdẽ: sub pena amissionis omniuꝫ
librorum et quinqꝫ librarũ ster-
lingorum pro singulis sic ven-
ditis ubiubi impressi fue-
rint preter penã pretax-
atam in decreto.

Cornicum oculos configere noli.

London stationer Henry Jacobi, who from 1505 commissioned several books in Paris in partnership with another stationer, Joyce Pelgrim, opened a shop in Oxford in 1512, but died in 1514. The only book he published in this short period is another tract related to Duns Scotus by Antonius Sirectus, printed for him by Wynkyn de Worde. In 1518 a printing press was operated briefly in Oxford itself by John Scolar, clearly supported by De Worde, whose founts of type were used. Scolar published five books, three of which were apparently in response to a demand for medieval scholarship that had also been evident in the choice of texts related to Duns Scotus. The first, the most substantial of Scolar's publications, is a commentary on Aristotle's *Ethics*. Two other works were by Walter Burley and date from the fourteenth century. Two much-reprinted textbooks by Stanbridge and Whittinton were intended for use in schools. In the following year another stationer, Charles Kyrfoth, published a *Computus* for use by Oxonians.

Fig. 113 a & b. The first publication of John Scolar in Oxford was given official status by a privilege granted to the University of Oxford 'under the seal of chancery' that protected it for seven years.

Joannes Dedicus, *Questiones moralissime super libros ethicorum Aristotelis*. Oxford, John Scolar, 1518. London, BL, C. 54.b.2, fol. A1 recto, N4 verso.

The selection of texts printed at and for Oxford must reflect the conservative taste of perhaps no more than one scholar. Something similar happened in Cambridge with a contrasting effect. Johann Siberch, from Siegburg, near Cologne, had been connected with the Cologne book trade as agent and publisher, had travelled, and had made some connections with distinguished and influential scholars in Cambridge, four of whom were sufficiently inspired to procure a loan of £20 from the university bursar to set up a press to be operated

Fig. 114. The first book printed in Cambridge was Bullock's address to Cardinal Wolsey, archbishop of York.

Henry Bullock, *Oratio ad Thomam cardinalem archiepiscopum Eboracensem*. Cambridge, John Siberch, 1521. London, BL, C. 38.d.32 (3), fol. a1 recto.

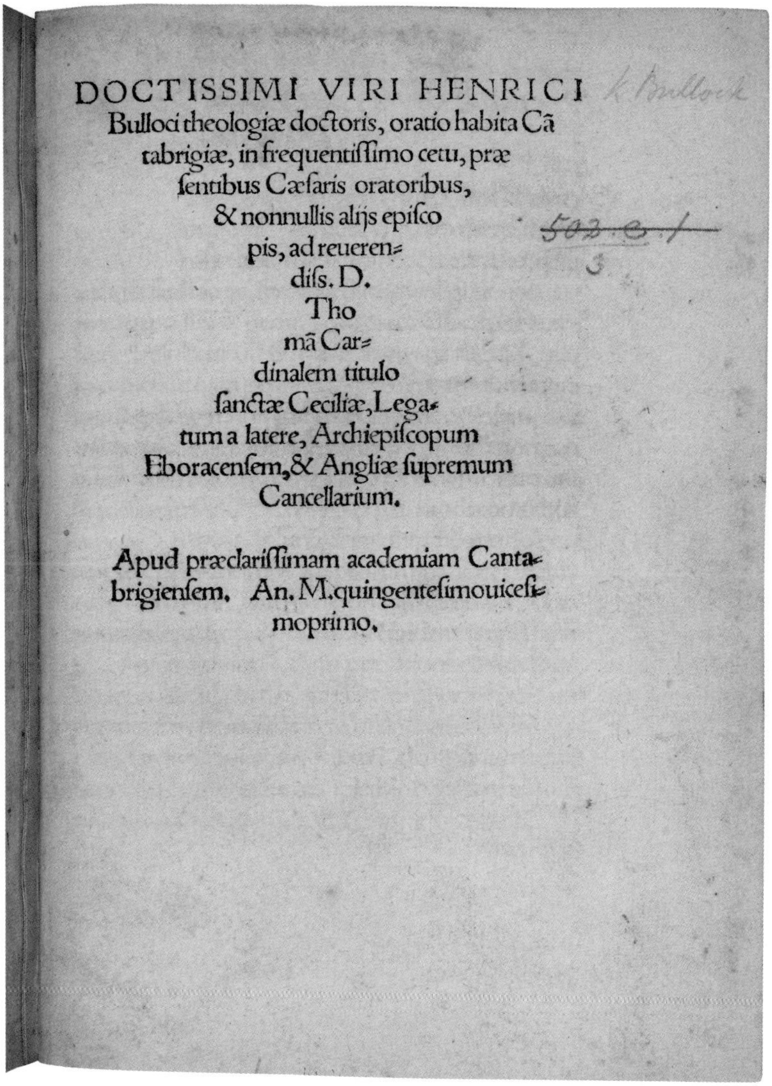

DOCTISSIMI VIRI HENRICI
Bullocí theologiæ doctoris, oratio habita Cā
tabrigiæ, in frequentissimo cetu, præ
sentibus Cæsaris oratoribus,
& nonnullis aliis episco
pis, ad reueren=
diss. D.
Tho
mā Car=
dinalem titulo
sanctæ Ceciliæ, Lega=
tum a latere, Archiepiscopum
Eboracensem, & Angliæ supremum
Cancellarium.

Apud præclarissimam academiam Canta=
brigiensem. An. M.quingentesimouicesi=
moprimo.

by Siberch. Of the four, Henry Bullock of Queen's College was the most active patron of the press. Its first publication was an oration by Bullock to welcome Cardinal Wolsey when he visited the university in 1520. It was followed by a brief translation from the Greek by Bullock of Lucian's *Dipsades*, accompanied by some Greek maxims, the first appearance of Greek movable type in England. Bullock displayed here his modern scholarship of Greek, which he had studied under Erasmus, no less, when the latter was in Cambridge. He is better remembered for a long letter addressed to him by Erasmus in 1516 than for his own works. One of the books published by Siberch is Erasmus's *Libellus de conscribendis epistolis*, dedicated to Bishop John Fisher, then Chancellor of Cambridge University. Unfortunately it was an unauthorized, garbled version that had proudly been brought to light, probably by Bullock. It aroused the author's fury, as he

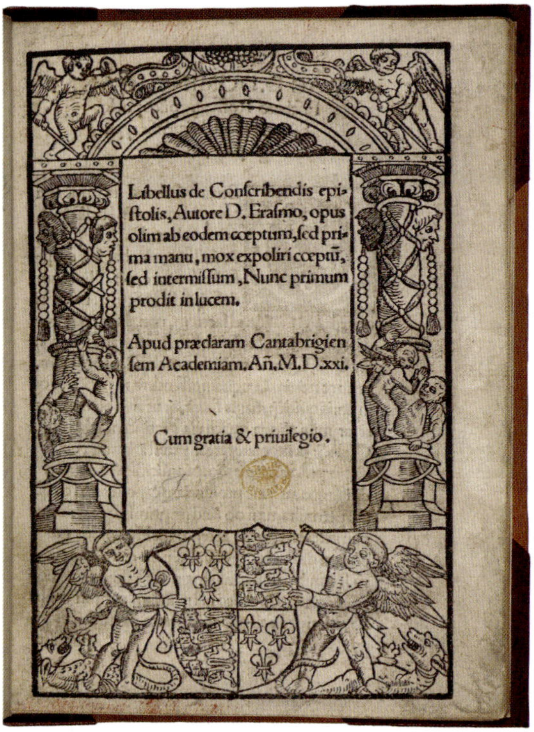

Libellus de Conſcribendis epiſtolis, Autore D. Eraſmo, opus olim ab eodem cœptum, ſed prima manu, mox expoliri cœptū, ſed intermiſſum, Nunc primum prodit in lucem.

Apud præclaram Cantabrigienſem Academiam. Añ. M.D.xxi.

Cum gratia & priuilegio.

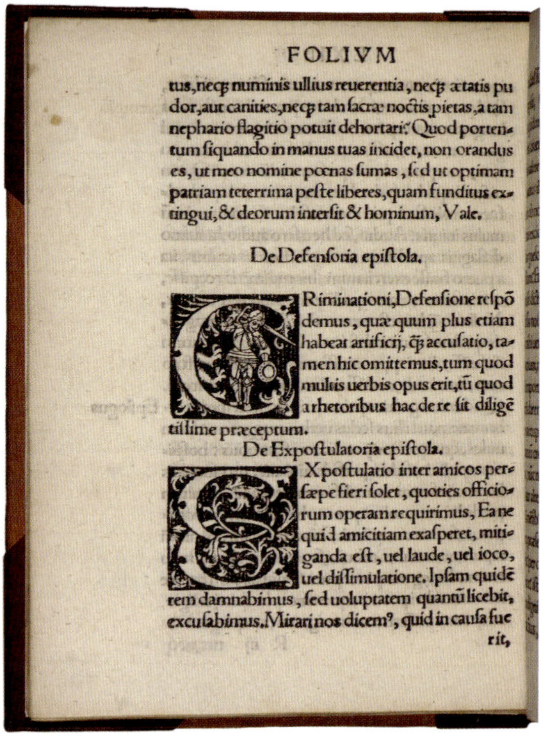

FOLIVM

tus, necq numinis ullius reuerentia, necq ætatis pudor, aut canities, necq tam ſacræ noctis pietas, a tam nephario flagitio potuit dehortari. Quod portentum ſiquando in manus tuas incidet, non orandus es, ut meo nomine pœnas ſumas, ſed ut optimam patriam teterrima peſte liberes, quam funditus extingui, & deorum interſit & hominum, Vale.

De Defenſoria epiſtola.

CRiminationi, Defenſione reſpōdemus, quæ quum plus etiam habeat artificij, q̄ accuſatio, tamen hic omittemus, tum quod multis uerbis opus erit, tū quod a rhetoribus hac de re ſit diligētiſſime præceptum.

De Expoſtulatoria epiſtola.

EXpoſtulatio inter amicos perſæpe fieri ſolet, quoties officiorum operam requirimus, Ea ne quid amicitiam exaſperet, mitiganda eſt, uel laude, uel ioco, uel diſſimulatione. Ipſam quidē rem damnabimus, ſed uoluptatem quantū licebit, excuſabimus. Mirari nos dicem⁹, quid in cauſa fuerit,

Fig. 115 a & b. In spite of the decorous execution of the book, its fine type and initials, the splendid title-page with the boast that this was the first edition, Erasmus thoroughly disapproved of its publication. Siberch began the book with a long introductory letter addressed to bisop John Fisher, Chancellor of the university. Its defensive tone suggests that he may have been aware that all was not in quite proper order.

Desiderius Erasmus, *Libellus de conscribendis epistolis.* Cambridge, John Siberch, 1521. London, BL, 96.b.1, fol. A1 recto, R3 verso.

forcibly expressed in a 'genuine' edition printed a little later in Basel by Froben. It was all most unfortunate, and Bullock's vanity may have been to blame. Siberch's reputation is redeemed, however, by his most substantial publication, the first edition (in 1521) of the great Oxford scholar Thomas Linacre's Greek–Latin translation of Galen on the Temperaments.

In all Siberch printed ten works between 1520 and 1523, several of them orations and other short works meant to flatter or satisfy vanity, but despite ephemeral purposes they are also manifestations of modern humanist learning. His enterprise depended on the short-lived enthusiasm of a small circle of scholars, and when no more commissions were forthcoming, he left.

In the first three decades of the sixteenth century, England witnessed a luminous constellation of scholars revolving round the great humanist Erasmus. His friendships with Thomas More, John Colet, Richard Pace, and Thomas Linacre were fostered during lengthy visits, and gave direction to their scholarly achievements. Erasmus strove to disseminate the text of the New Testament in the purest possible form, an objective that is known as 'evangelical humanism'. This concept gave direction to the establishment of St Paul's School by Dean John Colet, for which Colet himself, Linacre, its first high master William Lily, Erasmus, and Richard Pace wrote instructions and textbooks that were printed by Pynson and Rastell (and in the

¶A deuout treatise vpon the Pater no-
ster/ made fyrst in latyn by the moost fa-
mous doctour mayster Erasmus
Roterodamus/ and tourned
in to englisshe by a yong
vertuous and well
lerned gentylwoman of .xix.
yere of age.

Fig. 116. Thomas More's eldest daugter Margaret translated Erasmus's paraphrase of the Lord's Prayer when she was nineteen years old. The Latin text was published by Froben in Basel in 1523. In the learned household of the More family Margaret's translation was probably undertaken as an exercise; it was liked well enough by her father to persuade Berthelet to publish it.

Desiderius Erasmus, *Precatio dominica*, translated into English by Margaret Roper. London, Thomas Berthelet, c. 1524. London, BL, C. 37.e.6(1), fol. a1 recto.

case of Pace by Froben in Basel). Erasmus's own words on the subject of a Christian education, encompassed in his very popular *Enchiridion militis Christiani* (first published in 1504) were not printed in England in Latin, and a much-reprinted English translation was first published as late as 1533. Apart from textbooks for schools, very little of this flourishing renaissance of learning is reflected in printing in England.

Linacre (who died in 1524) was one of the towering figures in the world of classical learning, in particular of Greek. His principal contacts in the world of learned publishing were with Aldus Manutius in Venice, and with other learned printers in Basel and Paris, although Pynson began reprinting some of Linacre's other translations of Galen and of pseudo-Proclus in 1522, during his lifetime. The fact that Linacre made his new Galen translation available for publication by Siberch suggests that he welcomed the arrival in England of a learned press. The printers in Venice, Basel, Paris, and Louvain who worked for the world of learning are most famously associated with Erasmus, and it is undoubtedly due to his close associations with printers on the Continent that the Latin works of More and Linacre were printed by the same printers who had primarily been the publishers of Erasmus's works. The Latin version of Lucian's satires, jointly translated by Erasmus and More, was first published in Paris in 1506, followed by at least fifteen editions all printed on the Continent. Erasmus's best-known work, the *Encomium moriae* (In praise of folly), dedicated to More and written in his house, was first published in Paris in 1511 and went through many editions, but in England it was not published until 1663. A translation into English was published by Berthelet in 1549. Thomas More's famous *Utopia* was first printed in 1516 in Louvain by Dirk Martens (a printer well known to Erasmus), and subsequently in Basel and Paris. The works of Richard Pace, humanist diplomat, secretary to Henry VIII, and friend of Erasmus and Thomas More, were mainly published in Rome, Venice, Basel, and Paris, but Pynson published a Latin oration, and Siberch his Latin translation of an oration against Luther originally presented – in English – by Bishop John Fisher. In 1526 Pynson printed Pace's treatise on the Hebrew version of the Book of Ecclesiastes.

When the two greatest scholars of the English Renaissance, Linacre and More, presented themselves on the world stage, they would not do so through the contemporary printers in England, with the exception of Rastell whose family connection with More led to publications of More's English writing. There is not the slightest affinity between their ambit and that of Wynkyn de Worde and his followers, who all worked for an entirely different vernacular market. Pynson's association with grammatical works for St Paul's School, and hence with John Colet, William Lily, Thomas Linacre, and on a few occasions with More and Pace (who succeeded Colet), gave him a few opportunities, but his contact with the world of great learning remained largely limited to works of instruction. His market was not that of the world of great classical scholarship.

Only a few of the printers who worked in England between 1500 and 1535, often for only a couple of years, are more than elusive figures. The work of the many others was intermittent, dependent on circumstance, its survival fragmented, and there is simply not enough of it to build up coherent pictures of individuals. Producing books in print was usually not their principal occupation. In vernacular and especially popular publishing we can see them testing the boundaries of typographical expression, sometimes with quirky results. For scholarly works, in Latin, they were slow to equip themselves with the materials (roman, Greek and italic founts of type) that would stand comparison with the presentation in books imported from the Continent.

We can observe that the old dividing line between alien printers and Englishmen had begun to dissolve, but was being replaced by a distinction between importers of books (who often were aliens and provided a crucial link with the great printing businesses on the Continent), and printers who increasingly were indigenous Englishmen. From 1523 there had been incremental steps leading to the Act of 1534, limiting the number of alien journeymen and apprentices. The Act, virtually coinciding with the death of Wynkyn de Worde, was not only a controlling measure to stem a potential influx of heretical books, but also an incentive for a new generation of printers to step out of the shadows and begin a new, and more turbulent chapter in the story of printing in England.

Further Reading

A story of early printers and printing can only be a reconstruction, built by putting together the concrete relics of the past, and in the process pulling down parts of the imaginary edifices built by predecessors in what is called 'the archaeology of the book'. Each version of the story cannot be more than an interpretation of what over the centuries was left to us, a seemingly endless succession of variations. But the building blocks remain the same. The constant in any historical approach is the record of what survives, in this case the bibliographical record. The record of early books (manuscript and printed) may grow and become more refined – in recent years its most significant change is that it has become much more accessible. Here are the bricks with which any reconstruction of the story of early printing in England is put together.

Bibliographical record

The relics of early printing in England are well recorded. An overall view, and the first port of call, is A. W. Pollard and G. R. Redgrave (eds), *A short-title catalogue of books printed in England, Scotland and Ireland, and of English books printed abroad, 1475–1640*, 2nd edn, revised and enlarged, begun by W. A. Jackson and F. S. Ferguson, completed by K. F. Pantzer (3 vols, London, 1976–91), commonly abbreviated as STC. A frequently updated electronic version is available online (http://estc.bl.uk), as the English Short-title Catalogue, commonly abbreviated as ESTC, listing items printed in English or in the British Isles between 1473 and 1800.

Incunabula, i.e. items printed before the end of year 1500, have traditionally received special treatment. English incunabula were extensively described in E. Gordon Duff, *Fifteenth-century English books: A bibliography of books and documents printed in England and of books for the English market printed abroad* (London, 1917), recently revised and enlarged by the present author: Lotte Hellinga (ed.), *Printing in England in the fifteenth century: E. Gordon Duff's bibliography with supplementary descriptions, chronologies and a census of copies* (London, 2009).

More extensive descriptions of the items in the largest collection of English incunabula are presented in Lotte Hellinga (ed.), *Catalogue of books printed in the XVth century now in the British Library*, vol. xi: *England*, with contributions by Margaret Nickson, John Goldfinch, and Paul Needham ('t Goy-Houten, 2007), commonly abbreviated as BMC xi.

English book production should be viewed against the background of contemporary book production elsewhere. For the books surviving from the fifteenth century the overview exists in the Incunabula Short-title Catalogue (ISTC) database, available online via the British Library website (http://istc.bl.uk), and as part of the Heritage of the Printed Book (formerly Hand-Press Book) database of the Consortium of European Research Libraries. Each ISTC entry refers to extensive descriptions in numerous published catalogues and bibliographies of incunabula. Among those, the most important is the ongoing publication of an alphabetically arranged bibliography of all printing of the fifteenth century, *Gesamtkatalog der Wiegendrucke* (vols I–VII, Leipzig, 1925–40; vols VIII– , Stuttgart, 1968–). To date it has progressed to include 'Horatius'. The drafts for the forthcoming additions can be accessed online at http://gesamtkatalogderwiegendrucke.de. Complementary to it is the thirteen-volume *Catalogue of books printed in the XVth century now in the British Museum (Library)* (vols i–x, xii, London, 1908–85; vols xi, xiii, 't Goy-Houten, 2004, 2007), commonly abbreviated as BMC. The successive volumes are arranged in a sequence determined by the dates of the introduction of printing in countries or areas of Europe, and include extensive introductions to the history of printing in the area covered by the relevant volume. Of particular relevance to the present book are volumes viii (France) and ix (the Low Countries). Vol. xi (England) has already been mentioned.

Biography

Other source material consists of biographies partly based on documents regarding the lives and work of the printers in England who are the subjects of the present book. The first port of call should be the *Oxford dictionary of national biography* (Oxford, 2004), commonly abbreviated as *ODNB*, which provides almost invariably reliable references to primary and secondary sources. E. Gordon Duff, *The printers, stationers and bookbinders of Westminster and London from 1476 to 1535* (Cambridge, 1906), and *The English provincial printers, stationers and bookbinders* (Cambridge, 1912) still provide a comprehensive overview. In the introduction to BMC xi, pp. 5–19, I have provided brief biographical sketches of the printers in England in the fifteenth century. For monographs on individual printers, see below.

History of the book – general background

The most influential general introduction to the history of printing which gave new direction to the discipline known as 'history of the book' is Lucien Febvre and Henri-Jean Martin, *L'Apparition du livre* (Paris, 1958), which appeared in English translation by D. Gerard as *The coming of the book* (London, 1976). A classic overview of the spread of printing, including the early years, is S. H. Steinberg, *Five hundred years of printing* (Harmondsworth, 1955, and often reprinted). An edition revised by John Trevitt was published in 1996. Rudolph Hirsch, *Printing, selling and reading 1450–1550* (Wiesbaden, 1967), should now be used with some caution as its often-quoted figures are no longer accurate. A much shorter overview for the fifteenth and sixteenth centuries is presented in essays by L. Hellinga and D. J. Shaw in Simon Eliot and Jonathan Rose (eds), *A companion to the history of the book* (Malden, MA/Oxford, 2007), pp. 207–31.

There is a vast amount of secondary literature on printing and printers in the fifteenth century. The most up-to-date bibliography of this material, giving systematic access is Severin Corsten, Reimar Walter Fuchs, and Kurt Hans Staub (eds), *Der Buchdruck im 15. Jahrhundert: Eine Bibliographie* (2 vols, Stuttgart, 1988–93).

The printed book in England

In *The Cambridge History of the book in Britain*, vol. III, ed. Lotte Hellinga and J. B. Trapp (Cambridge, 1999), commonly abbreviated as CHBB III, the period 1400–1557 is covered by twenty-four specialist authors with essays on literacy, technique and trade, ownership in collections and by individuals, and reading and the use of books. The authors frequently summarize their earlier specialist studies, and the volume can therefore be considered as the most recent introduction to the interpretation of the bibliographical and biographical materials regarding the book trade in the British Isles during this period, and its influence on intellectual development. It largely supersedes H. S. Bennett, *English books and readers 1475 to 1557* (Cambridge, 1952).

The technique of book production

The present book pays scant attention to the technical procedures followed in the early printing houses in England, the techniques they applied for manufacturing movable type, typesetting, and printing. Printers in the fifteenth century did not reveal their techniques in writing, as some printers of later periods did in professional manuals. For early printing we depend on what can be observed in the books themselves (or rather, the interpretation of observations), and occasionally on details revealed in agreements in contracts, or disagreements recorded in the courts of law. The size of editions (the numbers of copies printed, or print run) is occasionally recorded in such documents. The first scholar to record features of incunabula and put them in a systematic order was Konrad Haebler, *Handbuch der Inkunabelkunde* (Leipzig, 1925), translated by L. E. Osborne as *The study of incunabula* (New York, 1933). Since then a considerable body of evidence for printing-house practices, based on particular instances, has come to light, but has not been gathered systematically. In BMC xi, pp. 19–36, I discuss in the section 'Methods of production' the printing-house practices that can be observed in English incunabula, primarily based on the items in the British Library described in the volume.

The classic study of printing technique in the context of its implications for textual transmission is Ronald B. McKerrow, *An introduction to bibliography for literary students* (Oxford, 1927). McKerrow's experience was mainly based on printing of the Elizabethan and Jacobean period, but much of this is also valid for the earlier decades of the sixteenth century. The techniques used in the printing of incunabula were different in several respects. Philip Gaskell, *A new introduction to bibliography* (Oxford, 1972), is also based on material from the sixteenth century on; his handbook is a more detailed guide to technique than McKerrow's. A brief introduction to early printing techniques is presented in Michael Twyman, *The British Library guide to printing: History and techniques* (London, 1998).

For the raw materials used in the printing houses, paper, founts of type and other typographical materials, I refer for the fifteenth century in the first place to the section 'Materials' in BMC xi, pp. 311–428, including essays on paper by Paul Needham and on printing types (followed by extensive illustrations) by myself. The founts of type used in England in the sixteenth century are described and illustrated in F. Isaac, *English & Scottish printing types 1501–1535* (Oxford, 1930). There is as yet no study of the paper used by English printers from the 1490s and in the sixteenth century.

Illustration

A complete inventory of woodcut illustration (with the exception of armorial woodcuts) is E. Hodnett, *English woodcuts 1480–1535* (London, 1935, repr. with additions and corrections 1973). For further discussion see Martha W. Driver, *The image in print: Book illustration in late medieval England and its sources* (London, 2004).

On the illustrations of successive editions of *The*

Canterbury tales see D. R. Carlson, 'Woodcut illustrations of the Canterbury tales', *The Library*, 6th ser., 19 (1997), pp. 25–67. On the illustration of Caxton's Aesop see Martin Davies, 'A tale of two Aesops', *The Library*, 7th ser., 7 (2006), pp. 257–88.

Recently a second fragment of the Lyonnese edition edition used by Caxton has come to light including the colophon revealing the printer's name as Jehan Rousset and the date 10 May 1482.

The trade in printed books

In the first instance I refer to the essays in CHBB III by Paul Christianson, Margaret Lane Ford, and Paul Needham on the importation of books, the organization of the trade, and the dissemination of books through the trade. Their work is a continuation of that of earlier generations, notably Duff (1906, 1912), and diverse articles by H. R. Plomer published between 1904 and 1929 in *The Library*. The subject was energetically pursued by Graham Pollard in two extensive articles: 'The names of some English fifteenth-century binders', *The Library*, 5th ser., 25 (1970), pp. 192–218, and 'The English market for printed books', *Publishing History*, 4 (1978), pp. 7–48. Important recent studies include three by Paul Christianson: *Memorials of the book trade in medieval London: the archives of Old London Bridge* (Woodbridge, 1987), 'Evidence for the study of London's late medieval manuscript-book trade', in Jeremy Griffiths and Derek Pearsall (eds), *Book production and publishing in Britain 1375–1475* (Cambridge, 1989), pp. 87–108, and *A directory of London stationers and book artisans 1300–1500* (New York, 1990). A further discussion is A. S. G. Edwards and Carol M. Meale, 'The marketing of printed books in late-Medieval England', *The Library*, 6th ser., 15 (1993), pp. 95–124.

On the early organization of the book trade in London see Graham Pollard, 'The Company of Stationers before 1557', *The Library*, 4th ser., 18 (1937), pp. 1–38, and 'The early constitution of the Stationers' Company', *The Library*, 4th ser., 18 (1937), pp. 235–60; Cyprian Blagden, *The Stationers' Company: A history, 1403–1959* (London, 1960); and Peter W. M. Blayney, *The Stationers' Company before the Charter, 1403–1557* (London, 2003). Blagden usefully clarifies the privileges of a citizen of London: 'to open a shop and sell retail within the City; aliens could deal only by wholesale and only with freemen. These advantages could only be obtained by purchase by those whose fathers were not citizens or who were not prepared to serve a full apprenticeship.'

Early ownership

Extensive bibliographical records include notes about ownership of individual copies. For English printing of the fifteenth century such data form part of the catalogue entries describing several major collections of incunabula (in order of publication: Pierpont Morgan Library, Cambridge University Library, Harvard College Library, Bodleian Library, British Library), but such data are not available for other major collections (e.g. John Rylands University Library, the Hunterian collection in the Glasgow University Library, the H. E. Huntington Library, and the Library of Congress). There is therefore as yet no general overview of early owners of fifteenth-century English books. There is none for books printed in the sixteenth century.

Early owners are discussed in chapters in CHBB III, in particular those by Margaret Lane Ford, 'Private ownership of printed books' (pp. 205–28), David N. Bell, 'Monastic libraries 1400–1557' (pp. 229–54), J. H. Baker, 'The books of the common law' (pp. 411–32), and Mary C. Erler, 'Devotional literature' (pp. 495–525). The last author presents a much more extensive discussion of ownership of devotional books by women in her *Women, reading, and piety in Late Medieval England* (Cambridge, 2002). For owners in the fifteenth century in the period preceding printing, but with observations that are also pertinent to the later years, see Kate Harris, 'Patrons, buyers and owners: The evidence for ownership and the rôle of book owners in book production and the book trade', in Jeremy Griffiths and Derek Pearsall (eds), *Book production and publishing in Britain 1375–1475* (Cambridge, 1989), pp. 163–99.

Printers had to work for an imagined constituency of future owners and readers. A new generation of scholars is now engaged on renewed interpretations, focusing on capturing the interaction between early printers/publishers in England and their (expected) readers, in particular in vernacular printing. This issue is discussed in a wider chronological context by Daniel Wakelin, *Humanism, reading and English literature 1430–1530* (Oxford, 2007). Concentrated on the first decades after 1476 is a collection of essays edited by William Kuskin: *Caxton's trace: Studies in the history of English printing* (Notre Dame, IN, 2006). The themes in this collection are elaborated and complemented in William Kuskin, *Symbolic Caxton: Literary culture and print capitalism* (Notre Dame, IN, 2008). A seminal work that influenced such recent approaches is Benedict Anderson, *Imagined communities: Reflections on the origins and spread of nationalism* (rev. edn, London, 1991).

Most of the works listed above have been used throughout the present book. The following have in addition supported particular sections.

Introduction

On the dissemination of the Gutenberg Bible see Eberhard König, 'New perspectives on the history of Mainz printing: A fresh look at illuminated imprints', in Sandra Hindman (ed.), *Printing the written word: The social history of books, circa 1450–1520* (Ithaca/London, 1991), pp. 143–73. See also the same author's *Zur Situation der Gutenberg-Forschung: Ein Supplement* (Münster, 1995). These two articles include summaries of several previous studies. See also his description of the leaf illustrated in fig. 1 above: 'A leaf from a Gutenberg Bible illuminated in England', in *British Library Journal* 9 (1983), pp. 32–50.The final observation on investment and marketing by the Strozzi is based on the study by Florence Edler de Roover, 'Per la storia dell'arte della stampa in Italia: come furono stampati a Venezia tre dei primi libri in volgare', *La Bibliofilia*, 55 (1953), pp. 107–17.

On Caxton

A biography published in the year of the Caxton quincentenary celebrations should head the list: George D. Painter, *William Caxton: A quincentenary biography of England's first printer* (London, 1976). Painter's analysis of the archival documents pertinent to Caxton's career remains the basis for any biographical account. Some of his premises regarding the chronology of undated editions are overtaken by more recent research.

N. F. Blake's systematic bibliography of secondary literature on Caxton is an indispensable research tool: *William Caxton: A bibliographical guide* (New York, 1985). Of the hundreds of publications listed by Blake I select as most used in the present book (in order of publication): William Blades, *The life and typography of William Caxton, England's first printer* (2 vols, London, 1861–3), W. J. B. Crotch, *The prologues and epilogues of William Caxton* (London, 1928 [Early English Text Society o.s. 176]), two further volumes by N. F. Blake: *Caxton and his world* (London, 1968) and *Caxton's own prose* (London, 1973), and my own *Caxton in focus* (London, 1982). Of the studies published since Blake's bibliography I have drawn most often upon Paul Needham, *The printer and the pardoner* (Washington DC, 1986) and a collection of essays on Caxton by Blake first published between 1964 and 1989: *William Caxton and English literary culture* (London, 1991).

Flemish manuscript production and the Burgundian court

On authors associated with the Burgundian court see Georges Doutrepont, *La littérature française à la Cour des Ducs de Bourgogne* (Paris, 1909).

On the Golden Fleece see the collection of forty-nine essays edited by Pierre Cockshaw and Christiane Van den Bergen-Pantens, *L'ordre de la Toison d'or de Philippe le Bon à Philippe le Beau (1430–1505): idéal ou reflet d'une société?* (Brussels, 1996), in particular Anne S. Korteweg, 'Les armoriaux: Un présent offert au chapitre de 1473: Le livre des Statuts avec armorial, La Haye KB, Hs 76 E 10' (pp. 50–5), and Danielle Quéruel, 'La Toison d'or, sa légende, ses symboles, son influence sur l'histoire littéraire' (pp. 91–8).

Several major exhibitions and their catalogues with additional essays by experts have contributed significantly to our understanding of the period: [L. M. J. Delaissé], *La miniature flamande: Le mécénat de Philippe le Bon* (Brussels, 1959; exhibition catalogue, Palais des Beaux Arts, Brussels), and *Vlaamse kunst op perkament: Handschriften en miniaturen te Brugge van de 12de tot de 16de eeuw* (Bruges, 1981; exhibition catalogue, Gruuthusemuseum, Bruges). See in particular the introductory essays in the latter by A. Vandewalle, 'Het librariërsgilde te Brugge in zijn vroege periode' (pp. 39–43), and A. Derolez, 'Middeleeuwse bibliotheken te Brugge' (pp. 45–54). A survey of Flemish manucript painting is provided by: G. Dogaer, *Flemish miniature painting in the 15th and 16th centuries*. Amsterdam, 1987. A recent exhibition on Charles the Bold was accompanied by a catalogue with a generous overview of the Burgundian court from its beginning until 1477: Susan Marti, Till-Holger Borchert, Gabriele Keck (eds), *Charles the Bold (1433–1477): Splendour of Burgundy*. Brussels, 2009.

On early printing in Cologne and Caxton

I have used four studies by Severin Corsten: *Die Anfänge des Kölner Buchdrucks* (Greven, 1955; Arbeiten aus dem Bibliothekar-Lehrinstitut des Landes Nordrhein-Westfalen), 'Ulrich Zell als Geschäftsmann', in Marinette Bruwier et al. (eds), *Villes d'imprimerie et moulins à papier du XIVe au XVIe siècle* (Brussels, 1976; proceedings of an international conference held at Spa, 11–14 Sept. 1973), pp. 83–103, 'Caxton in Cologne', *Journal of the Printing Historical Society*, 11 (1976–7), pp. 1–18, and 'Johann Veldener in Köln: Geschichte eines Problems', in C. Coppens et al. (eds), *E codicibus impressisque: Opstellen over het boek in de Lage Landen voor Elly Cockx-Indestege* (Louvain, 2004), vol. I, pp. 253–67.

Also Paul Needham, 'William Caxton and his Cologne partners: An enquiry based on Veldener's Cologne type', in H. Limburg, H. Lohse, and W. Schmitz (eds), *Ars impressoria: Entstehung und Entwicklung des Buchdrucks* (Munich, 1986), pp. 103–30.

Caxton's return to Flanders and his plans for a printing house

On Margaret of York and Charles the Bold see H. Vander Linden, *Itinéraires de Charles, Duc de Bourgogne, Marguerite d'York et Marie de Bourgogne 1467–1477*

(Brussels, 1936); P. Cockshaw, C. Lemaire, and A. Rouzet (eds), *Charles le Téméraire* (Brussels, 1977; exhibition catalogue, Bibliothèque Royale Albert 1er, Brussels); and Muriel J. Hughes, 'The library of Margaret of York, Duchess of Burgundy', *The Private Library*, 1984, pp. 53–78.

On the miniatures and engravings connected with Margaret of York see O. Pächt, *The Master of Mary of Burgundy* (London, 1948); Lotte Hellinga, 'Reading an engraving: William Caxton's dedication to Margaret of York, Duchess of Burgundy', in Susan Roach (ed.), *Across the Narrow Seas: Studies in the history and bibliography of Britain and the Low Countries presented to Anna E. C. Simoni* (London, 1991), pp. 1–15; and Thomas Kren (ed.), *Margaret of York, Simon Marmion and The Visions of Tondal* (papers delivered at a symposium organized by the Department of Manuscripts of the J. Paul Getty Museum in collaboration with the Huntington Library and Art Collections, 21–24 June 1990) (Malibu, CA, 1992). The manuscript of the *Traités moraux* is described in O. Pächt and J. J. G. Alexander, *Illuminated manuscripts in the Bodleian Library*, vol. 1, Oxford, 1966. (no. 352).

On Loys de Gruuthuse see Maximiliaan P. J. Martens (ed.), *Lodewijk van Gruuthuse: Mecenas en Europees diplomaat ca. 1472–1492* (Bruges, 1992; exhibition catalogue).

On manuscripts for Edward IV see Janet Backhouse, 'Founders of the Royal Library: Edward IV and Henry VII as collectors of illuminated manuscripts', in Daniel William (ed.), *England in the fifteenth century: Proceedings of the 1986 Harlaxton Symposium* (Woodbridge, 1987), pp. 23–41; Scot M. McKendrick, 'La grande histoire Cesar and the manuscripts of Edward IV', in P. Beal and J. Griffiths (eds), *English manuscript studies 1100–1700*, vol. II (London, 1990), pp. 109–38, and 'The *Romuléon* and the manuscripts of Edward IV', in Nicholas Rogers (ed.), *England in the fifteenth century: Proceedings of the 1992 Harlaxton Symposium* (Stamford, 1994), pp. 149–66.

On David Aubert see Richard E. F. Straub, *David Aubert, escripvain et clerc* (Amsterdam/Atlanta, 1995), and Danielle Quéruel (ed.), *Les manuscrits de David Aubert, 'escripvain bourguignon'* (Paris, 1999), in particular Jacques Paviot, 'David Aubert et la cour de Bourgogne' (pp. 9–16) and Pascale Charron and Marc Gil, 'Les enlumineurs des manuscrits de David Aubert' (pp. 81–100).

On Colard Mansion see Joseph van Praet, *Notice sur Colard Mansion, libraire et imprimeur de la ville de Bruges en Flandre* (Paris, 1829); [W. H. J. Weale], 'Documents inédits sur les enlumineurs de Bruges', *Le Beffroi*, 4 (1872–3), pp. 238–337; Lotte and Wytze Hellinga, *The fifteenth-century printing types of the Low Countries* (Amsterdam, 1966), pp. 28–9, 53–4; and Anne Rouzet, *Dictionnaire des imprimeurs, libraires et éditeurs des XVe et XVIe siècles dans les limites géographiques de la Belgique actuelle* (Nieuwkoop, 1975), pp. 136–9. Colard Mansion's manuscript of *Dialogue des créatures* (fig. 14) was extensively described with many illustrations by Eberhard König in his *Leuchtendes Mittelalter III: Das goldene Zeitalter der Burgundischen Buchmalerei 1430-1560*. Rotthalmünster, 1991, no. 15. [Antiquariat Heribert Tenschert Katalog XXVII]. The same catalogue (no. 14) includes an extensive illustrated description of the manuscript of *La penitance d'Adam*, written in a script that may have been the model for Mansion's first type.

On Caxton in Flanders see William Blades, *The life and typography of William Caxton, England's first printer. With evidence of his typographical connection with Colard Mansion, the printer at Bruges* (2 vols, London, 1861–3), and *The biography and typography of William Caxton, England's first printer* (London, 1877); and Lotte and Wytze Hellinga, *Fifteenth-century printing types of the Low Countries*, pp. 21–4, and 'Caxton in the Low Countries', *Journal of the Printing Historical Society*, 11 (1976–7), pp. 19–32.

On Caxton's activities as diplomat see W. J. B. Crotch, *The prologues and epilogues of William Caxton* (London, 1928 [Early English Text Society o.s. 176]). His letter in Dutch is examined in F. J. Bakker and J. Gerritsen, 'Collecting ships from Holland and Zeeland: A Caxton letter discovered', *The Library*, 7th ser., 5 (2004), pp. 3–11.

Caxton and Westminster

In addition to the general literature on Caxton listed above, see H. M. Nixon, 'Caxton: His contemporaries and successors', *The Library*, 5th ser., 31 (1976), pp. 305–26; Jeanne Veyrin-Forrer, 'Caxton and France', *Journal of the Printing Historical Society*, 11 (1976–7), pp. 33–47; and Ann Sutton, 'Caxton was a Mercer: His social milieu and friends', in N. Rogers (ed.), *England in the fifteenth century: Proceedings of the 1992 Harlaxton Symposium* (Stamford, 1992), pp. 118–48.

On the roundels inserted into Caxton's Psalter see Mary C. Erler, 'Pasted-in embellishments in English manuscripts and printed books', *The Library*, 6th ser., 14 (1992), pp. 185–206. On the illustrations in Caxton's second edition of *The Canterbury tales*: D. R. Carlson, 'Woodcut illustrations of the *Canterbury Tales*, 1483–1602', *The Library*, 6th ser., 19 (1997), pp. 25–67. On the illumination of the manuscript of Caxton's Ovid translation: K. L. Scott, *The Caxton Master and his patrons*, Cambridge, 1976. [Cambridge Bibliographical Society, Monograph 8]. A facsimile edition of the manuscript of Pierre de Vaux, *La vie de Sainte Colette* was published, with introductions, by Y. Cazauxe and other, Tielt, Leiden, 1982.

Printing at Oxford

See A. C. de la Mare and Lotte Hellinga, 'The first book printed in Oxford: the *Expositio Symboli of Rufinus*', *Transactions of the Cambridge Bibliographical Society*, 7 (1978), pp. 184–254; Ernst Voulliéme, *Der Buchdruck Kölns bis zum Ende des fünfzehnten Jahrhunderts* (Bonn, 1903; repr. Düsseldorf, 1978), pp. lxii–lxiv (on Theoderic Rood's connections in Cologne); and N. R. Ker, 'The vellum copies of the Oxford edition (1482) of Lathbury on Lamentations', *Bodleian Library Record*, 2 (1947), pp. 185–8. On the importation of books by Oxford stationers: Paul Needham, 'Continental printed books sold in Oxford, c. 1480–3', in: Martin Davies (ed.), *Incunabula: Studies in fifteenth-century printed books presented to Lotte Hellinga*, London, 1999, pp. 243–70.

Printing at St Albans

The primary sources on the history of the abbey and its tradition of historiography are discussed in three works by V. H. Galbraith: *The abbey of St Albans from 1300 to the dissolution of the monasteries* (Oxford/London, 1911), his David Murray lecture *Roger Wendover and Matthew Paris* (Glasgow, 1944), and an edited volume, *The St Albans chronicle 1406–1420* (Oxford, 1937; pp. lxi–lxii on St Albans script). See also George B. Stow, 'Richard II in Thomas Walsingham's Chronicles', *Speculum*, 59 (1984), pp. 68–102. Stow revises Galbraith's dates, but agrees that Walsingham was the author of the successive chronicles.

On John Whethamstede see R. Weiss, *Humanism in England during the fifteenth century* (3rd edn, Oxford, 1967), pp. 30–8.

Catalogues of the abbey's library are included in R. Sharpe et al. (eds), *English Benedictine libraries: The smaller catalogues* (London, 1996), pp. 538ff. (Corpus of British Medieval Library Catalogues, vol. IV).

Bale's passage mentioned on p. 97 is quoted in BMC xi, p. 11 and n. 1.

On the two earliest founts of type used at St Albans see Nicolas Barker, 'The St Albans press: The first punch-cutter in England and the first native typefounder?' *Transactions of the Cambridge Bibliographical Society*, 7 (1979), pp. 257–78.

On the monks printing at Subiaco see Lotte Hellinga, 'Three notes on printers' copy: Strassburg, Oxford, Subiaco', *Transactions of the Cambridge Bibliographical Society*, 9 (1987), pp. 194–204.

On Caxton's use of his own Chronicles to edit a section of the *Morte Darthur* see M. Takagi and T. Takamiya, 'Caxton edits the Roman War episode: *The Chronicles of England* and Caxton's Book V', in B. Wheeler, R. L. Kindrick and M. N. Salda (eds), *The Malory debate* (Woodbridge, 2000), pp. 169–90.

On the development of Caxton's use of the English language

See N. F. Blake, 'Caxton's language', in his *William Caxton and English literary culture* (London, 1991), pp. 137–47; Tim William Machan, 'Early modern Middle English', in William Kuskin (ed.), *Caxton's trace: Studies in the history of English printing* (Notre Dame, IN, 2006), pp. 299–322; and Jeremy J. Smith, 'From Middle to Early Modern English', in Linda Mugglestone (ed.), *The Oxford history of English* (Oxford, 2006), pp. 120–46.

Richard Pynson

See Pamela Neville, 'Richard Pynson, King's Printer (1506–1529): Printing and propaganda in early Tudor England' (unpublished PhD thesis, University of London, 1990); Pamela Neville-Sington, 'Richard Pynson', in *ODNB*, and 'Press, politics and religion', in CHBB III, pp. 576–607; and S. H. Johnston, 'A study of the career and literary publications of Richard Pynson' (unpublished PhD thesis, University of Western Ontario, 1977).

On archival documents concerning Pynson see H. R. Plomer, 'Pynson v. Squyr', *Transactions of the Bibliographical Society*, 6 (1903), pp. 137–41, and 'Two lawsuits of Richard Pynson', *The Library*, 2nd ser., 10 (1909), pp. 115–33; William Kuskin, 'Onely imagined', in William Kuskin (ed.), *Caxton's trace: Studies in the history of English printing* (Notre Dame, IN, 2006), pp. 199–240; and Peter W. M. Blayney, *The Stationers' Company before the Charter, 1403–1557* (London, 2003).

On Pynson's specialist areas of publishing see Nicholas Orme, *English schools in the Middle Ages* (London, 1971), and 'Schools and school-books', CHBB III, pp. 449–69. Also J. H. Baker, 'The books of the Common Law', CHBB III, pp. 411–32.

On Pynson's first official publications see Richard Beadle and Lotte Hellinga, 'William Paston II and Pynson's *Statutes of War* (1492)', *The Library*, 7th ser., 2 (2001), pp. 107–19, and K. Harris, 'Richard Pynson's *Remembraunce for the Traduction of the Princesse Kateryne*: The printer's contribution to the reception of Catherine of Aragon', *The Library*, 6th ser., 12 (1990), pp. 89–109.

Wynkyn de Worde

See Henry R. Plomer, *Wynkyn de Worde & his contemporaries from the death of Caxton to 1535* (London, 1925). For secondary literature about De Worde see the revised edition of James Moran, *Wynkyn de Worde, Father of Fleet Street* (London, 1960), enlarged with a chronologically arranged bibliography of secondary literature about De Worde up to the year 2003, ed. Lotte Hellinga and Mary C. Erler (London, 2003 [Wynkyn de Worde Society and the British Library]).

On De Worde's establishment see H. M. Nixon, 'Caxton, his contemporaries and successors', *The Library*, 5th ser., 31 (1976), pp. 305–26, and Peter W. M. Blayney, 'The site of the Sign of the Sun', in Robin Myers et. al. (eds), *The London Book Trade: Topographies of print in the Metropolis from the sixteenth century* (London, 2003), pp. 1–20.

The texts of the documents regarding the lawsuits in the aftermath of Caxton's death may be found in W. J. B. Crotch, *The prologues and epilogues of William Caxton* (London, 1928 [Early English Text Society o.s. 176]), appendices XXVII–XXIX (pp. clx–clxiii). On De Worde's denization see Lotte Hellinga, 'Wynkyn de Worde's native land', in Richard Beadle and A. J. Piper (eds), *New science out of old books: Studies in manuscripts and early printed books in honour of A. I. Doyle* (Aldershot, 1995), pp. 342–59.

On printing types used by De Worde see Lotte Hellinga, 'Tradition and renewal: Establishing the chronology of Wynkyn de Worde's early work', in Kristian Jensen (ed.), *Incunabula and their readers: Printing, selling and using books in the fifteenth century* (London, 2003), pp. 13–28. The chronological arrangement presented in this preliminary study is partly revised in BMC xi and the revised edition of Duff's bibliography, *Printing in England in the fifteenth century* (London 2009).

Other studies on Wynkyn de Worde I relied on are Mary C. Erler, 'Wynkyn de Worde's will: Legatees and bequests', *The Library*, 6th ser., 10 (1988), pp. 107–21, and A. S. G. Edwards, 'From manuscript to print: Wynkyn de Worde and the printing of contemporary poetry', *Gutenberg-Jahrbuch* 1991, pp. 143–8.

On the Grammarians' War see David R. Carlson, *English humanist books: Writers and patrons, manuscript and print, 1475–1525* (Toronto, 1993), pp. 138–41.

Publishing of devotional texts

See Anne Hudson, *Lollards and their books* (London and Ronceverte, 1985) and 'Lollard book production', in Jeremy Griffiths and Derek Pearsall (eds), *Book production and publishing in Britain 1375–1475* (Cambridge, 1989), pp. 125–42; Vincent Gillespie, 'Vernacular books of religion', *ibid.*, pp. 317–44; Nicholas Watson, 'Censorship and cultural change in late-medieval England: Vernacular theology, the Oxford translation debate, and Arundel's Constitutions of 1409', *Speculum*, 70 (1995), pp. 822–64, and 'The politics of Middle English writings', in J. Wogan-Browne et al., *The idea of the vernacular* (Exeter, 1999), pp. 336–52; Mary C. Erler, *Women, reading, and piety in late medieval England* (Cambridge, 2002); Susan Powell, 'Lady Margaret Beaufort and her books', *The Library*, 6th ser., 20 (1998), pp. 187–240 and 'John Mirk', in *ODNB*; and J. J. Rhodes, 'Syon Abbey's religious publications', *Journal of Ecclesiastical History*, 44 (1993), pp. 11–25.

On John Ryckes and *The ymage of love* see E. Ruth Harvey, 'The image of love', Appendix A in Thomas M. C. Lawler, Germain Marc'Hadour, and Richard C. Marius (eds), *The complete works of St Thomas More*, vol. VI, part 2 (New Haven/London, 1981), pp. 727–59.

Printers outside the mainstream

See generally E. Gordon Duff, *The printers, stationers and bookbinders of Westminster and London from 1476 to 1535* (Cambridge, 1906); Peter W. M. Blayney, *The Stationers' Company before the Charter, 1303–1557* (London, 2003); A. S. G. Edwards and Carol M. Meale, 'The marketing of printed books in late-medieval England', *The Library*, 6th ser., 15 (1993), pp. 95–124; Mary Erler (ed.), *Robert Copland: Poems* (Toronto, 1993); David J. Shaw, 'An unrecorded STC item: Johannes de Garlandia's *Multorum vocabulorum equivocorum interpretatio*, Paris, 1502', *The Library*, 7th ser., 5 (2004), pp. 359–69; and James E. Blodgett, 'Some printer's copy for William Thynne's 1532 edition of Chaucer', *The Library*, 6th ser., 1 (1979), pp. 97–113.

On John Rastell: E. J. Devereux, *A bibliography of John Rastell*. Montreal, London, 1999. On Berthelet's Gower: T. W. Machan, 'Thomas Berthelette and Gower's *Confessio*', in *Studies in the age of Chaucer* 18 (1996), pp. 143–66.

On humanists and printers see J. B. Trapp, *Erasmus, Colet and More: The early Tudor humanists and their books*. (London, 1991 [The Panizzi Lectures, 1990]); and J. B. Trapp and Hubertus Schulte Herbrüggen (eds), *'The King's good servant': Sir Thomas More 1477/8–1535* (London, 1977; exhibition catalogue, The National Portrait Gallery, London).

On provincial printing see Nicholas Orme, 'Martin Coeffin, the first Exeter publisher', *The Library*, 6th ser., 10 (1988), pp. 220–30.

On printing at Tavistock Abbey see Lucy Lewis, 'The Tavistock Boethius: One of the earliest examples of provincial printing', in John Hinks and Catherine Armstrong (eds), *Printing places: Locations of book production & distribution since 1500* (London, 2005).

On John Scolar in Oxford see Nicolas J. Barker, *The Oxford University Press and the spread of learning 1478–1978* (Oxford, 1978), pp. 4–6.

On the first press in Cambridge see E. P. Goldschmidt, *The first Cambridge press in its European setting* (Cambridge, 1955), especially ch. 1: 'Siberch's ten books' (pp. 1–20).

Illustrations

All items are in the collections of the British Library, unless stated otherwise.

All are reproduced in reduced scale.

The following abbreviations for primary bibliographical references have been used:

BMC: *Catalogue of books printed in the XVth century now in the British Museum (British Library)*. Parts i–x, xii, London, 1908–85; parts xi, xiii, 't Goy-Houten, 2004, 2007.

Duff: Lotte Hellinga, *Printing in England in the fifteenth century: E. Gordon Duff's Bibliography with supplementary descriptions, chronologies, and a census of copies*. London, 2009.

GW: *Gesamtkatalog der Wiegendrucke*, vols 1–7 Leipzig, 1925–40; from vol. 8: Stuttgart, 1968– (in progress).

STC: A. W. Pollard and G. R. Redgrave (eds), *A short-title catalogue of books printed in England, Scotland and Ireland, and of English books printed abroad, 1475–1640*, 2nd edition. Revised and enlarged, begun by W. A. Jackson and F. S. Ferguson, completed by K. F. Pantzer. 3 vols. London, 1976–91.

Fig. 1. *Biblia latina*. [Mainz, Johann Gutenberg, 1455], [DD]7 recto. GW 4201.

Fig. 2. Nicolaus de Lyra, *Postilla super totam Bibliam*. Rome, Conradus Sweynheym and Arnoldus Pannartz, 1471–2, [a]4 verso (detail). BMC iv, 1–15.

Fig. 3. *Biblia latina*. Mainz, Peter Schoeffer, 1472, [kk]7 recto (detail). GW 4211, BMC i, 28.

Fig. 4. Gasparinus Barzizius, *Epistolae*. Paris, Michael Friburger, Ulrich Gering, Martin Crantz, [c. 1470], [a]1 recto. GW 3675, BMC viii, 2.

Fig. 5. Gaius Plinius Secundus, *Historia naturalis*. Translated into Italian by Cristoforo Landino. Venice, Nicolas Jenson, 1476, [a]5 recto. BMC v, 176.

Fig. 6. Raoul Lefevre, *Recuyell of the histories of Troy*, translated from the French *Recueil des histoires de Troies* by William Caxton. [Ghent?], William Caxton, [c. 1473], [a]3 recto. STC 15375, Duff 242, BMC ix, 129.

Fig. 7. Maino de Maineri, *Dialogue des créatures*, translated from the Latin *Dialogus creaturarum* by Colard Mansion. Manuscript, Bruges, Colard Mansion, 1482, 1 recto. Collection Heribert Tenschert, Bibermühle, Switzerland.

Fig. 8. Raoul Lefevre, *Recueil des histoires de Troies*, here entitled *Le livre nomme Hercules*. Manuscript, probably Bruges, c. 1480. BL, Ms Royal 17 E. ii, 171 verso.

Fig. 9. *Statutes of the Order of the Golden Fleece*. Manuscript, Flanders, c. 1470–73. The Hague, Royal Library, Ms 76 E 10, 5 verso.

Fig. 10. Raoul Lefevre, *Recuyell of the histories of Troy*. [Ghent?], William Caxton, [c. 1473], [a]2 recto. (Cf. above, fig. 6). STC 15375, Duff 242, BMC ix, 129.

Figs 11, 12. Bartholomaeus Anglicus, *De proprietatibus rerum*. [Cologne, William Caxton, 1472], [f]5 recto. GW 3403, Duff 39, BMC i, 234.

Fig. 13. Thomas Aquinas, *Tractatus de beatitudine eternitatis*. [Cologne, Printer of Dares, before December 1472], [d]1 recto. BMC i, 213.

Fig. 14. Engraving ascribed to the 'Master of Mary of Burgundy' inserted in *Recuyell of the histories of Troy*. [a]1 recto. (Cf. above, fig. 6). San Marino (California), H. E. Huntington Library. STC 15375, Duff 242, Goff L.117.

Fig. 15. *Traités moraux et religieux*. Manuscript, Ghent, David Aubert, 1476. Oxford, Bodleian Library, Ms Douce 365, 115 recto.

Fig. 16. Jacobus de Cessolis, *The game of chess*, translated from a French version of *De ludo scaccorum* by William Caxton. [Ghent?] William Caxton, 1474, [a]2 verso (detail). STC 4920, Duff 81, BMC ix, 130.

Fig. 17. *Le dyalogue de la duchesse de bourgogne a Ihesu Crist*. Manuscript, Brussels, c. 1468–70. London, BL, Ms Add. 7970, 1 verso, 2 recto.

Fig. 18. *La vie passion et mort pour le sauvement du monde* and *La vengeance de la mort de Jhesu Crist*. Manuscript, Ghent, David Aubert, 1479. London, BL, Ms Royal 16 G.iii, 193 recto.

Fig. 19. *Dialogue des créatures*. Manuscript, Bruges, Colard Mansion, 1482, 7 recto. (Cf. above, fig. 7). Collection Heribert Tenschert, Bibermühle, Switzerland.

Fig. 20. Giovanni Boccaccio, *De la ruyne des nobles hommes et femmes*, translated from *De casibus virorum illustrium* by Laurent de Premierfait. Bruges, Colard Mansion, 1476, [G]9 verso. GW 4432, BMC ix, 132.

Fig. 21. Petrus de Alliaco, *Les sept degrés de l'échelle*. [Ghent? David Aubert? c. 1474], [d]9 verso. Duff 25, BMC ix, 131.

Indexes

GENERAL INDEX

AUTHORS AND TEXTS

Theological, religious, devotional

Literary and general interest

Books for schools, education

Books for universities and humanist scholarship

Legal texts, printed

Official publications